POLITICALLY RED

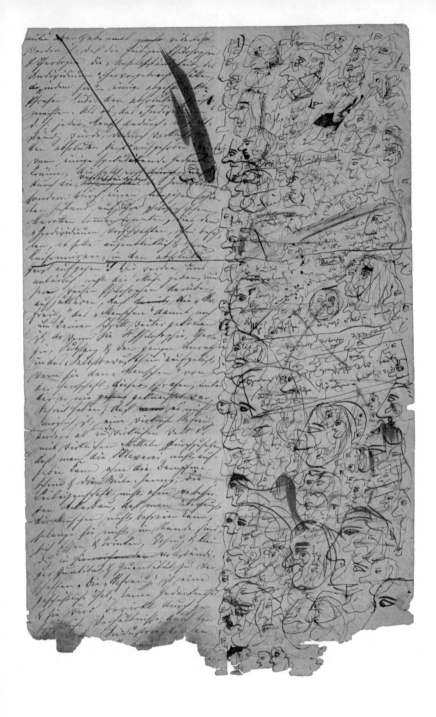

Karl Marx, manuscript page from the "Feuerbach"
section of *The German Ideology*, 1845–1846

EDUARDO CADAVA
SARA NADAL-MELSIÓ

POLITICALLY RED

THE MIT PRESS
CAMBRIDGE, MASSACHUSETTS
LONDON, ENGLAND

CONTENTS

Only since Marx have we begun to suspect what, in theory at least, *reading* and hence writing *means*.

—Louis Althusser

We start with our frontispiece. A threshold through which a reader passes in order to enter our book, it is itself a scene of reading. Belonging to the book but also preceding it, the frontispiece suggests that all books originate in earlier books, all pages are preceded by previous ones, all readings are mediated—and ours is no exception. In any given instance, it is a question of the particular constellation of texts that are set in motion. Here, we encounter a manuscript page from the never-completed Feuerbach section of what we now know as Karl Marx and Friedrich Engels's *The German Ideology*—a "book" they never titled or finished and which itself begins in a series of readings of, among others, Ludwig Feuerbach, Max Stirner, and Bruno Bauer. This ensemble of loosely arranged fragments represents one of their earliest sustained collaborations and is a window into the process of their production.[1] In particular, it points to the centrality of reading and writing in their political militancy. Their collaboration begins in a scene of reading that is at the same time a scene of writing and friendship: two friends in conversation, reading aloud, writing together, crossing out and editing each other's sentences, doodling, and also laughing—in fact, laughing so loudly that their neighbors complain to the landlord.[2] If we wonder how two people can make so much noise, it is because, even when they are altogether alone with each other, there is an entire crowd in the room with them.

Every scene of reading and writing involves a crowd: we never read or write alone. We always read through the medium of an increasing number of other readers and writers. Reading and writing are themselves labors of multiplication—and this multiplication is the direct effect of thinking with someone else's thoughts, someone whose "own" thoughts in turn also start elsewhere. Reading and writing are collaborative activities—they can become a means of massification, a matter of amplification, and, in the words of Walter Benjamin, a way of "setting the masses in motion."[3] There can be no mass movement, no mobilization, without the training that comes from a deep engagement with language and its capacity to produce unforeseen and incalculable effects. The many readers and writers we follow in our book all seek to move toward a different kind of production, one that, never exhausted by the calculus of capitalist productivity, can potentially lead to the emergence of an indeterminate but powerful mass.

As Benjamin writes in his 1934 essay "The Author as Producer," which he prepared for the Institute for the Study of Fascism in Paris and which also begins in a series of readings (of Marx, Bertolt Brecht, Ramon Fernandez, and Sergei Tretyakov):

> *An author who teaches writers nothing teaches no one.* What matters, therefore, is the exemplary character of production, which is able, first, to induce other producers to produce, and, second, to put an improved apparatus at their disposal. And this apparatus is better, the more consumers it is able to turn into producers—that is, readers or spectators into collaborators.[4]

Whatever else the writer might teach, he suggests, conveys "the exemplary character of production." He enacts and performs a production that, being nothing but a process of production, cannot be fully instrumentalized because it remains an activity with unpredictable aftereffects. If writing is a mode of production, a kind of labor, it turns "readers or spectators into collaborators," that is, into writers, into co-workers. Writers are first readers, and the interplay of writing and reading creates an apparatus—a network of historical relations—that intensifies and multiplies the forces of production at work within each text. This intensification and multiplication are mutually constitutive and operate through processes of replication, reproduction, and transformation that make readers writers in turn. In this way, a process of consumption is transformed into one of production, and what is produced, in addition to more readers and writers, is an apparatus that, mediating this transformation, creates the possibility of a mass of collaborators—even comrades. These comrades can potentially become Tretyakov's "operating" writer[5]—the writer who organizes, who engages in struggle rather than merely reporting it, who "intervenes actively" rather than remaining a spectator, who enacts a reconceptualization and expansion of what literary work does that, in turn, can extend to the masses and to the processes of their massification.[6]

All this is at play in the frontispiece we have put at the threshold of our book, since what we are confronted with in this page is nothing more nor less than the process of Marx and Engels's collaborative production. What has become known to us in assembled and edited form as *The German Ideology* can at most be considered a "work in progress," if not the preparatory drafts for later texts.[7] If the frontispiece embodies the process of their production, it is because it conveys what is true about all their texts, and not just this unfinished one. In general, the left-hand column on the printer's sheets was used for writing the text—this task was most often Engels's, since his handwriting was more legible than Marx's, but it also fell occasionally to Jenny Marx and, in other instances, to close friends—and the right-hand column was left blank for corrections and insertions, and mostly used by Marx to rephrase certain sentences and to note down additional ideas. What is remarkable about this particular manuscript page is, of course, the doodling that takes place in the right-hand column, over a few notes and phrases by Marx. The doodles are drawn by Engels and, because they most likely would have been drawn over the course of days, weeks, or even months—we can be sure he did not do them all in one sitting—what we see in them is the slow emergence of a mass through the movement of his pen. In this delineation of heads, the page archives the role of Engels's writing instrument in the construction and formation of masses, however heterogeneous and uncoordinated their constituents might be. This is possible not simply because of the doodling but also because of the interplay between the doodling and the writing. It points more generally to Marx and Engels's conviction of the force of writing as a means of mobilization. In their work, however, writing never takes place outside a moment of reading. If doodling is generally done in a state of distraction—a state in which the doodler is both present and absent at the same time—there is at least evidence here that Engels's doodling has a directionality to it. This directionality is legible not simply in the fact that, in his distraction, he draws heads—and heads within heads within heads, seemingly endlessly—but also in the fact that all the heads are looking to the left, toward a page from a fragment that belongs to Marx and Engels's writings on Feuerbach. If we have a mass before us, it is a reading mass—one that is oriented toward the reading of what would seem to be a fragment of a single text, but which, as we will see in a moment, is itself interwoven with an innumerable set of other texts.

What is so beautiful about the cumulative effect of Engels's doodling is the presentation of heads full of different heads, as if what is staged here, even if unwittingly, is the fact that we always think with others. Benjamin makes this point in "The Author as Producer" when, referencing Brecht, he claims that thinking politically involves "the art of thinking in other people's heads."[8] Engels's doodle would seem to be a rather extravagant demonstration of this dictum, since every drawn head is populated with other heads—there is no head here that can think alone. This mass is not a sum of individuals; each individual is already more than one, already related to an incalculable number of others, already a mass. If the page becomes an emblem for the activity of thinking politically, for the emergence of a mass through writing, or, more precisely, doodling, the distinction between doodling and writing emphasizes the fact that the formation of a mass cannot be entirely intentional or unidirectional. It emerges in an absentmindedness that, because of a process of multiplication and reproduction that resembles automatic writing, nevertheless generates a field in which heads can be coordinated, if somewhat haphazardly and without a strict design.

Indeed, if we look again at the doodle, we can see that the heads that compose the mass cannot be distinguished from one another. If the individual dissolves in the mass, the mass itself does not have a determinate face, which is why it might be more precise to say that we are looking not at a mass but rather at something that is *mass-like*. We could say that the heterogeneity of this restless, comical, and sometimes grotesque mass speaks to the kind of gathering Marx and Engels's labor calls into being, a gathering that will no longer be predicated on exclusion but on an ever-expanding and formless incorporation of the heads that inhabit us, sometimes against our will—heads of those we dislike and with whom we might disagree, and even of our enemies. This is why the mass remains unstable and unbounded; it threatens to become undone even if, surrendering to the momentum of its movement, it emerges as a force of transformation. Intentionality here proves to be multiple and impersonal, and not just human, since, beyond the animals that seem to be mixed in with the humans—rams, sheep, dogs, pigs, and even a snake—the human figures themselves often have animal-like snouts and features. This mass-like mass exceeds the human and recalls the several moments when Marx references the barbarous, animal-like characteristics of capitalist sovereigns and masters who, holding power, fight to keep it, brutally, violently, and in the most inhuman ways—when, that is, he refers to the "animal kingdom of politics" that has thrived on the principle of a "dehumanized world."[9] That we can put Marx's figure of the animalistic character of capital in relation to Engels's doodle suggests that—just as we cannot say that Engels is solely responsible for what is handwritten on the left side of the manuscript page—the doodle itself bears the traces of conversations and is therefore a collaborative archive. It cannot be extracted from the conversations and writings it reproduces, even if in displaced and fragmented ways, through the partially unconscious movement of the pen. This movement between doodling and writing is also legible in the fact that the same line of the pen can become either a word or a figure, and sometimes both. The pen literalizes the kinds of figurations that happen in language. This is clearer on the right side of the page when Engels seems to take the shapes of Marx's handwriting and, beginning with one of its strokes or curves, transforms the squiggle into a head or figure. To a large extent, the reading of the manuscript page depends on the unstable relation between writing and doodling, between language and figuration. Because of the duration of its extended production, the doodle brings together different temporalities. Marx and Engels continue to work on other texts and other pages before they finish the Feuerbach section and before Engels stops doodling—which means that, each time Engels returns to the doodle to add more heads, he brings the traces of their other intervening work to the lines he draws. As a consequence, the heads turned toward the page on Feuerbach have their heads filled with even more heads, with more texts, and not just those of Feuerbach.

We can see how this works by first turning to the text toward which the mass of heads is turned. As we have noted, it is from the fragments of writing that Marx and Engels devote to Feuerbach in the mid-1840s. On the left side of the page, below the crossed-out lines—referencing Feuerbach and the Young Hegelians against whom they are arguing, and with their usual sarcasm and irony—they write:

> We shall, of course, not take the trouble to explain to our wise philosophers that the "liberation" of man is not advanced a single step by reducing philosophy, theology, substance and all the rubbish to "self-consciousness" and by liberating "man" from the domination of these phrases, which have never held him in thrall. Nor shall we explain to them that it is possible to achieve real liberation only in the real world and by real means, that slavery cannot be abolished without the steam-engine and the mule jenny, serfdom cannot be abolished without improved agriculture, and that, in general, people cannot be liberated as long as they are unable to obtain food and drink, housing and clothing in adequate quality and quantity. "Liberation" is a historical and not a mental act, and it is brought about by historical conditions, the [level] of industry, com[merce], [agri]culture, [intercourse ...][10]

Even in this brief fragment, we get a glimpse of the extent to which Marx and Engels's critique of Feuerbach and the Young

Hegelians targets the language and "phrases" of these presumably leftwing political philosophers. The political stakes of Marx and Engels's critique cannot be separated from the way in which they inhabit and displace the rhetoric of these philosophers. They conduct their political work through what Althusser calls their insistent and characteristic "play on words."[11] In this instance, orthographical markers signal their distance from the concepts that their adversaries transform into abstractions. Putting the words "liberation," "man," and "self-consciousness" in quotation marks conveys not only that Marx and Engels mean something different by these terms than how these young ideologists understood them but also the extent to which the latter minimize the importance of production in the name of a critical consciousness that, for them, understands ideas to be the primary motor of history. These abstractions are incapable of transforming the historical conditions idealism obscures in the name of philosophy. Their efficacy is reduced when they are ascribed to agents that, believing they can control them, ossify them, turning them into linguistic corpses detached from the living movement of history—from the "play of words" that are Marx and Engels's *real* means.

In spite of their allegedly "world-shattering" phrases, the German philosophers subjected to Marx and Engels's critique betray their political and philosophical conservatism by insisting not on real political interests, but on pure thoughts. Rather than attend to the specific historical and social conditions that capitalism creates, requires, and sustains, these conditions are silenced by an idealism that is complicit with capital through the logic of abstraction they share. What the abolishment of slavery, serfdom, and capital demand is a forceful reconceptualization of the conditions of liberation itself and, for Marx and Engels, this requires a transformation of our relation to the "phrases," words, and concepts that dominate these debates over what "real liberation" might be. When Marx and Engels suggest that "real liberation" can only be achieved "in the real world and by real means," when they say that "liberation" is "a historical and not a mental act," they do not distinguish liberation from thought, but only from thought that would be reduced to the idealism of the mind or consciousness. As Althusser puts it, thought and "mental" acts are here not "a faculty of a transcendental subject or absolute consciousness confronted by the real world as *matter*, nor is this thought a faculty of a psychological subject, although human individuals are its agents." "This thought," he goes on to say, is the historically constituted system of an *apparatus of thought*, founded on and articulated to natural and social reality. It is defined by the system of real conditions which make it ... a determinate *mode of production* of knowledges. ... This system of theoretical production—a material as well as a "mental" system, whose practice is founded on and articulated to the existing economic, political, and ideological practices which directly or indirectly provide it with the essentials of its "raw materials"—has a determinate objective reality ... "thought" is a peculiar real system.[12]

That thought in Marx and Engels can never be opposed to the material world is legible in the way in which the word "liberation" remains in quotation marks throughout the passage. The quotation marks emphasize that "liberation" is a phrase within the discourse of the Young Hegelians and, if there is to be *real liberation*, we must be freed from the phrases and concepts that move us toward different forms of subjection, and this can only happen when we no longer discount thought itself as a mode of production. This is exactly what we see enacted in this passage and what Marx and Engels perform when they suggest that *real liberation* cannot be divorced from the movement and transformation of the language we inherit. Within the logic of the passage, it can only be actualized if it can free itself from the quotation marks that would keep it as a concept—when, that is, we register *"the absence of a concept behind a word,"*[13] even when, and perhaps especially when, this word is "liberation." This is confirmed in a series of marginal notes that Marx puts on the right side of a page a little further on in the manuscript. There, noting the importance of "phrases in Germany"—emphasizing their role in the construction of *reality*—he writes simply "phrases and real movement." This is a rather remarkable addendum. It signals, in a wonderfully exact and condensed form, the politics of Marx and Engels's writerly strategy. There can be no "real movement" without phrases, but this means without phrases that work against other phrases that would presume a distinction between thought and matter, between knowledge and modes of production. Or, to put it another way, *real movement* can only take place in relation to phrases that refuse to be arrested, to stand still, and to be instrumentalized. This is made legible in the passage toward which the masses are drawn—literally *drawn*—because, belonging to a larger context, it incorporates the modes of production that make it possible. We need only register that the passage already weaves together a constellation of concepts that will remain permanent interests throughout the rest of Marx and Engels's lives: capital, revolution, liberation, slavery, technology, the relation between theory and practice, historical and mental conditions, subjectivity and impersonal agency, and—as pointed to in a scarcely visible marginal note underneath Engels's doodle—the relation between "philosophical liberation and real liberation."

Not simply the fragment of a page, then, our frontispiece is rather an archive of the entire Marxian corpus, even if the traces on its surface appear and unfold in accordance with the intense massification that occurs in Marx and Engels's process of production. What the doodled mass on the right side of the page reads, then— what may help constitute it as a mass, even if an as yet unnamed and unidentifiable one—is an excerpt that carries within it the entirety of Marx and Engels's collaboration. These heterogeneous heads are in turn inscribed within an ever-expanding context that includes not simply the "[g]eological, hydrographical, etc., conditions. The human body. Needs and labor,"[14] that Marx has scribbled underneath Engels's doodles, but also the *real world* of a given historical society, its particular means of production, and its relation with other global structures. If real liberation can ever be possible, it cannot be an abstraction, but—like the abolition of slavery, serfdom, and poverty, each of which bears reference to the world of racial capitalism—can only be materialized, if it can ever be materialized, through acts of reading and writing that come with the transformative, and sometimes violent, force of interruption and deposition. This is part of the active refusal legible in Engels's doodle.

The doodle is itself a mode of thinking, but one that comes in the form of distraction—in the form of what unfolds in relation to an indeterminate end, even if it follows patterns of repetition, reproduction, and transformation. The doodle corresponds to a moment in which writing is suspended. It pertains to a different kind of labor, one that can no longer be abstracted and counted as labor within the logic of capital, since it is not oriented toward an end. It is fugitive labor and, in its suspension or refusal of writing—in its delay of writing—it has relays with the general strike as a force of deposition. In a very real sense, what Marx and Engels manage to convey is the possibility of a suspension that can gather into a mass. What we have before us in the frontispiece is an emblem for what a text might look like, with the pen as its implement, if it were capable of enacting the movements of a mass strike. We could say that Marx and Engels are among the first writers who try to write and think like a mass, who, understanding the political force of thinking and writing, repeatedly demonstrate that writing and reading are social forms and, more specifically, the making and unmaking of social forms. If the frontispiece is a living archive of a collaborative process and its conditions of possibility, the drafts, crossings-out, additions, and superimpositions make it at times impossible to identify the origin of the text in a determinate fashion. These marks also give evidence of the violence that Marx and Engels direct toward the sanctity of the text—a violence that becomes, in their hands, a modality of reading, the index of a certain political criticality, and an openness to endless transformation (what in *The Holy Family* they call a "permanent revolution"[15]). In fact, one of the problems that emerges most forcefully in our book is violence, not just political violence but all the different manifestations that violence can take—among others, femicide, genocide, slavery, racial violence, environmental violence, carceral violence, enforced poverty, and the denial of the right to education. Because these different violences appear under the same name, they often prove difficult to disentangle. Marx and Engels—but also Benjamin, Rosa Luxemburg, W. E. B. Du Bois, and Fredric Jameson, some of the other readers and writers we engage in our book—share a sense of the inevitability of certain forms of violence and an absolute condemnation of others, with full cognizance of the added risk that the polysemy of the word entails. While the violence implicit in reading and thinking in other people's thoughts eliminates the possibility of an innocent reading altogether—that reading and thinking are mediated means that no reading or thought can escape the risk of complicity—not all readings are guilty in the same way. This is why, Althusser notes, if "there is no such thing as an innocent reading, we must say what reading we are guilty of."[16] If there are forms of guilt and violence that must be assumed and others that must be avoided, the distance between them is not always apparent, and the possibility of complicity never disappears. This critical distinction between instantiations of violence and guilt in Marx and Engels is legible in their dissection of the language of the Young Hegelians. They unleash the force of their critical violence in the direction of the less visible but no less violent complicity between idealism and capitalism in order to interrupt it. The fierceness of their criticism is astonishing at times—in their aggressive sarcasm, biting irony, and parodic caricature of their enemies. This violence has its analogy in the intensity evident in their constant revisions on the page, a palimpsestic record of different interventions. Marx and Engels never lose sight of the total violence that is the experiential infrastructure that fuels capitalist abstraction and that spills over like an ink stain onto their pages. The fact that political violence also has been perpetrated under the name of Marx (as we know, there have been—and still are—several Marxisms, including nationalistic and totalitarian ones) would hardly surprise him; he is a keen observer of the ways in which language can be mobilized by counterrevolutionary and reactionary forces—forces that belong to the kind of instrumentalized violence against which his writings "forewarn and forearm" us.[17]

The problem of differentiating the distinct forms of violence that are inevitably inscribed within acts of reading and writing can be read in the materiality of the frontispiece's page—not only in the false antagonism between the two sides of the manuscript but also in the illegibility that extends well beyond the letter and the doodle: in the hidden figures, the erasures, the smudges, the ink blotting, the pen trials, the crossing out and writing over, and in the damage to the page's edges, as a result of which words and sentences are missing. The two columns, the writing on the left and the mass of heads on the right—always on the verge of becoming undone by the force of their own massification—begin to move in each other's direction. Two heads, for instance, cross over onto the left side of the page—they are faintly visible in its upper half—and, in doing so, seem to pull the other heads in their direction, introducing movement into our experience of the page that violently undoes the distinct integrity, stability, and even sovereignty of the two columns. It is tempting to read this dissolution as a displacement of another emblem for the relation between the masses and a figure of authority, indeed, of another frontispiece: the famous frontispiece of Thomas Hobbes's *Leviathan*, which itself appears as an emblem of absolute sovereignty, with the mass of anonymous and undifferentiated subjects facing the sovereign and upholding royal power. In Marx and Engels's communist version, the anonymous heads do not face a sovereign but instead the text. If the text occupies the position of Hobbes's sovereign—if in Marx and Engels the text rules—this text refuses sovereignty not only because its authority is shared but also because this shared authority is scattered and massified. At the same time, the doodled mass—beginning to transgress the border of the text—would seem to refuse to accept the text's precedence and authority, and even seems ready to overtake it with its proliferation, a proliferation that Marx and Engels's writing paradoxically sets into motion.

These multiple exchanges between the two sides of the page—preventing either side from being a "side"—are instances of what

Althusser calls "thought power,"[18] a power that emerges in the interplay between different productions of knowledge and that corresponds to an activation of imaginative and experimental literary strategies that can intervene politically within the text at hand. This intervention can be registered in the work Marx and Engels do when, focusing on the "phrases" and language of Feuerbach and company, they expose the complicity between the philosophers and the violence not simply of their language but also of their relation to capital. In this text in particular they amplify their critique by animating and releasing the critical potential of literary works in the direction of their ideological targets.[19] The force of these literary works has its analogue in the torsions Marx and Engels exert on the writings of the Young Hegelians and is related to the freedom evident in the mad proliferation of a doodle that contaminates the written traces on the page. Their sarcastic tirades—beginning with a play on words, a mode of literary doodling—create the space for an infinite number of permutations to emerge from the finite boundaries of the page. Their "thought power" may be inscribed within a determined system of sociopolitical, ideological, and cultural practices, but it gathers its force by moving these determinations toward a set of literary tactics that liberate the pen and the mind—that enable them to read, to write, and to doodle in a manner that is as free as it is fugitive. It is perhaps useful to give one example of this strategy in order to confirm that Marx and Engels's critique of the Young Hegelians—a critique that has enormous political stakes for them—can best be registered in what they do with language in general, and with just one literary resource in particular. Tracing their use of this literary text in their critique of the philosophers will give us another glimpse into the process of their production and demonstrate that, expanding their number of collaborators, they can find comrades on their bookshelves.[20] In this instance, they use Miguel de Cervantes's *Don Quixote* as part of their political arsenal.

The digressive and critical deployment of Cervantes's novel allows them to suspend the distinctions among fiction, philosophy, and political analysis. Don Quixote's fidelity to an outmoded "history"—to an abstract, idealist political philosophy—is likened to that of the Young Hegelians and, in particular, to that of Bauer and Stirner. Cervantes is used most extravagantly in the "Leipzig Council" section of *The German Ideology*. There Marx and Engels assert that these two idealist philosophers are uninterested—to the detriment of their thought and their politics—in the processes of material life and in the materiality of production more generally. They open the section with an evocation of Wilhelm von Kaulbach's famous painting *The Battle of the Huns*, which depicts the ghosts of fallen warriors fighting in the air above the battleground. Taking their point of departure from the painting, they write:

> [The struggle of the Young Hegelians] is not a battle over earthly things. The holy war is being waged not over protective tariffs, the constitution, potato blight, banking affairs and railways, but in the name of the most sacred interests of the spirit, in the name of "substance," "self-consciousness," "criticism," the "unique," and the "true man." We are attending a Council of Church Fathers.[21]

In theatrical fashion, Marx and Engels introduce the members of this Council and invent a series of ironic and sarcastic nicknames, metaphors, and allegories for Bauer and Stirner in relation to two highly literary and critical conceits. The first of these, the "Leipzig Council," is, in Robert Kaufman's words, "a burlesque of both the Old and the New Testaments, with the Young Hegelians (called 'Saint Bruno' and 'Saint Max') brought under charges in Marx and Engels's parody of the Inquisition."[22] The second, reinforcing the first, entails the relentless, digressive, and critical use of *Don Quixote*. Citing long passages from Bauer and Stirner, Marx and Engels inscribe these two figures into their own *Quixote*, alternately associating them with Sancho Panza and Don Quixote, and sometimes with both simultaneously. Here we will simply cite two examples of the way this rewriting works. First, a passage that accuses Saint Max of producing a historiography of illusory ideas, a history of spirits and ghosts: "Since Saint Max shares the belief of all critical, speculative, modern philosophers that thoughts, which have become independent, objectified thoughts—ghosts—have ruled the world and continue to rule it, and that all history until now has been the history of theology, nothing could be easier for him than to transform history into a history of ghosts. Sancho's history of ghosts, therefore, rests on the speculative philosophers' traditional belief in ghosts."[23] And second, a passage that suggests that Stirner's argument often is supported by a series of appositions which have no clear relation with one another:

> Against these painstaking distinctions and petty questions there stands out in strong relief the indifference of our Sancho for whom it is all the same and who ignores all actual, practical and conceptual differences. In general, we can already say now that his ability

to distinguish is far inferior to his ability not to distinguish, to regard all cats as black in the darkness of the holy, and to reduce everything to anything—an art which finds its adequate expression in the use of the apposition. Embrace your "ass," Sancho, you have found him again here. He gallops merrily to meet you, taking no notice of the kicks he has been given, and greets you with this ringing voice. Kneel before him, embrace his neck and fulfill the calling laid down for you by Cervantes in chapter 30. The apposition is Saint Sancho's ass, his logical and historical locomotive, the driving force of "the book," reduced to its briefest and simplest expression.[24]

Identifying Sancho's ass with the appositives that enable Stirner to move from one part of his sentences to another confirms the way in which Marx and Engels achieve their political critique by intervening in minute and precise ways in their antagonists' sentences—in this instance, through the mediation of Cervantes. *Don Quixote* becomes an active agent in their analysis of ideology and of different modes of production. As Marx and Engels well knew, *Don Quixote* is one of the great meditations on the relations between fiction and reality, between ideas and materiality. It is no accident, then, that they turn to Cervantes here, since, like them, Cervantes also proceeds in his novel through a series of literary discussions, critical commentaries, and philological debates that, despite their seeming randomness, converge around a series of reflections on the meaning, interpretation, and materiality of words.

The displacements and misunderstandings that occur between Sancho and Quixote become a lens through which to read the displacements and misunderstandings that characterize Bauer's and Stirner's philosophico-political writings. The play of names and nicknames that Marx and Engels circulate within their parodic and sarcastic argument also has its precedents in the plurality of masks, names, and pseudonyms behind which Cervantes often presents himself, and the novel itself evokes the modern world that these two communists inherit: a world that bears the traces of imperialism and colonialism, immigration and migration, poverty and the unequal distribution of wealth and power, death and depopulation, and the vicissitudes of the transition from feudal economies to capitalism, a world that confronts its myths with its realities, a world that, cut off from its realities, prefers to dream. If Quixote dreams through the lens of chivalric romances, however, Marx and Engels launch a critical attack against the romances and delusions of the young Hegelians through the very language of Cervantes's picaresque, which in their hands becomes a polyphonic, literary communism.[25]

In this regard, the theatricality and even literary madness of what we call *The German Ideology* can be read as a daring foray into the danger and unruliness of literary masses. As is the case with Don Quixote, a reader among readers, the act of reading is never innocent or without danger; it carries a transformative madness within it. Despite the fact that Marx and Engels never publish this satirical, allusive, and riotous set of readings, the assembled fragments of *The German Ideology* may be the underground infrastructure of the Marxian project—the site of its convulsive and unbounded creativity from which later and more systematic texts will emerge.[26] It may even be the unruly literary mass at the heart of the Marxian letter.

★

This book has its origins in an invitation to write a review of Fredric Jameson's 2020 book *The Benjamin Files* for the journal *Cultural Critique*. Jameson's book appeared in the midst of a global pandemic, in the context of the rise of racism in general and anti-Black violence in particular, an upsurge of authoritarianism and fascism around the world, an intensification of different forms of inequality, an escalation of conflicts and wars of all kinds, an increase in the dispossession of populations and in forced migrations, and an acceleration of environmental catastrophes globally. There was something remarkable about reading and thinking about this book in a moment of political volatility and communal grief and to write about it in the aftermath of the January 6, 2021 attack on the US Capitol. In what way can a text resonate with the historical moment in which it appears, even if it does not address the most urgent issues of that moment directly and even if its focus references other historical moments? How can a text become a resource for thinking about the present? How does a historical moment affect the way we read a text, either one that belongs to that moment or one that does not? Our book began, then, in a collaborative scene of reading and in conversations about the relation between texts and history, language and activism, reading and political work. While we tried to remain as attentive as we could to Jameson's reading of Benjamin—and we believe we have done so—we inevitably began, in Benjaminian fashion, to read not only what Jameson said but also what he did not; we began to read what remained invisible in his text, but which nevertheless left its traces on his pages. Increasingly, these readings began unfolding in relation to a growing number of references, often historical references that were not mentioned at all in his text, but which were signaled at its edges and in its omissions. Of these, the most significant one for us was a parenthetical remark that Jameson makes in relation to the question of why socialism has never flourished in the United States—a remark that, at its end, attributes this absence to "race." Hardly mentioned, just one word in a parenthesis, almost silenced there, the word "race" jumped out at us. It could only become louder and stronger—so much more resonant and forceful—because of the worldwide demonstrations that took place in the aftermath of the murder of George Floyd in the summer of 2020. Jameson does not pursue the matter, but, for us, the word became an opening to a vast archive—one related to the history of Black grief and suffering and to the violent history of racial capitalism.

This already heterogeneous archive in turn opened up to several others—in ways that seemed at times random and at other times strictly necessary, but always in a manner that compelled us to trace this ever-expanding assemblage of figures and motifs in their movement, and in their entanglement with one another. This process of opening, unfolding, and expanding continued throughout the writing of the book, determining it, often without our knowing where we were being led until we found ourselves in the midst of another set of disparate materials. This process of expansion accounts for the book's form, which emerged without a predetermined plan, but with the felt responsibility of following each trace as it led us to another one, always in unexpected directions. This movement seemed to have a will of its own, even when driven by the materials themselves, and at every step we were compelled to catch up to our own improvisations—*by reading more*. But this is what reading is: a process of amplification and massification that moves in a wandering wayward way, in an itinerant, incomplete, and asymmetrical exchange between the moment in which a text is written and the moment in which it is read, with these moments themselves permeated and fissured by other moments and other texts. We use the word "wayward" here in the sense that Saidiya Hartman gives it:

> Wayward, related to the family of words: errant, fugitive, recalcitrant, anarchic, willful, reckless, troublesome, riotous, tumultuous, rebellious and wild. ... The social poesis that sustains the dispossessed. Wayward: the unregulated movement of drifting and wandering; sojourns without a fixed destination, ambulatory possibility, interminable migrations, rush and flight, black

locomotion; the everyday struggle to live free. ... Wayward: to wan-der, to be unmoored, adrift, rambling, roving, cruising, strolling, and seeking. To claim the right to opacity. To strike, to riot, to refuse. To love what is not loved. To be lost to the world. It is the ... insurgent ground that enables new possibilities and new vocab-ularies. ... It is a beautiful experiment in how-to-live. ... [It] is an ongoing exploration of what might be.[27]

In everything that follows, we have discovered this waywardness not only in the writers we read—all of whom understand that to "be lost to the world" means staying close to it in all its uncertainty, all of whom are devoted to the proliferation of new possibilities—but also in the movement of language itself. As Hartman puts it, "wayward" is *related to the family of words* and, as such, is, like language, "errant, fugitive, recalcitrant, anarchic, willful, reck-less, troublesome, riotous, tumultuous, rebellious and wild." At the same time, if reading is wayward because it refuses to stop, to stay still, to move in a straight line, this does not mean it is not motivated—that it does not pause or slow down, riot or go on strike, is entirely without direction, even when this direction remains indeterminate. Instead, its waywardness is a form of experimentation and improvisation that, "rebellious and wild," like the unruliness of the Marxian letter, comes with the force of an insurgency that "enables new possibilities and new vocabular-ies," "an ongoing exploration of what might be."

If our initial motivation and momentum were prompted by Jameson's book, we have departed from it in order to read it more expansively, in order to experience what it might mean to live a life of reading and writing that loves "what is not loved," that aligns itself with the dispossessed and the vanquished. Moving beyond ourselves—in our collaboration but also by creating coalitions across various archives—we repeatedly have experienced the rich-ness of all the resources we have encountered and that, in turn, have reinforced us in this political work. Because this journey began with our first conversations about Jameson, however, rather than rehearse the trajectory of our book, we will stay closest here to the consequences of our first divergence from him. We trust that the wonder of our journey will become legible in the pages that follow, and we hope that the exhilaration and passion we have been fortunate to experience in this unexpected process of reading and writing can be conveyed. The wonder we have experienced in all the readers and writers we read here—and in our own collabora-tive practice—is what enables a reading to become red.

★

Experiencing Jameson reading Benjamin, registering the effects this reading has on him and his protestation against them, and thinking about the different historical contexts he evokes and in which he writes, wittingly or unwittingly, enabled his book to become an entry into the several archives we bring together here—all of which, we believe, can be used as resources for doing political work today and, in particular, antiracist work. As we demonstrate in relation to our frontispiece, a particular mode of reading historically—one inflected in a literary way—can collaborate with the text at hand in order to maximize its creative and political potential. This potential can become activated differently at different moments, and this is what makes a text a resource. A text is not always what it can become, but what it can become is its greatest strength; its potential is what can transform it into an invitation to imagine a different future. In our case, we began reading one single book, but it quickly drew us to several possible worlds—worlds that appeared in the process of reading, as we brought our own archives into contact with all the ones inscribed in Jameson's language, and beyond it. Opening up Jameson's text from within these worlds introduced a series of breaks around which we could imagine different plural collectivities emerging.[28] This is why, remaining a thread in our book, Jameson is now one figure among many others. These multiple worlds could have been generated from any of the writers in our book, but we have decided to preserve the traces of the book's beginnings as a review of Jameson's book—in order to underscore not simply how circumstantial and unpredictable the unfolding of our book has been but also how its trajectory cannot be disentangled from its starting point. *Politically Red* not only belongs to the aftereffects of the unruly mass of the Marxian letter but is meant to intensify them.

This is why we began with our frontispiece. It is a manifesto for reading and writing—and one we have followed. The threshold the reader must cross, it is a palimpsestic set of textual and visual protocols for reading and writing—the archival trace of different temporalities that bring together what is visible on the page with what remains invisible in it. It is the first of several indices in our book that political work can take place at the level of sentences and, in particular, in the force of their processes of figuration— especially when these processes are not reducible *just* to language. An emblem of the mode of collaboration we have embraced throughout, the frontispiece operates within a logic in which the reader cannot read our book without having read the frontispiece but also cannot read the frontispiece without having read our book.[29] This reading loop is legible throughout the book and accounts for why it requires a reader able to move backward and forward, to return to pages already read and to read them differently after having read other parts of the book. It is also legible in the relation between the main body of the text and our footnotes—a necessary supplement that, invisible to the reader as he or she reads, deepens and intensifies the initial reading and calls for a second one. This exchange between what is visible and invisible— what Althusser calls "the organic link binding the invisible to the visible"[30]—structures the protocols of reading that we enact here and that, as we already have noted, often begin in the margins of a text: in parentheses, ellipses, elisions, dashes, footnotes, and at the edges and limits of what is said and left unsaid. It is a matter of reading what is invisible, illegible, inaudible—what belongs to the structure of a text, whether it is linguistic, visual, historical, or something else altogether but what also functions like a clandestine infrastructure that binds the text with its silence. This is why so much of what follows involves reading peripheral moments as places of elaboration and experimentation.

Capitalizing on the homonymic play between "red" and "read," *Politically Red* traces the relations between political engagement and different forms of literacy. Like Marx and Engels, it begins in the conviction that sentences belong to the possibility of mass formations, collective action, and insurrectionary politics. Insisting on the relation between language and action, between action and what exceeds language, it offers a new lens through which to approach the long history of thinking about the relations between theory and practice. In a series of titled sections—each one introduced by a visual and textual epigraph, and organized around a particular figure or phrase—we follow the way these figures and phrases get recast, activated, and set in motion in relation to other figures and phrases. Because the writers we read either anticipate or incorporate the language of other writers, we can trace the movement and trajectories of their political lexicon, even when it does not follow a straight line. This lexicon includes words and phrases like accumulation, capitalism, class consciousness, colonialism, communism, fascism, general strike, genocide, hopelessness, indigeneity, literacy, masses, messianism, race, reproduction, revolution, socialism, technology, theology, and violence. In each instance, *Politically Red* takes these words and phrases, recontextualizes them, and then moves them in multiple, and often unexpected, directions. Emphasizing their mobility and plurality, demonstrating that there is no single concept behind them, it points to a new way of thinking about political action in general—one that has its starting point in the writers we read and whose language we inevitably inherit and transform.

These writers—often linked to Marx but not always—form a plural coalition, what we call a "red common-wealth." This common-wealth represents a shared wealth of resources from which we can draw to work against capital and its various forms of violence, and against racial violence in particular. Following Raya Dunayevskaya, who, situating race at the heart of Marx's writings, devotes much of her activist writing to what she calls the "Black dimension,"[31] our common-wealth insists that only a Marxism that is antiracist can be true to its critical force. After Black Marxism, Marx must be read differently, and more deeply— which means, among other things, with an acknowledgment of his force within Black Liberation movements, including today's. Black radicalism belongs to the history of communism and has questioned this history as much as it has contributed to it. For this reason, we have put our introduction under a militant aphorism from the poet Amiri Baraka. It resonates profoundly not only with our title but also with the arc of our book. Our entire book, in all its movements, could even be said to be condensed in this single line, which carries the weight of the "red common-wealth" Baraka evokes in his 1991 essay on the relation between the blues and Black aesthetics. In the essay, in a fragment that— operating like an undercurrent throughout *Politically Red*—is on its way to becoming a sentence, he writes: "The Red what reading did re adding reproducing revolution."[32]

Gisèle Freund, Walter Benjamin at the Bibliothèque Nationale, Paris, 1937

I. POLITICALLY READ

Reading is class struggle.

—Bertolt Brecht, *The Mother* (1931)[1]

What does it mean to read or to write? In what way are reading and writing a means of doing political work? Why is it that, in his preface to *Reading Capital*, Louis Althusser insists that "only since Marx have we had to begin to suspect what, in theory at least, *reading* and hence writing *means*"?[2] Although we could start anywhere to answer these questions, we wish to begin by considering the trajectory of Fredric Jameson's readings and writings for now more than 50 years, since he remains the best-known and most longstanding American Marxist critic today. In particular, we are interested in the fact that, after his early essay on Walter Benjamin in 1969, after having written extensively on Theodor Adorno and Bertolt Brecht as well as several other thinkers associated with Benjamin, he finally writes a book on this rather singular reader and writer in a moment marked by the rise of both old and new fascisms, and publishes it on election day, November 3, 2020. What is it that makes this particular act of reading and writing so necessary at this very moment, and what does it tell us not only about Benjamin and Jameson—about Jameson's relation to Benjamin and Benjamin's relation to Marx—but also about the political stakes of this act for both of them?

It is not surprising that, in reading Jameson's *The Benjamin Files*—his latest and most extended interpretation of Benjamin—we discover several things about Jameson. As we know, every act of reading reveals as much about the reader as it does about the object being read, even when two of the terms that this encounter between Jameson and Benjamin will question are "reader" and "object." What is more surprising is that the more closely we look at Jameson's book, the more closely we attend to his engagement with the strangeness of Benjamin's writings—even at the level of sentences, and perhaps especially at the level of sentences—the more we can register the profound transformation of Jameson's writing that occurs because of this encounter. Jameson's book is more "writerly" than any of his previous books. There is a peculiar mimetic contagion that seems to infiltrate his style, that helps account for the citationality of his text—itself a kind of homage to Benjamin's own penchant for quotation. It is as if this most recent encounter with Benjamin's writings transforms Jameson's mode of reading and writing. This transformation is legible in the way in which the Marxist critic traces and reenacts what he calls Benjamin's "spatial sentence," a sentence that, if read properly, can become "as broad as the world."[3] Already in his 1971 *Marxism and Form*, he had noted that any reading of "a literary or philosophical phenomenon—if it is to be really complete—has an ultimate obligation to come to terms with the shape of the individual sentences themselves, to give an account of their origin and formation."[4] In other words, in order to read a sentence, we need to reconstruct the world or worlds that made it possible and that the sentence in turn calls into being. If Jameson offers an intellectual physiognomy of Benjamin, this physiognomy resonates in the pedagogy implicit in tracing a sentence in space in order to understand its shape, to register an archive of figures that confirms that space is always traversed by a network of historical relations, in Benjamin's words "intertwined time," space-crossed time.[5]

It would seem that this return to Benjamin enables Jameson to formalize things he may have wanted to say earlier but could not until this latest passage through Benjamin's writings. It also permits him to go further in the direction of exposing himself to the risk of reading, and to the attendant risks that, for him, are implicit in any effort to bring about political change through reading and writing, something he knows better than most since he has had recourse to literary and philosophical texts in order to do his political work throughout his entire career. We should not forget that Marx, too, passed through literature and philosophy in his analyses of, among so many other things, capital, religion, history, ideology, law, rights, nationalism, and various political forms of social organization.

Jameson seems particularly aware of the risks of reading—and perhaps especially the risk to himself of reading Benjamin—when early in the book he suggests that reading involves "a physical displacement within the reading mind itself, a regulated spasm in which the mimetic categories are unexpectedly substituted for one another like the prestidigitation of a shell game or the unmistakable tremors of an underground detonation. This writer has visibly tampered with our mental infrastructure; his sentence has reached inside the mind with an imperceptible violence that ought to be illegal and denounced as such" (*BF*, 22–23). He later refs to the violence of this "reading effect" as "an unusual pedagogy which has to do with the perceptual levels within the mind, a kind of pedagogical surgery that can be characterized as a cultural revolution within the reading process" (*BF*, 35). Evoking the decade-long Great Proletarian Cultural Revolution that began in May 1966, initiated by Mao in his effort to reassert his control over the Communist party—by mobilizing the Chinese masses against it—Jameson points to the violence that characterized this revolution. Because he links this violence and this revolution to a transformation in the activity of reading, he reminds us that the Cultural Revolution was furthered by the printing and circulation of its official handbook, the Little Red Book, a pocket-sized collection of quotations from Mao that offered a blueprint for Red Guard life.

During the 1960s, this little book is said to have been the most printed book in the world, with more than a billion copies printed. Like the effect that Jameson claims Benjamin's writings have on him, the Little Red Book offered a pedagogy for the Red Guard that aimed to create a mass political formation whose mimetic proliferation could, in its most ambitious version, transform the world into communism. This possibility involves a process of reading that, concomitant with "a kind of pedagogical surgery," requires the internalization of a script of identification—of a series of party lines and images in which the reader can see himself or herself, as if in a mirror. This effort to inscribe a reader within the ideologemes of a particular political formation is made explicit in an editorial entitled "In Praise of the Red Guards" that appeared in the September 23, 1966 issue of the *Peking Review*. There we read:

> The Red Guards have been nurtured in their growth by Mao Tse-tung's thought. The Red Guards say, and say it well: Chairman Mao is our red commander and we are the young, red soldiers of Chairman Mao. What our Red Guards love most of all is to read Chairman Mao's works and follow his teachings, and their love for Mao Tse-tung's thought is most ardent. They carry with them copies of *Quotations from Chairman Mao Tse-tung*. They take as their highest obligation the study, dissemination, application, and defense of Mao Tse-tung's thought.

The emphasis on the role of reading in the formation of the Red Guards cannot be overestimated. This identificatory reading practice was meant to ensure that the reader could be more easily inscribed in the revolution's red doctrine and therefore presumably be more able to flourish under the light of its optative rays.

In the words of the same editorial, "Like the red sun rising in the east, the unprecedented Great Proletarian Cultural Revolution is illuminating the land with its brilliant rays."[6]

If Benjamin's writings present a pedagogy, even an *unusual* one, it is because his training manual for reading, writing, thinking, and even doing politics provides an explicit *counter* to the processes of identification and indoctrination that—in accordance with at least one logic of reproduction and perhaps the most violent one—wish: (1) to produce a homogeneous and identifiable mass formation; (2) to subject a populace to a predetermined and fixed set of ideological positions; and (3) to intensify the cathexis with an authoritarian leader. Unlike the Little Red Book, Benjamin's pedagogy underscores the relation between reading and violence in order to suggest that, without an understanding of the stakes of this relation in all its different manifestations, it is impossible to understand the violence of the Chinese Cultural Revolution—a violence that is inseparable from its instrumentalization of reading. The former never could have happened without the latter. Even before the Cultural Revolution—the period during which Jameson writes his first essay on Benjamin—Benjamin already had associated the violence of this contagion of mimesis with the possibility of transforming the way we read and think. He insists that we submit ourselves to this violence in the strictest form of mimesis by literally copying out what we are reading, as if reading can only really take place if we trace, if we follow and repeat, the very movement of sentences as they wind their way in a paragraph or a text and, in so doing, record the activity of thinking *in this movement* that reading traces in the mind. In this instance, then, staying close to the text means staying close to its depths and enigmas, to what, within the text, prevents the assertion of a fixed and stable identification and, instead, disperses the reading self across heterogeneous landscapes and possibilities. As Benjamin writes in the "Chinese Curios" section of *One-Way Street*:

> The power of a country road when one is walking along it is different from the power it has when one is flying over it by airplane. In the same way, the power of a text when it is read is different from the power it has when it is copied out. ... Only he who walks the road on foot learns the power it commands, and of how, from the very scenery that for the flier is only the unfurled plain, it calls forth distances, belvederes, clearings, prospects at each of its turns like a commander deploying soldiers at a front. Only the copied text thus commands the soul of him who is occupied with

it, whereas the mere reader never discovers the new aspects of his inner self that are opened by the text, that road cut through the interior jungle forever closing behind it: because the reader follows the movement of his mind in the free flight of daydreaming, whereas the copier submits it to command. The Chinese practice of copying books was thus an incomparable guarantee of literary culture, and the transcript a key to China's enigmas.[7]

The more closely we follow the movement of a text, Benjamin suggests, the more able we are to experience the many worlds and landscapes that exist within it. The copyist—surrendering himself to the power of a text that, as he traces and reproduces it, commands his soul—is inscribed in an activity of writing that is his and not his at the same time. It is precisely this lack of full agency, this inability to control the effects of a text, that guarantees a future for literary culture, for the inventiveness and even unpredictability that can come from copying a text faithfully—an activity that, in remaining faithful to the text, remains near its enigmas. Holding the key to China's enigmas does not mean understanding them—if understanding here means unlocking them and revealing their hidden mysteries—but rather holding onto and opening up the essentially enigmatic nature of reading and writing. Benjamin confirms this point by recalling the Chinese artistic practice of copying and its relation to creativity. Chinese artists learned by imitating ancient masters, and tracing was a primary pedagogical source for artistic training and workshop practice. They copied in order to master the techniques and styles of an earlier master, not in order to confirm their lack of originality, their impoverishment in relation to their forebears, but to produce a singularly inventive work—a possibility incorporated into the very act of copying.

What is perhaps most interesting to Benjamin here—and something to which we will return later—is a mode of reproduction that, however exacting it may be, nevertheless clears a path for something singular to emerge. But, as he suggests, the artist does not pass through what he or she inherits only in order to find his or her "own" voice. Instead, this passage through the past requires an absorption of the artist into the work, the disappearance of the artist in relation to the work and therefore in relation to all the precursors whose traces remain inscribed in the work's surface and to whom the artist is indebted, consciously or unconsciously. Benjamin makes this point in an early version of his *Berlin Childhood around 1900*: in a section titled "The Mummerehlen," he

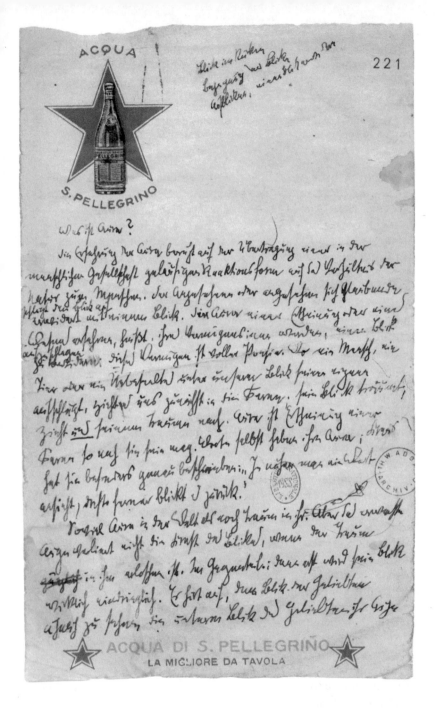

Walter Benjamin, "Was ist Aura?" Draft page from "The Work of Art in the Age of Its Technological Reproducibility," between 1936 and 1939

recalls a Chinese legend that returns him to the relation he had with the assorted items of porcelain *chinoiserie* that, during his childhood, were among his favorite objects and that, via a work of dissemblance and pantomime, he came to resemble and even enter. Despite their kitsch quality, Benjamin notes:

> Of all the things I used to mimic, my favorite was the Chinese porcelain. A mottled crust overspread those vases, bowls, plates, and boxes, which, to be sure, were merely cheap export articles. I was nonetheless captivated by them, just as if I already knew the story which, after so many years, leads me back again to the work of mummerehlen. The story comes from China, and tells of an old painter who invited friends to see his newest picture. This picture showed a park and a narrow footpath that ran along a stream and through a grove of trees, culminating at the door of a little cottage in the background. When the painter's friends, however, looked around for the painter, they saw that he had left them—that he was in the picture. There, he followed the little path that led to the door, paused before it quite still, turned, smiled, and disappeared through the narrow opening. In the same way, I too, when occupied with my paintpots and brushes, would be suddenly displaced into the picture. I would resemble the porcelain which I had entered in a cloud of colors.[8]

Benjamin's childhood relation to different modes of mimesis, imitation, and copying is a permanent motif in his autobiographical writings. Here the adult writer recalls the child painter he was and tells a Chinese story that he reproduces a number of times in his writings, including in his "Work of Art" essay.[9] It is as if, even as a child, he already knew the story he would later recall, but also as if he already was an actor within it. Like the old Chinese painter, he too finds himself displaced into the work—in his case, he is transported in "a cloud of colors" into the painted porcelain. The idea of vanishing into a work of art via a shifting medium—in this instance, a cloud, but also the colors which, he notes, color him and even disguise him[10]—is a direct counterpart to Benjamin's tendency to disappear into an act of reading that is also an act of writing.[11] The transience of both activities is experienced as so many fleeting instances of resemblance and assimilation, momentary configurations in which mimicry and imagination, the past and the present, coincide to reveal the enigma of reading and writing in the form of a dialectical thought-image, what Benjamin calls a *Denkbild*.

Benjamin returns to his proposition on the Chinese practice of copying, and of calligraphy in particular, in a short 1938 review, "Peintures chinoises à la Bibliothèque Nationale" ("Chinese

Paintings at the Bibliothèque Nationale"). There, challenging the prevailing assessment of the works of the Ming (1368–1644) and Qing (1644–1911) dynasties as unoriginal, he points to the wonder of the works, a wonder that begins in an act of copying that is also an act of painting, thinking, writing, and reading, but one that takes its point of departure from a pluralization and scattering of its subjects:

The subjects of these calligraphies, which constitute, in a way, part of the painting, are multiple. They sometimes contain commentaries and references to illustrious masters. ... "Chinese calligraphy, as an art," says the erudite Lin Yutang, "implies ... the cult and appreciation of the abstract beauty of line and composition in the characters, when these are assembled in such a way that they give the impression of an unstable equilibrium. ... In this search for the history of Chinese calligraphy, we see that practically all the organic forms and all the movements of living beings that exist in nature have been incorporated and assimilated. ... The artist ... seized upon the stork's thin stilts, the hare's bounding contours, the tiger's massive paws, the lion's mane, the elephant's ponderous walk—and weaves them into a web of magical beauty."

Chinese calligraphy—this "ink-play," to borrow the phrase that Monsieur Dubosc uses to designate the paintings—thus appears as something eminently in motion. Although the signs have a fixed connection and form on the paper, the many "resemblances" they contain set them moving. Expressed in every stroke of the brush, these virtual resemblances form a mirror where thought is reflected in this atmosphere of resemblance, or resonance.

Indeed, these resemblances are not mutually exclusive; they become intermingled, constituting a whole that solicits thought the way a breeze beckons to a veil of gauze. The term *xieyi* ("idea painting"), which the Chinese reserve for this notation, is significant in this regard.

An essential feature of the image is that it incorporates something eternal. This eternal quality expresses itself in the fixity and stability of the stroke, but it is also manifest, more subtly, thanks to the fact that the image embodies something that is fluid and ever-changing. It is from this blending of the fixed and the mutable that Chinese painting derives all its meaning. It goes in search of the thought-image. "In China," says Monsieur Sallers, "the art of painting is first and foremost the art of thinking." And thinking, for the Chinese painter, means thinking by means of resemblance. Moreover, just as resemblance always appears to us like a flash of lightning (since nothing is more transient than the appearance of a resemblance), the fleeting and changeful character of these paintings merges with their penetration of the real. That which they fix is no more immutable than a cloud. And this is their true and enigmatic substance—it consists of change, like life.[12]

Emphasizing the multiplicity of the calligraphic character's subjects, the traces of commentaries and references to precursors borne by its lines and brushstrokes, and the instability that is inseparable from the work's presumed equilibrium, Benjamin not only points to the mobility of these calligraphic paintings but also to the way in which they bear the traces of whole archives, even nonhuman ones. As he puts it, "practically all the organic forms and all the movements of living beings that exist in nature have been incorporated and assimilated" into the works, into "a web of magical beauty." The multiplicity of traces in the surface of these works—the result of, in his rather wonderful phrase, "ink-play"—forms a mirror whose reflections are constantly in motion, miming the movement of thought as it moves from one resemblance or echo to another. Even as the figure seems fixed on its paper support, even as it points to something "eternal," this "eternal quality" is only legible in the image as something "fluid and ever-changing." Benjamin here evokes the "petrified restlessness" he associates with Baudelaire but also with the "dialectical image" which—like the fleeting, fugitive resemblances that whirl within Chinese paintings and in such a way that they can never be read in isolation from one another and can never therefore emerge *as such*—"appears to us like a flash of lightning." What the works fix is the enigmatic, always changing signature of life as transience.

Because this movement is linked not simply to the pluralization of the work's subjects but also to the pluralization of the artist's brushstrokes—since each stroke carries a nexus of historical relations—we can again register the difference between the wished-for transparency of the Little Red Book and Benjamin's insistence on the enigmatic archive in every calligraphic sign. Benjamin's thought-image—not that different from the Chinese "idea painting"—becomes the calligraphical index of a reading and writing practice that distances itself from individual expression in order to become emmeshed in the multiple resonances of an "ink-play" that, incorporating the traces of innumerable "illustrious masters," ceases to belong to anyone in particular. In contrast to the readings of the Red Guard, where every word can be traced to Mao as an immutable source, Benjamin's calligraphic musings move toward the impersonality that will define his reading and writing practice, one organized around a pluralized logic of resonance and resemblance that remains faithful to the transience and mobility of the wondrously rich—and also painful and violent—historical experience of social beings. In contrast to the Little Red Book, Benjamin's writings mime the sociohistorical indices that swirl within any text and that, anchoring but also fissuring any sense of collectivity, point to the intense multiplicity and plurality of experiences that appear as infinitely layered Chinese boxes, just as the artist-writer-reader does. As he suggests, every act of reading involves a subject that can never be fully personalized without incurring a loss of experience. If he adopts the mobility and liquidity of the phrase "ink-play" to describe the gestural strokes of the Chinese painter's brush, it is because this phrase alone can capture the transient nature of reading and writing in their mutual implication.

The disappearance of the self, the impersonality we see enacted here by Benjamin, is distant from the modes of identification Mao's Little Red Book demands; it instead enacts an intensification of experience that requires an untethered subject—a subject willing to sacrifice identitarian certainties in order to participate in an event of disindentification and pluralization. As Benjamin would have it, the more closely we engage with a text, the more extended our reading, the more this activity affects not only our reading and writing but also our capacity to remain just ourselves. In the instance of *One-Way Street*, for example, which Jameson describes as a "dangerous stimulant," the pages we "absorb" transform our relation to reading and writing—against our will and knowledge (*BF*, 17). It is as if only in surrendering ourselves to the language of multiple others can we begin to navigate our way through a text, as the archive of relations that we are and that we become. Reading and writing—like any political act—reveal themselves to be entirely collaborative and collective. We can never enact them by ourselves, and this is why Benjamin resists—except in letters, he claims—using "I" in any of his writings and why we might say that Jameson, in his own engagement with Benjamin, can only begin to reveal the destruction, beginning with the destruction of the self, that is at the heart of all reading: what Benjamin calls "the perilous critical moment on which all reading is founded."[13] If reading is perilous, it is because its collaborative and collective character—when we read, we never read alone—inscribes us within a community but, in doing so, deranges our identity and even that of the community. What is at stake for Benjamin is the possibility of imagining a practice of reading and writing that, strictly speaking, begins neither in a collective nor in an individual, but in what we are calling the "impersonality" of reading. This structure of impersonality ensures, even when the copyist is rigorously faithful to the text being reproduced, a relation to what remains hidden in the "interior jungle" of a text—the "distances, belvederes, clearings, [and] prospects" that not only "guarantee" the future of literary culture but also keep "China" a place full of "enigmas." If to copy a text faithfully requires that we remain faithful to its enigmas, nothing is perhaps more enigmatic than an act of reading and writing that, relying on earlier acts of reading and writing, nevertheless manages to invent something singular, enables the traversal of a path of thinking that finds new roads to follow, or new paths in old ones, and is even "commanded" to do this by the text itself. In the "Chinese practice of copying books," "[s]trength lies in improvisation" and all the "decisive blows" must be "struck left-handed" (*OWS*, 447).

In his 1979 essay "Marxism and Historicism," Jameson already had pointed to the impersonality of reading in a passage that describes both the reader and the writer whose work he or she engages as "different modes of production," and their encounter as an "essentially collective confrontation of two social forms."[14] There he makes clear that the activity of reading not only transforms the reader but also judges him or her—as the "social formation" of which he or she is the living and constantly changing archive. We cite the passage at length since, in essential ways, our reading of *The Benjamin Files*—and of the Marxist inheritance and pedagogy to which, in its unfolding, this reading takes us—will be nothing more nor less than a demonstration of its consequences for any reading that would present itself as political and, in particular, as *politically red*.[15] Jameson writes:

> We must try to accustom ourselves to a perspective in which every act of reading, every local interpretive practice, is grasped as the privileged vehicle through which two distinct modes of production confront and interrogate one another. Our individual reading thus becomes an allegorical figure for this essentially collective confrontation of two social forms.
>
> If we can do this ... [w]e will no longer tend to see the past as some inert and dead object which we are called upon to resurrect, or to preserve, or to sustain, in our own living freedom; rather, the past will itself become an active agent in this process and will begin to come before us as a radically different life form which rises up to call our own form of life into question and to pass judgment on us, and through us on the social formation in which we exist. At that point, the very dynamics of the historical tribunal are unexpectedly and dialectically reversed: it is not we who sit in judgment on the past, but rather the past, the radical difference of other modes of production (and even of the immediate past of our own mode of production), which judges us, imposing the painful knowledge of what we are not, what we are no longer, what we are not yet.[16]

Jameson here reminds us, and this is perhaps one of the greatest discoveries of Western Marxism, that the base is intertwined with the superstructure in the mind, is inseparable from the shaping of thinking through form, even if this form is in turn in flux. Jameson has been faithful to this discovery throughout his career and, following him, we can understand that Marxism has always been another name for the act of reading. If this passage could just as easily have been written by Benjamin, it is because both Benjamin and Jameson inhabit Marx's language in similar ways. That they return to literature as a resource for doing political work time and time again, that they write in a literary fashion, confirms their fidelity to the Marxian letter—to the "place" where literary texts become writerly events. It is because neither Benjamin nor Jameson stop reading even as they write that we are privy to the effects of reading in their minds but also in their writing. This is why their sentences are historical. In response to György Lukács's "history is the perpetual breaking of form" (cited in *BF*, 143), Benjamin and Jameson add that these breaks occur in the mind through language and are materialized at the level of the sentence. These sentential breaks imply that reading is an act of destruction, but one without which there can be no political work in the Marxist sense. As Benjamin puts it in his 1934 essay "The Author as Producer" (an essay that Jameson singles out as one of his greatest):

> the tendency of a literary work can be politically correct only if it is also literarily correct. That is to say, the politically correct tendency includes a literary tendency ... this literary tendency, which is implicitly or explicitly contained in every *correct* political tendency of a work, alone constitutes the quality of that work. The correct political tendency of a work thus includes its literary quality *because* it includes its literary *tendency*.[17]

This polemical passage asks us to consider the relationship between politics and style and, in doing so, not only challenges received notions of what each of these terms may mean but also encourages us to imagine a future that, coming as literature, can perhaps realize what Jean-Luc Nancy calls "literary communism."[18]

Glenn Ligon, *Red Hands #2*, 1996

II. MULTIPLICITY

Ad plures ire [To go to the many]

—Latin proverb

Every historical act can only be performed by "collective man," and this presupposes the attainment of a "cultural-social" unity through which a multiplicity of dispersed wills, with heterogeneous aims, are welded together. ... Since this is the way things happen, the importance of the general question of language comes to light.

—Antonio Gramsci, Notebook 10, *Prison Notebooks* (1932–1933)[1]

In the rather striking opening of his book—titled "Wind in the Sails" and taking its point of departure from Benjamin's famous claim that what matters for the dialectician "is having the wind of world history in one's sails" and knowing how to set them (*AP*, 473)[2]—Jameson insists that thinking and writing are indistinguishable in Benjamin and that the movement between words and concepts in his work produces an uncertainty and indeterminacy that makes it impossible for us to settle on any one of them as a key to his thought. If "history is change as such" (*BF*, 2), it is not surprising, Jameson suggests, that the "changeability and variability" of Benjamin's vast reservoir of concepts are the writer's way of remaining faithful to the transience, fleetingness, contingency, "variability," and "historical ephemerality" that, for him, are history's signature and index (*BF*, 3). The only works Benjamin can write are works that destroy themselves, that can only appear as a process of destruction and bear the force of their own dissolution within them—as the cipher of the violence through which they are formed and deformed in the very movement of their coming into existence, and as the consequence of all the different temporalities inscribed within them. In Jameson's words, destruction is "a Benjaminian *gestus*," a "modus operandi" (*BF*, 7). This is why, he adds, Benjamin "could not write a traditional book"—from the *Trauerspiel* to the *Arcades Project* and beyond (even if we consider *One-Way Street* his one "book," it is less a book than simply "the new form that the impossibility of the book brings forth in its place" [*BF*, 9]).[3] This is largely because Benjamin's works carry the traces of their own finitude. Penetrated by a sense of finitude and violence, they are riven and interrupted by a force that prevents them from remaining identical to themselves.

This force of dissociation is legible in the way in which Benjamin's language immediately distances itself from itself. As Karl Kraus writes, in a sentence that Benjamin cites in the essay he devotes to the critic, "The closer one looks at a word, the further it looks back."[4] This sentence gives us a "formula" or "protocol" for reading Benjamin but also for his experience of language and of things in general. It suggests that every word or sentence in Benjamin has other voices, other words and sentences, in it, even "behind" it. He can never write as an "I" or speak only in his own voice. The act of reading becomes an involuntary conjuring of a distance, however close we may think we are to this or that text. Every word, every sentence, shows itself to be a "constellation," in the strict Benjaminian sense, and the multiplicity this constellation brings together makes it, in Jameson's words, a "destructive weapon, an instrument to be wielded against system and above all against systematic philosophy" (*BF*, 4). It is because the constellation of words and concepts that circulate in Benjamin's works—among others, allegory, aura, citationality, dialectical image, experience, happiness, impersonality, legibility, masses, media, messianism, mimesis, monad, montage, multiplicity, origin, redemption, reproducibility, revolution, similitude, theology—are intertwined and entangled with each other, can never exist in isolation from the others, that, in the end, reading can only encounter its own incompleteness. This multiplicity of words and concepts belongs to what Benjamin will later think in relation to the masses, the Baudelairean crowds, and the still unthought collective that might help inaugurate a future that will not negate itself by petrifying the past (*BF*, 13). But it also registers a multiplicity of figures and voices within Benjamin's language that corresponds to an almost machine-like citational structure.

What characterizes the interior mechanism of Benjamin's language—what Jameson calls his "style"—is the way in which its figures cinematically fade out into one another before any one of them has a chance to assert itself. They are evoked only to be transformed by different figures or mobilized into different contexts in a violent movement of extraction and displacement. As we have noted, the shifting movement that we understand as the signature of Benjamin's language is his way of remaining faithful to a process of destruction, what Jameson identifies as the "violence of [his] critical practice" (*BF*, 29). This violence is at the heart of Benjamin's citationality, something that is already evident in his earlier essays but gets its first extended enactment in his 1928 *Trauerspiel* book. Benjamin's *Trauerspiel* tells us that history can only *be* history as long as it is the withdrawing trace of its own transience. Only when it is no longer history—that is to say, no longer an empirical, historical fact among others—can it survive as history and as the possibility of history. The *Trauerspiel* presents itself as an anthology of baroque figures, a history of the surviving linguistic figures of the past, and, in particular, of the linguistic emblems of a literary past. This unstable relationship between figuration and the transience of legibility points to the necessity—the political necessity—of training new and emerging collectivities in the reading of the images, figures, and emblems of history and, in particular, of the reproducibility inscribed within them.

As Benjamin demonstrates, the baroque's emphasis on the inevitability of repetition, on the citational and scriptural character of history, suggests that the notion of an original or unique work of art is almost as difficult to sustain in the German baroque mourning play as it will be with the emergence of photography and film. The *Trauerspiel* should be read as a self-proliferating recitation of history—in particular, of a prebourgeois history—and, more provocatively, as a violent masterpiece of unoriginality (Jameson refers to it as "a tissue of citations" [*BF*, 35]). Benjamin's language surrenders itself to innumerable others—a Shakespeare, a Calderón, a Gracián, or any number of the baroque writers he considers here—whose language enters his text fragmentarily through a process of extraction that is both violent and destructive. Once gleaned from a historical text, this fragment, or even just a word, enters into a logic of analogy with other fragments and other words. The mechanism of analogy becomes an antidote both to causality and to a naive understanding of creativity; it underscores the fact that history is only political if it is simultaneously form and the breaking of form.[5] The similitude or conceptual affinity that travels from one text to another signals the movements of what can become legible, which appears as a series of endless emblems carrying enigmas across several different temporalities. As Baltasar Gracián puts it in his definition of *conceptismo*, they are inscribed within "un acto del entendimiento que expresa la correspondencia que se halla entre los objetos" (within "a mental event that expresses a correspondence between objects"), and their itinerancy relies on the intensification of polysemy, allegory, paradox, emblem, enigma, and ellipsis.[6] Gracián can illuminate the past insofar as his writings can be read as contemporary through a logic of analogy that bypasses literary history—a paradoxical refracting technique that freezes their contextual history to reveal structural similarities that dialectically illuminate the simultaneity of past and present. It is in the possibility of our being able to read this relation and difference that we can begin to register what Benjamin means by history as a pathway to politics, which is his absolute priority, especially when his approach often seems so curiously abstract.[7] If Benjamin returns to Gracián and other baroque writers, it is certainly in recognition of their inescapability for his thought, but also because, wanting to specify the means of his analyses (what makes them possible but also what in them may help us bear witness to an uncertain and open future), he releases and mobilizes the resources and critical potential he finds in the baroque in order to realize the promise of transformation—of revolution, of a future, of a potential redemption—in his present moment. Benjamin writes in the hope that, if he can transform our relation to language, even to words or phrases, he can perhaps change more than just language: he can perhaps change the social relations in which we live. The potential of this transformation is performed at the level of his sentences in a citationality that, in his essay on Kraus, he associates with the possibility of hope. As he puts it, writing of Kraus's practice of citation and linking it to a despair that we will see later is indissociable from the possibility of revolutionary change: "Only when despairing did he discover in citation the power not to preserve but to purify, to tear from context, to destroy: the only power in which hope still resides that something might survive this age—because it was wrenched from it."[8] This hope is most legible in his "Work of Art" essay, but it is already evident in his *Trauerspiel* book.

It is not what art and literature in themselves are that interests Benjamin but rather how they operate in the mind, how they shape and transform the mind. Aesthetics, understood as a repository of beauty and a space of contemplation, is regressive and compensatory and, for Benjamin, authoritarian and even fascist. It is exactly the relation between aesthetics and fascism that will later prompt his reconceptualization of the work of art as an impersonal mass-like object that can more easily resist its instrumentalization by fascism. In his *Trauerspiel* work, Benjamin already notes that the baroque spectacle depends on a manipulation of the aesthetic for the sake of political legitimation. Baroque sovereigns domesticated the aesthetic in order to secure their own position, and Gracián's *Agudeza y arte de ingenio* (Subtlety and the art of genius) is a *conceptista* training manual for the development of a strategic and political defense against such royal abuses. Absolute sovereigns relied on public spectacles to master in a self-contradictory fashion the arrival of new concepts of secularized power and political autonomy. The rise of European fascism during the 1920s and 1930s urges Benjamin to return to this conceptual and figural armature and to seek similar resources that can become weapons against the present rise of fascism. In its most extreme formulation, Benjamin's work understands the very grounding of action in figuration as an instance of political work. Figuration emerges throughout as a historical and concrete abstraction of phenomenological essences that evades both philosophy and aesthetics. In Jameson's reading—and we will return to this later—the secularization of religious abstractions traces the conceptual movement of Benjamin's historical figurations, often in strange and unexpected ways.

Jameson insists that the reader never lose sight of Benjamin's strangeness, of the lateness and anachronism of his literary taste, and, ultimately, of his style, especially as it relates to the centrality of figuration in his thinking. Benjamin's "canon"—which is part of his strangeness, including as it does not simply names we recognize but also an array of lesser-known and even marginal figures—is more than a question of taste (Jameson refers to his "private canon" as "totally unorthodox" [*BF*, 136]). It signals a series of structural choices—what Benjamin calls "elective affinities"[9]—each of which, if read properly, allows us to trace Benjamin's active and complicated relation to tradition: in the sense that what is at stake for him is the possibility of activating what he inherits (the resources he finds in *his* tradition of writers) in the direction of political work in the present. If, as he puts it in his "Work of Art" essay, "the uniqueness of the work of art is identical to its embeddedness in the context of tradition" (*WA*, 256), it is because its singularity—like that of Benjamin's writings—emerges from its engagement with earlier works that, in a real but unpredictable manner, prefigure and even destine Benjamin's writings to realize their shape through various forms of displacement. This is particularly legible in the violence structured into Benjamin's practice of citation, which involves the removal of words or sentences and their unexpected reinscription elsewhere.

This activity of citation reenacts the displacements, the distances and separations, that fracture subjectivity—a subjectivity that has been subtracted in the service of making legible a deeper and more enduring version of time and that, for Benjamin, is destined to survive histories that presume linearity, causality, and continuity. Just as a room is better seen when its inhabitants have left, history becomes more intimate when the "I" has been removed, in this instance by embedding it in a tradition that works against tradition, even as it carries its most critical moments forward. According to Jameson, these writerly gestures maximize "the techniques of cultural revolution," since, among so many other things, they trace "the ways in which instruction comes to society." The figures in Benjamin's canon "are always the objects of pedagogy" and, Jameson adds, "this is the deeper secret of his political and aesthetic kinship with Brecht" (*BF*, 42). As we will see, Benjamin's effort to extract, multiply, and fragment voices is not simply part of his "unusual pedagogy"[10]; it is also his way of mobilizing a certain version of communism against fascism, something that will be explored more fully in his later works. As Jameson notes, it is precisely Benjamin's passion for the "multiplicity" of voices that most interests him, and this is "yet another symptom of his not unpolitical fascination with the multiple, with the masses as such" (*BF*, 34). He goes further later in his book when he insists that "[m]ass politics lies at the very center of Benjamin's thought" (*BF*, 207).

Cassio Vasconcellos, *Múltiplos: É Nóis!*, 2011

III. MASSIFICATION

[P]roletarian class consciousness ... fundamentally transforms the structure of the proletarian masses. The class-conscious proletariat forms a compact mass only from the outside, in the minds of its oppressors. At the moment when it takes up its struggle for liberation, this apparently compact mass has actually already begun to loosen. It ceases to be governed by mere reactions; it makes the transition to action. The loosening of the proletariat masses is the work of solidarity. In the solidarity of the proletarian class struggle, the dead, undialectical opposition between individual and mass is abolished.

—Walter Benjamin, "The Work of Art in the Age of Its Technological Reproducibility (Second Version)" (1936)[1]

While Jameson is careful to highlight Benjamin's "anti-aestheticism" (*BF*, 213),[2] he is at times at pains to reconcile it with the writer's belief in the redemptive qualities of style—as a source of impersonality, and even a technological one, since language appears as a series of techniques, each of which belongs to a complex of different technologies. In the end, technology provides both Benjamin and Jameson with a means of overcoming an aesthetic understanding of style, of preventing, that is, the reduction of style to an aesthetic matter. As Jameson reminds us, there are always in Benjamin "secret correspondences between seemingly unrelated dimensions of the world" (*BF*, 49)—in this instance, between style and politics, between technology and a new conception of art, a conception of art that is itself inseparable from a thought of multiplicity and masses (*BF*, 178). All this is presented and confirmed in Benjamin's essay "The Work of Art in the Age of Its Technological Reproducibility."

Following Benjamin, Jameson suggests that reproductive technologies not only alter "the traditional relation between form and content" (*BF*, 199) but also bridge the distance between form and content by depersonalizing it. Becoming figures of mass consciousness—of the subjectivity of the many, and therefore not a subjectivity at all (something Benjamin enacts in what we might call the *unruliness* of the mass citationality of his writings)—they bear within them the possibility of countering fascism's aestheticization of the one, even as there is always the danger of their being mobilized in a fascist direction when their multiplicity is given a face. Despite the always-present possibility of political complicity, however—what, in "On the Concept of History," Benjamin calls "danger"[3]—technological reproduction can still potentially advance new historical forms that reconceptualize politics through the analogy of imperfect repetition. It is precisely when a repetition or reproduction is not perfect that something singular, something perhaps even revolutionary, can appear. It is important to make this distinction, Jameson reminds us, because not all forms of the *new* "are advanced; there is, for example, the fascist version of aestheticization" (*BF*, 156), which seeks to reduce the many to a namable community or even nation. Against this fascist gesture, Benjamin will disperse the "many" even further—making the "many" into the many more—by suggesting that whatever or whoever belongs to the many is already "mass-like."

If Benjamin claims that there can be no Marxism without a conception of production and reproduction that is neither teleological nor a sign of progress—a conception that introduces imperfections and differences, fissures and breaks, multiplicities and pluralities, within these processes—it is because the end of capitalism must itself pass through reproduction as a technology, as a process of formation and transformation. In Benjamin's terms, the formation of what he would call a *mass subject* coincides with the end of aesthetics, or rather with its neutralization in the name of a politics of the masses. As we have suggested, however, even the word "masses" has to be reconceptualized and distanced from a mass that would be identifiable, that would have a "face." In Benjamin, this work of reconceptualization—something performed in the movement of his writing because for him the crisis of our existence is inscribed within "the very heart of language"[4]—is already a means of doing political work. In our present context, this suggests that technology becomes a means of engaging the historical "dialectic of the individual and the masses" (*BF*, 200), since it is capable of transformation through the plasticity of both perception and form. To be more precise, it puts perception through a process of "massification"—and this because it is a mediating force in our relation to the world (ibid.).[5]

What Benjamin proposes is a politicization of reproducibility. This means that there can be no thought of what political praxis might be that does not move through technology in order to resist it, by multiplying and intensifying the imperfections of its repetitions and by registering the impersonality of politics in general. In Jameson's words, Benjamin's "deeper theoretical solution" involves the "abandonment of categories which, like those of ethics or aesthetics, presuppose the domain of the individual and its limits and limited function, and aims to substitute the wholly new categories of number, masses, multiplicities, in which an experience like aura has no place, but in which, perhaps, a different kind of Experience might be available" (*BF*, 189). We might begin here with Benjamin's reconceptualization of the artwork into a *mass* artwork that does not belong to any one single tradition, that becomes instead a source not for cult or exhibition value, but for what Marx would call "non-value," a Nietzschean transvaluation that, in the hands of Benjamin, becomes even more legibly political in the context of Weimar Germany but also today.[6]

The entirety of Benjamin's "Work of Art" essay can be read as a critical response to the fascist effort to mobilize the language of art toward the production of an organic community that, whether in the form of the German people or nation, presents itself as a work of art in the fascist program of self-formation and self-production. That the German nation seeks to describe itself as a *Gesamtkunstwerk*, as a total work of art, by attributing to itself the values we traditionally assign to the work of art—originality, mystery, eternal value, and genius—accounts for why, on the eve of military catastrophe, in the midst of the increasingly gathering forces of fascism, Benjamin writes about the work of art. Everything he claims about the work of art corresponds to his analysis of a national-political formation that claims to be an artwork. Benjamin responds to this situation by mobilizing the so-called forces of mass aesthetic production toward political ends—something already at work in fascism—but toward a politics whose infinitely mediated relations prevent it from organizing itself around a particular form of instrumentality, a guiltless economy that spells a mysterious form of happiness. As Jameson notes, "number will now play a central part as a fundamental organizational category of Benjamin's thinking. The masses, for him, determine new categories, a new form of thinking" (*BF*, 178).

As a first step, Benjamin associates the masses with the masslike character of the work of art. "The violation of the masses," he writes, "whom Fascism, with its *Führer* cult, forces to their knees, has its counterpart in the violation of an apparatus which is pressed into the production of ritual values" (*WA*, 269). This relation between the masses and the violence of technical reproduction can be read throughout Benjamin's essay—in his discussion of the breakdown of the traditional distinction between production and reproduction that he suggests occurred in the middle of the nineteenth century and that he associates with the introduction of first photography and then film, and also in his discussion of the disintegration of aura. As he explains, in a passage that associates these processes of breakdown and disintegration with the medium of film:

> *It might be stated as a general formula that the technology of reproduction detaches the reproduced object from the sphere of tradition. By replicating the work many times over, it substitutes a mass existence for a unique existence. And in permitting the reproduction to reach the recipient in his or her own situation, it actualizes what is reproduced.* These two processes lead to a massive upheaval in the objects handed down from the past—a shattering of tradition which is the reverse side of the present crisis and renewal of humanity. Both processes are intimately related to the mass movements of our day. Their most powerful agent is film. (*WA*, 254; italics in original)

The techniques of reproduction, Benjamin suggests, disperse the unique occurrence of the artwork into a mass whose reproduction sets it into circulation and motion. No longer to be understood in terms of the traditional values of singularity and originality, this mass-reproduced artwork belongs to a network of unforeseeably mediated relations that comes to itself as a reproduced mass. It is associated within the motility of Benjamin's passage with the movement of the contemporary masses. What links the artwork to the masses is that both have their origins in techniques of reproduction. They are both produced, that is, according to the structure and operation of technological reproduction. This means that contemporary mass movements begin in their reproducibility: they belong to the production and reproduction of images and to their mobilization in film. For Jameson, it is precisely "this unity of the masses, beyond any individual perception or personal feelings, which reveals its enormous power—that of the General Will—beyond all particularities or singularities"; and, as he goes on to note, "[t]he new media are its 'training ground'" (*BF*, 205). Benjamin's interest in the production techniques of film and photography corresponds to his conviction that what takes place on a film set or in a photography studio is related to what takes place outside this same set or studio, with "what is political in a situation of massification" (*BF*, 215): the emergence or mobilization of images.

For Benjamin, it is precisely this mobilization—one that gives the masses a figure or form—that lies behind the fascist mobilization of masses. In the epilogue to the "Work of Art" essay, for example, he explains that "the increasing proletarianization" and the growing formation of the masses are "two sides of the same process." "Fascism," he says, "attempts to organize the newly pro-letarianized masses while leaving intact those property relations which they strive to abolish. It sees its salvation in granting expression to the masses—but on no account granting them rights" (*WA*, 269). If, following the logic of total mobilization, fascism offers the masses self-expression, this self-expression becomes a means for the masses to give themselves a face in which they can see themselves reproduced. As Benjamin explains in a discussion of the weekly newsreel:

> A technological factor is important here, especially with regard to the newsreel, whose significance for propaganda purposes can hardly be overstated. *Mass reproduction is especially favored by the reproduction of the masses.* In great ceremonial processions, giant rallies, and mass sporting events, and in war, all of which are now fed into the camera, the masses come face to face with themselves. This process, whose significance need not be emphasized, is closely bound up with the development of reproduction and recording technologies. In general, mass movements are more clearly apprehended by the camera than by the eye. A bird's-eye view best captures assemblies of hundreds of thousands. And even when this perspective is no less accessible to the human eye than to the camera, the image formed by the eye cannot be enlarged in the same way as a photograph. This is to say that mass movements, including war, are a form of human behavior especially suited to the camera. (*WA*, 282)

What make a mass mass-like, Benjamin explains, are the techniques of reproduction and photography that enable a mass to see itself in the face as if it were looking into a mirror. If fascism allows the masses to view themselves according to the laws of self-reflection, if it gives a face to the masses by means of an aesthetically instrumentalized media, Benjamin claims that the masses can never have a face because they are impersonal, like the machine that produces them—a machine that, composed of innumerable technologies and bearing several histories within it, is nevertheless inseparable from the material forms of language, writing, and reading that enable it to work, or to *almost* work. It is because of the glitches in the system—what Benjamin seeks to intensify and even accelerate—that the masses can never be a signification. Unable to constitute an identifiable community, they are instead the name of a common dispersion into multiplicity. If fascism "realizes that the more compact the masses it mobilizes, the better the chance that the counterrevolutionary instincts of the petty bourgeoisie will determine their reactions," the proletariat "is preparing for a society in which neither the objective nor the subjective conditions for the formation of masses will exist any longer."[7]

Jameson's obsession with totality, inherited from Lukács, meets its interruption in Benjamin's technological imagination. Reading Jameson's analysis, we might wonder if Benjamin found the answer to Lukács's greatest challenge in *History and Class Consciousness*, if his theory of mass consciousness through technology collapses the distance between individual standpoint and class consciousness and escapes its instrumentalization by fascism with its emphasis on number, masses, multiplication, intensification, and acceleration. Throughout Jameson's analysis, Lukács often emerges as Benjamin's silent interlocutor, down to his interest in physiognomy and characterization (although in Benjamin's case, and through his reading of Baudelaire, physiognomy becomes the blind spot of the masses, rather than its average). As Jameson notes in his chapter on "The Physiognomic Cycle," in a passage about the way in which Baudelaire's concern with numbers anticipated Benjamin's interest in masses:

> Benjamin assures us that "the masses" haunt every page of *Les Fleurs du mal*, even where they remain unmentioned and unthematized (and there is a sense in which the same is true of Benjamin himself). Clearly, however, whatever his affective relationship, he was aware of the deeper category at work. He quotes *Fusées*: "The pleasure in being in a crowd is a mysterious expression of sensual joy in the multiplication of number. ... Number is in all. ... Ecstasy is a number ... " To which Benjamin adds, rather enigmatically, "Extract the root of the human being!" One assumes that this is meant to refute the idea that the individual, added up, makes the foundation of the mass; rather, it is the other way around—the collective is the constituent part of the individual (when the latter exists). (*BF*, 104)[8]

If "Baudelaire anticipated him in this discovery of sheer number as a category," Jameson adds later, for Benjamin, number "encompasses the masses, mass production, abstraction (allegory) and the multiple as well as multiplicity" (*BF*, 114). At stake in this entanglement of the individual and the collective—an entanglement we have been tracing in Benjamin's sentences as well as in his thoughts on the massification of the masses—is nothing less than the question of universals. Abstraction here names the absence at the center of the individual—an absence that is neither a void nor an emptiness, but a mass of relations. This mass—more unwieldy, unruly, and internally incommensurable than what Jameson here calls a "collective"—interrupts the individual's "subjectivity" with numbers. This is why, he suggests, even if only parenthetically, the individual—a figure whose temporality has been displaced and even shattered through different forms of reproduction, displacement, and mediation—may not exist. The question which remains largely undeveloped, if not unanswered by Jameson, however—even if it is signaled here and there—is what a politics of pure mediacy would look like. What kind of politics is possible in the interplay between singularity and the impersonal, when intentions and agency remain indeterminate and moved by the "wind of world history" without ever being fully able to control the setting of the sails?

Walter Benjamin, "Literature for a More Fully Developed
Critique of Violence and Philosophy of Law," n.d.

IV. GENERAL STRIKE

> Instead of the rigid and hollow scheme of an arid political action carried out by the decision of the highest committees and furnished with a plan and panorama, we see a bit of pulsating like that of flesh and blood, which cannot be cut out of the large frame of the revolution but is connected with all parts of the revolution by a thousand veins.
>
> —Rosa Luxemburg, "The Mass Strike" (1906)[1]

These questions about the mediated character of all agency are most directly addressed in Benjamin's 1921 "Toward the Critique of Violence." Although it has been read extensively, during the last three decades especially, it remains one of Benjamin's most enigmatic and inscrutable essays.[2] One reason for its difficulty is that it is almost impossible to contextualize it either in relation to the nexus of texts to which it belongs—within Benjamin's corpus but also beyond it—or in relation to the historical and political contexts to which it responds. The recent critical edition of the essay put together by Peter Fenves and Julia Ng is the most ambitious effort to date to address this difficulty. In addition to presenting a meticulous new translation of the essay, this edition provides the most extensive textual apparatus we have for it. Nevertheless, as Ng notes in her "Afterword"—pointing to the elusiveness of the context in which Benjamin's essay was imagined—the essay

> belongs to a shifting complex of politically oriented writings in various stages of completion. The project on a "futuristic politics" that Benjamin first mentioned in June 1919 in conversation with Scholem had, over the years, taken on a number of guises, sometimes envisioned as a book with several articulated chapters, sometimes as a series of essays, sometimes simply designated within quotation marks as "Politics." His final mention of the project as such occurred in 1927, when in July he wrote in a letter to Scholem that during his recent trip to Corsica, a "convolute of irreplaceable manuscripts" containing "years' worth of preliminary studies pertaining to 'Politics'" had gone missing.[3]

That Benjamin's project continues to transform in time is not surprising, since the events and contexts to which he responds themselves keep shifting and changing. If he strives to find a language that can match what is always metamorphosing into something else, he imagines a text that would approach the complex entanglements that not only constitute and deconstitute the political domain but also make a critique of violence—the effort to differentiate different forms of violence and the possibilities for overcoming them—such a vexed task. Although his project shifts for the next several years, we can piece together different statements in his correspondence and surmise that "Toward the Critique of Violence" belongs—along with the now lost "The True Politician" (which was to be the first part of his proposed trilogy), a planned consideration of the biological sciences and of Paul Scheerbart's 1913 *Lesabéndio*, and *One-Way Street*—to what he calls in a letter from January 24, 1926, the "arsenal" of his "political works."[4]

Benjamin publishes *One-Way Street* in 1928—the same year as his *Origin of the German Trauerspiel*, a book that could be said to further his critique of violence in the direction of an exploration of sovereignty, power, and political agency. At the same time, the concerns of his 1921 essay and, in particular, of his larger project on politics are referenced directly in, among other texts, his essays on the "Work of Art," Eduard Fuchs, and the "Concept of History," and in a text he writes on *Lesabéndio* during the last year of his life. That he continued to imagine an expanded critique of violence is confirmed by a bibliography to which he gave the title "Literature for a More Fully Developed Critique of Violence and Philosophy of Law," and which was among the papers he carried with him when he fled Paris in June 1940. In what follows, we trace this ongoing concern through an entirely unexplored reference in his "Critique of Violence" essay—one which remains silent and displaced, not only in this essay but also throughout the rest of his corpus. Because he never leaves the question of the relation between violence and politics behind, all of Benjamin's writings—especially if we follow the function of this secret reference, along with the enduring traces of his proposed project on politics—can be considered a critique of violence.

In the wake of World War I, Benjamin scans the political landscape and registers the near impossibility of imagining justice. Everything around him is organized in relation to different forms of violence and power, and this even after the devastation these forces brought about during the war and its aftermath. If violence and power are critical to political and juridical discourse, it is increasingly difficult to overcome their destructive effects, because law itself sanctions the use of violence, especially when it is a matter of securing particular political ends. Benjamin's critique of violence delineates a standpoint from which the legitimation of violence can be evaluated. That he can raise this question already suggests that the distinction between legitimate and illegitimate violence is not secure and that, instead, what is at stake is the possibility of differentiating, in his words, "the sphere of means itself, without regard for the ends they serve," of differentiating, that is, violence from its instrumentalization.[5] Recalling that "critique" does not simply mean a negative evaluation and that its etymological roots can be found in the Greek *krino*, which means to "divide" or to "judge," we can register the double gesture that governs Benjamin's essay, not only in terms of the intellectual debates it engages over violence, morality, and justice (debates that are countersigned by, among others, Spinoza, Kant, Marx, Darwin, Georges Sorel, Hermann Cohen, Erich Unger, and Kurt Hiller), but also in regard to the complex and volatile political context in which he is writing.

If Benjamin aims to provide a prolegomenon to what he calls the "historico-philosophical" (*CV,* 41) critique of violence, it is because his essay works simultaneously in at least two registers— as a metaphysical enterprise on the model of Kant (and especially in relation to Kant's *Critique of the Power of Judgment, Groundwork for the Metaphysics of Morals,* and *Toward Eternal Peace*), and as a moral and political engagement with what he refers to as the "legal circumstances" of "contemporary Europe" (*CV,* 42) in the aftermath of World War I. This helps explain the perplexing experience of encountering at least two different texts superimposed on one another: what Anthony Auerbach has called "an almost parodic amalgam of philosophical, juridical, and theological abstractions"[6] and what we can see as a series of references, direct and indirect, to the recent war, the failed revolution, the parliamentary crises and constitutional turmoil punctuating the contemporary political landscape, the figure of the great criminal, the right to strike, the death penalty, juridical capitalism, the violence of peace treaties, military violence and general conscription, and the omnipresence of the police state. While the latter matters are linked to socialist and anarchist debates on militarism, war, and violence that had appeared in various guises in the preceding decades, Benjamin's treatment of them belongs to his often idiosyncratic, but nevertheless political, way of proceeding. At every step, he gives us examples that confirm our intimate relation to violence of all kinds and, in particular, to violence that is sanctioned or unsanctioned by the law. While it is impossible to demonstrate this in every example Benjamin presents to us, we will trace in a moment the way in which his essay consistently offers "more and something different than may perhaps appear" (*CV*, 39).

It is important to present in more detail at least some of the background against which the essay is written. As Ng reminds us, Benjamin moved back to Berlin in 1920, "a little more than a year after the Spartacist and Bolshevist uprisings and their bloody suppression by government troops and the Freikorps and mere months before the Kapp Putsch and the government's call for a general strike in response. This was then quickly followed by the Ruhr uprising, the quelling of which resulted in the deaths of hundreds of revolutionary workers." "In short," she goes on to write, "it was a time of revolutionary and counterrevolutionary movement of government and countergovernment," during which different forms of violence were evident everywhere, both inside and outside the present legal order.[7] In Benjamin's words, what is needed in the face of all this violence, in all its various manifestations, is a "critique of all legal violence"—that is, a "critique of legal or executive power"—and this critique cannot "be accomplished with a less ambitious program." The legal order, he adds, must be challenged "root and branch" (*CV*, 46).

Benjamin begins his critique by suggesting the need to get beyond an impasse in legal, philosophical, and political debates over violence. These debates, he suggests—which help shape particular state formations and not only justify state violence in relation to the rhetoric of "just ends" or "just means" but also work to solidify state power through this justified violence—repeatedly mobilize contradictory terms and arguments and, in doing so, remain complicit with the violence they presumably attempt to overcome. Law must be understood to be inseparable from violence.[8] Violence is what makes the law the law (*CV*, 48). All law, however distant it claims to be from its violent origins and from the forces which maintain it, enacts its irreducible relation to violence. Violence itself decides what violence is justifiable for what ends; it becomes a calculus that, designed to justify its continuity, is brutal in its instantiation.[9] Just ends and just means are anything but just, and thinking beyond them demands a suspension of the causality that binds them together. As Ng notes, instead of considering "just ends as a way to 'justify' the means (as natural law does) or justified means to 'guarantee' the justness of ends (as positive law does)," a critique of violence—a critique of "violence as a principle" (*CV*, 39)—requires "a temporary suspension of the question of ends and their justness."[10] What is clear is that the inability to articulate criteria for evaluating the justness of any violence requires a reconceptualization of the terms of the debates in which Benjamin intervenes. As part of this reconceptualization, he introduces a series of categories—natural and positive law, law-positing and law-preserving violence, political and proletarian general strikes, and mythic and divine violence—all of which will prove to be as unstable as the circumstances in which he writes his essay, as each one works to formalize these same circumstances in order to move beyond them.

Having experienced military defeat, mass demobilization, and the toppling of its imperial ruler, postwar Germany found itself in a state of political confusion and pervasive violence. In November 1918 revolution broke out. Workers went on strike and into the streets. Workers' councils, on the model of the councils established by the Russian Revolution in 1917, emerged everywhere. Within a few days the entire country was in turmoil. Once the imperial order collapsed, Kaiser Wilhelm II abdicated his throne on November 9, 1918, and the German military was compelled to negotiate for peace. Within hours, the first German Republic was called into existence twice, dividing along the lines that had fractured German socialists at the outbreak of the war in 1914 and initiating a violent struggle for state power. In an effort to preempt the revolutionary forces that might be moved to establish a constitutional council, and aiming, in particular, to secure the succession of the Socialist Democratic Party (SPD), Philipp Scheidemann announced the German republic from the balcony of the Reichstag. Karl Liebknecht soon after declared "a free socialist Republic of Germany" from the balcony of the Imperial Palace, pledging revolution. Unwilling to cede full control to the insurgent workers' movement, the German capitalist class united with the reformist SPD, which, with its leader Friedrich Ebert, promised to restore order. The SPD claimed it wanted a peaceful, democratic transition to socialism, but it soon revealed its counterrevolutionary ambitions—its desire to establish its rule and keep the previous order as intact as possible. Against the demand that, as in Russia, power be given to the workers' councils, it insisted that elections to the National Assembly take place in January 1919. It countered the momentum of the workers' movement with support from the imperial regime's most reactionary quarters. It is in this context that the SPD's Gustav Noske formed the Freikorps, an armed militia composed mostly of former officers in the imperial army. One of its first tasks was to put down the uprising of militant workers in early January. The Spartacist uprising advanced with support from the Communist Party of Germany (KPD) and the Independent Social Democratic Party (USPD), and included the occupation of buildings by workers, mass demonstrations, and a general strike. The SPD blamed the uprising on the leaders of the newly formed KPD, particularly Rosa Luxemburg and Liebknecht, and Noske called in the Freikorps to crush the uprising, who carried out their extralegal police work with brutal violence and without effective regulation. Workers occupying the building of the main SPD newspaper *Vorwärts* were executed. On January 15, Luxemburg and Liebknecht were captured, tortured, and murdered.[11]

The SPD-led government signed the Treaty of Versailles in June 1919. Because the Treaty imposed harsh penalties on Germany for having started the war, including the loss of territory, reparations payments, and demilitarization, the government was blamed not only for the treaty's humiliating terms but for Germany's defeat itself. As Benjamin notes, "peace" treaties—he puts the word "peace" in quotations marks because he views it as a "correlative" of the word "war" and as a law-positing force (*CV*, 44)—simply replace the violence of war with that of peace. In Germany's case, the government—now subject to new laws—did not dissolve the Freikorps militias as the peace treaty required and continued to rely on them to suppress left-wing agitation. In 1920 the Freikorps staged its own coup d'état—the so-called Kapp Putsch. As Howard Eiland and Michael W. Jennings summarize, on March 13, a military brigade and the Freikorps

> seized control of the government district in Berlin, declared an end to the Social Democratic government, and named Wolfgang Kapp, a right-wing civil servant, as the new chancellor. ... Deprived of the support of large parts of the army, the government countered in the only way it could, through the declaration of a general strike. This action, together with the refusal of much of the bureaucracy to follow the directives of Kapp, led to the collapse of the putsch.[12]

After the failure of the attempted coup, Freikorps militias continued to crack down on left-wing activities on behalf of the government but also on their own initiative.

Although Benjamin does not mention it explicitly, he certainly has the SPD's shifting political positions in mind when he notes that the corruption of law-positing violence becomes legible whenever such violence seeks to preserve itself. By turning away from its revolutionary origins toward self-preservation, the SPD turns against the communist forces whose own positing force it now views as hostile to its authority. It calls for a general strike but instrumentalizes it in order to interrupt the Kapp Putsch challenge to its government. It proves itself capable of counterrevolutionary violence and, in doing so, turns against the principle of law-positing violence to which it owes its existence. This is why, Benjamin notes, it must disintegrate—it must experience a process of decay and ruin in its own internal self-destruction and its eventual replacement by another political formation, another legal structure. Like the violence on which it depends, all positing is "demonic-ambiguous" (*dämonisch-zweideutiger*; *CV*, 56). Every positing and every law is subject to a more powerful law that demands that it expose itself to another positing, and another law. This more powerful law is the law of historical change—an act of self-preservation, a consolidation of power, dictated by the ambiguity, which is evident in the SPD's actions, of being both means and end.

Benjamin further elaborates this logic of the decay of political and legal forms—a decay that occurs when law-positing violence becomes law-preserving violence, when these two forms of violence prove to be mutually constitutive. He references the suppression of the mass Communist uprisings in the Ruhr region during the spring of 1920, again by the SPD's Freikorps, the "indeterminacy of the legal threat" evident in the death penalty, which, for him, confirms that there is something "rotten in law" (*CV*, 47), the SPD parliament, which has forgotten the revolutionary violence from which it was born, and the general strike, to which we will return and which can be mobilized either for or against the state, as is evident in the 1919 doctors' counterrevolutionary strikes, which can be seen as part of a broader series of strikes by members of the bourgeoisie against the Spartacist movement. But, he suggests, the mixing of these two forms of violence—positing and preserving—is perhaps most evident in the modern institution of the police and, in particular, in the "ignominy" (*das Schmachvolle*) of its authority (ibid.). As can be seen in the Freikorps—which, as an extralegal quasi-police force deployed by the state, already blurs the boundaries of the law and, in doing so, tells us what is true of all policial structures— the police do not restrict themselves to simply enforcing the law, to just preserving and protecting it. Instead, they dictate it, they make themselves "rechtsetzend," "law-positing," they destroy the pretense of a distinction between these two kinds of violence. As Benjamin puts it, with the police, the separation of law-positing and law-preserving violence is annulled. ... It is law-positing—for its characteristic function is not the promulgation of laws but the adoption [*Erlaß*] of any given decree with the claim to legality [*Rechtanspruch*]—and it is law-preserving because it places itself at the disposal of these ends. The assertion that the ends of police violence are always identical with, or even connected to, the ends of the remainder of law is thoroughly untrue. Rather, the "law" ["*Recht*"] of the police basically denotes the point at which the state, whether from impotence or because of the immanent connections of every legal order, can no longer guarantee through the legal order the empirical ends it wishes to achieve at any price. Therefore, the police intervene "for security reasons" in countless cases where no clear legal situation exists. (*CV*, 48)

According to Benjamin, the police are everywhere the force of law exists: "The violence of this institution is shapeless [*gestaltlos*], like its nowhere-tangible, all pervasive, ghostly appearance in the life of civilized states." But "though policing may, in specific respects, look everywhere alike," he goes on to note—emphasizing a distinction between monarchies and democracies and therefore pointing to what he sees as an intensification of police violence with the SPD and its Freikorps—"there can ultimately be no denying that its spirit is less devastating in absolute monarchies, where it represents the ruler's power [*Gewalt*], in which there is a unity of full legislative and executive power [*Machtvollkommenheit*], than in democracies, where its existence, elevated by no such relation, bears witness to the greatest conceivable degeneration [*Entartung*] of power [*Gewalt*]" (ibid.).

If, as Benjamin asserts, "the critique of violence is the philosophy of its history" (*CV*, 59), what appears "closest at hand" within this history—in particular, what Benjamin understands as the constantly shifting political contexts of "contemporary Europe"—is "a dialectical back-and-forth in the formations of violence into its law-positing and law-preserving kinds" (*CV*, 60). He elaborates this "law of its oscillation" by noting that "all law-preserving violence, in its duration, indirectly, through its suppression of hostile counterforces, weakens law-positing violence, which is represented in it. ... This lasts until either new forms of violence or ones earlier suppressed gain victory over the hitherto law-positing violence, thereby founding a new law, with a new decay." What is at stake is the possibility of "breaking through this cycle that spins under the spell of mythical forms of law" in order to imagine a revolutionary violence that would inaugurate "a new historical era" by "de-posing law together with all the forms of violence on which it depends, just as they depend on it, and finally, therefore, on deposing state violence" (ibid.). This deposing of law and of state violence requires its own violence, but a violence that would open history onto a nonteleological temporal order.[13] It would break with the forms of law. In the wording of Pablo Oyarzún, it would not be,

> in any sense of the word, a "legal" violence, a violence justified by law and by the ends that it might serve and secure. Unalloyed violence, pure violence, violence as a means that is neither justified nor unjustified, a means in itself as it were, a violence that is absolutely indifferent to ends and for this very reason is immediate—this is, in a word, violence "beyond the law" (*jenseits des Rechtes*). Here "beyond" does not imply an unattainable and unimaginable vanishing point, a sort of transcendence; it is the work of deposing legal violence that opens this "beyond" in the first place.[14]

Benjamin explores the possibility of this revolutionary violence in his discussion of the general strike and, in particular, of the possibility for a certain type of strike—namely, the proletarian general strike—to exceed the limits of the right to strike, turning the right to strike against the law and its calculations. As he argues, the right to strike that is meant to protect the law against the possible violence of class struggles must be transformed into a means for deposing the law.

In order to make this case, Benjamin joins a discussion of the mediacy of language—linked to questions of massification and technological reproducibility—to that of the proletarian general strike. Benjamin's discussion of the strike may be viewed in the context of the strategic debates on the politics of striking which led in 1872 to the expulsion of the Anarcho-Syndicalists from the First International and whose most well-known political document was Luxemburg's 1906 *Mass Strike: The Political Party and the Trade Unions*. However, Benjamin explicitly refers only to Georges Sorel's 1908 *Reflections on Violence*. In a performative appropriation of Sorel's text, a text that is itself mediated by Luxemburg's writings on revolution and the mass strike, Benjamin distinguishes between the political general strike and the proletarian general strike. If the first works to reverse the relation of domination but, in doing so, still preserves and reinforces state violence, the second seeks to abolish the state altogether. Benjamin cites Sorel in his description of the supporters of the political general strike: "The strengthening of state power [*l'État / Staatsgewalt*] is the basis of their conceptions; in their present organizations the politicians (namely, the moderate socialists) are already preparing the ground for a strong centralized and disciplined power [*pouvoir / Gewalt*] that will be impervious to criticism from the opposition, and capable of imposing silence and issuing its mendacious decrees. ... The political general strike demonstrates how the state will lose none of its force [*force / Kraft*], how power is transferred [*la transmission / Macht*] from the privileged to the privileged, how the mass of producers will change their masters." "In contrast to this political general strike (whose formula, incidentally, seems to be that of the recently elapsed German Revolution)," Benjamin adds, "the proletarian general strike sets itself the sole task of annihilating [*Vernichtung*] state power [*Staatsgewalt*]" (*CV*, 52).[15] Annihilating state power altogether, this general strike strikes against any kind of end, any outcome that would reconstitute a particular political form or calculation.

As Jameson explains, emphasizing Benjamin's attraction to the proletarian general strike:

> violence only appears as a nameable and thereby theorizable issue after the fact. It is only after the "violent" act has taken place that we are able to identify it as an example of the pseudo-universal called "violence": indeed the "critique" of violence announced in Benjamin's title is meant to warn us that it is, in this sense, violence itself which performs its own auto-critique and unveils itself as ideological in the very moment in which its concept is then able to appear in time as though it had always been present. Benjamin seeks—and it is a radical move which may not at first be apparent in its consequences—to suspend and bracket any consideration of ends as such. He thereby neutralizes all of the judgments on violence which seek, either positively or negatively, to defend or denounce it in terms of ends, results, overarching values and the like, in order to examine what is called violence as pure means, in its own internal structure. (*BF*, 141–142)

According to Jameson, Benjamin's essay begins in the conviction that violence can only be a means of overcoming end-oriented violence, a means of justice, if it is pure means—if it is nothing but mediation, a force of impersonality that constitutes subjects as mediated, and therefore no longer as subjects, either individual or collective. For Benjamin, the proletarian strike is pure political violence, pure means without any determinate end beyond the strike itself, or beyond its force of annihilation—something Benjamin identifies with the criticality of violence itself. It retains the risks and promises of its violent incalculability. Directed toward the annihilation of state violence—but itself positing *nothing*—the strike suspends all positing violence. Without intention, entirely noninstrumental, "a teleology without final purpose" (*GS*, 2.3:943), a political event that shatters all determinations of the political, it scans as nonviolent. In Benjamin's words, "a nonaction, which after all is what ultimately constitutes a strike, cannot be described as violence at all. Such a consideration doubtless made it easier for state power [*Staatsgewalt*] to concede the right to strike once it was no longer avoidable. The validity of this statement, however, is not unrestricted because it is not unconditional. It is true that omitting an action or even a service can be a pure means wholly lacking in violence if it amounts simply to a 'severing of relations'" (*CV*, 43). The strike appears in all its unmediated mediacy. It enacts a hope in the midst of hopelessness (or, as Benjamin puts it at the end of his essay on Goethe's *Elective Affinities*, even if it were to take place "[o]nly for the sake of the hopeless ones" in the name of whom we have "been given hope"[16]), and does so in order to reveal the revolutionary possibilities that open up through the sheer mediacy of all social relations. If Benjamin associates the proletarian general strike with what he calls "divine violence"—pure, unmediated violence—it is because God is another name for mediacy. This mediacy has its extrahuman analogue in language, whose linguistic essence is, like God, unutterable. Language moves toward what cannot be expressed, working to intensify this expressionlessness by multiplying its directionality and by refusing to be directed or instrumentalized. This can be confirmed by reading Benjamin's 1916 language essay in relation to his later "Critique of Violence" essay, since each—taking its point of departure from a desire to imagine a conception of language or a form of violence that would be noninstrumental—can be read as the political complement of the other. Both language and the proletarian general strike are means of effecting a force of deposition—not as means to an end but as sheer means.

Rosa Luxemburg, age 36, at her desk in her Berlin apartment, 1907

V. ROSA'S CASKET

So now Red Rosa has also passed away.
Where she lies none can say.

—Bertolt Brecht, "Epitaph 1919" (1919)

Hic Rhodus, hic salta!
Here is the rose, here dance!

—Karl Marx, *The Eighteenth Brumaire of Louis Bonaparte* (1852)[1]

If Benjamin's language moves toward what cannot be expressed,
if the pure mediacy of language that he places at the center of his
critique of violence works to suspend the possibility of expression
and action, to enact a linguistic version of the proletarian general
strike—if it is a means of interruption and fragmentation—it is
because his essay is itself a *critical strike*. We already have begun
to suggest the various elements of violence that are its target.
We need to remember that Benjamin is not against all forms of
violence—his argument is not a pacifist one—but only against
those that remain bound to the law, those that can be given a
determinate form and are instrumentalized either in order to posit
law or to preserve it. But the essay also enacts a different kind of
strike, one that can only be read as a deliberate effort to refuse to
name the figure most directly associated with the general or mass
strike, Rosa Luxemburg. It is surely one of the great mysteries of
the essay that Luxemburg is not mentioned explicitly even once.
By the time Benjamin writes his essay, she was the best-known
theorist of the proletarian mass strike, and her writings had been
critical to the Marxist project in Germany and, in particular,
in Berlin for many years already. Along with Liebknecht, Clara
Zetkin, and Franz Mehring, Luxemburg founded the group Die
Internationale (The International), which became the Spartacus
League in January 1916, and in December 1918 she helped found
the Communist Party of Germany. Together with Liebknecht and
Zetkin, Luxemburg also had initiated the communist newspaper
Die Rote Fahne (*The Red Flag*) right after her release from prison in
November 1918, a newspaper devoted to the theory and practice of
socialist mass movements. Only Lenin exerted the same degree of

influence over Marx's reception in the aftermath of his death. But, while Lenin viewed the revolution as merely a "means to an end," a means for the overcoming of capitalism and the installation of socialism, Luxemburg sees revolution—appearing in the formlessness of a mass strike that is realized only when it disappears into a sociopolitical network of shifting forces—as the embodiment of a socialist practice that coincides with ceaseless movement and that has no other end than abolishing ends altogether. Her understanding of revolution resonates with Benjamin's own demand for a politics of pure means and is closer to his view of revolution than Sorel's is. He also would have shared her stance against the war, her view of the inhumanity of capitalism and the corruption of social democracy, and would have appreciated her effort to invent a political language and strategy linked to Marx but deeply inflected by the wars, mass strikes, and armed revolutions she had experienced in the previous decades.

We know that she was on his radar. Scholem had introduced Benjamin to Luxemburg in 1915 as they engaged in antiwar activities, distributing prohibited writings.[2] His brother, Georg, had given him a copy of Luxemburg's prison letters as a birthday present in 1920—which he read before writing his essay and which he praised in a letter to Scholem at the end of December 1920 for their "incredible beauty and significance" (C, 171). But perhaps most critical to her visibility for Benjamin is the fact that, after her dramatic assassination on January 15, 1919, Berlin was besieged by the largest mass demonstrations and funeral processions in its history, all in response to the murders of Luxemburg and Liebknecht, and to the deaths of others who participated in the Spartacist uprising. These events could not have gone unnoticed by Benjamin and would have affected him deeply. Given Georg Benjamin's own relations to the Spartacists, to the USPD and then the KPD,[3] and the extralegal violence with which Luxemburg was murdered, it would have been impossible for Benjamin not to have her close to him as he wrote his essay. Since she is not named in the essay explicitly, however, we are compelled, in the words of Hugo von Hofmannsthal, "to read what was never written"[4] (a task that Benjamin associates with that of the historical materialist). Benjamin's omission—an omission that ensures that Luxemburg functions *sub rosa* throughout the essay—is itself part of his critical strike. This "nonaction"—which, as a strike, "cannot be described as violence at all" (*CV*, 43)—corresponds to his wish not to instrumentalize her. At a moment in which she has been entirely instrumentalized—by the left as an iconic martyr and by the right as an extremist and terrorist—Benjamin abstains from mentioning her in order to minimize the risk of his contributing to her further instrumentalization (in this he anticipates Trotsky's own effort to minimize her instrumentalization, especially by Stalin, in his 1932 "Hands Off Rosa Luxemburg!"[5]). Refraining from naming her, Benjamin engages in a militant negativity that he values philosophically as well as politically. At the same time, he massifies and multiplies her by incorporating shifting traces of her throughout his essay; because of this dispersal and massification, she remains indeterminate and unnamable. As he puts it in a fragment titled "Death," written around 1920 if not earlier, when "the *individual* dies ... there occurs a shattering. The individual is an indivisible yet inconclusive unity; death is in the realm of individuality only a movement."[6]

Within Benjamin's essay, Luxemburg functions as what Werner Hamacher calls an "afformative strike": she does not appear in a determinate way, but only as a series of "ellipses, pauses, interruptions, and displacements" with which she at the same time can never be fully identified.[7] As an absent figure, she cannot be presented; she remains a displaced ellipsis. Yet because of this deposition and negation, she becomes an absent figure capable of containing—functioning like one of the many boxes in Benjamin's corpus—the enigma of the role of violence in politics. Her absence already had been monumentalized in the January 25 funeral procession that memorialized the thirty-three revolutionaries killed during the Spartacist uprising and buried in a mass grave in the Berlin-Friedrichsfelde cemetery. The dead included Liebknecht, but, because Luxemburg's body, having been thrown into the Landwehr Canal in Kreuzberg after her assassination, had not yet been recovered, only an empty casket was buried in her stead. Benjamin's entire reflection on violence takes the form of an afterimage of Luxemburg's murder and could be said to be another empty casket—a casket in a modernist "mourning play" that entombs not Luxemburg but her missing body.[8] This afterimage condenses all the forms of violence he seeks to differentiate, even if, in the end, they demonstrate and enact their irreducible entanglement and complicity. With Luxemburg, Benjamin can point, in the most discreet of ways, to what she represents—the abolishment of the state and its violence, which had been so forcefully directed against her. As a figure of the proletarian general strike, it is not surprising that she had to be neutralized or annihilated by the state and, in this instance, by a state with presumably socialist origins. In Benjamin's taxonomy, she is a figure for the "great criminal" precisely because, in defying the law, she reveals the violence of the legal system itself.

The mass-like challenge Luxemburg embodies prompts a violent and gendered assassination—a femicide that is simultaneously law-preserving and law-destroying since, among other things, she is assassinated by the Freikorps.[9] Benjamin observes this very degeneration in the practice of the Social Democratic state during the bloody repression led by Noske against the Spartacist insurgency. These historical events persuade him that the democratic "police" bear witness to "the greatest conceivable degeneration [*Entartung*] of power [*Gewalt*]" (*CV*, 48). For Benjamin, however, Luxemburg cannot be annihilated altogether. On the contrary, beyond any determinate position that would instrumentalize her, she survives as an inexpressible and unrepresentable force. Benjamin echoes this strategic modality of silent survival, safe from further instrumentalizations, in *One-Way Street*. There, in a passage referencing Karl Kraus and titled "Monument to a Warrior," Benjamin makes an argument for the necessity of keeping a name silent. If we replace the masculine pronouns he uses to refer to Kraus with feminine ones, the sentences read: "Nothing more desolating than [her] acolytes, nothing more godforsaken than [her] adversaries. No name that would be more fittingly honored by silence" (*OWS*, 469). As he puts it in his early essay "The Metaphysics of Youth," it is "the silent one" who "is the unappropriated source of meaning."[10]

This insistence on silence is legible throughout Benjamin's writings and perhaps has its most extended elaboration in his 1936 essay "The Storyteller." There he writes about the silence and muteness that follow historical convulsions like World War I, in particular the way in which soldiers returning from the war can be read as embodied emblems of the speechless transmission of violence and trauma. In her essay on the place of silence in Benjamin's writings, however, Shoshana Felman points to an earlier encounter with death, also related to the war, and one that led Benjamin to encrypt another missing body in this other text (as he does in his essay on violence). According to Felman, Benjamin's most emblematic silence may be the one organized around the mourning of his friend, the poet Fritz Heinle, who, with his fiancée Rika Seligson, committed a double suicide in protest of the German invasion of Belgium in 1914. Benjamin recounts the event eighteen years later in his 1932 *A Berlin Chronicle*, in an account that retreats from the event as much as it mentions it. In Felman's words, the text "cannot go directly either to the proper name of the dead friend or to the actual story of his death. Temporally as well as spatially, the story keeps moving in circles, as though around an empty, silent center." But Benjamin encrypts his dead friend more discreetly in an unpublished essay he writes between 1914 and 1915 in which he presents a reading of two poems by Friedrich Hölderlin (another F. H.). Benjamin's text on Hölderlin's lyric poetry is an "implicit dialogue with Heinle's work, a dialogue with Heinle's writing as well as with his life and with his death."[11] Focusing on "The Poet's Courage" and "Timidity," as two dissonant versions of the same poem in which, as he puts it, "the rhyme words themselves are not named,"[12] Benjamin silently references the "courage" of Heinle's suicide and what he perceives as the "timidity" of his own survival. As Felman notes, "the underlying, understated evocation of the dead is present and can be deciphered everywhere." All of Benjamin's writings, she suggests, can "be read as a work of mourning, structured by a mute address to the dead face and the lost voice of the young friend who took his own life in desperate protest in the first days of the First World War."[13]

Benjamin's encryption of Heinle in his essay on Hölderlin is a precedent for his encryption of Luxemburg in his later essay on violence. The earlier essay is a testament to what he calls "the plastic structure of thought ... a plasticity which is, as it were, buried and in which form becomes identical with the formless." This plasticity effectively dissolves the borders between the two versions of the poem, overcoming the difference between the cowardly and the courageous, and ensuring the survival of the dead in those who are left to mourn them. Heinle's memory is finally registered—without mentioning his name—as "the center of this world [which] by rights belongs to another," a reminder that the past survives in the present and that the movements of language and thought involve the transits from one mind to another and can never be said to belong to a single person.[14] If Benjamin's textual crypt for his dead friend works to preserve his memory, his inability to name him directly—to name him only through the similarly initialed avatar Friedrich Hölderlin—marks the trauma he experiences because of this death. In Luxemburg's case, her anonymity within his violence essay is a means of memorializing her but also of protecting her from instrumentalization. Her encryption in the essay is itself a political event—an event that destroys any determination of the political even as it deranges what we think of as an event, since it takes place inside and outside a text at the same time, at the border that inevitably connects the text to violence, even as it seeks to exceed this same violence.

This reconceptualization of the political occurs because of the mediums in which it takes place. In Benjamin's essay, these mediums are language and, in particular, the suspension of language's capacity to name, which, as we have suggested, is a linguistic analogue to the proletarian general strike and its force of interruption. Benjamin's language could be said to enact Luxemburg's theory and practice of the mass strike at the level of his sentences—as they activate, disperse, interrupt, and massify any attempt to conceptualize either violence or the emergence of the strike. The ceaselessly changing and altering form of mass movements has its counterpart—finds a transient form—in the movements of Benjamin's writing.[15]

The singularity of Benjamin's textual crypt lies in its failure to conform to any law and order. It comes in the form of a *strike* that targets the traditional oppositions that govern political discourse, something he registers in the force of Luxemburg herself. Within the orbit of *this* strike, Luxemburg is a phantom limb—and within an essay that is more than simply divided, and that may only grant us access to its secrets through routes that are not just topographical but plurally marked by different overlapping and sedimented histories and temporalities. Its effects are perhaps most legible in the retranscription of the concepts that Benjamin explores in his essay and that work to "de-signify" any monosemic understanding of violence. In his outline for a never-completed development of an extended critique of violence, he changes the title of his essay to "A Dismantling of Violence" in order to suggest a critical decomposition of violence. This decomposition has its complement in the fragmentation and decomposition of Luxemburg herself—something that happens both inside and outside Benjamin's essay. If the essay's notorious difficulty and abstraction disguises and hides a female body, it also obscures its disguise in this encryption. It hides Luxemburg as it holds and preserves her by constructing a series of partitions—between divine and mythic violence, law-positing and law-destroying violence, the political and proletarian general strikes, and different instrumentalizations of natural law—that eventually unravel around her missing body, a body whose clandestine inclusion calls into question these very partitions. In other words, the crypt that Benjamin's essay is can only keep its secret by fragmenting itself—like the body it wants to protect and preserve. In order to register the effects of this gesture, we have to gather the various traces it leaves behind and decipher them through a forensic act of readerly interpretation. As we will see, Luxemburg's body and work get dispersed across other names and figures—minimally, she appears in the guise of the "great criminal," Sorel, Niobe, and, in another kind of plurality, the company of Korah and as a counterpoint to Kurt Hiller—and, in doing so, she becomes a shifting frame through which we can read Benjamin's simultaneously abstract and concrete but always elusive treatment of violence.[16]

One of the most ingenious ways in which Benjamin enciphers Luxemburg in his text is by inscribing her within Sorel's text, or, more precisely, by evoking her language alongside his discussion of Sorel—and sometimes in it—as if to recall to us the fact that Sorel's text is already in proximity to her, is already inhabited by her.[17] Although Sorel only explicitly cites Luxemburg's *Reform or Revolution*, he surely knew her *Mass Strike* and, at different moments, he simply ventriloquizes her views on the mass strike and revolution without mentioning her. At the same time, there are differences between Luxemburg and Sorel that get accented by the way in which Benjamin contextualizes his evocations (in the case of Luxemburg) and citations (in the case of Sorel) of their writings. In the end, he is closer to Luxemburg than to Sorel, and this becomes increasingly legible the more we recall not only the specific arguments made by these two thinkers of the strike but also the argument that Benjamin makes. If Sorel becomes a mask for Luxemburg—it is impossible not to register that "Sorel" is an anagram of "Rose L"—Benjamin uses Sorel's language neither to silence her nor to exemplify the loss of her voice.[18] Instead, he inscribes her now suppressed and silenced voice into Sorel's text in order to have us hear it, as if we were listening to a secret—a secret that eventually unravels Sorel's text. As he notes in *One-Way Street*, "[c]riticism is a matter of correct distancing" (*OWS*, 476). Evoking Luxemburg through Sorel permits him to distance himself from the Spartacists in an auratic play between distance and proximity that facilitates his critical task—as it walks a tightrope between philosophical abstraction and the extremity of Germany's political climate—and, in the long run, confirms his closeness to their means of political insurrection. Their own mode of resistance involves distancing themselves from different state forms that reiterate and reinforce violence, oppression, and capitalist inequalities in order to engage and dismantle them.[19]

If Benjamin draws his distinction between the political general strike and the proletarian general strike from Sorel—something that he also could have taken from Luxemburg's own distinction between a narrower or more general sense of the mass strike—Luxemburg's silent presence within Sorel's text unsettles its certainties. In particular, it enables Benjamin to release the critical potential of her writings against the elements in Sorel that remain tied to direct action, instrumentality, and mythical violence, despite Sorel's claims to the contrary, despite, that is, his own effort to complicate these concepts. While Sorel claims that the general strike is "the myth in which socialism is wholly comprised, i.e. a body of images capable of evoking instinctively all the sentiments which correspond to the different manifestations of the war undertaken by socialism against modern society"—that "the myth of the general strike dominates the true working-class movement in its entirety" (RV, 118 and 31)—Luxemburg resists the idea that a constellation of ideas alone can move the masses. Instead, like Benjamin—who also disputes the suggestion that a mythical affective image of the future can galvanize the masses— she insists that there is no formula, no myth or "recipe," that can mobilize them. In her words:

> Whether great popular demonstrations and mass actions really take place, in whatever form, is decided by an entire set of economic, political, and psychological factors ... that are incalculable and which no party can artificially produce. ... The historical hour posits each time the suitable forms of popular movement and *itself* creates new, improvised, and previously unknown methods of struggle; it enriches and amasses the arsenal of the people without concern for any of the pronouncements of the parties.[20]

It is precisely Luxemburg's sense of the mass strike as pure means, as a movement without a determinate shape or end, that draws Benjamin's attention. For her, masses do not exist before they emerge as forms in movement—she refers to *"the method of motion of the proletarian mass"* (MS, 141). They may not even survive their success or their defeat, and therefore cannot be interpellated or directed in any determinate way without ceasing to be masses in their becoming. Luxemburg's insistence on plasticity and becoming as the essential features of the mass strike distances her from Sorel's penchant for strict oppositions—his confident assertions, for example, that myth distinguishes political and proletarian general strikes. The conceptual impurity of mass movements—because they emerge as multitemporal and multidirectional historical events—calls for a capacious formlessness capable of gathering and containing other forms. This plasticity can affect its origin as well: a movement can begin as a political strike and, in the course of its development, gather the force of a proletarian strike. While Luxemburg can contain all of

Sorel's antagonistic pairings, Sorel cannot contain the formlessness that is at the core of her masses and that is the changing repository of their historical force. Very much like Benjamin, Luxemburg radicalizes Sorel's nominal anarchism by adopting a far more extensive understanding of formlessness as a force of deposition that breaks from a politics of ends. As she puts it, in a passage that resonates with Benjamin's own insistence on the strike's aleatory politics:

> The mass strike, as the Russian Revolution has shown us, is so protean a phenomenon that all the phases of political and economic struggle, all the stages and moments of the revolution are reflected in it. Its applicability, its effectiveness, the moments of its origin—all are constantly changing. It suddenly opens new and wide revolutionary vistas where the revolution seemed already at a dead end, and where it is impossible for anyone to count on it with any degree of certainty ... it is a ceaselessly moving, changing sea of phenomena. And the law of motion of these phenomena is clear: it does not lie in the mass strike itself, not in its technical peculiarities, but in the political and social relation of forces in the revolution. (*MS*, 140–141)

If the strike suspends any politics oriented toward violently posited ends, it is because it is the sheer medium of the political: the only politics that, constantly in motion, cannot be instrumentalized. It anarchically unsettles every form of directionality, which is why the first part of *The Mass Strike* is devoted to extracting and distancing the concept of the strike from a narrow sense of anarchism, where it nonetheless has its origins. Returning to Engels's 1873 denunciation of Bakunin[21]—appropriating his "authority" for her cause—Luxemburg argues that the historical experience of the Russian Revolution, and the political training it embodies and offers, fundamentally alter the concept of the strike, transforming it into the most powerful political implement of socialism in its democratic struggle for rights. She differentiates her "mass strike" from that of the French and Italian "syndicalists" who instrumentalize it in order to achieve reduced, reformist goals—in this case, workers' rights *in lieu of* democratic gains like universal suffrage—and who, not unlike a policial understanding of revolutionary formations, believe that leadership holds the key to a successful outcome. Recalling the lessons of the Russian Revolution, Luxemburg insists that her conceptualization of the mass strike follows the complex, multiple, and unpredictable gathering of the proletarian masses—who are formed in the

activity of the mass strike and not in accordance with any precon-
ceived and abstract theoretical scheme. It is worth noting that,
throughout her political and dialectical reading of the Russian
Revolution, Luxemburg does not propose a theory of "spontaneity," as often has been assumed, but instead a theory of political
incalculability, of risk and potential. While she uses the language
of spontaneity and direct action to speak about the sudden uprising of the proletariat, in each instance these mass movements
arise in relation to historical experience—in relation to a multiplicity of unpredictably mediated relations. As she puts it, "It is
absurd to think of the mass strike as one act, one isolated action.
The mass strike is rather the indication, the rallying idea, of a
whole period of the class struggle lasting for years, perhaps for
decades ... every one of the great mass strikes repeats, so to speak,
on a small scale, the entire history of the Russian mass strike,
and begins with a pure economic, or at all events, a partial trade-
union conflict, and runs through all the stages to the political
demonstration" (*MS*, 141 and 144). Unlike Sorel's anarchist version
of direct action, Luxemburg's direct action is entirely mediated
by historical forces that influence "the action of the strike in a
thousand invisible and scarcely controllable ways" (*MS*, 141), in
"a fight in the midst of the incessant crashing, displacing, and
crumbling of the social foundation" (*MS*, 148) that proceeds not
"in a beautiful straight line but in a lightning-like zig-zag" (*MS*,
168). This is why "strike action itself does not cease for a single
moment. It merely alters its forms, its dimensions, its effect. It is
the living pulse of the revolution and at the same time its most
powerful driving wheel ... [it is] *the method of motion of the proletarian mass*, the phenomenal form of the proletarian struggle in
the revolution" (*MS*, 141).[22] Insisting on the political training necessary for transformation, Luxemburg argues that the historical
experience of the strike amounts to a "living political school," an
"actual school of experience," that is part and parcel of the "high
degree of political education" that revolutionary change demands
and implements (*MS*, 130). The lessons of this political education
system are cumulative and transmitted across generations and
nationalities in an "endless series of ever-spreading and interlac-
ing economic struggles," in "a series of preparatory insurrections"
(*MS*, 133 and 139), that no single myth would be able to name or
fully contain, which is why they remain a source of revolutionary
potentiality.[23]

In contrast to Luxemburg's oceanic mass strike, Sorel conceptualizes the proletarian strike as a myth, as a quasi-military

strategy that relies on direct action and on what he calls "a will to act" (*RV*, 28), a subjectivist vitalism that—in Sorel's case, originating in the writings of Henri Bergson—would soon be appropriated by fascist discourse. Like Sorel, fascism also understood myth as the great motive force behind its political aestheticism, an aestheticism that, as we already have seen, is one of Benjamin's targets in his artwork essay. Although it would be misleading to suggest that this vitalist myth enters fascist rhetoric solely by way of Sorel, his work greatly influenced the former syndicalists-turned-fascists Georges Valois and Enrico Corradini, both of whom embraced myth as a means of intensifying the revolutionary zeal of the proletariat—the means whereby the proletariat would ready itself for the coming revolution. Benjamin's choice of Sorel as Luxemburg's masculinist cover is therefore rather remarkable, since it introduces her many refusals of myth in all its various guises as covert forces hiding within the certainties of Sorel's authority as a writer and as an activist anarcho-syndicalist whose insistence on the force of the general strike—and the corresponding violence of its mythic action (something both Benjamin and Luxemburg contest)—is often militaristic, and even muscular, in tone. It is hard to imagine prose that would be less Benjaminian than Sorel's! Luxemburg's antiwar and antimilitaristic stances—"present" simply by virtue of her inscription in Sorel's text—serve Benjamin well as a subtle counter to this masculinist strain in Sorel's writing. The traces of Luxemburg's language cast a shadowed light on the interplay in Sorel between his professed revolutionary practice and his nevertheless at times legibly reactionary theories. She becomes a means of accenting the fragments from Sorel that can be reclaimed for a revolutionary project, while at the same time exposing the elements that need to be left behind, or at least require this textual intervention. She enables Benjamin to work between the lines of Sorel's text and to take advantage of its contradictions in order to remap it in a more revolutionary manner. Emphasizing that no text can follow a single line—that the language of a text moves in several directions, something that is true for his text as well—Benjamin draws our attention to his effort to signal a sinuous path through what, because of Luxemburg's intercession, we might call the "ruins" of Sorel's text, if not of his "masculinity."[24]

That Benjamin presents Luxemburg through the mediation of a male other interrupts and fissures all traces of Sorel's masculinity from within. At the same time, this act alienates her from herself, permits her to appear in this alienation—and from the distance at which death has now put her. But, if Luxemburg and Sorel deconstitute one another precisely in their relation, this exchange of sexual identities, this textual crossdressing, would itself have been a recognizable feature of Weimar culture, and one in which Benjamin himself participated. Beyond the sexual experimentation and fluidity of gender identity that characterized the period—and that was given institutional support by the Institute for Sexual Science (Institut für Sexualwissenschaft) inaugurated in Berlin in July 1919—writers and artists explored different sexual orientations, often at the same time, and took on different pseudonyms and alter egos as part of these experiments. Benjamin himself posed for a photograph with his friend Alice Croner in 1921 dressed in drag and, in the same year, Marcel Duchamp famously took on the persona of "Rrose Sélavy" (another Rose) in order to mark not only the role of eros and sexuality in our everyday life but also the instability of identity, the performativity of gender, and the possibility of embodying more than one sex simultaneously. "Rose Sélavy" first appears in New York in 1920 as the author of Duchamp's sculpture "Fresh Widow," and then adds an additional "r" to her name when she signs Francis Picabia's 1921 collage *L'Oeil Cacodylate* (*The Cacodylic Eye*). When Duchamp is photographed by Man Ray in 1921 as "Rrose Sélavy," Rrose's hands are those of Germaine Everling, then Picabia's girlfriend. Drawing on established drag conventions in an era when drag performances were very much in vogue in France but also elsewhere (crossdressing was for a time legal in Weimar), Duchamp's performance also pluralizes the concept of authorship, something that is further intensified when the surrealist poet Robert Desnos later writes under the Rrose Sélavy alias. In regard to Luxemburg in particular, in his 1919 eulogy for her and Liebknecht, "A Requiem for Karl Liebknecht and Rosa Luxemburg," Trotsky already had used gender-bending tropes in his description of the "complementary" nature of the two Spartacists. As he puts it, "If the intransigent revolutionary Liebknecht was characterized by a feminine tenderness in his personal ways then this frail woman was characterized by a masculine strength of thought."[25] The pluralization and multiplication of identity, the impersonality of a writer's language, is something we have seen before, but the specificity of this Luxemburg-Sorel "couple" permits Benjamin to delineate, in this performative way, the various complicities and antagonisms not only between these two writers—both of whom claim to be heirs of Marx—but also between their different political stances.

Intensifying Luxemburg's presence within Sorel's text, Benjamin confirms the multiplicity of voices that inhabit any writer's language and, in this particular case, this pluralization signals the clandestine circulation and massification of Luxemburg's voice itself. Luxemburg's voice is always massified—it is mediated, transformed, ventriloquized in distorted forms, even if at times it was violently silenced. But, if it is not just hers, this is also because—beyond the archive of all the leftist, Marxist writings she reads, of all the literature, philosophy, economics, and anthropology she absorbs, of all the experiences and relations she lives that leave their traces in her—it already is that of the masses themselves. As Trotsky notes in his eulogy for Luxemburg and Liebknecht—written immediately after their assassination—she is "the personification of the proletarian revolution."[26] This personification gets enacted when, in the last text she writes, "Order Reigns in Berlin!," written the day before her death, she joins her "I" to that of the revolution and has it speak through her. Declaring that Berlin's "'order' is built on sand," that "the revolution will 'raise itself up again clashing,'" the revolution, speaking for her, proclaims "to the sound of trumpets: *I was, I am, I shall be.*" It is moving that these are Luxemburg's last written words, since they are themselves archivally massified. "Raise itself up again clashing" is a line from a poem by Ferdinand Freiligrath, a close friend of Marx, entitled "Abschiedswort" (A word of farewell). Marx published the poem in the final issue of the *Neue Rheinische Zeitung* after the defeat of the 1848 revolution; the entire issue was printed in red ink. "*I was, I am, I shall be*" is a line from another of Freiligrath's poems, "Die Revolution" (The revolution), written in 1851, in which the line is spoken by the Revolution itself. Inscribing her own farewell in the words of Freiligrath—speaking her last words, her own farewell, through the farewell of a journal devoted to democratic rights and in the aftermath of both the 1848 defeat and the recent defeat of the Spartacists—Luxemburg not only ventriloquizes her voice through the voice of another but also through the more impersonal voice of the Revolution itself. The defeat of the Spartacist uprising—one in a series of historical defeats—does not mark the end of the revolution, which is why it can announce its future. As Luxemburg puts it,

> the individual fights of the revolution formally end with a defeat. But revolution is the only form of "war"—this, too, is its particular life principle—in which the final victory can be prepared only by a series of "defeats." ... The whole path of socialism, as far as

Man Ray, *Marcel Duchamp as Rrose Sélavy*, ca. 1920–1921

Alice Croner and Walter Benjamin, 1921

revolutionary struggles are concerned, is paved with sheer defeats. ... Where would we be today without those "defeats" from which we have drawn historical experience, knowledge, power, idealism! ... How does the defeat in this so-called Spartacus Week appear in light of the above historical question? Was it a defeat due to raging revolutionary energy and a situation that was insufficiently ripe, or rather due to frailties and halfway undertakings?

Both! ... The leadership failed. But the leadership can and must be created anew by the masses and out of the masses. The masses are the crucial factor; they are the rock on which the ultimate victory of the revolution will be built. The masses were up to the task. They fashioned this "defeat" into a part of those historical defeats which constitute the pride and power of international socialism. And that is why this "defeat" is the seed of the future triumph.[27]

Luxemburg's mobilization of defeats, of their accumulation as constitutive elements of historical experience, is the closest she ever comes to a political prognosis. The secret of international socialism is that accumulated defeats are the necessary sediment and unspoken hope that conjure "the seed of the future triumph." Benjamin appropriates this logic, already present in Marx, and matches it with an incipient love of secrecy and encoding as the means for a clandestine mode of preservation and activism. His treatment of Luxemburg in "Toward the Critique of Violence" presents us with an early version of this counterintuitive and future-oriented revolutionary logic—one that gets enacted in the language of his text—as well as an example of secrecy as an act of safekeeping, as a gesture in the direction of a future that might inaugurate and even realize a *"new historical era"* (*CV*, 60).

Max Beckmann, *The Martyrdom* (plate 4) [*Das Martyrium* (Blatt 4)], from *Hell* (*Die Hölle*), 1919

> What might be the relationship between experiment in language
> and the violence of the modern world, between a truncated sen-
> tence and a truncated life? What drives syntax askew, makes
> language stall completely or spill over its proper borders ... ?
>
> —Jacqueline Rose, *On Violence and on Violence against Women* (2021)[1]

In Benjamin's essay, Luxemburg is inscribed in a series of allegorical transformations and figures that prevent any simple or
univocal identification between her and a determinate name,
whether it be individual or collective. Putting aside Benjamin's
own penchant for pseudonyms and alter egos, we might note that
Luxemburg and the Spartacists often took on different names—
especially when engaged in clandestine activities—including
Spartakus and Junius as collective and historical names, respectively.[2] Within Benjamin's essay, Luxemburg is encrypted in his
discussion of the Greek myth of Niobe, something that becomes
more legible when the myth is put in relation to a letter she writes
in 1917 while she is in prison and that Benjamin reads just before
writing his essay. Benjamin evokes the Niobe myth—a myth about
violence, numbers and massification, and the mutual instantiation of borders and the law—in order to illustrate what he calls
"mythical violence," a form of violence that, for him, involves the
violent imposition of law. Like that of Luxemburg, Niobe's fate
highlights the excessive violence that—responding to a perceived
threat or strong challenge, especially one made in the name of
equality—erects legal limits, separations, and demarcations that,
in turn, enable the sovereign state to declare who is inside or outside the law. In the mythical story, Niobe is accused of boasting
that she had more children than the goddess Leto, mother of
Apollo and Artemis. In retaliation for her claim—which is factu-
ally correct since she had twelve children, the so-called "Niobids"
(the exact number of her children varies from one version of the
myth to another, but it is always a matter of proliferation and
massification)—Leto orders Artemis and Apollo to kill all of Niobe's
children in front of her and to leave them unburied for nine days.
After their burial, Niobe is returned to her native Mount Sipylus
and transformed into a stone, a stone that eternally mourns and

weeps over her dead children. In Benjamin's reading of the myth, Niobe's fate cannot be understood as a punishment for a crime or transgression; it must be seen as the establishment of a boundary stone "marking the border between men and gods" (*CV*, 55) that did not exist previously. Niobe's transgression only exists retroactively, according to the perverse logic of a self-positing law, as the gods' violence "establishes a law far more than it punishes the transgression of an existing one" (ibid.). Accordingly, the law does not put an end to violence. It maintains and preserves violence as its foundational force. As Benjamin puts it, law-positing violence establishes "not an end that would be free of, and independent from, violence but, on the contrary, an end that, under the name of power, is necessarily and intimately bound up with it" (*CV*, 56). This cruel and excessive violence is revealed as the founding act of the law, as its bloody birth against the background of innocent deaths. The law behaves like a border staked on the violent exclusion of those it does not protect: in this instance, Niobe's children. One could say that Luxemburg's violent murder is used in a similar manner and functions primarily as a reminder that communists like her cannot expect protection from the law because, declared to be outside the law and therefore a threat to the state, they can be executed with no consequences. Indeed, despite being identified, Luxemburg's murderers were never held accountable for their crime.[3]

With the example of Niobe, Benjamin's critique of the relationship between violence and the law extends to those whose existence the law acknowledges but does not protect, making them more vulnerable to further violence and terror.[4] As the myth of Niobe demonstrates, murder is not alien to the law. It creates the law and is considered foundationally necessary whenever the designation and demarcation of illegal subjects suits the state and its legal system. The myth of Niobe must be understood as a conceptual extension of Benjamin's critique of violence, and as a mythical formalization of the history and structure of the law, a reminder that in his materialist thinking history and critique cannot be disentangled.

At this point in his difficult and multifaceted argument, however, Benjamin further qualifies the resilience and impregnability of legal borders when he adds that "when boundaries are laid down, the adversary is not utterly annihilated" (*CV*, 56). He leaves open the possibility that the "adversary" (be it a Niobe or a Luxemburg) may persevere in her plight, even when condemned to be "an eternal, mute bearer of guilt"—the one who must relentlessly and silently mourn the dead and memorialize the violence that led to this death, who becomes a sign that marks the violent act that inaugurates the law as a gravestone for justice. Furthermore, if Niobe's fate enacts a separation and border between gods and humans under the coercive threat of violence, at the same time, once she is metamorphosed into a weeping stone, she also endures as the marker of an extended grief for the violence against her children. A monument to what violence "leaves behind" (*CV*, 55), to the force of mythical violence, Niobe is stripped of her human form and transformed into a thing-like state that remains capable of animation and signification, even if she remains mute. As Michelle Ty puts it, "[b]y force, Niobe is silenced, no longer able to represent herself in speech, while further being made to testify—univocally yet without uttering a word—to the history of violence to which she has been subjected. Though mute, tearful Niobe is not released from the economy of signification but is deposited fixedly within it." Embodying the division between hierarchically differentiated realms, her tale confirms that mythic violence "leaves behind a residuum of what it destroys."[5] Niobe becomes a figure that binds the natural world with that of human sentience, and specifically in relation to the pain and loss to which they are fated under the onslaught of violence.

That Luxemburg's fate resembles that of Niobe is confirmed in her prison letters, which Benjamin read with great interest. In her numerous letters to friends and collaborators, Luxemburg establishes a series of connections and transferences among the violent exploitation of the natural world, the destruction of life under capitalism, and the state violence complicit with it. A selection of her correspondence with Sophie Liebknecht, written while in Breslau prison, was published shortly after her assassination. Their publication and editorial success quickly countered the myth of "bloody red Rosa" that was circulated and leaned on in order to justify her murder. Like many other Germans at the time, Benjamin read the letters. Greatly moved by them, he continues to reference them in the 1930s. In addition to her already influential political pamphlets, and her volumes on capitalism, revolution, colonialism, and violence of all kinds, Luxemburg's correspondence exhibits a wide range of complicities and an inspiring alertness to the smallest details of her surroundings. Her love of nature and her frequent identifications with birds, her commentaries on literature and music, her heartfelt belief in friendship and collaboration, and her commitment to the liberatory possibilities of mass movements are truly striking.[6]

Among the letters, the one most directly related to the myth of Niobe is the letter she writes to Sophie Liebknecht on December 24, 1917. In the letter, included in the selection of letters that Benjamin reads, Luxemburg—if not turned into stone, certainly imprisoned within Breslau's stone walls[7]—weeps, in echo of Niobe's own mournful tears for her children, as she registers the cruelty and violence of Europe's Great War. After offering an incisive assessment of the Russian October Revolution, reflecting on her third Christmas in prison, describing the sounds she hears at night while lying awake in her cell, speculating on the kind of flowers that could compose the bouquet she knows Sophie had picked up in Steglitz Park, and discussing poems by Stefan George, Luxemburg's letter, smuggled out of prison and therefore uncensored, takes a sudden and poignant turn:

Oh, Sonyichka [Sophie Liebknecht], I've lived through something sharply, terribly painful here. Into the courtyard where I take my walks there often come military supply wagons, filled with sacks or old army coats and shirts, often with bloodstains on them. ... They're unloaded here [in the courtyard] and distributed to the prison cells, [where they are] patched or mended, then loaded up and turned over to the military again. Recently one of these wagons arrived with water buffaloes harnessed to it instead of horses. This was the first time I had seen these animals up close. They have a stronger, broader build than our cattle, with flat heads and horns that curve back flatly, the shape of the head being similar to that of our sheep, [and they're] completely black, with large, soft, black eyes. They come from Romania, the spoils of war. ... The soldiers who serve as drivers of these supply wagons tell the story that it was a lot of trouble to catch these wild animals and even more difficult to put them to work as draft animals, because they were accustomed to their freedom. They had to be beaten terribly before they grasped the concept that they had lost the war and that the motto now applying to them was "woe unto the vanquished" [*vae victis*]. ... There are said to be as many as a hundred of these animals in Breslau alone, and on top of that these creatures, who lived in the verdant fields of Romania, are given meager and wretched feed. They are ruthlessly exploited, forced to haul every possible kind of wagonload, and they quickly perish in the process. —And so, a few days ago, a wagon like this arrived at the courtyard [where I take my walks]. The load was piled so high that the buffaloes couldn't pull the wagon over the threshold at the entrance gate. The soldier accompanying the wagon, a brutal fellow, began flailing at the animals so fiercely with the blunt end of his whip handle that the attendant on duty indignantly took him to task, asking him: Had he no pity for the animals? "No one has pity for us humans," he answered with an evil smile, and started in again, beating them harder than ever. ... The animals finally started to pull again and got over the hump, but one of them was bleeding ... Sonyichka, the hide of a buffalo is proverbial for its toughness and thickness, but this tough skin had been broken. During the unloading, all the animals stood there, quite still, exhausted, and the one that was bleeding kept staring into the empty space in front of him with an expression on his black face and in his soft, black eyes like an abused child. It was precisely the expression of a child that has been punished and doesn't know why or what for, doesn't know how to get away from this torment and raw violence. ... I stood before it, and the beast looked at me; tears were running down my face—they were his tears. No one can flinch more painfully on behalf of a beloved brother than I flinched in my helplessness over this mute suffering. How far away, how irretrievably lost were the beautiful, free, tender-green fields of Romania! How differently the sun used to shine and the wind blow there, how different was the lovely song of the birds that could be heard there, or the melodious call of the herdsman. And here—this strange, ugly city, the gloomy stall, the nauseating, stale hay, mixed with rotten straw, and the strange, frightening humans—the beating, the blood running from the fresh wound. ... Oh, my poor buffalo, my poor, beloved brother! We both stand here so powerless and mute, and are as one in our pain, impotence, and yearning. —All this time the prisoners had hurriedly busied themselves around the wagon, unloading the heavy sacks and dragging them off into the building; but the soldier stuck both hands in his trouser pockets, paced around the courtyard with long strides, and kept smiling and softly whistling some popular tune to himself. And the entire marvelous panorama of the war passed before my eyes.[8]

In this extraordinary passage, Luxemburg offers her own critique of violence, giving us a glimpse into the ellipses around which Benjamin's essay is written. It is not that Benjamin does not engage what is not said in his text directly—he does, as we already have demonstrated—but Luxemburg goes further into the details of a singular and contingent experience of violence. This incident is at once familiar and quotidian, but is intensified and expanded by the state of emergency of a war that provides the historical context for Luxemburg's reflections. More than the stories of Niobe or the Korah, Luxemburg's letter goes to the heart of the experience of the endlessly entangled brutality that underlies war and capitalism and that reverberates—even in "quiet times," as she often reminds us[9]—in the experiences of class, labor, the prison system, immigration, and the constant plunder of nature, but of a nature that is intimately bound to us.

The passage begins with the blood of soldiers soaking the garments that are sent in military supply wagons to the prison for mending, one form of conscripted and brutal labor seeping into another—in perfect continuity, however different they are—and as part of a barbaric cycle with no end in sight. In one single sentence, Luxemburg transforms the prison courtyard where the scene takes place into an allegory of life under capitalism. Before our eyes, she literally materializes her argument against Germany's imperialist war as yet another aftereffect of capitalism's relentless plunder. The passage, raw as it appears, is also a condensation of Luxemburg's life-long study, analysis, and criticism of the ruthless logic of capitalism. The Romanian buffaloes that carry the loads of military supplies are "the spoils of war" but also the immigrants that, upon crossing a border, become the "draft labor" that fuels capitalism's greed, a modality of economic conscription. The loving patience and observational detail of Luxemburg's description of the black buffaloes is typical of the treatment of nature exhibited throughout her prison letters, with nature becoming a reservoir of beauty, freedom, and life capable of undoing the logic of imprisonment because it ignores the enforcement of captivity. In this instance, however, the freedom of the buffaloes grazing the Romanian prairies is merely an imagined and mournful memory lost long before the beginning of her narration of the prison yard scene. The violence of the border is enacted not only allegorically but also physically by the soldier beating the buffalo to press him across the threshold of the prison gate. The soldier's brutality, which is only superficially an act of personal sadism, is one more instance of the transmission of violence through the compromised agency of the conscripted soldier, an instrumentalization moving against another instrumentalization, and even within it. When the soldier exclaims, justifying his abuse of the animals, "no one has pity for us humans," he identifies with the broken skin of the buffalo. At once subject and object of violence, his "agency" echoes and reverberates with his own unfreedom. Luxemburg's "woe unto the vanquished"—a phrase that should be understood in all its depth and that Benjamin variously incorporates more than once into his writing, especially in his notes to his late essay on the concept of history—is the red thread woven into the entire passage. It can refer to any of the characters involved in the scene, including the soldier, the buffalo, and Luxemburg. That she refers to the sad eyes of the buffalo as those of "an abused child" underscores the future violence inscribed in every single act of violence, not only because it appears as an act of transmission but, above all, because it forecloses the possibility of a different future. Like the myth of Niobe, Luxemburg's is a story of cruel violence against children, here in the form of the buffalo, and, also like Niobe's, it is a story of witnessing and mourning. In another instance of displaced, compromised, and vicarious agency, Luxemburg's tears are not her own but the buffalo's, yet the buffalo's tears are not just his own, for he is the allegorical figuration of the shared fate of the vanquished, who are "powerless and mute, and are as one in [their] pain, impotence, and yearning." Niobe's children become proleptic figures of Luxemburg's children of the revolution, the vanquished with whom she identifies and in whose name she writes, the vanquished for whom, like Niobe, she weeps. In the world of Luxemburg's letter—in perfectly Benjaminian fashion—the prison courtyard becomes a capitalist panorama. In her words, "the entire marvelous panorama of the war passe[s] before [our] eyes." Not for nothing, the Spartacists' well-known motto would be "socialism or barbarism."[10] Luxemburg's letter stands as a powerful indictment of capitalism's pervasive barbarism and plunder but also as an instance of the revolutionary empathy that, identifying with the vanquished masses, gestures in the direction of another way of being in the world, one that is simultaneously relational and impersonal, even as it takes its point of departure from a singular instance of the violence against which it stands. Like Niobe, Luxemburg's imprisonment—her confinement in stone—confirms the inextricable relation between violence and the law, a violence whose mythical reach can only be interrupted by another violence, but one that, having no relation to the law, would strike in the name of justice, in the name of a new historical era. It is to the possibility of this other violence that Benjamin next turns.

Willy Römer, *Spartacists behind Barricades Made of Rolls of Newspaper in Front of the Rudolf Mosse Publishing House, Schützenstrasse, January 11, 1919. Occupation of the Newspaper District*

> This is the divine violence that moves, like a storm, over humanity to obliterate all traces of guilt.
>
> —Judith Butler, *Parting Ways: Jewishness and the Critique of Zionism* (2012)[1]

It is because of what Benjamin calls the "perniciousness" of the historical function of mythical violence that, for him, the most urgent task is its annihilation. In his words, "[p]recisely this task introduces once again and for the last time the question of a pure, immediate form of violence that might be capable of putting a halt to mythic violence" (*CV*, 57). His "once again and for the last time" suggests not only that he again imagines the possibility of a violence beyond all legal and mythical violence but also that, although he will gesture in the direction of this possibility, it must necessarily be his last effort in the face of this gesture's inevitable failure, or at least the unpredictability of its success. It is as if he already alerts us to the fact that he will simply once more suggest the difficulty, if not the impossibility, of achieving justice, or of providing us with a determinate path toward it. As we will see, in the same way that his critique of violence can never be finished—it is because violence is everywhere that he can only move "toward" such a critique—the violence he imagines beyond violence can only be "pending" (*CV*, 60), waiting for its moment, still to come. Nevertheless, in the final pages of his essay, Benjamin erects yet another demarcation; polemically, that is, since it will soon implode, like all the other previous terms he sets against each other, and this because of the explosive semantic violence of his sentences. He extracts justice from the law in order to imagine the possibility of a justice that can be neither entirely instrumentalized nor beholden to the violence of the law and its ends. A violence beyond human and legal violence, the violence of justice would presumably be a "bloodless" violence that promises a different historical order. He conceptualizes this "violence beyond violence," this pure means without ends, by turning, as he so often does throughout his more political writings, to religious figures, in this instance to the figures of Korah and "divine violence."

It is not surprising that Benjamin sets a biblical story against the myth of Niobe, especially since the story to which he turns— that of Korah and his horde, the Israelites who, having been freed from oppression in Egypt, challenge the authority of Moses and Aaron as they journey to take possession of the promised land—is, like the Niobe myth, also a story of numbers and massification, violence and punishment, and equality and inequality. The Korah story belongs to the fourth of the five books of Moses, to the book titled Numbers because of its relation to the counting of the people in the twelve tribes of Israel—before and along their thirty-eight-year journey across the desert to the promised land.[2] The story is obsessed with counting. It contains not just population counts but also statistics, tribal and priestly figures, and other numerical data. For a story devoted to counting, what is of interest to Benjamin is what cannot be counted, who counts and who does not, and what remains unaccounted for and even incalculable. In other words, if Benjamin is drawn to the story of Korah, it is surely because it falls within one of the most enigmatic, poetic, miscellaneous, and contradictory books in the Bible—with one of the longest and most complicated histories of conflicting interpretations (what we receive are the shards of a story because the story already has been shattered in its transmission). It is also because it furthers his exploration of violence against the backdrop of his encrypted references to Luxemburg and the Spartacists, who demanded that everyone count, even as they knew that counting within the sphere of politics—where every number, enumerating who belongs and who does not, bears something uncountable within it—demonstrates the uncertainties of counting. Benjamin's critical reading of biblical materials is often inverted and ironic, even heretical in its exegesis. It is not unusual, we will see, for him to recontextualize these materials in a series of reflections that, clearing a path for different interpretive possibilities, enable him: (1) to reconceptualize what the political is or may be, especially in relation to religious and theological figures; (2) to register the communal work and play in Talmudic study[3]; and (3) to demonstrate that his relation to Judaism takes place within activities of reading and writing rather than through an active faith—activities that, in each instance, enact a mode of distancing that, in a counterattack, permits him to gesture in the direction of what, for him, is most urgent and most at stake in any given context.

The book's first four chapters consist of a detailed census of the tribes of Israel conducted in the wilderness. The generally used

Hebrew title for the book, Bemidbar, simply means "in the wilderness," and we can imagine that Benjamin finds this wilderness of interest—not simply as a description of the context in which the events in Numbers take place but as a figure for the "wilderness" that is biblical language, the wilderness of numbers, and the wilderness of the story of Korah itself. The story of Korah's rebellion against the leadership of Moses and Aaron in chapter 16 is the focus of Benjamin's retelling of the story, although he neglects many of the story's details, especially those elaborated in chapters 17 and 18. In the biblical story, Korah and 250 Levites—"community chieftains," "men of renown"—assemble against Moses and Aaron and declare: "You have too much! For all the community, they are all holy, and in their midst is the LORD, and why should you raise yourselves up over the LORD's assembly?" Moses responds by telling them that they should acknowledge everything that they have. Not understanding what they already have received by having been chosen by God, he goes on to say, and not accepting the authority God has granted him and Aaron, they have offended God, demonstrating that it is they who "have too much," not him and Aaron. He declares that God himself will make clear who is holy and who is not. He instructs them to gather their fire-pans and to bring them to the tabernacle in the morning and to burn incense as an offering to God. Their ongoing complaints and challenges, however, anger Moses, and he tells God not to "turn to their offering." When God appears, He tells Moses and Aaron to separate from the rest of the community so that He can "put an end to them in an instant." They plead with Him not to manifest His rage against the entire community if only some have offended Him. God then asks Moses and Aaron to separate and divide the community, and Moses turns to them and, encouraging them to distance themselves from the offending members of the community, says:

> "By this shall you know that the LORD has sent me to do all these deeds, that it was not from my own heart: If like the death of all human beings these die, and if the fate of all human beings proves their fate, it is not the LORD who has sent me. But if a new thing the LORD should create, and the ground gapes open its mouth and swallows them and all of theirs and they go down alive to Sheol, you will know that these men have despised the LORD." And it happened, just as he finished speaking all these words, the ground that was under them split apart, and the earth opened its mouth and swallowed them and their households and every human being that was Korah's, and all the possessions. And they went down, they and all that was theirs, alive to Sheol, and the earth covered

over them, and they perished from the midst of the assembly. And all Israel that was round about them fled at the sound of them, for they thought, "Lest the earth swallow us." And a fire had gone out from the LORD, and consumed the two hundred fifty men bringing forward the incense.[4]

This double annihilation still does not prevent further complaints, since "all the community of Israelites murmured on the next day against Moses and against Aaron, saying, 'You, you have put to death the LORD's people.'" God again decides to eradicate all the complainers, this time by means of a plague, and, again, Moses and Aaron intervene: "And Moses said to Aaron, 'Take the fire-pan and place fire upon it from the altar and put in incense and carry it quickly to the community and atone for them, for the fury has gone out from before the LORD, the scourge has begun.'" Aaron follows Moses's instructions and, standing "between the dead and the living," he holds the scourge back with his offering and by atoning for the people, but not before another 14,700 people are killed (Numbers 17:1–17). As David Lloyd notes, "it is not God's violence that is expiatory but Aaron's. ... Expiation appears as the prerogative of the lawful priest, who establishes a boundary between the worthy and the unworthy, the saved and the doomed, rather than as a quality of divine violence."[5]

In Benjamin's reading, the story exemplifies the difference between divine expiatory violence and retributive mythical violence, between incalculability and calculus. If, we will suggest, the story's details would seem to belie this reading, they point to a relation rather than to an absolute break between these two forms of violence. What seems at first inconsistent eventually reveals itself to be a rather extraordinary rereading of the biblical story in terms of questions of privilege, class, wealth, inheritance, and the circulation of capital—all in the name of a revolutionary annihilation of all the laws that support these capitalist traits, and of the lexicon with which we speak about violence, since, for Benjamin, divine violence can be neither manifested nor represented. Unlike mythical violence, it cannot be "disclosed to human beings" (*CV*, 60). It proceeds not through the unfolding of a natural order but rather through "the introduction of a *creative caesura*"—in Moses's words, "a new thing the LORD should create"—that, interrupting "the regular succession of things," points to the invention, the conditions, of a new era.[6] The features of this new era can be deduced from several of the story's details, but we can perhaps begin with Benjamin's own response to the story. As he puts it:

Just as God is opposed to myth in all spheres, so divine violence runs counter to mythic violence. Indeed, divine violence designates in all respects an antithesis to mythic violence. If mythic violence is law-positing, divine violence is law-annihilating; if the former establishes boundaries, the latter boundlessly annihilates them; if mythic violence inculpates and expiates at the same time, divine violence de-expiates; if the former threatens, the latter strikes; if the former is bloody, the latter is lethal in a bloodless manner. The legend of Niobe may be contrasted by way of example with God's judgment on Korah's horde. The judgment strikes privileged ones, Levites; it strikes them unannounced, without threat, and does not stop short of annihilation. At the same time, however, precisely in annihilating, it is also de-expiating, and one cannot fail to recognize a profound connection between the bloodless and the de-expiating character of this violence. For blood is the symbol of mere life. (*CV*, 57)

Setting aside the distinctions he makes between mythical and divine violence—we will return to them in a moment—Benjamin claims that "[t]he legend of Niobe may be contrasted by way of example with God's judgment on Korah's horde." Since the distinctions he makes in these sentences—as with all the others in the essay—are not sustainable, this claim suggests that the example in question here is nothing but an example of contrast and, in particular, of the way in which contrasts do not hold. Reminding us that all contrasts are relational—that opposing terms inhabit one another and cannot be altogether distinguished—it is significant that the one trait with which he identifies Korah and his horde is that of privilege, which also depends on distinctions. Korah's interest is to minimize the distinction between him and Moses and Aaron in order to maintain the one between his and his horde's privilege and the rest of the community. If Korah challenges the authority of Moses and Aaron—if he challenges their privilege—it is not in order to eliminate privilege, but instead to achieve parity with it. As Fenves notes, the fact that Moses, Aaron, and Korah are all privileged "indicates that they are willy-nilly exponents of law in accordance with the recently articulated theorem 'all law [*Recht*] was the privilege [*Vor-recht*] of kings or grandees.'" "Privilege equals law," he goes on to say, "even in the case of the grandee named Korah, who expresses the identity of one with the other, *Recht* with *Vor-recht*, through an appeal to the supposed sanctity of 'the whole community' (Numbers 16:3)."[7] Korah's challenge is less a rebellion or insurrection than an appeal made in the name of a system of laws and privilege—in the name of protecting and keeping the privilege he and his horde already enjoy. It is an appeal for the protection of wealth, property, nobility, and power—not really for *all* the community, since Korah's wealth and property have depended on enslaved labor and different forms of exploitation, all legalized under the laws of the privileged—but, in particular, for the propertied elite who wish to maintain their privilege and who refuse to be subject to, to be different in status from, Moses or Aaron. The exchange between Moses and Korah—with each mirroring the other's accusation, with each stating that the other already has "too much"—casts in relief the stakes of their argument, not the least of which, and this beyond the particulars of their own interests, is a reconceptualization of what wealth means and which wealth is more valuable—material or spiritual wealth. It is because their discussion does not threaten the state but rather insists on privilege within it that it is a discussion about how, in Sorel's words, power can be "transferred from the privileged to the privileged" (*RV*, 171). This mirror effect between Moses and Korah is interrupted by God's violence because He privileges Moses over Korah, and this because Moses favors spiritual wealth over material wealth.

In this book of counting, that is, Korah miscounts because what counts for him is the privilege of wealth, class, property, and inheritance, all of which are intimately connected to his declared wish to be equal in power to Moses and Aaron. God's strike against Korah and his horde is, among other things, a strike against their insistence on the relations between capital and religion—a strike that Benjamin himself will repeat more generally in his short 1921 essay "Capitalism as Religion," arguing that religion would not have been able to become capitalist if capitalism had not already been essentially religious.[8] The target of God's strike becomes legible in the consequences of His divine violence: he strikes the Levites "unannounced, without threat, and does not stop short of annihilation." The medium of His destruction is the earthly world, which opens its mouth, swallows Korah and his horde alive, together with all their possessions, and, closing its mouth, seals them inside Sheol, as Fenves notes, "without ever breathing a word or marking the site."[9] The implications of this gesture are far-reaching in the context of Benjamin's encryption of Luxemburg, since, in many respects, this act of divine violence makes way for precisely the potential destruction of capital and its system of privilege and wealth that was Luxemburg's ambition. Indeed, the moment Korah and his horde are buried with their property, it can no longer circulate; it no longer belongs to the logic of capital. The burial of their possessions also ensures that their surviving children will inherit not material wealth but, instead, something different and not quantifiable. Assuming they can learn from this example of God's "educative violence" (*CV*, 58), they will inherit spiritual wealth from the ruins of Korah's capitalist religion. This transformation of material wealth into spiritual wealth has its most tangible manifestation in God's directive to Moses shortly after. There God asks Moses to tell Aaron's son to gather all the fire-pans whose ruins have been left behind by His conflagration and, because they have now become holy, to "make of them hammered sheets as plating for the altar" as "a sign for the Israelites," in remembrance of them, and as a warning that no one should become like Korah and his community (Numbers 17:1–5). If Korah becomes a sign (26:10), he is the sign of what needs to be annihilated in the name of a potentially new order. To the extent that it obliterates law and privilege, divine violence moves in the direction of a revolutionary cause.

If the earth erases the traces of the devastation left in the wake of this violence, it is because divine violence cannot be represented or manifested. In this, it is an analogue not only to Luxemburg's ideas of the general strike and revolution, since they too cannot be represented, but also to Luxemburg herself, since, even if she appears as the embodiment of both the general strike and the revolution, she also cannot be represented. Within the logic of Benjamin's essay, she must remain hidden, if not buried. Sheol keeps what cannot be represented. As a figure of the void, it recalls Luxemburg's position within Benjamin's essay. It is a space of illegibility, of negativity and indistinction, where there is no clear border between the living and the dead. In some versions of the story, the voices of Korah and his horde can still be heard from below the ground. In both Benjamin and Luxemburg, this illegibility is a principle, what Jacqueline Rose calls a "revolutionary creed."[10] In the essay, as in Sheol, we cannot know what, if anything, can or should survive, and this uncertainty is at the heart of what Benjamin means by revolution. In this, he pays homage to Luxemburg's own sense of revolution, and the mobility of his language corresponds to the shifting movement of the Spartacist's masses. This mobility also adds to the meaning of the German word *Streik* and brings it in relation to its more ambiguous English "strike." As Hamacher notes, "it should be kept in mind that the origin of the German word *Streik* in the English word *strike* would have been more widely remembered in the 1920s than it is today; in the nineteenth century it was still common in German texts to use the word *strike* in its English spelling. Engels's works are one of numerous examples. Benjamin would have been familiar with this spelling and with the meaning of the English word."[11] When God strikes against Korah and his horde—when His rage opens up and effects their transfer to Sheol—this transcendental strike does not simply expose the conditions of historical action but also suspends its previous forms and inaugurates the possibility of another history, one no longer dominated by capital and its monied distinctions and privileges, but rather by the promises of Luxemburg's mass strikes, in all their deposing force.

This deposing force—also an effect of the mobility of Benjamin's language—is at work even within the distinctions he draws between mythical and divine violence, since, in the end, the example of the story of Korah undoes each of these distinctions, dividing them along different lines and refracting them in multiple directions. None of them continue to stand, which can be registered very easily if we just consider the story's details. If, for example, unlike mythical violence, divine violence annihilates law and abolishes boundaries, it nevertheless also depends on several law-preserving gestures, especially those of Moses, and on innumerable distinctions and borders—between who is included or excluded from God's chosen people, who is holy and who is not, who is devoted to God and who strays from Him. This force of dissolution annuls all the other distinctions Benjamin makes. The divine violence of God is not immediate or "unannounced," since it passes through the mediation of Moses—first in a negotiation, when he asks God not to annihilate everyone but only those who have offended Him, and then in his prophecy of the earth swallowing Korah and his horde, which is the script God follows. Within the story of Korah, no one speaks in their own voice, not even God. Everyone's voice is mediated by another, if not by several others, with the result that everyone's agency is scattered. As Ariella Azoulay puts it, God Himself is "the very paradigm of an absence of agency."[12] Unlike mythic violence, which "inculpates and expiates at the same time," divine violence "de-expiates." It de-poses the logic of opposition because, annihilating agency by scattering it, it obscures the distinction between the guilty and the guiltless, between agency and its duplication, revealing the complicity between them. If Moses—who is identified with the law, minimally with Mosaic law—threatens Korah and his horde, when God strikes after Moses's intervention, his strike is not without threat (he cites Moses, as it were). Finally, if mythical violence is "bloody," divine violence is never simply on the side of "bloodlessness," since, within the story, 250 Levites are burned to death. Within the logic of Benjamin's reading, "bloodnessness" is never just "bloodless" but, instead, the sign of what never belongs simply to "mere life," of what exceeds what is just human—the impersonal and even the extrahuman. The more closely one considers the examples and traits Benjamin attributes to mythical and divine violence, the more the distinctions between them break down—the more they point to the destructive, unsettling, and deposing force of his language, and of the essay's own critical strike. In each instance, it is the movement of Benjamin's language that destroys the possibility that any word, concept, or, in our context, act of violence could ever be monosemic or calculable, which is why the essay in turn enacts a linguistic violence. The dismantling of each word, concept, or act of violence becomes synonymous with the act of reading the essay performs and also demands.

As Benjamin announces in the very first sentence of his essay, "[t]he task of a critique of violence may be described as the presentation of its relation to law and justice" (*CV*, 39). While he associates violence with both law and justice, he nevertheless distinguishes them, suggesting that violence can only be a means of justice if it is pure means. It can only be just if—striking in a medial way, and with an impersonal force—it annihilates the law and its end-oriented violence. This force of mediation circulates throughout the entirety of Benjamin's essay and can be traced, even if in encoded and displaced ways, in the appropriations, refractions, exchanges, and allusions that constitute the movement through which his text opens onto history—and confirm that his voice and agency are thoroughly differential and dispersed. In order to close our reading of Benjamin's essay, we want to demonstrate this point "once again and for the last time"—at least here—by tracing the relation of his language to that of two of his contemporaries, the first his longtime friend and interlocutor Gershom Scholem, and the other the pacificist and activist Kurt Hiller. The first is unnamed in the essay but mediates Benjamin's discussions of fate, time, myth, law, and justice, and the second enables Benjamin to reinforce his encryption of Luxemburg in a further enactment of the critical strike his essay is.

While the story of Korah carries most of the weight of Benjamin's discussion of divine violence, his understanding of justice is indebted to a 1919 essay by Scholem that, only published posthumously, he read in draft form with great admiration in October 1918.[13] In the essay, entitled "On Jonah and the Concept of Justice" ("Über Jona und den Begriff der Gerechtigkeit"), Scholem argues that in the story of Jonah prophecy functions as a pedagogical means of transmitting the idea of justice, and that it is Jonah's failure as a prophet that ironically teaches him the truth about justice.[14] Jonah misunderstands prophecy because he conflates prophecy with fate. He believes that prophecy is a script that is actualized in the unfolding of human history. He believes it predicts the future. Scholem, however, insists that *"all* prophetic concepts are concepts of distance,"[15] and, in particular, they mark the distance between the present and an unpredictable future. A prophesied future can change from one moment to the next, especially when a judgment that would realize the prophecy alters in relation to changed and unpredictable circumstances and, in this way, distancing itself from the prophecy, simultaneously opens onto a responsibility toward the political (this is why Scholem can state that, in the end, what Jonah does "is essentially politics"[16]). That a judgment can change suggests that a judgment is suspended endlessly across time; from the point of view of justice, the present is eternal, and therefore never present. This duration and suspension constitute the structure of justice. Justice must be understood here as a deferral of the execution of judgment—especially in relation to a judgment about punishment, since punishment is a matter of law. Justice is instead a form of suspension and delay that interrupts the law's causality, undoes the distinction between guilt and guiltless, and breaks down the logic of the relation between a doer and a deed, which supports all forms of positing, indebtedness, and violence that can be instrumentalized.[17] It corresponds to a deed without a determinate fated agent behind it. In Scholem's words: "The deed void of meaning is the just deed. To act in deferral implies to eliminate meaning. The meaningful deed is the mythical one and answers to Fate. *Justice eliminates Fate.* Isaiah 65:19–24 not only indicates the elimination of Fate in messianic time but also provides the method of this elimination in the idea of deferral."[18]

The resonances of the passage with Benjamin's effort to differentiate mythic from divine violence are striking. They illuminate the political and religious stakes of Scholem's and Benjamin's shared denunciation of the role of fate in myth (which Benjamin explores directly and more fully in his 1919 essay "Fate and Character"). If justice must remain without meaning, and thus illegible, it is because it is a figure of suspension and postponement that, rather than merely negating the deed, interrupts it so that it becomes, as in Benjamin, detached from its ends. According to both Scholem and Benjamin, justice can only be just if, like divine violence, it is pure means—if it is read as a question that cannot be answered but that in its very positing effectively suspends and deposes the logic of ends, which sustains the worlds of myth and law. Because of this, justice—again like divine violence—has the power not just to annihilate life, but above all to annihilate the laws that govern life and thereby reduce it.

The medial character of prophecy, which is the source of its distancing effects, reverberates with Benjamin's expansive understanding of the activity of reading—as the creation of a distance through linguistic mediation. As Marc Caplan reminds us, prophecy is a linguistic performance capable of transforming even the divine deed into a "replication of an event that had been textually foretold in the language of its own revelation."[19] As Benjamin would have it, this divine power "acquires attestation" through "religious tradition" and is therefore not only already mediated but cannot even be acknowledged without precedent and without indebtedness (CV, 58). There is, however, an even more striking resonance between Scholem's text and Benjamin's essay, one that references not only justice but also the "just ones" and, in particular, their death. "[T]he circle of events completes itself in the unsaid," he writes, adding that "the death of the just ones is hidden."[20] These two sentences bear on our present reading. Benjamin's concealment of Luxemburg—a necessity that, at once rhetorical and political, relegates her to the "unsaid"—becomes, via Scholem, a means of referencing her justness. Scholem's lines become events in Benjamin's essay; they reinforce his valuation of Luxemburg's ethico-political force. Benjamin's silent evocation of both Scholem and Luxemburg is intensified with the suggestion that the realm of justice must remain detached or distanced from the certainty of ends—only in this way is it unable to be instrumentalized and made legible by myth.

As we already have noted, besides its being a force of instrumentalization, this mythical legibility is defined by a structure of guilt and retribution that identifies a doer with a deed. Justice, on the other hand, requires a forgiveness that, suspending judgment, eliminates the dividing line between the guilty and the guiltless—and, in doing so, demonstrates its strike against the system that, organized around the creation and attribution of guilt and debt, we call "capitalism." For both Scholem and Benjamin, this reconceptualized forgiveness hinges on a temporality that remains exterior to human history, since human history—bound to legal and religious structures of all kinds—relies on retribution, guilt, punishment, and sacrifice. If, as Benjamin remarks, forgiveness finds "its most powerful figuration in time" (*GS*, 6:98), it is because time becomes the condition that makes justice possible by embracing delay, retraction, and refusal. This negative understanding of time as delay—as the retraction of both the deed and its punishment—announces the "storm of forgiveness" that "is not only the voice that drowns out the criminal's scream of terror" but also "the hand that expunges the traces of his misdeed—though the earth be laid to waste thereby"; it becomes "the thunderously loud oncoming storm of forgiveness before the ever-approaching court."[21] This "ever-approaching court" appears in Scholem under the guise of the "Last Judgment," an essential theological figure in several of Benjamin's texts. This impending judgment can only be counteracted by a forgiveness that follows from justice as an act of infinite deferral. In Scholem's words:

> Justice is the idea of the historical annihilation of divine judgment, and just is that deed which neutralizes divine judgment upon it. Justice is the indifference of the Last Judgment; this means that justice unfolds from within itself the sphere in which the coming of the Last Judgment is infinitely deferred. Messianic is that realm which no Last Judgment follows. Therefore the prophets demand justice, in order infinitely to eliminate the Last Judgment. In just actions, the messianic realm is immediately erected.[22]

According to Scholem, the force of justice lies in its strike against the very principle of action that subtends the law. If the law assumes that every action can be traced back to an intentional subject, and if this assumption is what enables it to assign guilt and retribution, what preserves its judicial and law-positing power, justice suspends judgment, action, and execution altogether. It annihilates the entire legal order by deactivating and disabling the law's reliance on matters of agency, causality, calculability, and judgment, and, in its force of interruption and delay, it ensures a distance between judgment and its execution, between cause and effect. Its neutralization and deferral of action rhymes with the force of Benjamin's revolutionary strike, which, in the end, is the most important political figure in his essay. In its final paragraph, he declares that, if "pure immediate violence" could be "secured beyond law," this would "prove that, and how, there is a possibility of revolutionary violence, which is the name reserved for the highest manifestation of pure violence through human beings" (*CV*, 60).

We will turn to Benjamin's quasi-secular appropriation of messianism later—to his insistence that messianism cannot be reduced simply to a religious or theological concept, to his conception of a time that, in its delay, in its nonarrival, inaugurates historical time, or, more precisely, initiates a time that begins with forgiveness—but here we only wish to note that the constellation of justice, Last Judgment, messianism, and delay emerges from an encounter between Scholem and Benjamin that leaves its traces in Benjamin's essay. That Benjamin's language can be shown to be entirely mediated, and not just by Scholem, is just one more indication of its impersonality, one more confirmation that Benjamin is never a single "doer" behind any of his sentences. The impersonality of his language moves in accordance with what he calls in his 1916 essay on language the "continua of transformation." "[W]hat is communicated in language," he writes, "cannot be externally limited or measured" because "all language contains its own incommensurable, uniquely constituted infinity,"[23] an infinity that is inseparable from its "method of movement." We can see how this method of transformation works in our next example—an example that again demonstrates that Benjamin never writes alone.

Like Benjamin and Scholem, Hiller in his 1919 essay "Anti-Cain" writes against the background of innumerable indices of the violence that characterized the early Weimar period.[24] He writes in favor of an uncompromising pacifism, arguing that an absolute refusal of all violence is the only means of achieving peace. Benjamin read earlier texts by Hiller with admiration, but here he goes against what he perceives to be Hiller's naïveté in relation to the inescapable ubiquity of violence; indeed, much of his essay incorporates traces of Hiller's anti-violence tract.[25] As Lisa Marie Anderson notes in the preface to her recent translation of Hiller's essay, "[t]he thoroughgoing critique of violence Benjamin wanted to carry out was necessitated at least in part … by the talk of 'pacifists and activists' like Hiller about militarism and compulsory military service—talk that utterly failed to account for the 'law-preserving' function of legal violence," not to mention the violence within all legal forms, including peace treaties.[26] There would be more to say about the ways in which Hiller's text circulates in Benjamin's essay, but, in regard to our interests, we will focus on their respective stances on Luxemburg and the Spartacists, with Hiller's stance explicitly stated and Benjamin's, not surprisingly, taking the form of an ellipsis.

We will begin with the final sentences of Hiller's text and then move to the passage in which he directly references the Spartacists and their leaders. Hiller closes his essay with a reference to the biblical commandment against killing. He writes: "Thou shalt not kill. Thou shalt not kill even for the sake of an idea. For no idea is more sublime than the living."[27] Hiller advocates for the extension and secularization of the biblical commandment to Germany as a whole; Benjamin responds by noting that Judaism permits violence in instances of self-defense, adding that "[n]o judgment of the deed follows from the commandment. ... [T]hose who base the condemnation of every violent killing of a human being by fellow human beings on the commandment are wrong" (CV, 58). Recalling Scholem's essay on justice, Benjamin goes on to say, in a sentence that emphasizes the commandment's ethico-political dimension, that "[t]he commandment exists not as a standard of judgment but as a guideline of action for the agent or community that has to confront it in solitude and, in terrible cases, take on the responsibility of disregarding it" (CV, 58).[28] Criticizing Hiller for his belief in what Benjamin calls the "dogma of the sanctity of life" (CV, 59), he cites an excerpt from another passage of Hiller's essay:

> If I do not brutalize, if I do not kill, then I will never establish the empire of justice, of eternal peace, of joy. This is the reasoning of the intellectual terrorist, of the noblest Bolshevik; this was the reasoning of the Spartacist leaders who were deliberately and treacherously slain by military officers loyal to Ebert. We profess, however, that higher still than the happiness and justice of an existence—stands existence itself. We demand that no one be permitted to take the life of one brother in order to bring freedom to another.[29]

Ventriloquizing the perspective of the "intellectual terrorist"—whom we can assume is represented not simply by "the noblest Bolshevik" but also by Luxemburg and Liebknecht—Hiller condemns any argument that justifies violence in the name of justice and peace. Reversing the equation, he argues that violence is exactly what prevents justice and peace since, in his view, these can only flourish when the sanctity of "existence itself" is revered and protected. For him, such existence can only be preserved through an absolute pacifism, which is why the violence of the Spartacist uprising is no more acceptable than the violent murders of Luxemburg and Liebknecht.

Benjamin declares Hiller's thinking here "false and lowly" (CV, 59) and suggests that his conceptualization of existence is naive, especially since it does not understand that "mere life" is not the same as life. We will return to this distinction in a moment, but what is most remarkable here is that, when Benjamin quotes this passage, he omits the phrase "of eternal peace, of joy" in its first sentence and, more significantly, in its second sentence, the phrase "of the noblest Bolshevik" and the second part of this sentence, "this was the reasoning of the Spartacist leaders who were deliberately and treacherously slain by military officers loyal to Ebert." He omits, that is, a likely reference to Lenin and more specifically the reference to Luxemburg and Liebknecht. Within the context of our argument that his essay is organized around the missing body of Luxemburg, what is important is that he deliberately transports her—along with her two comrades—into what we could even call the "Sheol" of his text, but in a manner that deepens the stakes of his encryption of her. This gesture puts a spotlight not only on his refusal to name Luxemburg directly—for all the reasons we already have given—but also on his refusal even to reference her. Removing the Spartacists and displacing them into the void of his text, he hides them and, in doing so, he reiterates what we already have seen in Scholem—that "the death of the just ones is hidden." Extracting Hiller's reference to Luxemburg and the Spartacists, Benjamin preserves them at a distance and in relation to his argument against Hiller, suggesting that, despite whatever violence Hiller attributes to them, they are the "just ones." His extraction is itself a form of critical strike; putting Luxemburg in a differentiated space, he indicates that she cannot be contained in Hiller's formulation. She exists outside it, since, among other things, her definition of "life" cannot be circumscribed within Hiller's. Hers is "aggregate," more expansive and mass-like, and, because of this, moves beyond the moralism of Hiller's pacifism and, in particular, his narrow conception of life as existence. The very omission of Luxemburg and the Spartacists in his citation not only returns their force of deposition to them but also provides a rather astonishing example of the way in which Benjamin enacts politics at the level not simply of his sentences but also of his citations.

His omission signals his defense of revolutionary violence against its suppression. His militant reading of Hiller furthers his essay's critical strike, something that is legible in the sentences that precede his own discussion of the commandment "Thou shalt not kill." Speaking of what he calls the forms of "educative violence," he writes:

These forms are thus not defined by God immediately exercising divine violence in miracles but rather through moments of bloodless, striking, de-expiating implementation [*Vollzug*]. Through

Ludwig Mies van der Rohe, *Monument to the November Revolution*, Berlin-Lichtenberg, 1926

the absence, in the end, of all positing of law. To this extent, it is doubtless justified to also call this violence annihilating; but it is annihilating only in a relative sense, with regard to goods, law, life, and the like, never absolutely with regard to the soul of the living.— Such an extension of pure or divine violence will certainly, and especially today, provoke the fiercest attacks, and one will respond to this extension by saying that, directly in accordance with its justification [*Deduktion*], it unleashes lethal violence on human beings against one another under certain conditions. This is not to be conceded. (*CV*, 58)

It is impossible to draw out all the connections between this passage and the details of our argument here, but, somewhat telegraphically, the passage can be coordinated with at least three neuralgic points, each of which can be read in relation to Benjamin's covert references to Luxemburg: (1) Although he associates divine violence with a force of annihilation, this annihilation is not total. Instead, it targets all the features related to the live burial of Korah and his horde—"goods [property, that is], law, life, and the like"—but does not annihilate "the soul of the living." If the valence of Luxemburg's burial within Benjamin's text runs counter to that of the burial of Korah and his horde, it is not only because of its anticapitalist register but also because it suggests that Luxemburg's existence is not entirely annihilated by the extinguishing of her material body (this is just one trait of the difference between Luxemburg's conception of life and Hiller's conception of "existence" or "mere life"—and one that requires a reconceptualization of "life" itself—with the other being her sense, and Benjamin's, too, that life is aggregated and more than just human). Besides its insistence that Luxemburg's annihilation and murder cannot silence her, that the "soul" of everything she represents remains living, the passage also demonstrates that Benjamin's language can never be taken at face value; his differential characterization of the word "annihilation" is part and parcel of his political strategy here. (2) Benjamin's discussion of divine violence is not restricted to biblical exegesis; "pure or divine violence" can be extended into the present—as he puts it, "especially today"—and this can be seen in the way he extends the story of Korah into a story about the Spartacists, with the Spartacists more closely aligned with the anticapitalist gesture of God's striking annihilation. Bringing together the strike of divine violence with that of Luxemburg's masses, he offers a context in which the deposing force of both God and the Spartacists, or God and the revolutionary masses, provokes "the fiercest attacks," as is evidenced by the crushing of the Spartacist uprising by the Freikorps and the sheer brutality of Luxemburg's murder. It is always what is most threatening to the state and its capitalist structures of privilege, wealth, and power, he suggests, that unleashes the greatest violence. And (3) the greater and more forceful the justification of divine and revolutionary violence becomes, the more it unleashes incalculable violence against calculated violence. In recalling the cycle of violence that divine violence and the revolutionary strike are meant to interrupt, he nevertheless suggests that certain conditions—no doubt at least the ones in which he is writing—require violence, and even lethal violence. This point "is not to be conceded." It is here that he turns more directly to his criticism of Hiller, and to the nonapplicability of the commandment "Thou shalt not kill"—"especially today."

For Benjamin, Hiller's strict prohibition of violence is rooted in an impoverished understanding of existence. In the same way that he alerts us to the multiple valences of the word "annihilation," he notes that the word "existence" itself has to be read in at least two registers—he refers to the word's "double sense"—and suggests that, in the lines he cites from Hiller, the word "existence (or better, life)" must not be reduced, as Hiller understands it, to "mere life." It should instead mean "the unshakeable aggregate of the 'human being.'" He reinforces his point by insisting that "[u]nder no condition does the human being coincide with the mere life of a human being, just as little with the mere life in this being as with any of its states and qualities, indeed not even with the uniqueness of its bodily person" (*CV*, 59). Hiller's proposition, he suggests, "owes its plausibility to this ambiguity" (ibid.); it can only make sense if the word "life" is more than "mere life." For Benjamin, the only "life" worthy of its name is a life that exists in the process of aggregated becoming and is not reducible either to the singularity of a body or to just being human. In both instances, bodies and humans are more than just bodies and humans. They are archives that—like language's "incommensurable, uniquely constituted infinity"—bear the traces of several worlds, superimposed or overlaid upon one another. Benjamin again makes his argument by analyzing language, in this instance the words "life" and "existence," and he reconceptualizes what these terms mean. In the process, we experience a writer whose language, never just his, becomes, as he will put it years later, "something living," something that lives "in the rhythm, in which sentence and countersentence displace themselves in order to think themselves" (*GS*, 5:526). It is because his engagement with language is meant to develop weapons against all forms of legal violence that his activities of reading and writing do not require a political practice; they are in every instance a political, and even militant, practice. He turns every concept against itself by means of sentences that move relentlessly toward negation, toward an active critical strike that is at the same time a revolutionary one. What is remarkable is that the force of this strike becomes increasingly legible in an intensified and accelerated manner in the essay's last paragraphs—as if they themselves acquire an irresistible and unstoppable momentum of their own through a "mimetic contagion" of the force of deposition that dominates the closing moments of his essay. By the time we reach the end, nothing is left standing, since nothing has been left untouched by the destructive force of his language. The pure violence of the revolutionary strike, the human extension and counterpart of divine violence, must recoil from itself, must itself go "on strike," must be "pending" (*waltende*) (*CV*, 60). Contra Hiller, this pending violence does not merely oppose or negate violence but rather deposes it, because only in this way can it announce the end of all mythical violence and, in particular, the end of state violence, the very concrete and urgent target of Benjamin's essay. In his words, "only the idea of its ending [*Ausgang*] makes possible a critical, incisive, and decisive attitude towards its temporal data" (*CV*, 59–60). Only by imagining, even prophesying, the end of violence can we imagine the possibility of moving beyond the oscillating rhythms of law-preserving and law-positing violence, of moving beyond the law and into the uncharted territory of "a new historical era." If it is only through the revolutionary strike of pure means that the cycle of violence spinning "under the spell of mythical forms of law" (*CV*, 60) can be interrupted, this interruption has already been taking place "here and there" (ibid.). The Spartacist uprising and the militancy of a Rosa Luxemburg stand as the most recent glimpses into what a total deposition might look like, as it opens and announces this new historical epoch. As Benjamin knows, the task now is to extend these brief moments into a temporal duration that takes the form of a revolutionary, even a messianic, waiting that is simultaneously an act of radical refusal.

John Heartfield, *The Voice of Freedom in the German Night—On the Wave*, 1937

VIII. THEOLOGICAL FIGURATIONS

> It lies in the nature of the religious movement called capitalism
> to hold out until the very end ... to the point where the world has
> been taken over by total despair, which is exactly its secret *hope*.
> This is the historically unprecedented, the unheard-of character
> of capitalism: it is a religion which offers not the reform of exis-
> tence but its complete destruction, it is the expansion of despair to
> the religious condition of the world in the hope that this will lead
> to salvation.
>
> —Walter Benjamin, "Capitalism as Religion" (1921)[1]

It is impossible not to register the pervasiveness of theological
language in Benjamin's corpus. Jameson insists that Benjamin's
language is saturated with theological language and concepts, including references to angels, the Greek *apokatastasis*,
and Jewish mysticism, and terms like "reconciliation, redemption, the Messiah, allegory and myth" (*BF*, 12). He argues that
the writer's "recourse to theological language" persists "from
the beginning of Benjamin's career to its end" and that it forms
the background against which "his politics must also ultimately
be grasped" (ibid.). As Jameson puts it, "theology, like historical
materialism, is a whole code or language field, a constellation
in its own right" (*BF*, 221).[2] It is legible everywhere in Benjamin
but perhaps most famously in his "On Language as Such and
On the Language of Man," "Toward the Critique of Violence,"
"Capitalism as Religion," "Theological-Political Fragment," "The
Task of the Translator," *The Origin of the German Trauerspiel*, and
"On the Concept of History." In his *Arcades Project*, he acknowledges this persistence when he writes: "My thought is related to
theology as the blotter to ink. It is saturated with it. But if the
blotter had its way, then nothing that was written would remain"
(*AP*, 471; translation modified). At the same time, he elaborates
his sense of the atheological elements within theology—those
elements which suggest that Benjamin's writings are, strictly
speaking, neither "theological" nor "secular"—in a response to
a March 1937 letter from Max Horkheimer, describing his philosophy as "something that forbids us to conceive of history as
fundamentally atheological, little as it may be granted to us to
try to write it with immediately theological concepts" (*AP*, 471).[3]

If, as we have seen, Benjamin's language does not coincide with itself—instead, it exceeds itself, riddled as it is with paradoxes and contradictions that ask to be read together, always referring elsewhere—he here suggests that it is simultaneously theological and not theological (not theological in the traditional sense, that is, not in its religious valence). Its theological elements appear even as they withdraw; they are written and erased at the same time. As with blotting paper, the oversaturation of these theological elements in Benjamin's thought must be erased in order to preserve, to keep legible, the intended trace, even if part of this trace is transferred to the blotter. The time of language is that of an ending without end: a transfer or transmission takes place, even if this transfer or transmission can only convey the inescapable oscillation between legibility and illegibility that structures the possibility of redemption—or, in Benjamin's understanding of the term, of the messianic.

To press it even further, Jameson states that the messianic needs to be thought in relation to "the peculiarly dialectical structure of what Benjamin meant by 'hope'" (*BF*, 12), but also to his concept of happiness, since the latter is "indissolubly bound up with the image of redemption" (*CH*, 390). These concepts (the messianic, hope, happiness, and redemption), Jameson suggests, belong to the "'theological' dimension of Benjamin's view of history" (*BF*, 233), and, we might add, of his politics. There is nowhere in Benjamin's corpus where he dissociates theology from history and politics, even as he reconceptualizes each of these terms, and all the related terms that form the ever-widening constellation of figures that nearly always turn into each other and therefore can never be thought in isolation from one another. Benjamin insists on the communist underpinnings of this act of reconceptualization in a 1931 letter to Max Rychner: "if I were asked to express it in brief: I have never been able to conduct research and to write in anything other than, if I may put it this way, a theological sense—namely, in accordance with the Talmudic teaching about the forty-nine levels of meaning [*Sinnstufen*] in every passage of Torah." He goes on to note that "in [his] experience, even the most pedestrian communist platitude possesses more hierarchies of meaning than does today's bourgeois profundity, which always only has one meaning, that of an apologetic" (*C*, 372–373).

If Benjamin identifies his mode of research and writing as "theological," it is explicitly in the sense that these activities begin in the conviction of the inexhaustible multiplicity of meaning. In other words, what makes a text "theological" is the fact that it bears within it at least "forty-nine levels of meaning," as does the Torah. This suggests that, for Benjamin, all texts—insofar as every text is multiple, plural, unable to be identified with a single meaning—are effectively "sacred" texts, and their sacredness is characterized by precisely their inability to be contained or circumscribed within a determinate or fixed significance. Making every text a sacred text leads to a nontheological theology, to what we might call a "secularized hermeneutics" that can never fully leave behind its theological figurations. Distinguishing the massification that is legible in even the "most pedestrian platitude" of communism from the shallowness of "bourgeois profundity," Benjamin identifies communism with the richness of the sacred and, in turn, the bourgeoisie with its "apologetics." Here he uses a technical term that refers to the religious discipline of defending religious beliefs and, in contemporary usage, to a practice of argumentation that is identified with debates over religion and theology. Beyond his suggestion that both communism and bourgeois ideology have a "theological" dimension, he further distinguishes the pluralization of reading that is communism's signature from the bourgeois effort to insist on a single, identifiable meaning that can be instrumentalized in the direction of its counterrevolutionary ideologies. In his letter to Scholem, Benjamin counters this bourgeois "apologetics" with a communist one, but a communist apologetics that can never be reduced to a single party line, since, for him, communism exceeds the positions of the Communist Party.

If Benjamin's interest in communism begins at least as early as his engagement with Luxemburg, it is intensified in 1924 through his reading of Lukács's *History of Class Consciousness*, a text he engaged for the rest of his life in different ways and contexts, and through his relation with the Latvian Bolshevist Asja Lacis.[4] Indeed, communism and historical materialism form a red thread throughout the rest of his work. Setting aside his suspicions of any sort of teleology within the communist endeavor—within any communist position that would instrumentalize a concept of ends or progress—he asserts his attraction to what, in a letter to Scholem from September 1924, he calls the "political praxis of communism," declaring it an "obligatory attitude."[5]

He makes this point again in another letter to Scholem, this time from April 17, 1931, in which he responds to his friend's accusations that he is misguided in his belief that he can bring together his interest in language with the materialism at the heart of communism, that he cannot overcome his bourgeois conditions

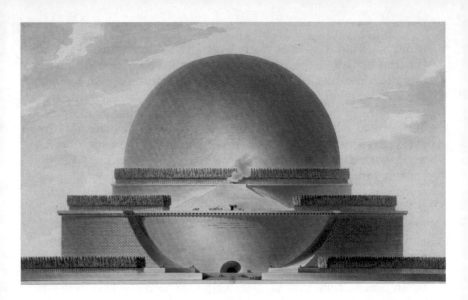

Étienne-Louis Boullée, *Cenotaph for Newton* (geometric elevation), 1784

and counterrevolutionary tendencies, and that his efforts to "suspend" any clear identification with either a metaphysics of language or the communist revolution must inevitably fail. In a passage that demonstrates the rigor with which Benjamin attends to the always-present possibility of political complicity—the almost inevitable complicity with the very positions he strives to overcome—he evokes his complicated relations to both his bourgeois circumstances and the Communist Party but also again insists on a commitment to *his* communism, a communism that can neither be identified with the Party's concept of revolution nor with that of the bourgeoisie:

> But do you really want to impede me with my little writing factory located right in the middle of Berlin West quite simply because of my imperious need to distinguish myself from a neighborhood that for certain reasons I must accept—do you want to prevent me from hanging a red flag out of my window, saying that it is only a little piece of cloth? If someone produces "counterrevolutionary" writings, as you quite correctly characterize mine from the Party's point of view, should he also expressly place them at the disposal of the counterrevolution? Should he not, rather, denature them, like ethyl alcohol, and make them definitely and reliably unusable for the counterrevolution at the risk that no one will be able to use them? Can one ever be too clearly distinguished from the pronouncements and the language of people whom one learns more and more to avoid in life? Is not this clear distinction, if anything, understated in my writings, and should it be increased in a direction other than the Communist one? (*C*, 378)

This rather remarkable passage offers us a glimpse into Benjamin's multifaceted approach to the subject of his critical inquiry—here that of a communist writing and reading practice that cannot be contained by any party orthodoxy. He turns the object of his inquiry around in his hand to better observe it from different angles, in accordance with what, in his letter, Scholem calls Benjamin's capacity for "polemical rotation."[6] It is as if Benjamin were playing chess with himself, while remaining certain throughout of the impossibility of either concluding or winning the game. Here he strings a series of rhetorical questions together that, through a series of kaleidoscopic turns, manage to put his subject, communism, at angles that make it at once more distant, complex, uncertain, and, above all, more difficult to instrumentalize *in the name of communism* (or, for that matter, in the name of bourgeois or religious ideologemes). He begins by placing his "little writing factory" in the midst of a West Berlin bourgeois neighborhood, signaling the impossibility of ever fully displacing his cultural lineage and class alliances—even through a militant intellectual labor that refuses to be aestheticized, or to become mere cultural capital. He then considers the hypothetical and slightly comedic scene of him putting a little red flag out on his balcony, as if to announce his alliance and commitment to a communist revolution that the little red flag can scarcely signify unequivocally or even contain, and this because what is most revolutionary in communism survives any symbolic effort to represent it.[7] As the passage develops, the humility of the raggedy communist flag stands in inverse proportion to the force of the unbounded revolutionary communism of the color red, as it begins to saturate the movements of Benjamin's prose, even if discreetly and almost invisibly, as his language continues to move in the direction of communism, despite all its hesitations.[8] Insisting that the revolutionary impulse cannot be reduced to a single ideological party configuration, the passage points to the impossibility of containing the color in one place. Like the sacred text that can appear in innumerable guises, the little red flag circulates even when it no longer appears as a red flag but rather in the guise of language that, as Scholem notes, colors Benjamin's idiomatic sense of communism "in phraseology that is conceptually close to Communist phraseology" (*C*, 374)—even if, as we can see from Benjamin's reply, it remains differentiated from it.[9]

In fact, his following four rhetorical questions ironically delineate and perform Benjamin's resistance to ideological entrapment, a gesture that begins with his use of quotation marks around the word "counterrevolutionary." If his writings are "counterrevolutionary," this is: (1) because the Party would consider them such because his conception of revolution exceeds that of the Party's platform (it can only misread and mislabel them as negations of what they truly are); and (2) because his "counterrevolutionary" gesture cannot be identified with a counterrevolutionary movement that views itself in strict opposition to communism. But Benjamin makes clear that, for him, the most revolutionary gesture is the one that cannot be instrumentalized, absorbed, incorporated by any political formation—either communist or counterrevolutionary—and that, instead, seeks to achieve an impossible *Umfunktionieren* of any ideologeme that would seek to install itself in a fixed manner. He compares this negative process to the process of using ethyl alcohol as a solvent that denatures and kills the microbes that keep a substance alive, a form of preservation that relies on partial destruction. Yet that minimal difference, not always visible to the naked eye, and taking the modest form of an orthographical mark, is the dangerously small distance that destroys and preserves the concept of revolution, that separates revolution from counterrevolution, and communism from party orthodoxy (as Benjamin knew well from the Communist International's condemnation of Lukács's *History and Class Consciousness* that same year). By the end of his chess game—a politically charged chess game without terminus—Benjamin can only reinforce his commitment to a communism that will not betray itself without self-destructing, and that finds a rather singular expression in the self-defeating movements of this letter to Scholem. But, as always in Benjamin, the experience of defeat becomes a vital condition for moving forward differently.

Postage stamp printed in USSR, ca. 1967, in celebration of the
fiftieth anniversary of the Great October Revolution, including
S. Karpov's 1924 painting *Friendship of the Peoples*

IX. MESSIANIC PROMISES

No Messiah, only that would be a Messiah.

—Werner Hamacher, "Messianic Not" (2014)[1]

Because there is no single key to Benjamin's politics, his messianism cannot be thought solely in relation to what messianism traditionally has meant within religious, philosophical, or political discourse (where it generally has been associated with the transcendence of history, with what is outside time or in the future, with the affirmation of a determinate messiah figure). It must be considered a finite messianism—as a historical event, that is, even if it can never be reduced to a historical concept or category—and this because it is what, within history, interrupts history. It is because it is a structural feature of historical existence that, as Benjamin tells us in his theses "On the Concept of History," the task of the historical materialist is to establish "a conception of the present as now-time shot through with splinters of Messianic time" (*CH*, 397). If there is no moment for Benjamin that is not touched—"shot through"—by the messianic, it is because the messianic is not a negation of time, but rather a differential structure of time in and as history.

Benjamin's messianism therefore names a structure of experience that cannot be reduced to any kind of religious messianism (either Jewish or Christian, for example), or to any recognizable utopianism. Like Kafka, who renounced Judaism in the name of Judaism, Benjamin could be said to renounce messianism in the name of the messianic (this explains why, in his reading of Benjamin, Derrida can refer to a "messianism without religion, even a messianic without messianism"[2]). The "messianic" refers, at every moment, to the coming of an indeterminate, unpredictable, and irreducibly heterogeneous future, a future that would not arrive with the Messiah—since the Messiah never arrives, or at least never on time—but instead as a temporality of waiting that restructures our sense of the future itself. In Jameson's words, the Messiah "is available to do something rather different to temporality and in particular to its future dimension, to its way of conceptualizing futurity" (*BF*, 12–13). Nothing is more "present" than this messianic waiting, which is why, never contemporaneous with itself, it can neither be presented nor represented. Since what is coming is beyond knowledge and perception, this waiting can never be oriented around a determinate expectation. Because the future remains unpredictable and unprogrammed, this waiting is linked to a promise and a demand that, within the context of our finitude, urgently call for a revolutionary commitment to interrupt the course of history. Linked to the possibility of a singular future, Benjamin's messianism points, as he puts it in his theses, to the "arrest of happening" (*CH*, 396), to what we would call a "finite politics." Benjamin emphasizes this association between messianism and finitude in his early "Politico-Theological Fragment." There, referring to a nontheocratic and thoroughly messianic politics, he explains that "Nature is messianic by reason of its eternal and total passing away,"[3] and asks us to imagine a *politics of transience*.

It is because the messianic refers to the transience, transformation, and change which structure existence that it bears constant reference to the experience of an emancipatory promise—but a promise that, remaining open, promises what cannot be promised, and therefore what is left to be realized. That the messianic promises a futurity that is always open to something else means for Benjamin that we must oppose any effort to predict or organize the future. "Whoever wants to know how a 'redeemed humanity' would be constituted," he warns us, "under which conditions it would be constituted, and when one can count on it, poses questions to which there is no answer. He might as well ask about the color of ultraviolet rays" (*GS*, 1.3:1232). We might recall here, as Benjamin does, Marx's claim in an 1869 letter to Edward Beesly that "whoever drafts programs for the future is a reactionary" (*GS*, 2:194). As Jameson reminds us, Benjamin's angel of history "cannot turn its face toward the future" (*BF*, 219), but this is also why, insisting on what Benjamin gains by never letting go of the language of theology, he adds, "[t]he theological code ... has one particular conceptual space in which it proves to be the privileged instrument in what is, in any case, an impossible situation: and that is the realm of the future" (*BF*, 231). Indeed, "[t]heology reserves a uniquely specific virtue for the domain of the future: it is called hope" (*BF*, 240), and, as we have seen, "hope is the sign of a future for those who are hopeless" (*BF*, 242).

Jameson already signals near the beginning of *The Benjamin Files* the constellation of concepts to which he will return in his final chapter—redemption, hope, messianism, and revolution—and which we have been tracing and wish to elaborate further (and in relation to what we already have been emphasizing: masses, technology, and happiness). There, he claims that "Redemption (*Erlösung*) ... must be understood in a collective rather than an individual way. It governs Benjamin's thinking, if not of history as a whole, then at least of the past and the dead: it functions for him as a debt and an obligation and is assimilated for him to communist and revolutionary ideals. ... There, too, the notion of the Messiah will necessarily find its place, along with the peculiarly dialectical structure of what Benjamin meant by 'hope'" (*BF*, 12).

As Hamacher notes in a more detailed way, *Erlösung* (thought, as Benjamin does, more prosaically as *Einlösung*) involves

> a redeeming of possibilities which are opened with every life and are missed in every life. If the concept of redemption points towards a theology—and it does so without doubt and *a fortiori* in the context of the first thesis, which mentions the "little hunchback" of theology—then this is not straightforwardly Judeo-Christian theology, but rather a theology of the missed or distorted—hunchbacked—possibilities, a theology of missed, distorted or hunchbacked time. Each possibility that was missed in the past remains a possibility for the future, precisely because it has not found fulfillment. For the past to have a future merely means that the past's possibilities have not yet found their fulfillment, that they continue to have an effect and demand their realization from those who feel addressed by them. When past things survive, then it is not lived-out (*abgelebte*) facts that survive; rather what survive are the unactualized possibilities of that which is past. There is historical time only insofar as there is an excess of the unactualized, the unfinished, failed, thwarted, which leaps beyond its particular Now and demands from another Now its settlement, correction and fulfillment.[4]

"The kind of happiness that alone can prove itself," he adds, "is not past happiness, it is the happiness that was possible in the past but was missed. Happiness is the *festum post festum amissum*."[5] Happiness is "assigned (*verwiesen*)" to redemption insofar as it is, or was, a possible happiness that was missed. What is required, as Benjamin notes in his 1929 essay on surrealism, citing Pierre Naville, is an "organization of pessimism," a pessimism—born from a sense of the missed and uncompleted desires in the past and from an uncertainty about the possibility of retrieving this lost possibility—that he refers to as "the call of the hour."[6] Incomplete in the past, happiness—here another name for *organized pessimism*—strives for completion in the future, displaying in this way the temporal structure in which Benjamin is interested, in which a past is referenced secretly to a moment of redemption in the future. Redemption names—without doing so in a fixed or determinate manner—the possible completion of an incomplete happiness. Benjamin identifies what he calls "pessimism all along the line" with the "Communist answer."[7]

Paradoxically, communal despair is the secret hope of happiness, the redemptive quality of mass subjectivity, and another name for politics. As Benjamin notes in his *Arcades Project*, "[t]here vibrates in the very idea of happiness (this is what that noteworthy circumstance teaches us) the idea of salvation. This happiness is founded on the very despair and desolation which are ours. Our life, it can be said, is a muscle strong enough to contract the whole of historical time. Or, to put it differently, the genuine conception of historical time rests entirely upon the image of redemption" (*AP*, 479). He already makes a similar point in "Capitalism as Religion," but there the identification between despair and hope is even more explicit: "The nature of the religious movement which is capitalism entails endurance right to the end, to the point where God, too, finally takes on the entire burden of guilt, to the point where the universe has been taken over by that despair which is actually its secret *hope*."[8]

If redemption must be collective, if despair is communal, and if both have to be mediated by not simply a God but a Messiah that never arrives, or arrives too late, this is because mass subjectivity does not correspond to a subjective standpoint but to the impersonal objectivity of technology. The impersonal can be the site of mass consciousness because it does not belong to anyone in particular; it is the shared fate of the many, the origin of a secular hope. Just as the language of pure mediacy interrupts instrumental language, only an impersonal understanding of hope can interrupt the structure of guilt as credit in capitalist totality. The extraordinary powers of language are the extraordinary powers of the impersonal—analogous to the function of the *gestus* in both Brecht and Kafka. An existence that is "transient in its totality" can only be represented figuratively through an impersonal hope that has no meaning but contains infinite possibility. The only true political collectives must be either pre- or postindividual, made up of either the dead or the unborn, of those who arrive either too early or too late. It is in this context that we can begin to understand what Benjamin means when he writes that "[t]he secular order should be erected on the idea of happiness,"[9] an idea that he associates with both revolution and the messianic. As he writes in his "Paralipomena to 'On the Concept of History'":

Once the classless society had been defined as an infinite task, the empty and homogeneous time was transformed into an anteroom, so to speak, in which one could wait for the emergence of the revolutionary situation with more or less equanimity. In reality, there is not a moment that would not carry with it *its* revolutionary chance—provided only that it is defined in a specific way, namely as the chance for a completely new resolution of a completely new problem [*Aufgabe*]. For the revolutionary thinker, the peculiar revolutionary chance offered by every historical moment gets its warrant from the political situation. But it is equally grounded, for this thinker, in the right of entry which the historical moment enjoys vis-à-vis a quite distinct chamber of the past, one which up to that point has been closed and locked. The entrance into this chamber coincides in a strict sense with political action, and it is by means of such entry that political action, however destructive, reveals itself as messianic.[10]

Messianism is also another name for the abolition of the distance between the individual and the masses, for the endless tactics of incorporation that undergird true revolutionary politics, for a politics of multiplication and impersonality. Benjamin puts it clearly here:

In the solidarity of the proletarian class struggle, the dead, undialectical opposition between individual and mass is abolished; for the comrade, it does not exist. Decisive as the masses are for the revolutionary leader, therefore, his great achievement lies not in drawing the masses after him, but in constantly incorporating himself into the masses, in order to be, for them, always one among hundreds of thousands.[11]

Indeed, hope, futurity, and even happiness, as temporal conceptualizations of the political, are directly dependent on class consciousness and can only have a negative structure, and Benjamin, as the bourgeois intellectual that he is, can only make way for it through self-destruction. In Jameson's words, "our access to the very idea of hope is class-conditioned, and it [is] useful at this point to register Benjamin's most significant pronouncements on the subject of social class. Everything he wrote was steeped in his awareness of himself as a bourgeois intellectual and of the inevitable limitations this class status imposes: 'the intellectual who espouses the proletarian cause will never himself become a proletarian'" (*BF*, 240). As Benjamin himself puts it in a review of what Jameson calls Siegfried Kracauer's "white-collar analysis in *Die Angestellten*":

This left-radical wing may posture as much as it likes—it will never succeed in eliminating the fact that the proletarianization of the intellectual hardly ever turns him into a proletarian. Why? Because from childhood on, the middle class gave him a means of production in the form of an education—a privilege that establishes his solidarity with it and, perhaps even more, its solidarity with him. This solidarity may become blurred superficially, or even undermined, but it almost always remains powerful enough to exclude the intellectual from the constant state of alert, the sense of living your life at the front, which is characteristic of the true proletarian.[12]

Hope and happiness—in their most politicized valences—remain exterior to Benjamin, "an external experience; a reality to be glimpsed from the outside and at a distance" (*BF*, 242). They belong to others; never to Benjamin as an individual, as a subject who would be punctual, self-identical, or "one self," except perhaps when he is "one among hundreds of thousands," when he is plural and mass-like. In a final secularization of a religious figure, hope can only come to existence where it is absent. In Jameson's words, "[t]here is certainly a logic in the idea that, where hope is unnecessary, it need not or cannot exist; or, better still, it has a reason for existing only where it is absent and desperately needed" (ibid.).

As Kafka would famously put it in his own version of this insight, "the Messiah will come only when he is no longer necessary; he will come only on the day after his arrival; he will come, not on the last day, but on the very last."[13] Kafka is Benjamin's companion in this act of self-destruction. Benjamin's linguistic and formal understanding of theology allows him to reappropriate theological categories that, once detemporalized, can be harnessed to express the possibility of a new "subjectivity" and a new "consciousness" no longer trapped in individual singularity and its guilt economy: a mass subjectivity that performs but does not signify within the totality of that guilt economy.[14] The possibility of this transformation, of this revolution, requires a means of exceeding and getting beyond what, in his essay "Fate and Character," Benjamin calls the "guilt nexus of the living" (*der Schuldzusammenhang des Lebendigen*),[15] which he reads as the link between religion and capitalism as forms of individual subjectivity. The only possibility for redemption, for hope or happiness, depends on the effort to experience a liberation from this "guilt nexus," from this preordained program that inscribes us within an inheritance of debt and guilt that prevents us from acting, if not on our own—since this is never possible—at least with some measure of responsibility, at least with the possibility of an uncertain leap into an indeterminate future. For Benjamin, historical time can only begin when this context of guilt and debt is shattered, when it is annihilated. But this force of annihilation always has been at work even within the capitalist-religious system of guilt and debt and perhaps can be understood in relation to the "secret index" that the past carries within it and "by which it is referred to redemption" (*CH*, 390). It is precisely out of the self-devastation inscribed within the Christianity of capital that the messianic can emerge as a counterhistory whose time is a time still to come, and especially because it never arrives.

Benjamin's reflections on the messianic cannot be reconciled with the utopianism so many of his readers attribute to him (and this is also why Jameson warns us against any idea of "Progress," which for both him and Benjamin "illustrates the dangers of a propagandistic use of the future" [*BF*, 236]). Referring both to what is not yet and to what can never be present, the messianic can be said to correspond to a longing for a future that would be otherwise, that would not be the continuation of pasts but would, for the first time, expose the claim of these pasts to another time—a time dissociated from the time of labor and capital. A certain unorthodox Marxism, we might say, is exactly the articulation of this Benjaminian promise. Jameson insists that we should one day seek to understand Benjamin's relation to Marx much more expansively and precisely. We might then come to understand why, in the many worlds of Benjamin, any politics, any historical act, must pass through the messianic promise.

Paul Klee, *Angelus Novus*, 1920

X. BENJAMIN'S BOXES

You can of course keep shaking the box.

—Anne Carson, *Autobiography of Red* (1998)[1]

As Jameson tells us time and time again, the messianic is not a means of revelation. Instead, it is a mediatic figure that—like the famous *Angelus Novus* that Benjamin kept close to him throughout his life—bears the sedimentation of time within it. If it is never on the side of revelation, it is because, bearing all time within it, it points—if only obliquely since it has broken with referentiality altogether—to the transience of all things. If messianic power is *weak*, it is because it is traversed by time and finitude. Like happiness, it can never have a form, but it is this formlessness that gives this weakness its strength against forms of domination that would diminish its possibilities. It is only when happiness is in danger, when it seems impossible, that it can flash up. It can only take effect with the loss of the individual self, that is to say, when, like politics and revolution, it is communal and impersonal. Happiness requires this destruction of the self—this release from the "guilt nexus of the living"—in order to be experienced, even if fleetingly and in the midst of its impossibility. Like the messianic, it can only come at a time that is distorted, as a disfigurement or distortion of time, as what interrupts the continuum of time, its homogeneity. The most profound derailment of the possibility of happiness, though, is the derailment of happiness itself. It cannot perceive itself because it can never be present to itself. Like the truth of all of Benjamin's major concepts, the truth of happiness reveals the inability of happiness to present itself or to be represented. It is as if it is kept within a box that, full of time and history, can never be opened completely or reveal the entirety of its contents, because its contents can never be fully accounted for.

Benjamin's corpus is filled with boxes of all sorts. There are the boxes and crates that include all the books, letters, pamphlets, religious tracts, and leaflets he famously unpacks in his "Unpacking My Library" essay, opening them to the daylight after having kept them closed in darkness for two years and registering all the images, memories, cities, and experiences sealed within each text, as if each one was itself its own kind of box, filled with time. There is the "Reading Box" in his *Berlin Childhood around 1900*, into which he reaches his hand to pull out letters to form words and which made reading and writing so decisive for his life, and, in the same text, the "Sewing Box," which he understands is so much more than a box devoted to sewing but instead a box full of snow and flurries that become letters that, again, enable him to form words. There are the hidden interiors, the breakfast room, the vestibules, and even Goethe's study in Weimar, that we find in *One-Way Street*, again each one a sort of enclosure or box. Jameson actually refers to this book as a "box of chocolates that should bear the warning: addictive substances!," each one "plunging" us into a "state induced by riddles and puzzles," which, "too rich to be devoured all at once," require a slower labor of reading than we could perhaps ever imagine (*BF*, 17). There are of course all the boxes of index cards, all the card boxes, in which Benjamin kept the clippings and notes that would, as Jameson notes, "constitute the raw materials of the future *Arcades*" (*BF*, 19), itself a gigantic box full of passages and citations, an enclosed but always growing archive.

In each instance, these boxes become means of exploring the relations between what we can see and what we cannot, between interiors and exteriors, revelations and secrets, memory and forgetting, presence and absence, light and darkness, destruction and survival, and means of thinking about letters, words, sentences, paragraphs, and books, each of which, we are suggesting, is its own kind of box, or even its own series of boxes. It is not surprising that, collector that he was, Benjamin would not simply amass boxes and containers but would transform everything into a box. If boxes are ubiquitous in his work, it is also because they can become another name for the monad, for the dialectical image, and for every one of his major concepts. Like boxes, every one of his concepts reveals and conceals at the same time. Like boxes, they open up several worlds to us, even as they hold details and histories in reserve, away from sight, asking that we imagine what we cannot see directly, that we learn to read what can never be present, and that we do so *historically* and with political urgency. Reminding us that a surface is itself never just a surface but a box, an archival space, even when it seems to be just two-dimensional, Benjamin suggests it is the history inscribed within a surface that gives it a depth that remains inaccessible, even as it requires a process of endless and incomplete excavation.

If Benjamin's entire corpus therefore can be read as an effort to inaugurate and enact a history that does not offer itself to sight (with all the boxes of history, of "time filled full by now-time [*Jetztzeit*]" [*CH*, 395], just one more allegory of its fugitive, transient, and heterogeneous character), it is not surprising that his most famous figure for historical movement and responsibility—the angel of history that presides over his reflections on history—is pushed by the storm of progress toward a future into which it cannot see, to which its back is turned, and which bears witness only to catastrophe. Presumably describing Paul Klee's *Angelus Novus*—in a parenthetical remark, Jameson suggests, "entre nous," that Klee's work "has very little in common with Benjamin's description of it" (*BF*, 219)—Benjamin tells us:

> His face is turned toward the past. Where a chain of events appears before us, he sees one single catastrophe, which keeps piling wreckage upon wreckage and hurls it at his feet. The angel would like to stay, awaken the dead, and make whole what has been smashed. But a storm is blowing from Paradise and has got caught in his wings; it is so strong that the angel can no longer close them. This storm drives him irresistibly into the future to which his back is turned, while the pile of debris before him grows toward the sky. What we call progress is *this* storm. (*CH*, 392)

Writing of the trajectory of his book on Benjamin, Jameson identifies the angel with the figure with which he opens his first chapter: "in the end is our beginning: the angel's wings have very much the same problems as the boat's sails—they must be adjusted to catch the wind, to profit from the wind of history that is to propel them. This particular angel has been remarkably maladroit and has failed to reckon with the winds of a storm" (*BF*, 220).

Yet Benjamin's *Denkbild*, his "thought picture," is not exactly an image but an emblem, and there is no more powerful and enduring emblem in Benjamin than this small 1920 oil and water-color monoprint that famously accompanied him for most of his life as a writer. From his intention to begin a journal in the 1920s entitled *Angelus Novus* to the moment in his *Trauerspiel* book in which the death's head turns into an angel's countenance to his 1931 essay on Kraus in which Klee's *New Angel* appears as a "messenger of the old engravings" to his two 1933 essays entitled "Agesilaus Santander" to his famous description of Klee's work in the ninth of his theses "On the Concept of History," the angel is the circulating and displaced emblem that concentrates within itself all Benjaminian ruins. This is an angel that moves, circulates, and, above all, replicates and multiplies himself.

But, according to Jameson, the appearance of the angel in Benjamin's theses, in particular, marks a shift in their "polemical direction" and signals "a new contradiction" that "represents a narrowing of Benjamin's polemical sights and a return to his denunciation of the social-democratic belief in progress and the ideological vision of 'historicism' that underpins it," while at the same time suggesting that "everything is tainted by complicity" (*BF*, 236). Like the boat's sails, the angel registers his inability to "reckon with the winds of a storm" and, instead, suggests his lack of control in general. Indeed, the angel's muteness and blindness together suggest that the agency of historical meaning is something that must be thought away from intentionality, subjectivity, and even a sense of the human. Unable to gaze into the future, he can neither intervene in its direction nor redeem the past at which he stares (and therefore may not even see). It can neither "awaken the dead" nor "make whole what has been smashed."[2] It is this lack of agency—a structure of passivity that defines our relation to the movement of historico-political events (a passivity associated with the impersonal structure of our subjectivity, the movement of history, and everything that prevents us from seizing the present)—that makes the future unpredictable and our decisions and actions a matter of risk and danger. What the angel of history tells us, then, in all its muteness, is that political action and responsibility cannot be thought in terms of any knowing, intentional, strategic, and calculated intervention: they must instead be conceived in relation to the revolutionary chance of a world open to its own uncertainties, and to a future that can never be anticipated or controlled. In other words, political responsibility can only take place in a space that exceeds calculation, in a space that is not a determinate space; it is a space in which Benjamin suggests we must take a "tiger's leap" toward happiness (as he notes in "On the Concept of History," this leap does not take place "in an arena where the ruling class gives the commands" but "in the open air of history," as "the dialectical leap Marx understood as revolution" [*CH*, 392]).

In one of the two autobiographical texts he wrote while in Ibiza in 1933, Benjamin tells us that this same angel "wants happiness."[3] As an object, Klee's *Angelus* literally materializes the internal mechanism of Benjamin's theological figuration and its potential for the appropriation of theological concepts and images for political purposes. One of the innumerable boxes in Benjamin, it has remained closed much longer than most others—and this even though it is the one that has received perhaps the most critical attention. We have only recently been able to register that, among other things, it hides another hunchback that is the keeper of history's most intimate secrets.

This is confirmed by the rather remarkable discovery by the artist R. H. Quaytman—a discovery that will enable us to read what has never been *seen* within the box that Klee's *Angelus* is. As she was preparing for an exhibition at the Tel Aviv Museum, Quaytman visited the Israel Museum in Jerusalem and was granted a special viewing of the *Angelus Novus* (one of the most prized possessions of the Israel Museum).[4] She noticed something that had never been registered before—that Klee had purposefully glued this monoprint directly onto an old copper engraving. The edge of the engraving, discernible around all four sides of Klee's work, suggested a portrait of a single figure in a black robe made by someone with—these details are legible on the engraving just below the Klee image—the initials LC in the 1520s. She thought this fact was important to Klee's gesture of defacement—a defacement that is at the same time, in the materiality of its support, dependent on the very trace it obscures—but also to Benjamin's well-known description of the work, which situates the temporal past in front of the angel, not behind it. Working with the paper conservation department at the Israel Museum, Quaytman spent two years trying to uncover the identity of this hidden figure. Scientific imaging techniques such as X-ray and thermography failed to uncover it. On returning to her studio, however, Quaytman continued to search websites and databases from libraries and museum collections and, in early June 2015, she serendipitously found the engraving in a site from the regional government of Lombardy. The engraving was made by a relatively unknown engraver named Christian Friedrich von Müller in 1838 and, more interestingly, it was based on a 1521 portrait by Lucas Cranach of Martin Luther.[5]

If we take Benjamin at his word, the angel's body faces the past—while Benjamin states that the angel's face is turned toward the past, the eyes in Klee's monoprint are clearly looking to the side, toward the margins of the work, perhaps inviting us to register the edges of the engraving behind him—even as he is being driven "irresistibly into the future, to which his back is turned." What is so beautiful about Quaytman's discovery is that it helps us read the relation between Klee's image and the engraving behind it as a dialectical image in the strict Benjaminian sense: as an image, that is, "wherein what has been comes together in a flash with the now to form a constellation. In other words: image

R. H. Quaytman, *חקק, Chapter 29*, 2015

Christian Friedrich von Müller, engraving after a painting by Lucas Cranach, 1838

is dialectics at a standstill. For while the relation of the present to the past is purely temporal, the relation of what-has-been to the now is dialectical: not temporal in nature but figural" (*AP*, 463). It also suggests that, in order to move into an unseen future, we must pass through what we inherit, and what we inherit, and what we must think, are the histories of different forms of life, different modes of production and reproduction. In other words, what the materiality of Klee's drawing tells us is that we can only move into the future through a reflection on the various processes of reproduction that, one on top of the other, delineate the mediatic strata through which we encounter our relation to the past and the future—and to the ruined world in front of us. The future can only emerge through an engagement with a past whose multiple traces are before and behind us at the same time.

The threaded knot to which these relations belong becomes a means of reflecting on the disjunctive techniques and media of representation in general. In David Wills's words:

> such disjunction is certainly explicit once the angel is a figure drawn on the painted surface, once it is clearly no longer some ineffable spiritual emanation, some spirit or sprite. An angel embodied in ink, chalk, and brown wash is an angel fallen not just into incarnation but into technology; it has become artifact. The future it recedes into is a technological future that nevertheless occurs behind and in its back because it was always there, originarily, from the beginning. At the outside, one can say that the angel never was without technology, that a nontechnological angel has never been seen. Where anything resembling human corporeality begins, there technology begins also. If the angel doesn't see that, it is because it is that. In becoming history, in blasting itself dialectically out of the continuum, it has become the point at which, the flashpoint by means of which, as we see in the image, some techno-anthropic form comes to be. Indeed, it does not look like what we would normally call an angel; rather, a bodily form emerges from, and defines itself against, a nebulous background, simultaneously revealing itself as a rudimentary mechanicity—intersecting lines, triangles, tubes, and scrolls—a prosthesis of proteiform organicity and marionette, animation and automation.[6]

Klee's "angel" does not look like an angel. The figure is not an angel but, instead, a figure for a process of technological reproducibility that, beginning in different forms of citation and repetition, of reference and encryption, asks us to reconceptualize what a figure or subject can be—especially as each figure is always on the way to becoming another one, and indeed many other ones. Klee's invention of the oil-transfer drawing involved covering a sheet with black oil paint, placing it on a clean sheet of paper, and tracing a drawing placed on the oil sheet so that the line would be transferred. Technically speaking, these monoprints are a hybrid between original and reproduction, being both unique works and at the same time the product of a mechanical printmaking process, even if hands remain involved. They are repetitions with a difference and, when seen through a cinematic sensibility, they become akin to photograms in a film. In this way, once more through a sort of technological magic, the angel's wings begin to move, to flap and flicker in the kino-eye of the mind.[7]

This is why we might be led to believe that the truth content of Benjamin's many boxes, the coincidence of their content and form, can only be accessed through a magical kind of radiological technology—one that might be better able than Quaytman's failed radiological efforts to see what was behind Klee's monoprint—a power that would exceed the limitations of the optical, even if it retained a relation to regressive forms of technological mediation. In this instance, we could perhaps extend Jameson's insight that technological possibility is represented as much by the radiological as it is by reproducibility. But radiology never offers an unclouded or clear gaze inside a box, even when that box is the human body. The X-ray brings Benjamin closer to Maurice Blanchot and his "power of the negative."[8] In relation to the body, it offers images from the point of view of death, of bones and remains, in yet another instance of destructive and violent reading and in echo of the skeletal remains that appear everywhere in the medieval mystery plays Benjamin reads in the *Trauerspiel* (further evidence that in Benjamin the technological imagination exceeds and precedes modernity). Its danger is that, on the one hand, it offers too much for us to see, forcing us to glimpse in order to survive, and, on the other hand, its opaqueness and shadows point to transience, mobility, and duration as defense mechanisms against totalizing readings. It is in the X-ray's ambivalence—in the transition between it and other mediums, and the fight between the life and death of a technical medium—that Benjamin discovers the revolutionary chance of historico-political transformation. The legibility of the X-ray's arrested image is ephemeral because the freeze-frame cannot be held for too long without burning the film altogether. As Jameson remarks, the radiological technique "uses visuality itself against the very illusions inherent in it, the false appearances aroused by movement and encouraged by our pleasure in visual consumption" (*BF*, 223). If the *Denkbild* is an X-ray of the figures of history and an aftereffect of technological and temporal manipulation, it suggests that what is displayed will never be legible enough to be entirely consumed. While the camera seeks to create the illusion of the presence of a body in space and time, radiography instead charts objects according to their volumetric space and by measuring their density. If Benjamin treats every image like a box whose contents already remain inscrutable to the naked eye, the X-ray can only expose its incapacity to reveal all the box's secrets, even if it can offer us the traces of their fugitivity, and even if his boxes already integrate the radiographic imagination. As Benjamin notes, in a phrase that Jameson describes as "a radiological figure" (*BF*, 224), "[h]istory decays into images" (*AP*, 462).⁹

If the *Angelus* is an impenetrable box, if it has to be thought of as volumetric and dense, it is also because, like Benjamin's reconceptualization of the artwork, it is full of time and relations, a mass of sedimented forms of reproduction and media—from paintings to engravings to monoprints and beyond. Following what Jameson refers to as Benjamin's mode of reading from the "margins" and "fringes" (*BF*, 136), a mode of reading obliquely, with eyes slanted—again, it is not an accident that Klee's angel looks toward the edge of the work instead of directly at us—Quaytman's engagement with Klee's *Angelus* reenacts the eccentricity of Benjamin's philological sensibilities. The more she reads the work from its margins in order to reconstruct its internal structure, the closer she gets to the Benjamin who Jameson says would have "been happy to consider himself a philologist" (*BF*, 137). But the identification of the hidden figure behind Klee's monoprint is never given, even if it is eventually named. Luther remains invisible, without a face that we can see, and, in the end, is really the name not of an individual but of a network, a mass of historical relations that move across centuries from Cranach to Müller to Klee to Benjamin to Quaytman. In every instance, this network and mass pass through Benjamin, whose writings and readings move simultaneously (and cinematically) backward and forward, even if also in more entangled and multidirectional ways. Quaytman's discovery and identification of the reproduced portrait of Luther behind Klee's *Angelus* is therefore not an identification but the sign of another displaced or slanted reading whereby, with a logic that follows Benjamin's understanding of the work of art as mass-like, the defaced figure of Luther is at once contingent and abstract, singular and impersonal, the "name" of a knot of relations that remains to be unraveled.

Klee, Benjamin, and Quaytman reenact a series of displacements in which one figure points to another even as it already shifts in other directions. The box the *Angelus* is becomes an emblem of fugitivity and mobility—an emblem of resistance against critical readings that treat the angel as the identifiable center of the monoprint. Additionally, the flatness of Klee's drawing presents a visually ironic depiction of directionality, since the artist knew with certainty what he was painting over, covering up, and at the same time signaling toward. The *Angelus* functions like a baroque emblem whose enigma, in a recognizably Brechtian gesture, conceals and reveals at the same time. Klee's ironic gesture is as rhetorical as it is visual and works to construct his angelic box with its multiple temporalities—each one traversing the others—intensified by the different modes of reproduction in its monadic density.

whelming numbers in fact, beyond the disciplines of salvation; and this despite the fact that the West has been "buy-
ing" African natives for centuries. There is, I should
hazard, an instantaneous necessity to be divorced from
this so visibly unsaved stranger, in whose heart, moreover, one cannot guess what dreams of vengeance are
being nourished; and, at the same time, there are few
things on earth more attractive than the idea of the unspeakable liberty which is allowed the unredeemed.
When, beneath the black mask, a human being begins
to make himself felt one cannot escape a certain awful
wonder as to what kind of human being it is. What one's
imagination makes of other people is dictated, of course,
by the laws of one's own personality and it is one of the
ironies of black-white relations that, by means of what the
white man imagines the black man to be, the black man
is enabled to know who the white man is.

I have said, for example, that I am as much a stranger
in this village today as I was the first summer I arrived,
but this is not quite true. The villagers wonder less about
the texture of my hair than they did then, and wonder
rather more about me. And the fact that their wonder
now exists on another level is reflected in their attitudes
and in their eyes. There are the children who make those
delightful, hilarious, sometimes astonishingly grave over-
tures of friendship in the unpredictable fashion of children; other children, having been taught that the devil is
a black man, scream in genuine anguish as I approach.
Some of the older women never pass without a warmly
greeting, never pass, indeed, if it seems that they will be
able to engage me in conversation; other women look
down or look away or rather contemptuously smirk. Some

b/w

XI. AN UNUSUAL PEDAGOGY

Productive undoing is a difficult task. It must look carefully at the fault lines of the doing.

—Gayatri Chakravorty Spivak, *An Aesthetic Education in the Era of Globalization* (2012)[1]

In a very real sense, this hybrid, technologized angel-artifact is perhaps the most massive archive of all of Benjamin's writings. With him for most of his life, it bears references to nearly all of his most enduring concepts and concerns: including, among others, writing, history and its catastrophes, the relations among the past, the present, and the future, the mass-like character of all things, the relation between theology and politics, redemption and messianism, technological reproducibility, the depersonalization and nonhumanness of the subject, questions of agency and their inscription within networks of mediation that restrict intentional acts, and artworks (and conceptions of art) that can be politicized. While many critics have identified Benjamin with his angel, Jameson goes even further when he tells us that the angel is "the awkward Benjamin himself" (*BF*, 220). Whether wittingly or unwittingly, he qualifies Benjamin with a word that, in its late Middle English origins, combines "awk"—which means "backward" or "wrong way round"—with "ward," and, in doing so, suggests a *moving in the wrong direction*. This Benjamin-angel moves backward—is pushed backward by the "*storm* of progress"—into the future, which is of course Benjamin's own signature gesture and one that, no doubt to his great pleasure, would have satisfied Gracián's criteria for *ingenio*. As we have seen, Benjamin everywhere looks backward in order to think about his present. He draws resources from a past that, in his hands, becomes a lens through which he can view his particular historical moment—since one of his most fundamental axioms is that every moment is already full of time; it can only be thought by considering the past, the present, and the future all at once. The aftereffect of everything that has preceded it, it appears as a knot of historical relations and events that can neither be disentangled nor reconstructed in a linear and causal fashion. It is impossible to think of an event solely in relation to the temporal situation in which it occurs. It has to be thought in relation to all the history it has within it—like Klee's *Angelus Novus*. If Jameson's book closes by moving toward this emblem—and Benjamin's reading of it—it is because all of Benjamin's writings can be viewed as involving the necessary training and preparation that are required to begin to disentangle all the threads woven into this figure. We might even say that what is at stake in reading the figure of the angel of history is the possibility of reading any of Benjamin's figures—as the deeply historical and transforming archives that they are.

Jameson identifies a pedagogical dimension in Benjamin, the "unusual pedagogy" to which we have already referred and which, according to Jameson, involves "the shifting of perceptual levels within the mind" in order to produce "a cultural revolution within the reading process" (*BF*, 35). Since pedagogy only works if it can be transmitted, Jameson actually confirms the efficacy of Benjamin's training manual for reading historically, especially in moments of danger, by transmitting the writer's concepts in his reenactment of them—in his extraction, selection, and presentation of Benjamin's most emblematic figures. Indeed, the act of reading is a form of transmission, and, if there is a Benjaminian object that requires a particular kind of reading subject, it is the angel of history. As evidenced by Jameson's book, it is only when a reader is entirely embedded in the constellation of references and relations that form the boxes of a writer's corpus that he or she can even begin to read. What is perhaps most interesting—despite the rather extraordinary way in which Jameson, in this book more than anywhere else in his corpus of writings, takes on the concepts and even the cadences of the writer whom he is reading—is the way in which Jameson nevertheless tries to resist being "boxed in" by Benjamin, even as we time and again witness his failure. What get staged in this effort and failure are the risks and restrictions of embedding himself in the worlds of a writer, the reduced agency it entails. The more deeply a reader inhabits the works of a writer—the more deeply the reader enters a writer's words or sentences—the more profoundly he or she disappears into the writer's corpus. It becomes increasingly difficult to set the sails in relation to the "wind of world history" but also in relation to the force a writer's language can have on us. Like the "real collector" in Benjamin's "Unpacking My Library" who dwells in the objects he has collected, in a cloistered intimacy, the reader also disappears into the texts he or she engages. As Benjamin puts it:

inside him there are spirits, or at least little genii, which have seen to it that for a collector—and I mean a real collector, a collector as he ought to be—ownership is the most intimate relationship that one can have to things. Not that they come alive in him; it is he who lives in them. So I have erected before you one of his dwellings, with books as the building stones; and now he is going to disappear inside, as is only fitting.[2]

Similarly, within the trajectory of his book, Jameson increasingly disappears into Benjamin's figures, as Benjamin himself disappears into them, by withdrawing the "I" in his sentences so that someone else could one day inhabit them, take them over, and send them somewhere else, as Jameson does here. Indeed, he moves through several of Benamin's figures. He is the flâneur who, making his way through the streets of Benjamin's texts, the many paths and sentences the reader is asked to follow, understands, like the flâneur who writes with his gaze as he walks, that "[e]ach directed gaze is a sentence in the making, a formulation already virtual and implicit; the writing is already being done with the movements of the eye" (BF, 114). He is the gambler who takes his chances and makes his bets not only in relation to which texts he will attend to in order to reap the greatest gain but also in relation to yet another gamble, a temporal one, which "risks destroying temporality altogether" (BF, 93). He is the storyteller who pieces together the nonnarrative threads within Benjamin's corpus that, interrupting the linearity of any story, attend to the distance that prevents any story from being fully unfolded but lead us to an exploration of what cannot be experienced in experience—experience itself (BF, 166). He is the historical materialist who traces the relations between politics and theology but through his passion for language and literature; the one who, engaging the relations between history and historiography and among the past, the present, and the future, registers the inevitability of a complicity that he associates with the always-present danger of, without knowing it, reinforcing the very forms of domination he strives to overcome, and responds with an explosive force that, corresponding to a will to "expansion" and "intensification" (BF, 30), is most often legible in his writing. He is the insurrectionist who, like Blanqui, seeks to intervene in a context in which history repeats itself "over and over again in unimaginably vast cycles" (BF, 28) and does so from his own lifelong prison cell—a "prison-house of language," but one that Blanqui could also be said to have shared and in which style is inseparable from an insurrectionary politics and sentences are a form of action.

That Jameson finds himself inscribed within Benjamin's figures, that he finds himself scattered and extended across these different figures, each of which contributes to the dissolution of his own voice and his control over it, becomes a means of measuring the difficulty that structures the very possibility of insurrectionary political acts—the mediating conditions that restrain the voluntarism and agency of political action. While this is the question raised by Benjamin's angel—whose wish to stay, to waken the dead and restore what has been destroyed, is made impossible by the storm whose wind has "got caught in his wings" and prevented him from being able to close them—Jameson prefers the more mobile figure with which he begins his book, the "wind in the sails" that makes the work of the dialectician a difficult and precarious one. Like the figure of the angel, this earlier figure reduces the question of agency to that of directionality. What is at stake for the dialectician is the possibility of setting the sails in such a way as to take advantage of the force of the wind of world history—to enable it to move things in an emancipatory and revolutionary direction. But he needs to take into account not just the wind but also the moving and often turbulent undercurrents beneath the boat that, unseen and uncontrollable, intensify the precariousness of his task. In this scene, the chance that, for even a brief moment, the sail, the wind, and the undercurrent can align themselves in a direction that might offer a revolutionary opportunity demands that the dialectician be prepared, at that very moment—which "flashes up" (*CH*, 391) in a moment of danger—to "blast open the continuum of history" (*CH*, 396), to seize the opportunity and work to maximize its consequences. The question of directionality always has a political valence in Benjamin—especially in relation to its radical unpredictability— and it should be understood in temporal terms. Indeed, the spatial complexity of his allegory of the "wind in the sails" parallels the temporal complexity of his understanding of the revolutionary moment. But this allegory is just another of Benjamin's boxes.

This is why, we might say, Benjamin's boxes and figures are more militant than antiquarian. They are all elements of a pedagogical impulse that he develops and enacts throughout his life—an ever-widening constellation of emblems that require an exercise in the reading of history as an enigma. This pedagogy prepares us to engage a world that is always transient, metamorphosing and unfolding in multiple temporal directions. These shifting traces—exhibiting the discontinuities, the processes of "perpetual translation" (*BF*, 3) that, together, inaugurate a force of destruction—are mobilized within Benjamin's writing against any form of identity, intentionality, and capitalized indebtedness. It is precisely through the withdrawal of the individual into the impersonality of his many figurations that Benjamin hopes to ready us for the emergence of the fleeting and transient moment of political possibility and historical intensity. Removing his individual self for the benefit of a figure, however withdrawing this figure might be, he frees up a negative space for others to occupy and inhabit, a space that belongs to the uncertainty of a political future. As we have argued, the intensification of relationality in Benjamin's boxlike sentences strives to interrupt, displace, and transform the "guilt nexus of the living" by moving us to *choose* a debt to the future rather than to the past. Here, directionality and temporality become complicit in the topological undoing of the nexus that binds capitalism to religion, and in this way they transform the certainty of indenture into the indeterminacy of hope, neither of which can ever be disentangled from the other. This new nexus offers the possibility of a destructive force whose pessimism can enable a more energized future (*BF*, 80), whose sense of defeat can become the catalyst for revolutionary events (*BF*, 93). But even here, the task of the dialectician remains risky, unpredictable, and even a gamble in relation to several intersecting temporalities. In the end, there is no calculus for the political in Benjamin; the multiplicity of his figures remains a site of political incalculability, and this because the absence of the individual self—like Klee's faceless Luther—corresponds to the intensification of historical contingency.

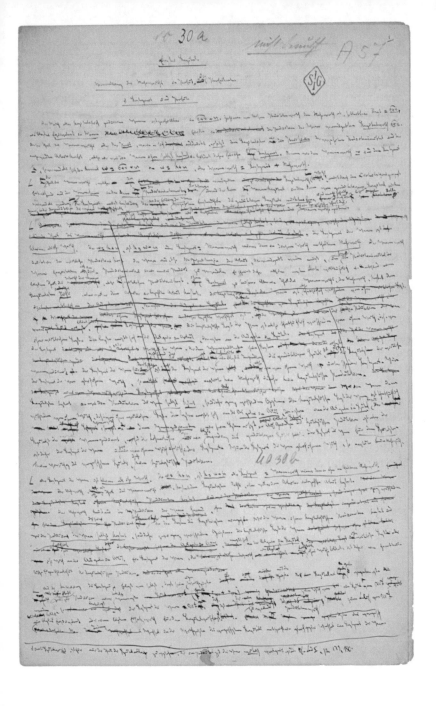

Karl Marx, draft page from the third volume of *Das Kapital*, 1870–1880

XII. A SHIP OF FOOLS

The crew are all quarrelling with each other about how to navigate the ship, each thinking he ought to be at the helm; they know no navigation and cannot say that anyone ever taught it to them, or that they spent any time studying it; indeed they say it can't be taught and are ready to murder anyone who says it can. They spend all their time milling round the captain and trying to get him to give them the wheel. ... They have no idea that the true navigator must study the seasons of the year, the sky, the stars, the winds ...

—Plato, *The Republic*, Book 6 (ca. 375 BC)[1]

If Benjamin attempts to set the sails of his writing so that he can better imagine—and perhaps even enable—the possibility of a new nexus capable of conjuring those who are no longer here or who are not yet here, the inability either to awaken the dead or to guarantee the life of the not yet born names an unchosen moment of danger through which the contingency of the present becomes the source of communal despair. This despair is legible in Benjamin's writings about the mass artwork, the proletarian general strike, and the angel of history—even when it remains an invisible undercurrent—and in Jameson's return to Benjamin in 2020 in the midst of the rise of old and new forms of authoritarianism but also of a global and deadly pandemic that has revealed the long histories of what Benjamin famously described as "the tradition of the oppressed" (*CH*, 392), along with all the inequalities, destruction, violence, and racism that have permeated these histories. In both writers, this despair, this hopelessness, nevertheless has the capacity to generate new forms of political action and activisms. Even so, in the end, seizing a political moment, setting the sails of world history in a way that can perhaps reap a political benefit in the midst of innumerable historical crises, and taking an existential risk are one and the same gesture. Only when the urgency and contingency of the present moment lead to a heightened sense of finitude in a communal sense, when our precariousness binds us together as a mass so that our fate is shared by millions of others, are we forced to imagine a world in which we can only survive if we no longer remain ourselves. Orienting ourselves toward a future that may never come, carrying within us a sense of communal finitude, we can perhaps only look in the direction of a hope that still depends on us, even if it can never belong to us.

If, as Jameson has recently stated, "the political is the heightened excitement awakened by the intersection of individual experience with the presence of the collective," and the life and value of a text lies in "the hidden kindling of a collective spark in its representations,"[2] then these representations are the sails that have to be set to catch the winds of collectivity. As Benjamin warns us, however, we do not yet have an adequate means of talking about a collectivity that emerges not only out of a communal sense of despair but also out of our shared incommensurability with one another (what Adorno calls in *Negative Dialectics* "the togetherness of the diverse"[3]). The dialectical writer is neither able to set the sails by "himself" or "herself" nor to align them in such a way that the winds will move him or her in an enduring revolutionary direction. But there are moments that come with the force of interruption and arrest the directionality of history in order to move it, even if just temporarily, in this revolutionary direction. These moments emerge and become part of the training that Benjamin's materialist historian—having passed through them, even if only in a fragmented and mediated manner—can later inhabit as part of his or her capacity to respond when, in a moment of danger, such a moment flashes up again. If, for Benjamin, one of these moments was the October Revolution, for Jameson, May '68 was a similarly critical moment—if we remember that, however punctual these moments may seem to be, they are of course full of time and history and it is this fullness that gives them their historical strength. In these two revolutionary events, these two Marxist dialecticians witnessed the possibility of breaks, of moments that, interrupting the flow of history, enabled the blasting of "a specific era out of the homogeneous course of history," and the attendant possibility of "blasting a specific life out of the era" (*CH*, 396). If these explosive events, these breaks and fissures, emerge from the contradictions and weaknesses of a political formation or system, from the "secret agreement between past generations and the present one," from a past that "carries with it a secret index by which it is referred to redemption" (*CH*, 390), they offer a glimpse into why Benjamin so often focuses his attention on the edges of things, on the margins or fringes of a text or, in the case of Klee's *Angelus*, of a boxlike image. It is precisely his attention to what, seemingly incidental or even just parenthetical, nevertheless permits the opening of several worlds, all of which have the potential to initiate a break around which a dispersed but forceful collectivity might appear.[4]

Citing a phrase from "Central Park" in which Benjamin refers to Baudelaire's "deepest intention," Jameson reminds us that "the vocation of revolution is 'to interrupt the course of the world'" (*BF*, 223).[5] What is at stake is a moment of urgency that, appearing in a series of images (and we should remember that, in Benjamin, images are never just visual but bearers of "a whole world" [*BF*, 7]), points, however evanescently, to the potential of inciting a mass movement. Responding to the "secret agreement" that enables a present to take advantage of the momentum of a past with which it registers a "structural similitude" (*BF*, 224), it refuses to be contained within a closed box, especially one that would carry a label meant to diminish its force. But this is why, Benjamin notes, the "historical index" of images "not only says that they belong to a particular time; it says, above all, that they attain to legibility only at a particular time" (*AP*, 462–463). In Jameson's words, "[w]e have to understand that the 'particular time' in question is our own present, the moment in which we find ourselves able to read this moment of the past and to grasp its 'now of recognizability'" (*BF*, 223–224). What is "properly historical here only reveals itself to a future generation capable of recognizing it; that is, a generation possessing developers strong enough to fix an image never seen before,"[6] and the capacity to mobilize it in a revolutionary direction.

Having arrived here, we might say that this is the very moment in which the force of our reading of Jameson's reading of Benjamin (and, in turn, of Benjamin's reading of Marx and Luxemburg) can begin to be measured. In particular, our reading points to the ways in which Jameson and Benjamin—and by extension Marx, Luxemburg, and, as we will see, W. E. B. Du Bois—remain powerful resources for doing political work today. Taking our cue from Jameson's and Benjamin's insistence that we read from the margins, the lacunae or ellipses, of a text, image, object, or even an event—this directive belongs to their respective pedagogical projects, which resonate deeply with one another—we wish to return to two such margins, the first a parenthetical remark in Jameson's book, the second a footnote belonging to Benjamin to which Jameson refers and which he claims could offer, if developed, "a wholly new theorization of political action" (*BF*, 199). In neither instance does Jameson himself develop his point, but these two remarks, belonging to what we might call the "undercurrents" of his text, open a space for extending his reading of Benjamin in a way that can perhaps set its sails differently and, in doing so, enable the text to move us in unexpected ways that can be activated politically precisely because it is timely and untimely at the same time.

We begin with Jameson's parenthetical whisper at the end of a passage (punctuated by two other parentheses that touch on the issue of complicity) in which he suggests the way in which, in the aftermath of different world revolutions, including, we can assume, the October Revolution, the force of American capitalism and commodification has been increasingly globalized. For him, this fact helps answer, even if inadequately, the question of why socialism has never yet been able to exist in America. In his final parenthesis, however, he suggests an answer that is "better" because it is at once more particular and more comprehensive:

> But when, in the 1920s and '30s, world revolution begins to recede and capitalism's production of the lifeworld is tendentially universalized, then—particularly in so-called Western Marxism—the problem of the theorization of superstructures returns in full force, and with Lukács's epoch-making *History and Class Consciousness* (and quite against his own political intentions), commodification becomes a political issue. Indeed, after World War II, it takes center stage as a crucial problem of political strategy and mobilization. The dangers of Americanization were recognized long before decolonization and the Cold War. Lenin could speak of the bribery of the working classes in a formula which will continue to be invoked as an explanation for their support for Hitler in the German elections of 1932, but which will come to seem inadequate (even if true) for answering the now hoary question of "why there is no socialism in America?" (whose better answer would seem to be "race"). (*BF*, 153)[7]

Even if commodification emerges as the social totality of the globalized world in which we live, Jameson's emphasis on the Americanness of the phenomenon provides a telescopic view into the specific historical realities, the particular practices of domination and oppression, "the bribery of the working classes," that capitalism would prefer to keep disguised, invisible, and anonymous—if only to make them more effective.[8] If Jameson suggests that "race" is perhaps a better explanation than "bribery" for why socialism has been impossible in America, it is not because this "bribery" is not at work—*it is* (it is what seduces and persuades workers to subscribe to capital, to imagine that it might share its bounties and—moved by its promise of freedom and autonomy, however minimal these might be for them—ensures their acquiescence)[9]—but because "race" prevents the working classes from uniting by dividing them, and proves to be yet another form of extortion. Capitalism encourages and even requires these divisions: it galvanizes its white workers to compete with one another, and also to believe they are better than other workers—most often workers of color or minoritized populations. They are encouraged to believe that they are therefore more deserving of capital's benefits, of greater status and privilege. It gathers its force from forms of racialization, and these forms are experienced as different structures of social fragmentation that at once support and contradict the system's totalization. If American capitalism is defined by its generalized racism and, in particular, its anti-Blackness—as race, class, and capital are entirely intertwined on every front—it is because the history of race relations is the direct social product of a system based on profit: race may even be the most pernicious and persistent of capitalist constructions.[10] It is founded on the commodification, exploitation, and extermination of Black subjects (and not only Black subjects), which is why resisting capitalism without simultaneously resisting racism is not just an ineffective political calculus but also a misreading of the depth of their complicity.[11]

Rather than realizing the promise of individual and social liberties, capital's insistence on autonomy depends on the success of a violent politics of oppression, of economic and ideological unfreedom, and thus of the destruction of autonomy. As Hamacher notes, this insistence "often has gone hand in hand with a process of disenfranchisement and even the massacre of countless persons and peoples. And this process—one hesitates to call it a process of civilization—has to this day continued to thrive on the massive, capitalist exploitation of individuals and peoples." "The process of capitalization is a process of the automation of the mechanisms of capital," he goes on to say,

> it is a process of the obliteration of labor, the obliteration of a violent history and of the particularity of the socio-economic and politico-cultural forces that sustain this autonomy, a process of the erasure of those who are always insufficiently paid and of that which cannot be counted. Whoever invokes the universalism of this freedom and this equality always invokes, whether or not he acknowledges it, this history of automatization, colonialization, and exploitation.[12]

The history of capitalism in America and beyond is always a history of the grief and grievances of the uncounted, of, in Benjamin's words, the "vanquished," the anonymous who toil for others. This is also why the fate of socialism, of anticapitalism, depends on the historicization of anti-Blackness as an archive of communal grief that is woven in often invisible ways into the very fabric of the "American" project—from its already heterogeneous and multidirectional beginnings to its presently multiple and intensely entangled configurations—like a structuring undercurrent. Race is another name for the history of American capitalism.

In a passage from the notes to his theses on history, Benjamin offers a critique of historicism that imagines what a history would look like if it began with the vanquished rather than with the victors, even if the danger of complicity, the danger of "empathizing" with the victor, still remains inevitable. Jameson himself returns to this passage in his book on Benjamin—as we have seen, in his discussion of race in particular—but he also had placed the final paragraph of *The Political Unconscious* under the sign of this passage, suggesting that, in the identification it makes between civilization and barbarism, it not only offers "an appropriate corrective to the doctrine of the political unconscious" but also points to the conditions for a Marxist "political praxis."[13] It is a passage that will help us frame our discussion of race, which is meant, as we have suggested, to confirm the radical political potential of the writings of these two readers of Marx—and of all those who follow—as a means for engaging the present.

Hoping to unleash the "destructive energies of historical materialism," Benjamin delineates "the three most important positions of historicism," each of which needs to be destroyed and overcome to clear a path for a revolution that, taking its point of departure from "Marx's theoretical sketch of labor under the dominion of capital," might finally "honor the memory of the anonymous" without whom history cannot happen, and certainly cannot be blasted out of its continuum.[14] Liberating itself "from the schema of progression within an empty and homogeneous time," the conception of history that motivates the historical materialist first attacks any form of universalist history—which he associates with a capitalist narrative and, in particular, a capitalist narrative that takes advantage of the "intellectual laziness" that divides the world into different peoples who can then be mobilized against each other—and secondly targets the concept of an epic narrative, which capitalism attributes to itself but which, after Marx, is no longer possible. In contrast to Lukács (who views the epic form as a sign of the world's cohesiveness), Benjamin remains resolutely against "the idea that history is something that can be narrated."[15] "In a materialist investigation," he explains, "the epic moment will always be blown apart in the process of construction. The liquidation of the epic moment must be accepted, as Marx did when he wrote *Capital*. He realized that the history of capital could be constructed only within the broad, steel framework of a theory. In Marx's theoretical sketch of labor under the dominion of capital, humanity's interests are better looked after than in the monumental, longwinded, and basically lackadaisical works of historicism." If Benjamin calls for a theorization of the critique of historicism that refuses to heed capitalism's demand for narrative instrumentalization, for its "lackadaisical historicism," he does so in favor of a "historical construction" devoted to the more difficult task of honoring "the memory of the anonymous." But, as he goes on to say, marking the third target of the historical materialist, this task involves confronting "the third bastion of historicism," which, according to him, is "the strongest and the most difficult to overrun," and this because of the difficulty of extricating oneself entirely from the allure of the victor. As he puts it, this difficulty

> presents itself as "empathy with the victor." The rulers at any time are the heirs of all those who have been victorious throughout history. Empathizing with the victor invariably benefits those currently ruling. The historical materialist respects this fact. He also realizes that this state of affairs is well-founded. Whoever has emerged victorious in the thousand struggles traversing history up to the present day has his share in the triumphs of those now ruling over those now ruled. The historical materialist can take only a highly critical view of the inventory of spoils displayed by the victors before the vanquished. This inventory is called culture. For in every case these treasures have a lineage which the historical materialist cannot contemplate without horror. They owe their existence not only to the efforts of the great geniuses who created them, but also to the anonymous toil of others who lived in the same period. There is no document of culture which is not at the same time a document of barbarism. The historical materialist keeps his distance from all of this. He has to brush history against the grain—even if he needs a barge pole to do it.[16]

The most difficult task of the historical materialist would seem to be writing a history that is not complicit with the long history of victors, especially when all their victories, all their conquests—coming at the expense of those they rule, and enforced by violence, oppression, and "horror"—have shaped, and even largely determined, not just histories but also the way they are written. These histories celebrate the victorious, the rulers, the "great geniuses," and not the vanquished who toil anonymously for their benefit. The celebration of "the inventory of spoils displayed by the victors before the vanquished" (an inventory that Benjamin calls "culture") is at the same time a celebration of the barbarism—the violence, the exploitation, the forces of domination—that, "stained with the guilt" of culture, has made history, in Jameson's words, "one long nightmare."[17] If the historical materialist is to keep a distance from this terrible complicity, he must "brush history against the grain." Following the logic of this passage—following its trajectory from beginning to end—brushing history against the grain means writing history against a historicism that privileges victors, writing history from the point of view of the vanquished, that is, rather than from that of the victors. As Benjamin puts it, "[t]he history-writing subject, is, properly, that part of humanity whose solidarity embraces all the oppressed. It is the part which can take the greatest theoretical risks because, in practical terms, it has the least to lose."[18] He emphasizes the difficulty of this task by offering us a rather remarkable figure: given the strength and longstanding traditions of writing history from the perspective of the victors, he suggests, writing a history from the point of view of those who remain uncounted and unheard, who toil for others anonymously, is like pushing or pulling a heavy barge, loaded with the bulk goods and values of capital, forward—and trying to direct it, against the muddy but invisible ground of cultural sedimentation, with a barge pole.

As is so often the case, Benjamin's figure enacts what he wants to convey, self-reflexively offering us a means of viewing the labor of the historical materialist differently. In this instance, we might say that the historical materialist's labor—inseparable from a labor of writing, regardless of the work that is being done—has to be read in relation to his skill at using the barge pole, a double for the political writer's stylus. Here, though, the writing instrument writes in water—marking the movement of the barge in relation to the tracings of movement this barge-pole stylus leaves behind as it moves through the water, but also in relation to the muddy mire against which the pole finds its position and then, using this unsteady position as a point of resistance, pushes off it in order to move the barge forward. The skillful handling of the barge pole is a form of reading that, taking its point of departure from this resistance, turning stagnation and inertia into movement, enables the historical materialist to move through capital's channels and waterways. But, if the barge moves forward, the inscriptions of movement left behind by this new writing instrument move backward, in another enactment of the way in which revolutionary writing—breaking the unity of the surfaces of capital and thereby interrupting the directional narrative of progress—can "brush history against the grain." At the same time that the historical materialist marks the distance from his usual writing tools, he also marks his distance from the victors by associating the muscular effort involved in moving and handling the barge pole with the work involved in pushing or pulling the barge, work that often was done not only by horses but also by anonymous laborers, often women. His is a labor that pulls him in the direction of the workers, of the masses. It is as if, in order to write from the perspective of the vanquished, the historical materialist must inscribe himself, even if through an act of writing that is also an act of manual labor, within the history of the unnamed. In doing so, however, in aligning his labor with that of the lowly worker who "toils for others," he also exposes the collaborative ground of his writing labor and, in particular, begins to write in collaboration with the vanquished. His capacity to direct the barge is indissociable from the collective labor that makes it possible, a fact that in turn prevents him, distances him, from asserting his individuality against this collectivity.

Benjamin's figure emphasizes—in its almost allegorical presentation of capital's endurance and vulnerability—not simply the difficulty in shifting the direction of the barge of capitalism but also the strength required to enable this work, a strength that, in Benjamin, comes with numbers. What gets staged is the training that the historical materialist has to undergo before either he or the dialectician can even begin to set the sails. Put another way, this training is the preparation necessary for taking advantage of even the most fleeting chance of revolutionary action. It involves a hands-on training in the long history of labor and capital, in the slow history of collaboration across different classes, races, and generations. It also includes a sense of the herculean effort involved in engaging the mire and mud of capital. While Benjamin already has suggested that reading and writing require the production of a distance capable of steering the historical materialist boat in unexpected and urgent new directions, he here invokes another body of water—this time the less tidal waterways of capital—in which liquidity serves as a placeholder for the possibility of transformation. But it is not surprising that this barge-pole writer and laborer finds his activist and revolutionary energy elsewhere—as we know, in Benjamin writing always begins somewhere else, never in the voice of an individual writer—on another barge and in relation to another stylus, one that belongs to Marx himself.

In a letter to Arnold Ruge, written in March 1843 while on a barge in Holland, Marx speaks about the way in which Germany is presently "ridden deeply" into a mire which it will soon "sink into" even further, about the ways in which the "new school" of radical critique has begun to prepare the populace to no longer be "deceived" about the capitalist system, with all its nationalisms and despotisms, and about a possible pathway to revolution that involves a government experiencing shame for its ethico-political failings in regard to its people and, in particular, to its most vulnerable populations. He writes:

> I am now travelling in Holland. From both the French papers and the local ones I see that Germany has ridden deeply into the mire and will sink into it even further. I assure you that even if one can feel no national pride one does feel national shame, even in Holland. In comparison with the greatest Germans even the least Dutchman is still a citizen. And the opinions of foreigners about the Prussian government! There is a frightening agreement, no one is deceived any longer about the system and its simple nature. So the new school has been of some use after all. The glorious robes of liberalism have fallen away and the most repulsive despotism stands revealed for all the world to see.
>
> This, too, is a revelation, albeit a negative one. It is a truth which at the very least teaches us to see the hollowness of our patriotism, the perverted nature of our state and to hide our faces in shame. I can see you smile and say: what good will that do? Revolutions are not made by shame. And my answer is that shame is a revolution in itself; it really is the victory of the French Revolution over that German patriotism which defeated it in 1813. Shame is a kind of anger turned in on itself. And if a whole nation were to feel ashamed it would be like a lion recoiling in order to spring. I admit that even this shame is not yet to be found in Germany; on the contrary, the wretches are still patriots. But if the ridiculous system of our new knight [Frederick William IV of Prussia came to the throne in 1840] does not disabuse them of their patriotism, then what will? The comedy of despotism in which we are being forced to act is as dangerous for him as tragedy was once for the Stuarts and the Bourbons. And even if the comedy will not be seen in its true light for a long time, yet it will still be a revolution.
>
> The state is too serious a business to be subjected to such buffoonery. A Ship of Fools can perhaps be allowed to drift before the wind for a good while; but it will still drift to its doom precisely because the fools refuse to believe it possible. This doom is the approaching revolution.[19]

From a distance, and with his perspective mediated and rein-forced by at least French and Dutch newspaper accounts of the political situation in Germany—another instance of the role and force of the technical media within the realms of history and pol-itics—Marx expresses his disdain for Germany's drift away from not simply the rights of its citizens, which it erases more and more every day as is increasingly legible to the outside world, but also from the ideals of the French Revolution, which, from Marx's perspective, even if still to be realized, nevertheless point to a future that remains open. Rather than embrace this future, however, the Prussian government insists on its despotic monar-chical system and, in so doing, reveals—as Marx puts it in another letter to Ruge, this time from May 1843—"for all the world to see," that, within despotism, "brutality is necessary and humanity impossible." "A brutal state of affairs can only be maintained by means of brutality," he goes on to say, noting that, in response to the revolution's effort to restore "man to his estate," to transform things into people and even to give them names, the Prussian king soon "put a stop to these un-German activities." But "the loss of respect both at home and abroad" cannot "remain with-out consequence"; the light cast on Germany's inhumanity leads not to national pride but to national shame, both inside and out-side its borders—a shame Marx admits he feels and believes can become a force of transformation.[20] This shame becomes possi-ble because Marxism—appearing as a kind of literacy for reading the capitalist system in all its authoritarian forms, with all its mechanisms of power, privilege, enslavement, and violence—has exposed the system's naked and "repulsive despotism" for "the world to see." Once we *see* the brutality, the processes of dehu-manization, without which capital would be unable to support itself, we become aware of the necessity of distancing ourselves from it. If we do not, we remain complicit in the suffering, grief, and death it produces and guarantees—and this because we are "forced to act" in the "comedy of despotism," either against our will or without our knowing it. If seeing this brutality cannot guarantee that we will not succumb to complicity, it is never-theless a necessary step and one without which we are unable to minimize this possibility.

Making what was previously invisible visible, the "new school" of radical critique urges us to register the absolutely intolerable world created by this despotism. It reaches back to the French Revolution and—mobilizing it as an example of what is possible and what can even be furthered, directing its critical potential against the Germany that had sought to suppress its possibilities—teaches us to "hide our faces in shame" on registering the distance between the revolution's democratic aspirations and "the hollowness of our patriotism," the "perverted nature" of our state. Marx suggests that this shame "is a revolution in itself" because it turns in on itself in anger over what we had before now permitted, effecting a transformation not simply in perspective but in the subsequent unfolding of action. Shame works by enacting a kind of "cultural revolution" within the activity of reading. Shifting our sensibilities, interrupting our complacencies, urging us to exceed ourselves and to accept our responsibilities for others, it potentially gives birth to resistance, even to an ethico-political set of revolutionary positions. There is no shame in experiencing shame, Marx suggests; on the contrary, what is most shameful is the shamelessness of capitalism—and its wide network of different forms of subjection. The experience of shame makes room for the shattering of the forms of capitalism: it enacts a kind of socialism of emotion that counters capitalism's wish to anaesthetize or deaden our passions. Shame is a social affect; it is activated by sociality, by relationality, by a loss of self that marks our belonging to communities far larger than us. It creates the possibility of new kinds of assemblages that respond to what is intolerable in the world; it is precipitated by an affect that is social, lived, experienced in a transformative way. If shame can be said to begin with an experience of powerlessness and impossibility, Marx suggests that it is at the same time active and affirmative, even in its negativity.

Marx underlines its mass relationality as a source of revolutionary potential, even if a "negative" one. In the words of Aislinn O'Donnell, "[t]o *see* the intolerable is not enough; one must see the possibility of something else."[21] It requires—at the very moment in which we experience the impossibility of living under the present conditions, in which we feel caught within an impasse or at the limit of hopelessness—"a sensitivity to the richness of the present, to the forgotten histories, excluded others, silenced voices, and unrealized world"[22] that Marx (along with Benjamin and Jameson) compels us to see and hear. An affirmative "negativity," shame names a first stage of preparation and training that, in turn, opens a path for a critical interpretation and reading of the present. The experience of shame takes the form of a body recoiling, an experience that can potentially expand and multiply in the experience of "a whole nation." Beginning in a shared admission of a generalized lack of agency, in the resistance to the collective feeling of "being forced to act" in someone else's comedy—the comedy of despotism and its "buffoonery," for example—this shared shame threatens, in this instance, the stability of the "Ship of Fools" that is the Prussian nation. As Marx puts it so vividly in his letter, this shame is first expressed as the bodily withdrawal of a complicit self, as the need to retreat "like a lion recoiling in order to spring." This retreat, however, is only the proleptic announcement of what Benjamin later calls, in a remarkable echo of Marx's image, "a tiger's leap" toward happiness. Taking place beyond the reach of the ruling class, this "dialectical leap" is, in Benjamin's formulation, the leap of "revolution." If it requires a recoil, a withdrawal, this recoil and withdrawal are a necessary step in the preparation for revolutionary action, in the effort to direct the movement of history against capitalism's capacity to absorb, appropriate, and subsume all threats to its modus operandi.

If the barge of capitalist nationalism continues to drift, apparently undisturbed, into a future it can scarcely conceive because of inertia and sheer lack of imagination, this slow drift is at once a figure of stasis and movement. It represents capitalism's continued need for a simulacrum of change in order to remain the same, to continue to thrive by maintaining the political status quo—a paradox Marx never tired of signaling in his writings. But the negative space of this status quo uncovers an emptiness or void. The barge's tendency to "drift" is a figure of passivity, a reminder that no one is at the helm. The comedic and buffoonish nature of this state of affairs in no way diminishes its danger and violence, which is why uncovering its mechanisms in all their comedic glory, however long this process of discovery and unearthing may take, simultaneously involves the wish to take over and to actively redirect the boat, to occupy the empty seat at the helm and enable the possibility of a new direction. The ship's drift is only a pantomime of movement, following a script with no apparent text (except for that of the long history of capitalism's "barbarism"). Shame carries within it the perverse realization that there is no active steerage but instead a "laissez faire" attitude that erodes rights and justice by simply not lifting a finger (the capitalist status quo would seem to be anti-labor in more ways than one!). There is a real barbarism in this complicit passivity. Indeed, Prussia's Frederick William IV is another figure for the Second Empire's Bonapartism and its disguising of barbarism as civilization. Like the new Bonaparte, he is

clumsily cunning, knavishly naive, doltishly sublime, a calculated superstition, a pathetic burlesque, a cleverly stupid anachronism, a world-historic piece of buffoonery and an undecipherable hiero-glyphic for the understanding of the civilized—[a symbol that bears] the unmistakable physiognomy of the class that represents barbarism within civilization.[23]

The ruling barbarism not only promotes the passivity of unfreedom in those who toil but also in the rulers themselves. In the world order of capitalism, there is only subjection, either blatant or carefully hidden. In his letter to Ruge from May 1843, Marx points to the unfreedom of the "lords of the world":

Of course, they are lords of the world only in the sense that they fill it with their presence. ... They require nothing more than a number of slaves to complete their society and slave-owners do not need to be free. If their ownership of land and people entitles them to be called lords and masters *par excellence* this does not make them any less philistines than their servants. ... The philistine world is the *animal kingdom of politics* and if we must needs acknowledge its existence we have no choice but to accept the *status quo*. Centuries of barbarism have produced it and given it shape, and now it stands before us as a complete system based on the principle of the *dehumanized world*.[24]

If the question is how we can turn this drift of the status quo, this drift of the "Ship of Fools"—a ship carrying Frederick William IV and a few other "lords of the world"—against capitalism, how we can exploit its tendency to treat movement as a form of stasis in order to accelerate its doom, Marx suggests that the experience of shame might be one possible route, since the structure of shame also bears tension, incommensurability, ambivalence, and even the possibility of intensified paralysis within it. If the lion must first recoil before it can spring, it is because its act is delayed and suspended: it knows it will leap, but, if its leap is to be effective, it has to happen at the right moment. Shame reveals our inability to remain isolated or disconnected from the history we share with others; it counters the individualism of liberalism and capitalism and its instrumentalization of a guilt economy. Taking shape through Marx's stylus as he travels on a barge, it becomes another name for the barge pole that can enable the historical materialist to "brush history against the grain."

Marx and Benjamin present their allegories of the movement and stasis of capitalism and its despotic character—structures that, like barges or ships drifting through mire, are difficult to dislodge and redirect—as letters to a revolutionary future.

Entrusted with the labor of reading the past and the present, they conjure a future that will no longer belong to the time of capitalism, a future that will have the ability and imagination to move the barge and ship (the "Ship of Fools" as well as the ship of state) in a different direction. They do this in the name of a future they cannot guarantee or predict but which they wish to call forth, even if this future may very well not include them. There can be no change of direction without a labor of preparation, a labor of reading and writing, a labor that embodies the history of labor and capital, and, even then, the timing of the lion's leap is everything, which is why, in the end—but an end that is at the same time a beginning—what is necessary is the untimeliness of the most timely revolution. As we have seen, this revolution is arduous and invisible and can only belong to those who literally "toil for others," like the many anonymous laborers to whom Benjamin refers. But this time, the possibility of a collective training in historical materialism—a training that, today, might include our reading Marx, Luxemburg, Benjamin, and Jameson, along with all the other readers and writers they invoke and engage and who form an ever-growing constellation around them (we will soon add W. E. B. Du Bois to this constellation)—enables acts of reading and writing whose aim is to ensure that the imagined "others" for whom we continue to toil can belong to a future these historical materialists can perhaps only imagine and announce. What these writers suggest is that preparing for a revolution is *still* working for others, but these potentially new collectivities must include the uncounted of the past, as well as those of the future. Here Marx's exploration of shame comes into contact with Benjamin's insistence on pessimism and Luxemburg's on defeat, and, together, they remind us that communal grief, the negation of agency and right, is at the root of political possibility and that, while it arises through class antagonism, it can potentially extend across different class identifications, before these are undone in a new and more inclusive formation that still remains to be named. We become when we realize we do not yet exist and we work to turn this negation into a possibility, but we must do so through a communal expansion of this lack and this grief, using it as a bond that rewrites the social contract in a manner that is truer to the ideals of the French Revolution—since it acknowledges the innumerable masses without whom this revolution never would have taken place. According to Marx, Prussia's betrayal of the ideals of the French Revolution affects not just Germany but the world in its complicity and interconnectedness. This betrayal binds the

German bourgeoisie to the French bourgeoisie, which in turn works to elide the radical ideals of the unnamed masses. All victories are a series of betrayals, until the arrival of a victory that can no longer be described by that name because it destroys the logic of defeat, subjection, and exploitation through which history is constructed.

The close kinship between Marx and Benjamin—and of course between Luxemburg and Jameson and these two political readers and writers—should be very clear by now. That Benjamin is a brilliant close reader and active interlocutor of Marx's texts is legible in all the ways in which his language is entirely infused by Marx's language, images, and conceptual movements, and by how much his analyses absorb the lessons of Marx's writing. Benjamin returns us to the full complexity of Marx's worlds by refusing to read him ideologically and instead by taking the more difficult and indirect path of finding what is most political in Marx in the movements and images of his sentences. It is in this act—an act not unlike that of Jameson as he insists that we stay close to Benjamin's sentences—that Benjamin makes all of us better readers of Marx.

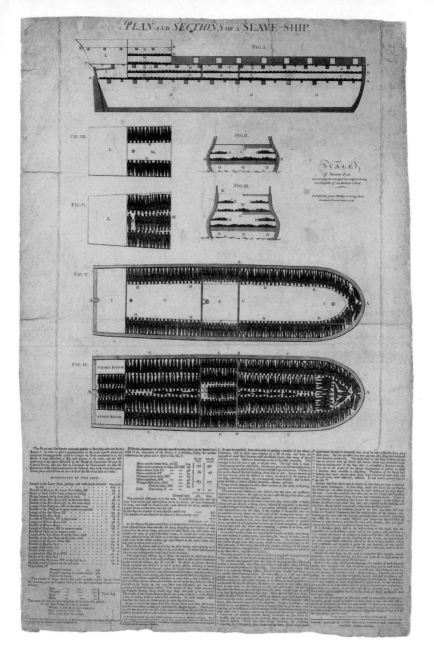

Plan and section of slave ship *Brooks*, 1789

XIII. COMMUNAL GRIEF

> Our histories never unfold in isolation. We cannot truly tell what
> we consider to be our own histories without knowing the other sto-
> ries. And often we discover that those other stories are actually our
> own stories.
>
> —Angela Y. Davis, *Freedom Is a Constant Struggle* (2016)[1]

If we trace the way in which each of these four historical materialists write, what we discover is a fierce pedagogy that, beginning at
the level of sentences, hopes to create a citizenry of the counted
and the uncounted that, together, might form an increasingly
activist "reading" community. This community—composed of
heterogeneous and at times even incommensurable constituencies—would begin in an understanding of the role of reading and
writing within the historico-political domain. It would direct its
work of reading, its labor of writing (with neither activity restricted
to the worlds of texts), toward understanding all the ways in which
capitalism's capacity to "bribe" different populations, to consistently invent new means for the division of these populations, to
further install and secure the violent realities of the "dehumanized world" it requires to continue its expansion, gives capital its
barbaric force. Even if it is still unnamed and not yet gathered
together, this community to come—eventually called into being
through the force and massification of critical acts of reading—
would seek to make us aware of our inevitable complicities with a
world of bribery that relies on constructed hierarchies among different classes, races, and genders. If this world seeks to prevent
the establishment of uncontrollable collectivities that—armed
with a literacy that would be dialectical, materialist, and attentive
to the anonymous millions, and even billions, who "toil for others," what Benjamin calls "a communist pedagogy"[2]—could begin
to introduce fissures and cracks within the edifices of capital, the
historical materialist works to intensify this shattering.

That this "communist pedagogy" should begin as early as possible is made clear in Benjamin's 1929 review of Edwin Hoernle's
Grundfragen der proletarischen Erziehung (Basic questions of proletarian education). Benjamin suggests that, in order to assist
in this training, we would need to invent a "Marxist dialectical

anthropology of the proletarian child" and to do so by keeping "detailed records—prepared according to the principles of materialist dialectics—of the actual experiences of working-class children in kindergartens, youth groups, children's theaters, and outdoor groups," all of which should be "introduced as soon as possible" to supplement Hoernle's "handbook." "It is in fact a handbook," he goes on to say,

> but it is also something more. In Germany, there is no orthodox Marxist literature apart from economic and political writings. This is the chief reason for the astonishing ignorance on the part of intellectuals, including left-wing intellectuals, about matters concerning Marxism. Hoernle's book gives us an authoritative and incisive account of education theory. By demonstrating its relevance to a question of fundamental importance, he shows us what orthodox Marxist thought is and where it leads. We should take this book to heart.

To "take this book to heart," however, involves supplementing "the political exposition [Hoernle] has given us with a philosophical one," and one that, as we are arguing, would insist on critical—what Benjamin calls here "polytechnical"—reading as one of the most "basic principles of mass education—principles whose seminal importance for young people growing up is utterly obvious." As he explains, "[c]ommunist education" must be "class struggle" on behalf of proletarian children. It "is a function of class struggle, but it is not only this":

> In terms of the Communist creed, it represents the thoroughgoing exploitation of the social environment in the service of revolutionary goals. Since this environment is a matter not just of struggle but also of work, education is also a revolutionary education for work. Offering a program for this, [Hoernle's] book is at its best. In the process, it meets up with a point of crucial importance for the Bolsheviks. In Russia, during the Lenin years, the important debate over single-subject or polytechnic education took place. Specialization or universal labor? Marxism's response is: universal labor. Only if man experiences changes of milieu in all their variety, and can mobilize his energies in the service of the working class again and again and in every new context, will he be capable of that universal readiness for action which the Communist program opposes to what Lenin called the "most repulsive feature of the old bourgeois society": its separation of theory and practice.

This is a remarkable set of passages. They emphasize the importance of Benjamin's "unusual pedagogy," a pedagogy that—at once literary, philosophical, historical, political, and communist—would seek to blast open "the hidden but precise functions of elementary and vocational schools, militarism and Church, youth organizations and Boy Scouts" that "act as the instruments of an antiproletarian education," and to replace them with a pedagogy for children that would sharpen the child's "consciousness, from an early age, in the school of poverty and suffering," in order to develop "class consciousness." "The proletarian child is born into his class—more precisely, into the next generation of his class—rather than into a family," he writes, adding that this situation, "like life itself, takes possession of him from the very first moment—indeed, while he is still in the womb."

Suggesting that the proletarian child is born into a network of relations, not just familial but also social, he tells us that "the proletarian family does not protect the child from the harsh lessons of social knowledge any more than his frayed summer jacket protects him from the biting winter wind." The transmission of this "social knowledge"—not simply through the child's participation in "revolutionary children's organizations, spontaneous school strikes, children's strikes during the potato harvest, and so on," but also before his or her birth—allows for the possibility that "everything from the subtle speculations of education theory to [the bourgeois class's] reproductive practice" might be interrupted, if not shattered altogether, by the collective consequences of this other kind of training, this "communist pedagogy."

But while the communal shame over the complicity between relative privilege and violent exploitation may not by itself be enough to interrupt the inertia of the capitalist barge and of the nation's ship of fools, it does set the stage, create the potential, for a collective lion's leap, for a revolutionary "tiger's leap," ready at the right moment. What Benjamin calls the "now of recognizability" is the moment in which an emerging mass, a newly emerging political collectivity, however fleetingly, helps the dialectician set the sails of revolution and seize the "wind of world history" from the hands of capital and its very real but nevertheless fabricated antagonisms. The effort to take advantage of a particular moment, to blast it out of history and to intensify its effects, has marked all revolutionary movements, even if they emerge from and lead to another experience of defeat, hopelessness, and communal despair. Marx, Luxemburg, Benjamin, and Jameson can be said to actualize their theorizations in their respective, but still interconnected, historical, social, and political contexts, and this because every one of their sentences is traversed and wounded by history. These contexts—at the same time a training ground for

THE SLAVE SHIP. *RA. 1840.*

In the possession of Miss Alice Hooper, of Boston, U.S.

Robert Hoskin, *The Slave Ship, after Joseph Mallord William Turner*, c. 1879

their activist pedagogy—include the bourgeois revolutions of the nineteenth century, the Paris Commune, the October Revolution, World Wars I and II, the Great Depression, the American civil rights movement, May '68, the opposition to the Vietnam War, and the long succession of global economic crises created by the history of capitalist violence. But, because Americanization can be understood as one name for the global unfolding of the earlier capitalist and nationalist scenarios that Marx, Luxemburg, and Benjamin address in their writings, it is Jameson's understated parenthetical word, "race," that sends an intolerable undercurrent of recognition through history's continuum, so that it is experienced as the site of a prolonged series of defeats, those of the unnamed and the uncounted, that simultaneously offers the hope for a mass transformation.

While Jameson's remark about the role of race within the history of America (and within the history of America's particularly expansive forms of global capital) may conjure and even seem to correspond to the demand for a racial reckoning that was so greatly manifested in the American summer of 2020, it is important to remember the limited agency of the historical materialist. Putting aside our not knowing exactly when this parenthetical note was written—we know Jameson's book was published on election day, but we do not know whether the note was written before or after the summer's events—and recalling the impersonal character of agency in general, Jameson's writerly act (an act that is already a reading of the racist infrastructure of American capitalism) has to be measured against the larger winds of world history. In the summer of 2020, those included the communal despair associated with a global pandemic, with a moment of national awakening and political possibility ignited by an intolerable experience of grief and shame, and with the growing resistance across different populations against Trump's patently racist programs—with Trump just an emblem and archival effect of a long history of white supremacist angst and violence. This is to say that, as the American Marxist that he is, "Jameson" is not just a proper name tied to an individual agent, but rather a "social form" whose task is to keep alive an entire archive of resistant readings that must be kept at the ready in the event that the moment of their needed materialization in political action and activism becomes legible. For Jameson, reading Marx or Benjamin in America today becomes a means of preparing us to seize the potential for transformation as it flashes up "in a moment of danger," before it is once more engulfed by the inertias of the historical continuum.

Only this training and readiness can enable us to read the shame of this America—and of all other Americas before it—as a means of activating a relational experience of the communal that is *both* painful and political, or rather, becomes political *precisely* because it is painful.

Communal grief is the key to understanding why Jameson's parenthetical "race" is at the center of any political reorientation of America, calling into being a new community that will acknowledge, grieve, and maybe even overcome its "barbarism" through a reckoning, through an experience of national and even global shame; a community that will mourn not just the unnamed and the uncounted, but itself as a perpetrator. If Marx and Benjamin were alive today, they might remind us that there is no document of capitalism that is not at the same time a document of inhumanity, inequality, and violence. The historical materialist should therefore dissociate himself or herself from it as much as possible, and encourage the uncounted to do so as well. If the projects and discourses of rights do not wish to neglect this counsel, they will have to define themselves continuously against the inhumanity, inequality, and violence that threaten them from within as well as from without. Always and at once motivated by a broader sense of democracy—but a democracy that would correspond to other, more radical and as yet untested forms than those we have with us today—they would begin in an aporetic praxis, one that would take its point of departure from what Hannah Arendt calls the "perplexities" of rights,[3] and the surprise of a world we have never seen before. They would move in the direction of a world beyond "bribery," exploitation, racisms, nationalisms, class ideologies, sexisms, and economic oppressions and displacements of all kinds. Only then would it be possible to begin to imagine a growing mass organized around the questions raised by Jameson's single word "race": What does it mean to understand America's past and present moments through race as the archive of communal grief? What kind of angel would be capable of awakening the dead and, redeeming the wreckage of the past, calling into being a new kind of "collectivity"? If, as Marx, Luxemburg, Benjamin, and Jameson tell us, new communal forms can never emerge from the individual, or even from the mere sum of individuals, what kind of expression will this new relational assemblage take? If this world can ever be inaugurated, it needs to begin, at least if we follow Jameson's discreet but massively consequential parenthetical murmur, with these questions.

Paul Nadar (1856–1939), W. E. B. Du Bois, identification
card for Exposition Universelle, 1900

XIV. A RED RAY; OR, SOCIOLOGY'S SUPPLEMENT

> Out of the depths of slavery has come this prejudice and this color
> line. It is broad enough and black enough to explain all the malign
> influences which assail the newly emancipated millions to-day. ...
> The office of color in the color line is a very plain and subordinate
> one. It simply advertises the objects of oppression, insult, and per-
> secution. It is not the maddening liquor, but the black letters on
> the sign telling the world where it may be had. ... Slavery, stupidity,
> servility, poverty, dependence, are undesirable conditions. When
> these shall cease to be coupled with color, there will be no color
> line drawn.
>
> —Frederick Douglass, "The Color Line" (1881)[1]

Jameson's "hoary question"—"why there is no socialism in
America?"—embeds a reference to Werner Sombart's 1906 sociological study, *Why Is There No Socialism in the United States?*
Jameson's parenthical suggestion—that "race" would seem to be a
better answer to this question than Lenin's insistence on capital's
capacity to bribe its workers—extends and racializes capitalist
bribery at the same time that it reads and corrects Sombart. In
his text, not translated into English until 1976, Sombart argues
that social democracy faced a unique series of obstacles in the
American context, including: (1) the working classes' embrace
of capitalism, fueled by the rewards of consumerism; (2) an
increasingly entrenched two-party system, which prevents the
emergence of other alternatives; (3) the illusion of universal
upward social mobility; and (4) the endurance of a frontier mentality. As Jameson's correction implies, each of these reasons can
be connected directly to the issue of race, a factor and explanation that Sombart minimizes (as the German sociologist puts
it: "[i]n explaining the circumstances of interest to us, we must
therefore exclude any argument based on racial membership"[2]).
We need only recall capitalism's entanglement with slavery and
its continued reliance on the exploitation of Black labor, Jim Crow
laws and the disenfranchisement of Black American citizens and
voters, an upward mobility often measured against the mainte-
nance of Black poverty, and a racist frontier mentality based on
the genocide of indigenous populations, to register the extent of
Sombart's neglect of race.[3]

Sombart's comparative charts and statistics, exactly contemporary to those of W. E. B. Du Bois, contrast the social and economic status of the American worker with that of the European worker—rather than point, as Du Bois does, to the ways in which race has prevented socialism from being fully embraced in the United States. Despite the fact that race does not seem to figure prominently in Sombart's analysis (he considers race only in relation to the immigration of ethnic Europeans rather than referencing the earlier forced migration of Black Africans), Black emancipation still offers a model for the formation of a third party, a socialist one that would be constituted by a diverse coalition of workers, united under the common cause of fighting capitalist exploitation:

> It might still be said that what one party managed to do using the battle cry of "Emancipating the Black Slaves" should be attainable by a party today, even in harder circumstances, when it has proclaimed the much more powerful and comprehensive slogan of "Emancipating the White Slaves from the Fetters of Capitalism" and of "Emancipating the Proletariat." If it really were possible to unite the broad sections of the working population on this program and in that way to awaken their class consciousness, it seems to me that no election machine, however complicated, and no monopoly of the major parties, however longstanding, would halt such a triumphant march.[4]

While Sombart imagines expanding the "battle cry" of abolition to include white workers and, more broadly, the proletariat, he insists on the difficulty of another party emerging today, noting that this effort would have to take place in even "harder circumstances" than in the past. These "harder circumstances" include a labor context in which coalitions among workers are now more difficult—because capital has mostly succeeded in dividing its workers and because party discipline is stronger and more established than it was in the mid-nineteenth century—and not as inclusive as abolition's effort to join the emancipation of Black slaves with other nonslavery interests. The context for this additional difficulty follows from the claim he makes in his previous paragraph that "at the time of the rise of the Republican Party, whose beginnings go back to 1854, conditions were considerably more favorable to the emergence of third parties."[5] If he suggests that the conditions were more favorable in 1854 for the battle cry of "Emancipating the Black Slaves," he certainly has the Kansas-Nebraska Act of 1854 in mind. This act allowed for the possibility that slavery could be extended into territories that previously had banned it (each territory now could decide the issue of slavery on the basis of popular sovereignty). Its passage led to bitter and intense debates over slavery in the United States, and many historians believe that this was the single most important factor leading to the Civil War. Marx himself, in a letter to Engels from July 1, 1861, writes that "the present war should actually be dated" from "the Kansas affair."[6] As Sombart notes, the Northern Whigs—who opposed the Kansas-Nebraska Act—reorganized themselves with other nonslavery interests to become the Republican Party. The success of this new party's emergence depended, he suggests, on: (1) the mobilization of the language of slavery in relation to white workers and the proletariat (this appropriation moves the rhetoric away from its origins in the struggle against chattel slavery and, generalizing it now to include "white slaves," risks minimizing, and even erasing, the devastating violence of anti-Black racism and its historical specificity in the antebellum period)[7]; and (2) the possibility that socialism in the United States would rely on the mobilization of abolitionist rhetoric, which, in turn, points to the possibility that abolitionism already was a form of socialism. We will return to this second point in a later discussion of Raya Dunayevskaya, who makes a similar argument—that abolitionism allowed for the possibility of imagining a socialist movement in America—but, for now, we wish to emphasize what Sombart misses here: that the force of Black emancipation, in its historical specificity, already contains the broad political force of a socialism capable of including a multiracial coalition of workers. In other words, although Sombart proposes a more "comprehensive" workers' coalition project, his study's overall neglect of the capitalist exploitation of Black populations in fact reduces the scope of his proposal by calling for an emancipation that effectively bypasses race—and its ontological, political, and historical force. Even if race is not entirely absent from Sombart's study, his marginalization and at times even erasure of Black workers suggests a refusal to pursue what would otherwise be the most evident corroboration of his statistical research: American workers of almost all ethnic backgrounds fare better economically and socially precisely when compared with disfranchised Black Americans, a comparison that, especially in the America of which he is writing, reveals the racism that sustains the illusion of white upward mobility and that keeps socialism from thriving in the United States.

This is especially surprising since Sombart was certainly aware of the centrality of race in America. In the same year that he published *Why Is There No Socialism in the United States?*, he also published Du Bois's essay "Die Negerfrage in den Vereinigten Staaten" ("The Negro Question in the United States") in *Archiv für Sozialwissenschaft und Sozialpolitik*, the journal which he edited with Max Weber and Edgar Jaffé.[8] In his essay, Du Bois insists on the irreducible relation between capitalism and an American caste system: "[i]t would have been strange if in the striving toward a new and powerful economic development a new stratum of people had not been suppressed and burdened, thus preparing the way for a new caste difference. In America, too, this happened, and the suppressed class was the Negro slaves." He goes on to detail the defeating labor conditions of Black "croppers" in the American South, who are "condemned to chronic bankruptcy"[9] by a legal and social system that makes it impossible for them to ever accrue any surplus or to participate in a capitalist economy without being instrumentalized, commodified, and dehumanized. He also argues that the living and labor conditions of the "black belt" are the direct cause of the massive exodus of Black populations to the northern cities, who flee in an attempt to experience what Sombart sees as the American working class's upward mobility, even if this yearning is often complicit with the system they wish to escape.

It is only by putting Sombart's and Du Bois's studies together that a more complete picture of American capitalism's inescapable relation to race begins to emerge. Both Sombart and Du Bois: (1) emphasize the critical role of workers' unions in the fight for improved working conditions, but Du Bois emphasizes the failures of these unions in relation to Black workers; (2) are equally alarmed by the increase in voter suppression laws, but Du Bois calls attention to the way in which these laws disproportionately affect Black citizens; and (3) wish to establish socialist coalitions to counter the inertias of capitalism, but Sombart's puzzling dismissal of race falls short of Du Bois's more inclusive and multiracial endeavor. Taken together, these concerns make Jameson's own parenthetical comment on race all the more salient. Du Bois pays particular attention to the early ideals of racial integration in organizations like the Knights of Labor and the American Federation of Labor—organizations which initially prohibited membership to any association that excluded Black workers and whose moral and activist disintegration can be traced to their later de facto support of segregation.[10] If, Du Bois suggests, a true workers' union can only succeed if it is also antiracist, the eventual failure of American workers' unions to incorporate Black workers only makes the need for workers to overcome their racism in the name of a broad sense of solidarity all the more legible. In Du Bois's words:

> Even the white workers are not yet intelligent, ambitious, and disciplined enough to defend themselves against the powerful encroachments of organized capital. The result for them too is long working hours, low wages, child labor, and lack of protection from usury and fraud. But for the black workers the situation is aggravated, first of all by racial prejudice that wavers between the doubt and mistrust of the best white elements and the glowing hate of the worst, and secondly by the miserable economic legacy that the freedman inherited from slavery.[11]

Du Bois's emphasis on the necessity of a broad interracial coalition points to the way in which racism has historically contaminated and disassembled the struggle for just and equitable working conditions. It is only when a coalition embraces full inclusivity that it can begin to claim its political force; the price of any compromise always has been the failure of socialism.

Du Bois makes this critical point, two years after having joined the American Socialist Party, in his 1913 "Socialism and the Negro Problem":

> In the Negro problem as it presents itself in the United States, theoretical Socialism of the twentieth century meets a critical dilemma. ... Can the problem of any group of ten million be properly considered as "aside" from any program of Socialism? Can the objects of Socialism be achieved so long as the Negro is neglected? ... The Socialists face in the problem of the American Negro this question: Can a minority of any group or country be left out of the Socialistic problem? ... The essence of Social Democracy is that there shall be no excluded or exploited classes in the Socialistic state; that there shall be no man or woman so poor, ignorant or black as not to count one. Is this simply a far off ideal, or is it a possible program? I have come to believe that the test of any great movement toward social reform is the Excluded Class. Who is it that Reform does *not* propose to benefit? If you are saving dying babies, whose babies are you going to let die? If you are feeding the hungry, what folk are you (regretfully, perhaps, but none the less truly) going to let starve? If you are making a juster division of wealth, what people are you going to permit at present to remain in poverty? If you are giving all men votes (not only in the "political" but also in the economic world) what class of people are you going to allow to remain disfranchised? ... The Negro Problem then is the great test of the American Socialist. The Socialist party finds itself in this predicament: if it acquiesces in race hatred, it has a

chance to turn the tremendous power of Southern white radicalism toward its own party; if it does not do this, it becomes a "party
of the Negro," with its growth South and North decidedly checked.
There are signs that the Socialist leaders are going to accept the
chance of getting hold of the radical South whatever its cost. This
paper is written to ask such leaders: After you have gotten the radical South and paid the price which they demand, will the result
be Socialism?[12]

From Du Bois's perspective, the responsibility for why socialism has not taken root in America lies also within socialism
itself—in its strategic refusal to incorporate Blacks into its ranks, a
refusal that corresponds to its willingness to further its project at
the expense of Black citizens, something that Jameson registers,
if only parenthetically. This refusal marks a complicity between
socialism and capitalism. As he puts it twenty years later: "[n]o
revolt of a white proletariat could be started if its object was to
make black workers their economic, political and social equals."
"It is for this reason," he adds, "that American socialism for fifty
years has been dumb on the Negro problem, and the communists
cannot even get a respectful hearing in America unless they begin
by expelling Negroes."[13] He further elaborates this complicity in
his 1931 essay "The Negro and Communism":

> Socialists and Communists attempted to show the Negro that
> his interest lies with that of white labor. That kind of talk to the
> American Negro is like a red flag to a bull. Throughout the his-
> tory of the Negro in America, white labor has been the black
> man's enemy, his oppressor, his red murderer. ... Socialists and
> Communists explain this easily: white labor in its ignorance and
> poverty has been misled by propaganda of white capital, whose
> policy is to divide labor into classes, races and unions and pit one
> against the other. There is an immense amount of truth in this
> explanation: Newspapers, social standards, race pride, competi-
> tion for jobs, all work to set white against black. But white American
> laborers are not fools. And with few exceptions the more intelligent
> they are, the higher they rise, the more efficient they become, the
> more determined they are to keep Negroes under their heels. ...
> Whatever ideals white labor today strives for in America, it would
> surrender nearly every one before it would recognize a Negro as
> a man.[14]

If Du Bois understands that capitalism consolidates its economic power, nullifies universal suffrage, and bribes white
workers with high wages and the lure of wealth and opportunity through different means of propaganda, he also declares

that none of these mechanisms can be disentangled from what he calls "race antagonism and labor group rivalry."[15] In response, he calls for a pluralized and collective formation, a coalition that would subsume this antagonism and rivalry by undoing the logic of identity that makes them possible. This coalition acknowledges the shared class interests that antagonism attempts to obscure by privileging division over a relationality that Du Bois intensifies, multiplies, and expands.

Like Marx, Luxemburg, and Benjamin, Du Bois makes it clear that the political potential of the "vanquished" can only emerge once their massiveness has overtaken the particular interests that present themselves as incompatible with one another. In Du Bois's workers' coalition model, the relationality and entanglement of a proletariat class that is even more vast than it may realize goes beyond the cliché of a strength in numbers in order to signal a political strength that can only result from the massification of a shared force. This force begins with the excluded and expands in the direction of those who do not even realize they are excluded (not just from the right to their labor but from the moral force that comes from taking responsibility for acts that remain complicit with the monstrosity of capitalism).

Reading Du Bois today—and reading Du Bois reading the entanglement of race and capitalism, especially after his deep engagement with Marx, beginning soon after the Russian Revolution—is to recognize the kind of painful repetition his work never ceases to register. The continued resonance of his writings confirms the endurance of forms of racism, all of which remain inscribed at every level of the capitalist system that requires them. As is the case with Sombart's wealth of sociological data and the sociologist's tendentious interpretation of it, Du Bois's texts give further evidence that, even if this entanglement can be extensively and accurately documented, it can still remain obscured, unread, and largely ignored. Du Bois's entire career as a writer, thinker, and activist can be read as so many efforts to find a language that can interrupt this violent system of erasure. He never ceases to experiment with different mediums, disciplines, and languages to express the unimaginable toll of racism in America, and he does so in order to gather and mobilize a massive wealth of evidence that remains unseen despite, or precisely because of, its vastness and pervasiveness.

To put it another way: the reflexivity of Du Bois's writing and thinking reveals a relentless effort to find a form that can match the experiential, temporal, and ontological complexity of Black life in America. This form—necessarily shifting in its shape from one work to another, as it recirculates and recontextualizes particular traits and even sentences—would uncover not just defeats but, more importantly, the traces of a collective historical agency, of an extraordinary political force that, in its movement, creates an archive that, saturated with grief, loss, and a devastating and at times crippling despair, is still filled with resilience, possibility, and hope. Such an archive, however, can appear only in fragments that are temporally multidirectional—appearing in innumerable broken and displaced narrative lines—and that demand a continued formal and conceptual creativity capable of expressing the *Erlebnis* of a people in search of a language that will neither instrumentalize nor commodify their being, or their movement.

This creativity already is legible in profoundly moving ways in Du Bois's contributions to the 1900 Exposition Universelle in Paris. His curatorial collaboration in "The Exhibit of American Negroes" relies on different mediums of visualization and visibility in order to present and reconceptualize the "Negro problem." One of the first displays in the exhibition includes a line that had appeared in 1899 and would continue to circulate through several of his later texts, becoming one of his most emblematic sentences: "The problem of the twentieth century is the problem of the color line." This line—echoing and citing the language of Frederick Douglass—not only marks the social and economic divides established by slavery, segregation, and colonization but also the racialization that emerges from a systemic insistence on white supremacy and from what came to be understood as the "Negro problem." The "Negro problem" was, on the one hand, a mystifying enigma—what Nahum Chandler has called "a problem for thought"[16]—and, on the other, a judgment on the Negro's inferiority that required and justified his or her enslavement or at least subjugation. Even more, in the words of Frederick Hoffman's 1896 *Race Traits and the Tendencies of the American Negro*, the Negro problem was "a hopeless problem"—a perspective that is itself a form of intellectual and conceptual violence related to the primal violence of slavery and its afterlives, and, in Hoffman's hands, predicting the eventual extinction of the race.[17] The Paris exhibition is meant not only to counter the racist representations of Blacks in the 1893 and 1895 Chicago and Atlanta expositions, respectively, but also the failures of Reconstruction to fully incorporate now freed Blacks into the American citizenry. The exhibition presents a persuasive account of Black accomplishments and possibilities, of their progress and promise, and, most importantly, of Black agency—and mobilizes all these against the white supremacist democracy that, in David Levering Lewis's words, continues to consign "all black people to the shadowy margins of the national life," where their "invisibility" remains "indispensable to the identity of white people."[18]

Relying on hundreds of photographs, social surveys, data charts and graphs, maps, patents, historical documents, and more than 200 books written by African Americans to render the complexity and plurality of Black life in America, Du Bois's project can be described as a "reformist empiricist" endeavor that begins in a belief in the emancipatory power of science and documentation, and in the social impact of the massive evidence of these materials and the weight he hopes they might carry.[19] It provides a counterarchive that challenges the long history of racist hierarchies and classifications that work to maintain white supremacy over Black populations, and especially the late nineteenth-century "race science" that serves to justify this supremacy. The exhibition relies on the science of sociology but—recognizing the limits of sociology—also on other forms of evidence which, together, promise to be the antidote to the demonstrably false claims of the so-called "science" of scientific racism. The more than 350 photographs that Du Bois includes in the exhibition, for example—mostly portraits of middle-class Blacks, a number of whom are pale skinned and even blonde—function as part of the counterarchive he presents in order to challenge the long legacies of racist taxonomies whose aim is to define racial identities and reinforce racial hierarchies at the turn of the century. In this way, Du Bois emphasizes the role of representation in the construction of identity and history and, in offering different representations of Black lives, creates a set of strategies that can counter and disrupt racial identification, and even the very idea of racial categorization altogether. As Shawn Michelle Smith notes, "[b]oth in method and content the American Negro Exhibit argued for the superior intellect and strength of character of a people who could make such advances just decades after emancipation, and in the face of segregation and devastating discrimination." Against the "vision of scientifically legitimized white supremacism," she adds, "Du Bois wields his own science in the Georgia Negro studies. He denaturalizes the color line, wrenching it from biology and biological explanations, to relocate it back in the terrain of social history, economics, and global politics."[20]

Already in *The Philadelphia Negro* of 1899, Du Bois used visual materials, in particular black-and-white charts and graphs, to

185

present the status of Black Philadelphians in relation and in contrast to the city's white population.[21] It is remarkable, however, how much more daring and experimental the 1900 color charts are than the charts and graphs he used just one year earlier—not simply in terms of design, color, and composition but also in the instability of the colors across the set of charts. Whereas the visual materials in *The Philadelphia Negro* are entirely in black and white—Du Bois reverses the valence of these two colors by associating black with white populations and white with black ones, but the colors' significance stays fixed within their new assignation—the colors of the later charts change their reference from one chart to the next and have to be read idiomatically in relation to the particular circumstances each chart maps and presents. Emphasizing the contingency, situatedness, and relationality of the colors requires a mode of reading that works against identification—and not simply because the charts are already abstractions of historical processes, movements, and shifting populations—and, in doing so, reinforces Du Bois's wish to displace the misidentifications that have governed the perception of the Negro in general, something that he further reinforces by pluralizing the mediums he incorporates into the project. The entire exhibition—with all its different materials from different moments and different places—can be viewed as an intervention not simply in relation to the then dominant ways of representing race and racial difference but also to the act of reading itself, an act without which, Du Bois believes, racism would not exist but also could not be resisted. The possibility of transforming prejudices against the Negro depends on the possibility of transforming the way we read. This reading requires a plurality of lenses—a refusal to read through a single lens, such as the lens of sociology in Du Bois's initial case—that keeps both the reader and his or her subjects and objects in motion.

Du Bois's extraordinary commitment—legible in the care with which he oversees the collective artistic production and design of the series of proto-modernist color charts and infographics included in the exhibition—points to his sense that sociology is unable to push forward his activist agenda by itself. It has to be joined with other practices and disciplines—in this case, with the visual arts. Du Bois's color charts enlist the power of striking and unexpected designs that far exceed the requirements of a simple delivery of data to his audience; as when he later turns to writing fiction to convey the devastation and hope of Black lives, he works here to capture his audience through an artistic rendering of both the relentless experience of racism in America and the progress that Blacks have nevertheless still made. His representation of data hopes to reach what Benjamin calls the "graphic regions of eccentric figurativeness" (*OWS*, 456–457). Take, for instance, the color chart that presents a tightly coiled red spiral that hypnotically unfurls around a numeric abstraction, "734,952," with an intensity that attempts to apprehend the massive exodus of Black rural populations, the dispersion of communities, the uprootedness of migration, and the dangers of spiraling out, unhinged, into the unknown. In the hands of Du Bois and his collaborators, the spiral becomes a narrative of at least one feature of Black life, or rather its visual abstraction. The combination of this centrifugal shape with the broken horizontal lines of the chart to which it is connected, and which represent the splitting of rural communities into urban locations of different sizes, each given a different color (green, blue, yellow), further accentuates the intensity of the spiral as a visual emblem. Red is the predominant color here, as it is in several of the charts, and, in this instance, it references the number of Blacks living in rural areas, all potentially looking toward the possibility of wending their way to more urban centers.

However, the charts exhibited in Paris employ a wide range of visual protocols and are not limited to proto-modernist geometric figures. The chart depicting the increase in the value of Black-owned land in Georgia stands out through its use of iconography rather than abstraction. The chart presents six drawings of burlap sacks, increasing in size in five-year increments from top to bottom (from 1875 to 1899), with a dollar amount inscribed on them, marking the value of land owned by Blacks in Georgia, and a year that serves as a caption. The visual language of the chart signals the sheer materiality of money through its inanimate "body" trapped in a heavy burlap bag, as if to highlight the social and physical effects of capitalism's foundational abstraction.[22] Each of the 63 charts in the exhibition can be read in its particularity, but, collectively, their aim, with their wide-ranging visual strategies, is to maximize the social impact and communicability of data that, if read and understood widely, would speak for itself.

But, as Du Bois knew well, no matter how imaginatively rendered, no matter how much "history writes itself in figures and diagrams,"[23] data can never capture the relationality and experimentalism of Black social life. While Du Bois's infographics can be understood as technologies that literally visualize the color line, they too fail in the end because they cannot express or contain the experience of racism in everyday life. In his capacity as

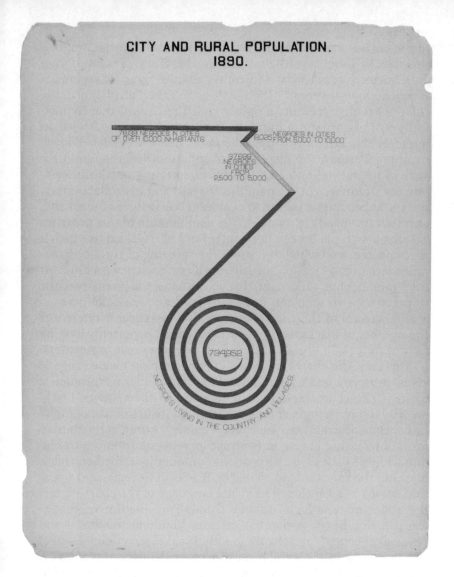

W. E. B. Du Bois, "City and Rural Population 1890," 1900

W. E. B. Du Bois, "Value of Land Owned by Georgia Negroes," 1900

one of the curators of the Paris exhibition—because of lack of funding, or at least for his passage—Du Bois makes the transatlantic voyage to Europe in steerage, while the graphs and prints travel ahead of him.[24] This small but significant detail (with its poignant echo of the Middle Passage, even if this time in reverse) cannot be represented in the sociological data of his charts. When Du Bois delivers his talk "Sociology Hesitant" in 1905, he calls attention precisely to the insufficiency of data and statistical analysis to record and convey the grief, loss, and daily forms of displacement and dispossession that racism produces and perpetuates. He insists instead on the "rhythms" and "incalculability" of human action.[25] His far-reaching critique of sociological positivism hinges on the question of collective historical agency and exceeds the bounds of sociology as a science of the calculable. This is why sociology must hesitate, pause, move slowly in front of what cannot be captured or comprehended. What cannot be fully counted and measured is the immeasurable anti-Black sentiment in the United States, what he calls the "glowing hate" that, while always present, often explodes in more violent forms that not only punctuate the entirety of Du Bois's life but also continue unabated, still today.

This hatred and its effects become even more legible to him in April 1899 when he confronts the lynching of Sam Hose in Atlanta and then, one month later, when he experiences the death of his nineteen-month-old son Burghardt. After being accused of killing his landlord and raping the landlord's wife, Hose is tortured and mutilated by a mob before being tied to a tree and burned alive.[26] The mob cuts off pieces of his dead body as souvenirs and sends them to businesses across the state for public viewing. While walking to the *Atlanta Constitution* office to submit a statement about the increase of lynchings, Du Bois receives news that Hose's knuckles are being displayed in a local grocery store and turns back. If, in a speech to the American Academy of Political and Social Sciences in November 1897, Du Bois expresses his belief in the power of scientific investigation to replace white supremacist propaganda with truth—he declares that "true lovers of humanity can only hold higher the pure ideals of science, and continue to insist that if we would solve a problem we must study it"[27]—in the aftermath of Hose's brutal murder, he questions the capacity of science to combat the increased intensity of white supremacist violence. "There cut across the plan which I had as a scientist," he writes, "a red ray which could not be ignored." He goes on to admit that "[t]wo considerations thereafter broke in upon [his] work and eventually disrupted it: first, one could not be a calm, cool, and detached scientist while Negroes were lynched, murdered, and starved; and secondly, there was no such definite demand for scientific work of the sort [he] was doing."[28] Du Bois's sense of defeat and disillusionment is deepened when his son, after a brief bout of diphtheria, dies in May when denied proper medical care.[29] These events form part of the context in which Du Bois begins curating and producing materials for the Paris exhibition and help account for the multipronged presentation that, after experiencing the limits of science in the face of violent systemic racism, he believes is now necessary to supplement his scientific efforts.

If the exhibition is meant to demonstrate Black capacity for upward mobility in all its different forms and contexts, then the race riots of the Red Summer, almost exactly two decades later, become a startling symptom of just how terrifying Black upward mobility is to virtually any other group in America's "melting pot," and a reminder that class (or Du Bois's preferred term "caste") in America was, and still remains, racialized. As Du Bois forcefully puts it in an article for the journal *The Crisis,* entitled "Returning Soldiers," the riots of 1919 have to be understood in continuity with the democratic promises that Black soldiers had been asked to defend during World War I and that, on their return, they are themselves denied in Jim Crow America: *"We return from fighting. We return fighting.* Make way for democracy! We saved it in France, and by the Great Jehovah, we will save it in the United States of America, or know the reasons why."[30] The lawful Black resistance against the violence of white supremacist mobs was in fact led by Black veterans who had returned from a European wartime encounter in which they had represented and defended American democratic values—as, in Adriane Lentz-Smith's words, both "emblems and agents" of a democratic struggle.[31] What is most pertinent here—what structurally guarantees the racism the soldiers continue to face and against which they exert their energy—is the complicity and contiguity between war and capitalism, and the fact that slavery and racism are coordinated with capitalism. As Luxemburg points out in her 1900 *Reform or Revolution,* "war has been an indispensable feature of capitalist development" and nations are "pushed to war especially as a result of their similarly advanced capitalist development."[32] Luxemburg's statement needs to be contextualized within her critique of orthodox readings of Marx, in which Marx is presumed to understand capitalist primitive accumulation as an early phase within capitalism's development.[33] In this critique, she rearticulates primitive accumulation as an intrinsic and ongoing feature of capital accumulation at large, a feature that is contiguous with both colonialism and war as modes of capitalist reproduction. Following Luxemburg's logic, the returning soldiers are twice victims of racialized capitalism and its need for primitive accumulation: first, as their instrumentalized agents in the war and, second, as they again become part of the exploited labor force of America's white colonial project.

W. E. B. Du Bois, Atlanta University, 1909

> To grasp the Black Dimension is to learn a new language, the language of thought, Black thought. For many, this new language will be difficult because they are hard of hearing. Hard of hearing because they are not used to this type of thought, a language which is both a struggle for freedom and the thought of freedom.
>
> —Raya Dunayevskaya, "The Black Dimension in Women's Liberation" (1975–1976)[1]

Du Bois would come increasingly close to Luxemburg's assessment in his magnum opus, *Black Reconstruction in America: An Essay toward a History of the Part which Black Folk Played in the Attempt to Reconstruct Democracy in America, 1860–1880*. There he famously argues that the slaves' general strike against slavery in the context of the Civil War is an example of Black collective agency and that it is world-historical in its importance.[2] In his reading, the Black masses of refugees escaping slave plantations transform the capitalist economy of the war into an unplanned social experiment that, unveiling and stretching the limits of American democracy, provides a model for world revolution. Emphasizing the essential role of the Black rebellion in the reconstruction of democracy in America, Du Bois—*brushing history against the grain*—challenges any heroic portrayal of the Confederacy, any effort to write the experiences of slaves and free Blacks out of the story of the war and Reconstruction, and any attempt to instrumentalize American history to guarantee the endurance of white supremacy. In the final chapter of his book, "The Propaganda of History," Du Bois traces the development of false and racist accounts of post-Civil War history in educational textbooks, academic scholarship, and popular culture. In his words, in a passage that still resonates today:

> This ... is the book basis upon which today we judge Reconstruction. In order to paint the South as a martyr to inescapable fate, to make the North the magnanimous emancipator, and to ridicule the Negro as the impossible joke in the whole development, we have in fifty years, by libel, innuendo and silence, so completely misstated and obliterated the history of the Negro in America and his relation to its work and government that today it is almost unknown.

This may be fine romance, but it is not science. It may be inspiring, but it is certainly not the truth. And beyond this it is dangerous. It is not only part foundation of our present lawlessness and loss of democratic ideals; it has, more than that, led the world to embrace and worship the color bar as social salvation and it is helping to range mankind in ranks of mutual hatred and contempt, at the summons of a cheap and false myth. (*BR*, 868)

Emphasizing the central role of Black agency in the unfolding of Reconstruction in order to counter its erasure in the annals of racist historiography, Du Bois reframes the history of Reconstruction altogether. The book is titled *Black Reconstruction* because he writes Blacks back into the history from which they have been historically effaced. He insists that they play the decisive role. In his words, his counterargument "changes, if not indeed revolutionizes, our attitude toward Reconstruction as part of democratic development in the United States."[3] As for Benjamin, what is at stake for Du Bois is the possibility of writing a materialist history that begins with the "tradition of the oppressed," with the vanquished—in this instance, the Black slave. This history would hear the clamor of the general strike and point to the slaves' emancipatory and revolutionary struggle, a struggle that, going far beyond the wish for their own liberation, has consequences, Du Bois suggests, for laborers and oppressed peoples around the globe.

Refusing to work, "downing tools," the "great labor force" of the slave slowly but irrevocably constitutes itself as a gathering historical force, a force that, as Du Bois notes, appears with the full strength of nature: "This was the beginning of the swarming of the slaves, of the quiet but unswerving determination of increasing numbers no longer to work on Confederate plantations, and to seek the freedom of the Northern army. Whenever the army marched in spite of all obstacles came the rising tide of the slaves seeking freedom" (*BR*, 82). The language he uses here—"swarming," "increasing numbers," and "the rising tide"—suggests the unbounded and uncontrollable historic force of this massive general strike, a force that comes, as he puts it, "like the great unbroken swell of the ocean before it dashes on the reefs" (ibid.).[4] The rhythms and cadences of his sentences themselves echo the trajectory of the slaves' mass movement in their flight. The half a million slaves who instinctively flee—without any certainty of the outcome of their flight, and at the greatest risk—manage to extract hope and possibility out of the hopelessness they experience in front of the most enduring and unimaginable violence. The general strike grows in numbers like the "great unbroken swell of the ocean," overwhelming everything in its path, until it hits the "reefs" of a system that strives to diffuse the strike, to absorb and recycle the fugitive slaves as different forms of labor—including soldiers, spies, laborers, and servants. Du Bois's language carries within it the long history of Black struggle that, resonating anachronistically across different historical periods, exceeds the scope of his analysis. This enduring struggle, which manifests itself in the amorphous but forward-moving unfolding of the general strike, proves capable of making or unmaking the premises of American democracy.

Du Bois presents his first thoughts on Reconstruction as early as 1901, but *Black Reconstruction* is not finished and published until 1935, in the context of the Great Depression, America's New Deal, Popular Frontism, the rise of foreign and domestic fascism, Stalinism, and the growing force of international Marxism and Black communism and antifascism (and, in relation to the red thread we are tracing, is contemporary to Benjamin's antifascist "Work of Art" essay). During the intervening three decades, Du Bois continues to experiment with a variety of forms in order to convey the historical experience of Blacks, including novels, short stories, essays, autobiographies, journalism, and, of course, sociology. If the imprint of experimentation is legible in all his writings during this period, it is most fully realized in the massive archive that is *Black Reconstruction*. There this experimentation appears in the discontinuities, repetitions, recursive structures, varied rhythms, different modes of citationality, multiple voices alongside and in his own, and the accumulation of different temporalities, geographies, and even literary and writerly genres that, together, make the book—and, we would say, even unmake it. Du Bois's act of writing becomes a measure of the difficulty of narrativizing a force of interruption. It is itself a practice of thinking, a means of enacting a mode of historiography that, remaining faithful to the disruptive power of the general strike, has profound relays with Benjamin's own protocols for writing history differently. His writing and thinking move in accordance with his sense of the incalculable unfolding of history, performing a mode of historiography that comes in the form of a juxtaposition and accumulation of archives, and this despite the racism and Jim Crow segregation that denied him access to innumerable archival collections, "[v]arious volumes of papers in the great libraries" that, as he puts it, "must have much of great interest to the historians of the American Negro" (*BR*, 870).

Nevertheless, among the things this monumental book archives—coming as it does in the form of another militant box, not unlike those overflowing and never entirely closed boxes we already have registered in Benjamin—are all the literary, historical, sociological, artistic, and political mediums he moves through and still carries forward throughout his writings. The mediated character of his writing is legible in the well-known citationality of his texts but also in the way in which even the revolutionary events he describes are mediated by his knowledge of similar events. These other events become a lens through which he reads the historical details at hand, and these details in turn become a means of reading later events. Following the logic of the book—its argument about the general strike and its consequences for the promises of Reconstruction but also the textual form this logic takes—this suggests, as Luxemburg does before him, that all revolutions are mediated forms. When Du Bois gathers as many voices as he can to convey the consequences of the multiplication and massification of the slaves' general strike, he evokes and incorporates a typology of revolution—drawing inspiration from anticolonial movements, the Haitian, French, and Russian revolutions, antifascist coalitions, and workers' movements—into *Black Reconstruction*'s archival structure. The events of 1865–1877 become a conceptual toolbox for *all* world revolutions before and after. In other words, *Black Reconstruction* is an assemblage that carries within it a visionary understanding of revolution as potentiality. Its joining of the past and the present is the textual event of the book. It dialectically embodies a form of writing history that is itself reconstructed and transformed by historical events and that activates and enacts Du Bois's conviction of the relation between texts and history—his belief in the power of texts to shape history and in the force of history to demand texts that might match it. In the same way that revolutions are mediated by other revolutions and could be said to relate to one another through dialectical forms of incorporation and expansion—Du Bois reads the slaves' general strike through the lens of the October 1917 Russian Revolution, for example, even as he sees it as a proleptic rewriting and reinterpretation of this later revolution[5]—Du Bois's text is mediated by other texts that relate to it through dialectical forms of appropriation, citation, intensification, and amplification.

Like Marx, Benjamin, and Luxemburg, his mode of writing history belongs not simply to the tradition of historical materialism, but to the most literary versions of it—which are the versions with the greatest fidelity to Marx himself.[6] This is especially legible in the fact that *Black Reconstruction* explicitly incorporates Marxian categories—among others, the dictatorship of the proletariat and the general strike—but in a way that, in its movement and language, in its rhetorical flourishes and imaginative recourse to literary modes of presentation, enacts Du Bois's own "experiment of Marxism."[7] If he mobilizes and recasts these terms through a labor of reading and writing, it is because he understands "Marx" as the name of a set of readerly and writerly strategies for doing political work. That Du Bois's text is mediated throughout by Marx is well known,[8] but the degree to which he moves Marx's terms to their limits—against the orthodoxies of Marxism and the Communist Party and in a way that would have given Marx great pleasure—remains less visible. In a 1935 letter to George Streator, declaring his sense of the mobility of Marx's own texts—their resistance to fixity of any kind—and marking a distinction between Marx and Marxism, he writes:

> I believe in Karl Marx. I am an out and out opponent of modern capitalistic labor exploitation. I believe in the ultimate triumph of socialism in a reasonable time, and I mean by socialism, the ownership of capital and machines by the state, and equality of income. But I do not believe in the verbal inspiration of the Marxian scriptures.[9]

As he writes *Black Reconstruction*, Du Bois is reading Marx intensely. He reads *Capital* and *The Communist Manifesto*, and we can assume he also read *The Eighteenth Brumaire*, and several of the articles Marx wrote on the American civil crisis. He reads *The Communist Manifesto* with his students at Atlanta University and, in 1932, he develops courses on "Karl Marx and the Negro" and the "Economic History of the Negro." In 1933, he writes an article for *The Crisis* entitled "Karl Marx and the Negro." He states that, at a moment in which "the world is so largely turning toward the Marxian philosophy ... [t]his little article seeks merely to bring before American Negroes the fact that Karl Marx knew and sympathized with their problem."[10] Although Du Bois points to the growing influence of Marxist politics in the 1930s, he moves quickly from his contemporary moment to emphasize Marx's stance against slavery in the United States, citing the letters Marx wrote to President Abraham Lincoln in the early 1860s, and pointing to Marx's sense of the signal importance of the slaves' rebellion. In a letter of January 11, 1860, Marx writes to Engels: "In my opinion, the most momentous thing happening in the world today is the slave movement."[11]

As Cedric Robinson famously notes in his landmark 1983 *Black Marxism: The Making of the Black Radical Tradition*: "[t]he development, organization, and expansion of capitalist society pursued essentially racial directions, so too did social ideology. As a material force, then, it could be expected that racialism would inevitably permeate the social structures emergent from capitalism." He goes on to say that he uses "the term 'racial capitalism' to refer to this development and to the subsequent structure as a historical agency."[12] If he then suggests that Marx and Engels underestimate the material force of racial ideology on proletarian consciousness and conflate the English working class with the workers of the world—he elsewhere claims that the "Black Radical Tradition emerged in 'the belly of the beast' ... as a response to the denial of historical agency within Marx"[13]—Du Bois turns to Marx precisely because he understands that this theorist of revolution and liberation is a powerful resource for thinking about racial capitalism, the world-historical agency of Black masses, and the period of Reconstruction in particular. As he puts it, "[t]he record of the Negro worker during Reconstruction presents an opportunity to study inductively the Marxian theory of the state" (*BR*, 459). What is most important to him, however, is Marx's understanding of the role of Black agency in the unfolding of the Civil War, an understanding that develops from Marx's own massive labor of reading and study. As Du Bois notes, "[t]he thing about [Marx] that must be emphasized now [i]s his encyclopedic knowledge. No modern student of industry probably ever equaled his almost unlimited reading and study."[14] *Black Reconstruction* is framed by Marx's Civil War writings, sometimes explicitly and other times more discreetly, but, despite the debates over when Du Bois turns to Marx, he already would have been introduced to Marx's ideas in his late teens by his early mentor, Timothy Thomas Fortune, who, in his 1884 *Black and White: Land, Labor, and Politics in the South*, offers the first Black Marxist reading of the history of the relations among race, capital, labor, and slavery, and, in particular, the history of the Civil War and Reconstruction.[15]

Marx himself begins studying the Civil War in 1861. He gathers his information from histories of American economics and law, writings and memoirs of leading political figures, and the British and American Unionist and Confederate press, most of which he reads in the British Museum Library. His work on the Civil War is composed mainly of writings he publishes in 1861 and 1862, in *The New York Daily Tribune* and in *Die Presse*, and of his correspondence with Engels and others until the end of the 1870s.[16]

Although he often is accused of viewing the struggle against racism solely through the lens of class struggle, Marx's Civil War writings make clear that racism motivates class struggle and also corresponds to what sustains and maintains capital itself. He insists on the centrality of slavery to the conflict in his October 1861 article for *Die Presse* entitled "The North American Civil War." There, writing against the weekly and daily papers of the London press, which, he writes, repeat "the same litany" on the war—that it is a "tariff war," that it "does not touch the question of slavery, and in fact turns on the Northern desire for sovereignty," and that it is "a war for the preservation of the Union by force"—he declares that the "whole movement" of the war rests "on the *slave question*," on "whether the twenty million free men of the North should subordinate themselves any longer to an oligarchy of 300,000 slaveholders; whether the vast Territories of the Republic should become planting grounds for free states or for slavery; finally, whether the national policy of the Union should take armed propaganda for slavery in Mexico and Central and South America as its motto."[17] Just a couple of weeks later, in an article titled "The Civil War in the United States" that argues against the "principle that only certain races are capable of freedom"—an argument that demonstrates his understanding that there can be no revolution against capitalist violence that is not also a revolution against racism—Marx insists that "[t]he present struggle between the South and the North is ... nothing but a conflict between two social systems, the system of slavery and the system of free labor," a war whose principle should be the elimination of "the root of the evil—*slavery itself*."[18] Documenting the resistance to abolishing slavery—resulting from the complicity between Southern slaveholding and Northern industrialization and the racism that subtends it—he traces a series of mass movements, all of which prepare the ground for the slaves' general strike in 1862. Delineating the different winds of world history that are ultimately moving in the direction of abolition, even if disparately and in accordance with shifting vectors, he points especially to: (1) the popular resistance against "the attempt to transform Kansas into a *slave Territory* by force of arms" in 1854; (2) the emergence of the Republican Party and its reinforcement of the abolitionist movement; (3) the opposition to the Dred Scott decision of 1857, which again identified the slave as property; (4) the raid on Harper's Ferry led by John Brown in October 1859; and (5) the Black revolt in Bolivar, Missouri in December 1859 in response to Harper's Ferry. He reads these events as "unmistakable signs of

Northern antagonistic agencies" that, first slowly, and then cumulatively and with increasing momentum, gather enough strength to "turn the balance of power."[19]

If, as Marx notes in relation to Lincoln's election in 1860, "the bombardment of Fort Sumter gave the signal for the opening of the war" and "the election victory of the Republican party of the North, the election of Lincoln as President, gave the signal for secession,"[20] in 1864 the "Address of the International Working Men's Association to Lincoln" (which Marx drafted, but which is signed by the 57 members of the Central Council of the International) describes the consequences of Lincoln's reelection in this way: "[i]f resistance to the Slave Power was the reserved watchword of your first election, the triumphant war cry of your reelection is, Death to Slavery." That the letter is signed by a mass of signatories rather than by a single author—even though Marx seems to have been responsible for writing the letter—and that it congratulates the American people instead of Lincoln is worth noting. It suggests Marx's understanding that neither Lincoln nor he are, strictly speaking, "individuals," but rather, in Jameson's words, "social forms," inscribed within a network of relations which diminishes their force at the same time that it increases it. For Marx, even Lincoln's Emancipation Proclamation is possible only because of the force of the slaves' rebellion and migration and because of the "military necessity" of additional soldiers, which pressured Lincoln further into an abolitionist direction. The decision to issue the Proclamation did not belong to Lincoln alone, in other words, which is why it could even be said to be impersonal or, more properly, displaced from any sense of intentionality, even in regard to its primary focus on the slave question in the United States. The letter itself makes clear that the war against slavery and racism offers an emancipatory promise for workers far beyond just America:

> From the commencement of the titanic American strife the working men of Europe felt instinctively that the star-spangled banner carried the destiny of their class. ... When an oligarchy of 300,000 slaveholders dared to inscribe for the first time in the annals of the world "slavery" on the banner of Armed Revolt, when on the very spots where hardly a century ago the idea of one great Democratic Republic had first sprung up, whence the first Declaration of the Rights of Man was issued, and the first impulse given to the European revolution of the eighteenth century; when on those very spots counterrevolution, with systematic thoroughness, gloried in rescinding "the ideas entertained at the time for the formation

of the old constitution," and maintained slavery to be a "beneficent institution," indeed, the only solution of the great problem of "the relation of labor to capital," and cynically proclaimed property in man "the cornerstone of the new edifice,"—then the working classes of Europe understood at once ... that the slaveholders' rebellion was to sound the tocsin for a general holy crusade of property against labor, and that for the men of labor, with their hopes for the future, even their past conquests were at stake in the tremendous conflict on the other side of the Atlantic. Everywhere they bore therefore patiently the hardships imposed upon them by the cotton crisis, opposed enthusiastically the pro-slavery intervention ... and, from most parts of Europe, contributed their quota of blood to the good cause.

While the working men, the true political powers of the North, allowed slavery to defile their own republic, while before the Negro, mastered and sold without his concurrence, they boasted it the highest prerogative of the white-skinned laborer to sell himself and choose his own master, they were unable to attain the true freedom of labor, or to support their European brethren in their struggle for emancipation; but this barrier to progress has been swept off by the red sea of civil war.

The working men of Europe ... consider it an earnest of the epoch to come that it fell to the lot of Abraham Lincoln, the single-minded son of the working class, to lead his country through the matchless struggle for the rescue of an enchained race and the reconstruction of a social world.[21]

There is much to say about this rather remarkable document—and the fact that Du Bois cites the entirety of the letter in *Black Reconstruction* (*BR*, 264–265)—but, for our purposes here, we will simply point to its emphasis on the war as a war against slavery and to its suggestion that the anti-Black racism of "white-skinned" workers has been a "barrier to progress," to the "true freedom of labor," that has had to be "swept off by the red sea of civil war." These details are linked to the possibility of progress for the international class struggle against capital itself, a possibility that depends on an understanding and overcoming of the racist structure of capitalism. After Lincoln's assassination and Andrew Johnson's assumption of the Presidency—and, in particular, his complicity with former slaveowners and his vetoes of all efforts at Radical Reconstruction—this possibility seemed less and less likely. In addition to a letter that Marx writes in the name of the International to Johnson in May 1865—to which Johnson unsurprisingly never replied—the London Conference of the International voted to send a third letter to America in September of the same year, but this time addressed "To the people of the United States of America." First congratulating the American people on the end of the war, the preservation of the Union, and the eradication of slavery, the letter closes with a warning about the dangers of not realizing a full and radical Reconstruction:

> Injustice to a section of your people has produced such direful results, let that cease. Let your citizens of to-day be declared free and equal, without reserve. If you fail to give them citizens' rights, while you demand citizens' duties, there will yet remain a struggle for the future which may again stain your country with your people's blood. The eyes of Europe and the world are fixed upon your efforts at re-construction, and enemies are ever ready to sound the knell of the downfall of republican institutions when the slightest chance is given. We warn you then, as brothers in the common cause, to remove every shackle from freedom's limb.[22]

It is not surprising that Du Bois is so interested in these documents and in Marx's Civil War writings in general—he refers to this last letter as a "bold" declaration "over the signature of Marx" (*BR*, 427).[23] He sees in the set of letters—all of which carry Marx's imprint, but, again, Marx as a figure for a broader coalition and movement—not simply the extraordinary significance of the Civil War for the ending of slavery and the need to realize the promises it has opened up but also the consequences of not acting decisively to eliminate the legacy of slavery altogether. This concern remains because of his sense of the force of white supremacy— including its capacity to fuel the white laborer's racism—and its ruinous consequences for democracy. "The upward moving of white labor was betrayed into wars for profit based on color caste," he writes, insisting on the racialized character of capitalism:

> the plight of the white working class throughout the world today is directly traceable to Negro slavery in America, on which modern commerce and industry was founded, and which persisted to threaten free labor until it was partially overthrown in 1863. The resulting color caste founded and retained by capitalism was adopted, forwarded and approved by white labor, and resulted in subordination of colored labor to white profits the world over. Thus, the majority of the world's laborers, by the insistence of white labor, became the basis of a system of industry which ruined democracy and showed its perfect fruit in World War and Depression. (*BR*, 40)

Already in his 1847 *The Poverty of Philosophy*, Marx links the enslavement of Blacks to the history of capitalist development, arguing that it is a condition for world trade and large-scale industry. As he puts it:

> Slavery is an economic category like any other. Thus it also has its two sides. ... Needless to say we are dealing only with direct slavery, with Negro slavery in Surinam, in Brazil, in the Southern States of North America.
>
> Direct slavery is just as much the pivot of bourgeois industry as machinery, credits, etc. Without slavery you have no cotton; without cotton you have no modern industry. It is slavery that gave the colonies their value; it is the colonies that created world-trade that is the pre-condition of large-scale industry. Thus slavery is an economic category of the greatest importance.
>
> Without slavery North America, the most progressive of countries, would be transformed into a patriarchal country. Wipe North America off the map of the world, and you will have anarchy—the complete decay of modern commerce and civilization. Cause slavery to disappear and you will have wiped America off the map of nations.
>
> Thus slavery, because it is an economic category, has always existed among the institutions of the peoples. Modern nations have been able only to disguise slavery in their own countries, but they have imposed it without disguise upon the New World.[24]

That slavery's place within capital is racialized is explicitly noted in a passage from the "Working Day" chapter in *Capital*—a chapter that Marx adds to his book after his consideration of events unfolding in the United States in the aftermath of the Civil War and a passage that Du Bois would have known well. As Marx notes, "[i]n the United States of America, every independent workers' movement was paralyzed as long as slavery disfigured a part of the republic. Labor in a white skin cannot emancipate itself where it is branded in a black skin."[25] This last sentence already appears in a letter that Marx sends to François Lafargue—the father of Paul Lafargue, the future husband of Marx's daughter, Laura—on November 12, 1866.[26] Like Benjamin and Du Bois, Marx often recirculates his language from one place to another. In this instance—an instance that points to processes of historical transmission and repetition that are indissociable from the activity of reading and writing—Marx's self-citation asks us to think these two moments together, to register the way in which the events of the Civil War and Reconstruction move him to reformulate and even rewrite certain parts of *Capital*. Anticipating Du Bois, Marx reminds us that the white laborer's emancipation depends on his or her solidarity with the post-Civil War Black struggle, with the work of Reconstruction.[27] He argues that the enslavement of Blacks relies on a color line and that the project of the emancipation of labor requires the overcoming of this color line—in this instance, the overcoming of the branding of Black skin, not simply in the literal sense of prohibiting the burning of Black flesh as a means of punishment or identification but also in the sense of branding Black labor as inferior to white labor.[28] In the latter case, branding implies a process whereby Blacks are declared inferior in order to justify their enslavement and subjugation. Marx makes this point explicitly in his 1849 *Wage Labor and Capital*. In his words,

> What is a Negro slave? A man of the black race. The one explanation is as good as the other.
> A Negro is a Negro. He only becomes a *slave* in certain relations. A cotton-spinning Jenny is a machine for spinning cotton. It becomes *capital* only in certain relations. Torn from these relationships it is no more capital than *gold* in itself is *money* or sugar the *price* of sugar.[29]

According to Marx, racial capitalism equates being Black with being a slave. The equivalence is not a natural one; it is the result of the requirements of certain economic and social relations, of an emerging capitalism that forces Blacks into slavery ("he only becomes a *slave* in certain relations"), and demands this process of dehumanization. Although slavery is inseparable from the various forms of violence that support it—all of which have devastating material and bodily consequences—it relies, Marx suggests, on a concept of racial difference that is as constructed as it is brutally destructive.

It is here that we can return more directly to Du Bois, since he too believes that race is a concept, a construct, a sociopolitical projection that gathers its force "only in certain relations." He confirms this in the subtitle to his 1940 autobiography, *Dusk of Dawn: Toward an Autobiography of a Race Concept*. To tell the story of his life, he suggests, is to tell the story of a race concept, since his identity cannot be dissociated from his inscription within this racialized conceptual framework. Throughout his life, Du Bois works relentlessly to convey "the strange meaning of being black." His dedication to this task is evident in the immensity of the research—the "almost unlimited reading and study"—to which he devotes his life in the name of countering the violence of white supremacy. This is why, we might say, the experimentalism of *Black Reconstruction* is as much related to his argument about the mass strike—and the way in which he presents it—as it is to his engagement with the way in which Marx works, the way in which he approaches a subject through reading and writing. As C. L. R. James notes in his 1971 lectures on *The Black Jacobins*—a book he writes while reading *Black Reconstruction*—Du Bois reads extensively on the history of revolution and, reading this history through Marx, "he [goes] further in regard to the demonstration of the essential verities of Marxism than anybody except perhaps Lenin and Marx himself."[30]

Black Reconstruction is a historical materialist text and, as Du Bois argues, the self-organizing of Black and white workers is an experiment of Marxism *before* their consciousness of either Marxist ideas or the Russian Revolution itself. If Du Bois imagines another means of writing history, he finds his model in Marx as a theorist of revolution—but a theorist of revolution who understands the labor of reading and writing at the heart of the revolutionary project. For both Marx and Du Bois, this labor is inseparable from its engagement with historical events. Their language works not by the accumulation of multiple associations around a strongly held center, but through the mobilization of terms from one shifting context to another. This mobilization names an engagement with changing historical and political relations, an intensification of a transformation in progress, wherein language works to alter and set in motion the shifting domains of history and politics and the historical and the political leave their traces in language. In the same way that the American Civil War transforms *Capital* as Marx is writing it, Du Bois's reading of the slave general strike is mediated by the Russian Revolution. In the midst of the Civil War, slaves and poor white workers following the slaves' growing momentum abandon the plantations just as, in the midst of war, the Russian peasantry rebel and abandon the army and, in doing so, mark the beginnings of revolution. Considering the period from the perspective of the fugitive slaves' politically marked flight—he repeatedly refers to the slave as a "refugee" in order to emphasize the slave's exclusion, illegibility, and experience of nonbelonging in both the North and the South—Du Bois insists on the relation between slavery and the capitalist world system. The moment the slave puts his tools down and refuses to work, he shatters not only the slave system but "racial capitalism" at large. It is important to register the force of what happens here, since Du Bois does not describe just any general strike. Indeed, the moment he describes a general strike *enacted by slaves*, the moment slaves "down their tools" and this act gets massified, he shatters the concept of the general strike—not only because the slaves' strike is, as he notes, unplanned and unorganized, but especially because the slave is not just a worker but also and above all a commodity and, as a commodity, condenses different moments and features of capitalism.[31] If Du Bois's language works to change language—here the language of the general strike—it does so in order to change much more than language. Because it seeks to materialize something new and singular, it potentially can change the relations in which we live. For him, the slave is a figure of primitive accumulation, commodification, exchange and use value, the money form, and, because the slave economy serves not just America but Europe and the rest of the globe, a universal equivalent. When the slaves refuse to work, the entire slave system—the entire logic of capital—experiences an existential crisis that strikes at the core of its capacity to reproduce itself.

The slaves' mass refusal surpasses the demands of a labor strike—even if not the unmediated and massified general strike discussed by Benjamin or Luxemburg—by refusing to limit its scope to the rhythms of capitalist production and reproduction. It is in the end the slaves who understand, even if not consciously, the true ontological extent of capitalism because they are the embodiment of the racialized logic of capital, in life but also in death, and even in their living death. In Marx's words, referencing the accumulation of death that capital demands in order to sustain itself, "capital does not *live* only on labor. A lord, at once aristocratic and barbarous, it drags with it into the grave the corpses of its slaves, whole hecatombs of workers who perish in the crises."[32] Capital lives in bodies and minds and reproduces itself as an existential modality that carries within its movement a figure, here the slave, that it can never fully absorb, unless it is as a corpse or a commodity. At the same time, it is the centrality of the slave to capital and its various economies—the slave does not exist before capital, and remains the condition of possibility of primitive accumulation—that makes him or her its potential gravedigger, capable of interrupting capitalism's destructive metabolism and auguring its demise.

What is at stake in *Black Reconstruction* is the possibility of giving an account of this revolutionary event and of finding a form that can express it, reenact or reconstruct it, even if this form is undone in the process. Given the signal importance of the slaves' general strike, it is remarkable how little time Du Bois actually spends on his description of it. In the chapter he devotes to it, the event is discussed in less than five pages, with the rest of the chapter—and even the rest of the book—focusing on the events that follow from it and, in particular, on the efforts to make sense of it, to reinforce its effects or diffuse them. The entire trajectory of the book is instantiated by this event: there would be no end to the Civil War nor a period of Reconstruction had it not occurred. We could even say that the sheer size of *Black Reconstruction* corresponds to the magnitude and historical density of an event that Du Bois painstakingly attempts to unfold in his text. "When Northern armies entered the South," Du Bois explains, "they became armies of emancipation. It was the last thing they planned to be. The North did not propose to attack property. It did not propose to free slaves. This was to be a white man's war to preserve the Union" (*BR*, 70). However, because it is forced to come to terms with a spontaneous "mass movement" that emerges as the moral legitimation and the material means of successfully reorganizing the war, the North comes to understand the fugitive slaves as strategic, as the very "meat and kernel" of the war (*BR*, 78). Both the North and the South register that, already in the first year of the war, the Negro had become

> contraband of war; that is, property belonging to the enemy and valuable to the invader. And in addition to that, he became, as the South quickly saw, the key to Southern resistance. Either these four million laborers remained quietly at work to raise food for the fighters, or the fighters starved. Simultaneously, when the dream of the North for man-power produced riots, the only additional troops that the North could depend on were 200,000 Negroes, for without them, as Lincoln said, the North could not have won the war.
> But this slow, stubborn mutiny of the Negro slave was not merely a matter of 200,000 black soldiers and perhaps 300,000 other black laborers, servants, spies, and helpers. Back of this half million stood 3 ½ million more. Without their labor the South would starve. With arms in their hands, Negroes would form a fighting force which would replace every single Northern white soldier fighting listlessly and against his will with a black man fighting for freedom. (*BR*, 99–100)

Du Bois suggests that the increasingly visible push for emancipation meant that "[t]he position of the Negro was strategic. His was the only appeal which would bring sympathy from Europe, despite strong economic bonds with the South, and prevent the recognition of a Southern nation built on slavery" (*BR*, 99). That the North and the South eventually understand the Negro's critical relation to the outcome of the war accounts for their respective efforts to instrumentalize his or her movements. Du Bois underscores the contrasts and relations between the political calculations of the North, wrapped in the language of abolitionism, and those of the South, disguising exploitation with the rhetoric of paternalistic duty and care. Before either side can instrumentalize the mass of Negro fugitives, however, what Du Bois uncovers—and hopes to reactivate through the movement of his own writing—is the slaves' general strike.

The difficulty, however, is that, as an event, the general strike remains illegible, mostly unrecorded, and unable to be represented. The refusal embodied in the slaves' general strike resonates with the event's refusal to be narrativized. Instead, its internally differentiated massification, its cumulative force—the innumerable, uncountable, and incalculable acts that comprise it and get furthered in its movement, slowly at first but then with increased intensity and acceleration—breaks down the categories and logic that sustain capital and undoes the concepts that would reinforce it. This work of shattering grows and expands like a radiating force that mimes the proliferation of the general strike, at times invisibly and at other times more ostentatiously. It is the negative absence around which *Black Reconstruction* is articulated. Appearing as pure force, even if in this negative and differentiated way, it circulates as a difficulty for thinking and writing. If it can only be imagined, it is because it is as difficult to capture as the wind—and this because, as Du Bois notes, "the slave entered upon a general strike against slavery by the same methods that he had used during the period of the fugitive slave" (*BR*, 73). The slaves' doubled gesture of putting their tools down and becoming fugitives initiates the general strike. The strike corresponds to the "lion's leap" the slaves take and that, despite their illiteracy, emerges from a period of waiting, an interval of study, that corresponds to a period of reading. In Du Bois's words:

It must be borne in mind that nine-tenths of the four million black slaves could neither read nor write, and that the overwhelming majority of them were isolated on country plantations. Any mass movement under such circumstances must materialize slowly and painfully. What the Negro did was to wait, look and listen and try to see where his interests lay. There was no use in seeking refuge in an army that was not an army of freedom; and there was no sense of revolting against armed masters who were conquering the world. As soon, however, as it became clear that the Union army would not or could not return fugitive slaves, and that the masters with all their fume and fury were uncertain of victory, the slave entered upon a general strike by the same method that he had used during the period of the fugitive slave. He ran away to the first place of safety and offered his services to the Federal Army. So that in this way it was really true that he served his former master and served the emancipating army; and it was also true that this withdrawal and bestowal of his labor decided the war. (*BR*, 72–73)

Du Bois begins by emphasizing how the plantation's isolation works against the possibility of a mass slave movement. He explains later in the same chapter that this isolation enables the slaveowner to control the flow of information, to restrict the knowledge slaves have of the world beyond the plantation, and eventually to support the South's war propaganda efforts. Together, these strategies are designed to prevent a kind of literacy among the slaves in relation to the unfolding civil crisis. But Du Bois points to the collective act of reading—appearing in the form of waiting, looking, listening, and studying—that eventually, slowly, gradually, expansively, becomes the ground of the general strike. Like Benjamin's dialectician, who tries to decide how best to set the sails in order to take advantage of the wind of world history, the slaves interpret the signs of the war and imagine in which direction their chances for greater safety might be. They engage in a form of critical reading meant to sort out the details of the conflicting narratives emerging from both the North and the South and, eventually coming to believe that the winds of freedom are blowing northward, they seek the Northern army and, joining it, decide the fate of the war.

Adding this labor of reading to the more general enforced labor that until now has defined their existence, the slaves display a different kind of literacy—one that cannot be reduced to alphabetic reading and that involves a lifetime of training in how to read the signs of their precarity. It is this mode of reading that, introducing a critical distance in the slaves' relation to their own labor, opens the possibility of the general strike. There can be no general strike, Du Bois suggests, without this labor of reading that prepares the slave to leap into mass fugitivity—a leap that, linked to an affirmation and a demand, interrupts the course of history through the slaves' cumulative agency. This waiting period—marking a moment between communal despair and infinite possibility, a pause, a hesitation (not unlike the pause and hesitation that Du Bois argues should be the signature of sociology itself)—is of the greatest interest to Du Bois, as it points to the brief moment of becoming that precedes the slaves' reinscription into capital. Once the slave reenters the labor force, even as a soldier within the Union Army, he is immediately instrumentalized and recycled within the system of capitalist and militaristic labor. Although it is nearly impossible for Du Bois to represent this transitional period of becoming, to linger in it, this is the moment around which, we have suggested, his entire book turns, even if, as we will see, he is committed to the institutionalization of the significance of this revolution—as this institutionalization is attempted by the government and the Freedmen's Bureau after the Civil War and in the present moment in which he is writing.

Du Bois seems keenly aware of the near impossibility of a form that could match this insurgent moment when he asks, "can we imagine this spectacular revolution?" The question dares his readers to imagine the world from the position of the slave and, in doing so, to be transformed through an experience that approximates the slave's revolutionary disruption of plantation logic. We are asked to imagine our "common humanity" with the slave, to imagine the experience of being "chattels and real estate" and then, "suddenly in a night," becoming "'thenceforward and forever free'" (*BR*, 149). Du Bois's answer to this question—the form that could at least approach this revolution—is *Black Reconstruction* itself, since this is a book that, as he imagines it, hopes to come to us in the very form—or more precisely, the very formlessness—of a general strike. In the same way that his account of the slaves' general strike insists on its slow emergence from innumerable acts of resistance and flight—unplanned, uncoordinated, disorganized, mostly related to singular acts of fugitivity that often have varied consequences but which nevertheless result from the same common, cumulative desire for freedom, what Du Bois elsewhere calls the "strivings" of the Black masses—his book gathers materials from widely varied and heterogeneous sources and, through a process of appositional expansion, citation and accumulation, overlaying and repetition, seeks to reenact this general strike, to reconstruct this mass movement through the very massiveness and even unwieldiness of his book, and to do so at the level of his sentences, paragraphs, and chapters. At the same time, the unwieldiness of his book is the register of the impossibility of containing what cannot be contained, what, in its measureless unfolding, exceeds narration and, in doing so, replicates, even if in a displaced form, the revolutionary emergence of an unforeseen but incrementally dynamic and massified force.

Finishing his book in the mid-1930s—in the context of the "ruin of democracy" he sees all around him, a ruined democracy whose "fruit," he writes, is "World War" and "Depression" (*BR*, 40)—he massifies both his sources and the story of revolutionary fugitivity. In order to do so, he engages in an enormous labor of reading that involves sorting through a vast archive of materials, listening to the many voices within them, and interpreting and disentangling the way in which these traces not only convey the intense debates over the future and meaning of American democracy but also insist on the Black agency inscribed within the general strike. His labor of reading follows the logic of the slaves' labor of reading and sorting and, in doing so, anticipates our efforts to read and sort through the multilayered, multilineal, and internally fissured and relentlessly mobile language of *Black Reconstruction* itself. Du Bois's insistence on this mobility is the measure of his commitment to a historical materialist approach to writing history that understands reading and writing as forms of engagement with the processes of historical becoming. If the slaves put down their tools in order to initiate their general strike, Du Bois *puts down his tools*—all his wisdom, his readerly and writerly strategies—on paper and, in this way, hopes to realize a general strike against white supremacist propaganda. This strike would begin by striking out the erasure of Black agency in the outcome of the Civil War and in the democratic possibilities of Reconstruction opened up by the slaves' revolutionary action. It would trace—in uncompromising detail—the profound social revolution made possible by their general strike and this even without their being fully conscious of what they were doing and accomplishing. As Du Bois puts it:

> in addition to [industrial and economic freedom], they wanted to know; they wanted to be able to interpret the cabalistic letters and figures which were the key to more. They were consumed with curiosity at the meaning of the world. First and foremost just what was this that had recently happened about them—this upturning of the universe and revolution of the whole social fabric is the question. (*BR*, 151)

Suggesting that knowledge depends on acts of reading and interpretation, he again points to the slaves' engagement in a labor of reading. This time the labor reveals the difficulty, if not impossibility, of fully understanding the magnitude of the "upturning of the universe" and the "revolution of the whole social fabric" that their general strike makes possible. Like that of Du Bois, the slaves' task is to read backward from the aftereffects of their actions and to "interpret" these effects—which Du Bois likens to "cabalistic letters and figures" whose mysteries have to be uncovered through a genealogical account of everything that led to this social revolution—in order to begin to comprehend actions that, because they were uncoordinated and unplanned, singular but reproduced differentially, almost seem to have taken place outside of any determinate agency. If there is agency here, if there is a voice that can be identified with the experience of Black agency, it is as fragmented, dispersed, and fugitive as the general strike itself. With the slaves, we are asked to imagine how a force of scattering and dispersal—a force that begins in histories of trauma, dispossession, and violence—can become a practice of solidarity that brings with it enormous democratic imperatives. But the absence of this determinate agency is again the point. As Du Bois suggests, it is in what is unrecorded, in what remains to be read and understood, in the emptiness where something might have been but was not, that the possibility of Black agency and the cabalistic secret of its own vitality, in all its fragmentation and incompleteness, can enact a breach that can then allow the task of reconstruction to begin anew.

Du Bois reenacts and reinforces this gesture by pluralizing and mobilizing innumerable voices in an abolitionist direction and, more precisely, in what he calls an "abolition-democracy" direction (*BR*, 225). This pluralization is legible therefore not only in the unplanned coalitions that emerge from the general strike and that include non-Black participants but also in the formal structure of his book. In addition to the vast archive of materials that he evokes, cites, and mobilizes within the book—anti-Negro tracts and books, propaganda pamphlets and texts, both racist and abolitionist writings on Blacks, monographs from varied disciplines that address the history of the Negro, biographies of Negro leaders who participated in Reconstruction, works by Negro historians and young Negro scholars, and all sorts of government reports, including congressional reports from various offices within the government, among them the Department of Education, the Bureau of Refugees, Freedmen and Abandoned Lands, Public Frauds and Election, and the Congressional Globe, testimonials and stories that arrive to him in different forms, many of them unwritten, citations from Marx and Frederick Douglass, and references to several of his own writings—Du Bois closes each of his chapters with a quotation. This time, unlike the bicultural epigraphs he puts at the head of each of the chapters in *The Souls of Black Folk*—lines from poems by white writers and fragments of Black "sorrow songs," all of them referencing the history of Black suffering and death, with the sorrow songs more particularly revealing their origins in the experience of Black Africans and their descendants—these closing citations are drawn from a far wider archive, one that includes writings by Black and white writers, men and women, American, German, and Irish writers, writers of African descent, gay writers and activists, and spanning the eighteenth, nineteenth, and early twentieth centuries. This broad multiracial and multinational coalition of texts includes passages from: Leslie Hill, the son of a former slave who, having gone to Harvard and studied with William James, becomes an educator, writer, and community leader; Percy Bysshe Shelley, the British poet and activist; James Rorty, the American radical poet and writer, and founding editor of the *New Masses* magazine; the lyrics of the collectively written "John Brown's Body," a popular Civil War eulogy for the abolitionist John Brown; Friedrich Schiller, the German dramatist and poet; Maurice Thompson, the American novelist, essayist, and naturalist; Jessie Fauset, the Black poet, essayist, novelist, educator, and literary editor for *The Crisis*; William Rose Benét, the American poet and essayist, and the older brother of Stephen Vincent Benét; James Jeffrey Roche, the Irish poet, journalist, and diplomat; Ralph Waldo Emerson, the American writer and abolitionist; L. S. Olliver, the radical political poet; Charles Erskine Scott Wood, the American author, civil liberties advocate, and attorney; A. W. Thomas, the American activist poet and author of the 1898 *Appeals to Reason: Poems for the People*; Fannie Stearns Davis, the American sentimental poet; James Weldon Johnson, the Black writer and civil rights activist, and, with Du Bois, a leader of the NAACP; Oscar Wilde, the queer Irish writer, playwright, and poet; and George Sterling, the American poet, playwright, and well-known proponent of bohemianism. The effects of these citations are the displacement of Black grief and suffering to other locations, a recodification that enables the history of Black despair to travel, to be transmitted elsewhere, but also—through this process of multiplication and amplification—to be related to communal grief across different global communities, even if it is not subsumed by it. In accumulating these citations, Du Bois declares that these archives can also belong to him, can also be part of his own set of resources, his own arsenal of linguistic weapons. Already in *The Souls of Black Folk*, he notes that his intimacy with the canon of Western literature and philosophy is part of the threat he represents to the world of whiteness:

I sit with Shakespeare, and he winces not. Across the color line I move arm in arm with Balzac and Dumas, where smiling men and welcoming women glide in gilded halls. From out of the caves of evening that swing between the strong-limbed Earth and the tracery of stars, I summon Aristotle and Aurelius and what soul I will, and they come all graciously with no scorn nor condescension. So, wed with Truth, I dwell above the veil. Is this the life you grudge us, O knightly America? Is this the life you long to change into the dull red hideousness of Georgia? Are you so afraid lest peering from this high Pisgah, between Philistine and Amalekite, we sight the Promised Land?[33]

In *Black Reconstruction*, moving through a series of sources that, becoming entangled with one another, inaugurate and enact a process of expansion, writing itself becomes an experience of amalgamation and rewriting, a demonstration of the massiveness and even inevitability of intermixtures, which Du Bois more than once identifies with the future and which is legible in the extent to which the book is composed of the language of others, of citations, sometimes several pages long. Given the mobility and instability of its shape, its historic sweep, and the degree of its citationality, Du Bois's *Black Reconstruction* presents a densely layered panorama of the embodied voices that, carrying the echoes of revolution and capable of moving backward and forward in time, recall and intensify other revolutions, past, present, and future. When Du Bois revisits the promise and failure of Reconstruction—from the vantage point of a Black Reconstruction, one that begins in an acknowledgment of the fugitive slaves' undoing of the capitalist slave system, of capitalism's processes of instrumentalization and commodification—in the name of an abolition-democracy, in the hope that he can inaugurate a more enduring reconstruction of this democracy in ruins, he also destabilizes the intellectual practices of contemporary Marxism. In particular, he unsettles orthodox readings of Marx's texts by saturating them with the problem of race, since, for him, Marxism can only be true to its name if it becomes part of an antiracist struggle—something he already has gleaned from Marx himself. Du Bois's vast archive of quotations can be read as an improvisational composition of voices that never sing in harmonic unison but that, in their multiple dissonances, manage to write and even enact the rhythms and cadences of a history that takes the form of a massive disruption, an upheaval that cannot be contained or bound—a clamor of becoming. *Black Reconstruction* comes to us as the revolutionary socialization of an archive, whereby voices are collected and juxtaposed, made to sing together in a cacophony that seeks to transmit not just a history but, more importantly, the experience of history as a disruptive event of collective becoming.

It is nearly impossible to reconstruct the enormous consequences of this democratic revolution—including the establishment of the Freedmen's Bureau, the redistribution of land, the expansion of voting rights, the opening of schools and an insistence on public education, the building of hospitals and the expansion of social benefits, the granting of civil rights and participation in governance, and the economic emancipation of labor—all in the name of realizing the promise of equality on which America was to have been founded. Du Bois spends hundreds of pages documenting this world-historical abolitionist—and, for him, Marxist—experiment, especially in the chapters "The General Strike," "The Coming of the Lord," and "Looking Forward." As he suggests, however, it is precisely the massive transformation that Radical Reconstruction implies and seeks to secure—and the success with which, backed by the government and the military, it tests "the whole theory of American government"—that accounts for the backlash against it, especially in "a government which more and more [i]s falling into the hands of organized wealth, and of wealth organized on a scale never before seen in modern civilization" (*BR*, 417). The revolutionary nature of Reconstruction, in other words, leads to its eventual unraveling because of the white counterrevolution it incites—a counterrevolution that is as capitalist as it is racist.

In "Back to Slavery," Du Bois presents a meticulous and rather extraordinary account of the intimidation, violent voter suppression, mutilations, dismemberments, lynchings, murders, and political coups with which the white South sought to regain its authority and dominance over its Black populations. He documents its coordinated resistance to the imposition of Reconstruction, and the North's eventual complicity with this "second" rebellion. It is because, Du Bois notes, "the North had never been thoroughly converted to the idea of Negro equality" that, when contemplating possibilities—"even granting that all the South said of the Negro was not true"—it paused: "Did the nation want blacks with power sitting in the Senate and in the House of Representatives, accumulating wealth and entering the learned professions? Would this not eventually and inevitably lead to social equality and even to black sons and daughters-in-law and mulatto descendants? Was it possible to contemplate such eventualities?" (*BR*, 758). Moved by their mutual desire to increase their capital and maintain the systemic machinations of white supremacy, the North and the South join forces around the issue of race to ensure that coalitions between free Blacks and white laborers will be impossible, that the disenfranchisement of workers, and especially Black ones, will be reinforced. Registering the racialization of the political and economic crises that unfold in the aftermath of the war, Du Bois explains:

> The race element was emphasized in order that property-holders could get the support of the majority of white laborers and make it more possible to exploit Negro labor. But the race philosophy came as a new and terrible thing to make labor unity or labor class consciousness impossible. So long as the Southern white labor-ers could be induced to prefer poverty to equality with the Negro, just so long was a labor movement in the South made impossible. (*BR*, 816–817)

In an extraordinary phrase that condenses everything around which the resistance to Reconstruction is organized—and that confirms the racialization at the heart of capitalism—Du Bois adds that "[t]here was but one way to break up this threatened coalition, and that was to unite the poor and rich whites by *the shibboleth of race*, and despite divergent economic interests. The work of secret orders in 1868–1872 [including that of the Ku Klux Klan, the White League, and the Knights of the White Camellia] frustrated any mass movement toward union of white and black labor" (*BR*, 817; our emphasis). According to Du Bois, this shibboleth—this social and racialized pact that does not even have to be articulated, even if it often is—is the password to the benefits of whiteness, to the detriment of what Du Bois calls the "dark races" of the world.[34] If Reconstruction fails, "[it does] not fail where it was expected to fail" (*BR*, 850–851). It does not fail because of any incapacity of the now freed Blacks—and of the coa-litions that organize around them and in support of them—but because of the enormity of the enemy, the massive and unrelent-ing machinations of racial capitalism.

Although Du Bois laments the failure of Reconstruction, he nevertheless believes the end of slavery and the revolutionary struggle of Reconstruction transform both the South and the North. This transformation is the result of the activism of freed people, abolitionists, and everyone who struggles to materialize a different kind of Union—one based on a strong and expansive abolition-democracy. Even if not realized, the potential for mul-tiracial working-class struggle created by the abolition of slavery is a critical step in the international class struggle, especially, Du Bois notes, as the United States increasingly becomes the center of world capitalism. If he refers to Reconstruction as a "splendid failure" (*BR*, 850), his monumental book can itself be considered a *splendid failure*. If neither was able to entirely transform the world, they have remained two of our greatest resources for imagining a future that would no longer be subject to the time of racialized labor and capital. Like the revolution that Reconstruction marks, Du Bois is also "Athanasius contra mundum" (*BR*, 851). His book testifies to the rather remarkable work that reading and writing can accomplish, work that always has the potential to be world-historical. In his words,

> This the American black man knows: his fight here is a fight to the finish. Either he dies or wins. If he wins it will be by no subterfuge or evasion of amalgamation. He will enter modern civilization here in America as a black man on terms of perfect and unlimited equality with any white man or he will not enter at all. Either extermination root and branch, or absolute equality. There can be no compromise. This is the last great battle of the West. (*BR*, 844–845)

That reading and writing are what give us our best chances in this battle, and not only this one, is confirmed in the 1938 commencement speech Du Bois delivers at Fisk University, on the fiftieth anniversary of his own graduation there. In a presentation to the students that he entitles "The Revelation of Saint Orgne the Damned" (in which Orgne is an anagram for "Negro"), he talks about the critical place of a democratic education—what it might look like and why it is so necessary. His almost Zarathustran Saint Orgne speaks oracularly from the Mount of Transfiguration on which he stands and offers the graduating seniors—all of whom represent a relation to the future—this dictum: "Blessed is he that reads and they that hear the words of this prophecy for the time is at hand. ... Fear not. Write thou the things which thou has seen."[35] If the romance that still exists to be realized is the transformation of reading and writing into action—or better, the full recognition that reading and writing are already acts and, in particular, political acts—this is because of what Du Bois calls the "Impossible Must," the dream of a multiracial revolution that, exercising "creative power," would overcome, among other things, "the lesions of race," the "segregation of color," and the "domination of caste."[36]

Glenn Ligon, *Debris Field (Red) #16*, 2020–2021

XVI. THE HAMMER OF SOCIAL REVOLUTION

You don't stick a knife in a man's back nine inches and then pull it out six inches and say you're making progress.

—Malcolm X, "Twenty Million Black People in a Political, Economic and Mental Prison" (1963)

No More Water, the fire next time.

—James Baldwin, *The Fire Next Time* (1963)[1]

On May 25, 2020, in Minneapolis, Minnesota, George Floyd's murder at the hands of police officer Derek Chauvin—with "Chauvin" a synecdoche for a broader system of police brutality and therefore not a single, lone actor, since, in nearly every instance, this system is channeled through its officers—was video-recorded by a Black teenage girl, Darnella Frazier, on her smartphone. The date marks simultaneously the date of the event and the beginning of the event's massification in social media. It inscribes the singularity of this act of violence within a vast archive of anti-Black hate and its reproduction in images. Despite this inscription, two distinct indices set this event apart as a dense confluence of references, echoes capable of extending into the past as well as into the future: first, the excruciating length of Floyd's asphyxiation, nine minutes and twenty-nine seconds, becomes a durational photograph, a site of temporal unfolding—because these minutes inevitably evoke the traces of the long history of Black death and suffering, the ongoing history of violence against Black bodies, the recorded event can be said to exceed all temporal measures—and, second, the staging of the image, the point of view it forces us to adopt, is one of passivity and complicity, distant from the event itself. Viewing it only through the mediation of technical media, we experience a helplessness in front of this unbearable scene—a scene that is unbearable because, full of time and history, filled with innumerable other images within the archive of Black death, it bears more weight than any scene or set of images should be asked to carry. At the same time, we become witnesses who potentially can be activated in the struggle against this murderous violence, witnesses who must choose between complicity and struggle.

Frazier's activist documentation already implies and expects a collective testimony: when she records, she does it because she knows, anticipates, and demands that others watch. The very moment she turns on her camera she begins to constitute a community through this seemingly limited but pivotal world-historical act. Inseparable from the activity of witnessing in which she is engaged, this act is at the same time a critical reading of the event. Confirming media technology's irreversible incursion into the realm of American politics and, in particular, testimonial video's role in recording racist violence, she bears witness to what would generally be just another event in the unassimilable history of Black death. At this particular historical moment, however, her recording exceeds its frame and explodes into the socius, calling forth the phantoms of earlier images of racism and imprinting them on the national unconscious with an unprecedented force. As we know, this call of conscience—drawing together the outrage, anger, and shame involved in watching the filmic record that gives this call its shape—generated global social protests that, together, brought what Martin Luther King, Jr. once called "the hammer of social revolution" crushing down on the history of systemic racism.[2] Widening the cracks and fissures that already had permitted us to see a common history of violence against Black people from slavery to colonialism, capturing the parallels in police violence against Black people across the globe, Frazier's video-hammer united protesters in a renewed global movement against the legacy of empires and its enduring racist symbols and, in particular, against all forms of racial capitalism, especially in the United States. The event of Floyd's murder passed into the media and became, in turn, an event that itself was an effect of the media; if it resonated so globally, this is perhaps because the response to his death already had an international dimension since this kind of violence and racial injustice is experienced around the world, but also, and perhaps most importantly, because, in the midst of the pandemic, the sense of shared mortality and communal despair was more legible and could be more easily activated and mobilized. But certainly his recorded murder became the spark that finally set the fire whose kindling had been accumulating for years, materializing "the fire next time" that James Baldwin had foreseen sixty years ago.[3]

Frazier's recording belongs to a long history of documenting violence against Black populations. A weapon of Black power, the camera, in all its different forms, has been part of a practice of critical Black memory, and its images—from Birmingham to

Emmett Till to the civil rights movement to the video of Rodney King's beating to the increasing documentation of police violence against Black bodies—have served as galvanizing forces, especially for Black political communities. Because these still and moving images cannot organize alone, even if they can energize, they have gone hand in hand with an activist training that— beginning with eighteenth- and nineteenth-century abolitionists and moving through the work of at least Frederick Douglass, Timothy Thomas Fortune, Ida B. Wells-Barnett, W. E. B. Du Bois, Zora Neale Hurston, Langston Hughes, Martin Luther King, Jr., Malcolm X, James Baldwin, Amiri Baraka, Cedric Robinson, Audre Lorde, Angela Davis, Toni Morrison, Robin D. G. Kelley, Patricia J. Williams, Saidiya Hartman, and Fred Moten—has sought to expand our understanding of what constitutes racism, linking it directly to the barbarism of capital. Within the context of what happened in the summer of 2020, the most relevant pedagogical frame had been largely articulated and developed by the Black Lives Matter movement.[4] The movement's effective reactivation of a Marxist archive (the three community organizers and Black feminists who cofounded the Black Lives Matter movement, Alicia Garza, Patrisse Cullors, and Opal Tometi, have explicitly situated their work in relation to Marx's writings[5]) has highlighted the entanglements of systemic racism and American capitalism, as the pervasive exclusionary and exploitative logic that undergirds the nation's founding structures and extends to other brutalized populations—the impoverished, the marginalized of any racial or ethnic background, who, recognizing their linked fates, have at different moments organized for social justice. Black Lives Matter did not invent this critical reading of America's social, historical, and economic realities. Black communists, the civil rights and Black Panther movements, had relied on these same Marxist resources as well, but Black Lives Matter has managed to vastly extend its activist community by appealing to the shocking precariousness of Black lives and by providing a critical and political lens through which to read the embeddedness of this precariousness in the everyday life of innumerable vulnerable communities. More importantly, it has done so in a way that reminds us that we are not only all implicated in this together—even if differently—but are also all at stake, managing to turn everyone into a participant—either an agent of complicity or an agent of change, and often both, which is why our historical materialists—Marx, Luxemburg, Benjamin, Du Bois, and Jameson—so often emphasize the need to be most vigilant in relation to our inevitable complicities. The archives of Black grief and Marxist ideological critique are here assembled together to politicize pain and mourning by experiencing them as sources of communal despair.

The communal despair that overtook tens of millions in the aftermath of Floyd's death may not have originated there—preceded as it was by too many other instances of deadly police force unleashed on Black citizens, instances that are violently cited and embedded in each new act of brutality. However, the images that were inscribed in the minds of a large part of the nation and around the globe, larger than ever before even if still insufficient, carried within them the force of multiplication and massification that, as Benjamin and Du Bois insist, can become a weapon in the fight against fascism, which now appears, once more, as white nationalism. Benjamin's reconceptualization of the work of art calls for a mass aesthetic that, unlike that of fascism and its many figurations, practices an infinitely mediated politics of relation in which the strength of numbers references the strength of a mass that cannot be collected under a single name, where Floyd can be read as at once singular and multiple, as a name that names something greater than a single individual, nothing less than a multitude. And this not only because technological transmissions act like an amplifier that reaches a wider number of witnesses but also, and much more importantly, because those witnesses cannot simply be transformed into a recognizable audience—which is all we ever are for both capitalism and fascism. No longer, or at least not at this miraculous and fragile "moment of danger," can this unrecognizable but nevertheless impactful audience consume images except as an activist reading community that reads them and, in doing so, recovers the agency that their complicity with capitalist consumption has long diminished and finally negated. The labor of reading critically and collectively not just words but also images, and the complex interplay between the two, is an act of embeddedness and historicization that moves backward and forward in time, recruiting and recalling images from the past in order to redirect those of the present and hopefully those of the future.

From the very beginning, the death of George Floyd was not just the death of an individual but an intolerable addition to an archive of Black deaths at the hands of a passive and complicit nation, a nation that had until very recently succeeded in a prolonged act of erasure, in the relentless production of the uncounted and the unnamed. Floyd's embodied temporalization of that archive, in which time becomes literally unbearable, awakens and gathers other deaths, some named but most unnamed, since they number in the millions, to put them at the center of the image's staging. The infinite temporal extension of the recording of Floyd's death manages to include and hold those who have remained uncounted, unnamed, and unmourned. The singularity of Floyd's death is its gathering force, the communal mourning it cries out for, and in the midst of a global pandemic that, once again, overwhelmingly takes its heaviest toll on Black, minority, immigrant, and impoverished populations, so that his death by asphyxiation acts as yet another amplifier of communal grief and rage. The particularity of George Floyd's death and the resonance of his words "I can't breathe," even the call for his mother, transform him into a concrete universal finally capable of expressing global pain without letting go of his singularity and its embeddedness in the history of slavery and its continuity in systemic racism. As a Black man living and dying because of the inequalities and the violence of American capitalism, Floyd is also capable of containing the uncounted hundreds of thousands of calculated deaths of American and global citizens whose lives were taken with impunity. He becomes an embodiment of Black grief as the singular index of a universal grief that cannot quite contain him—not a parenthetical "race" but an emblem capable of signaling the foundations of the world in which we all live, a world now organized around the enigma of George Floyd's singularity, an opacity that enables him to contain multitudes.

PRICE $8.99

JUNE 22, 2020

NEW YORKER

A MAN WAS LYNCHED YESTERDAY

I AM A MAN

NELSON

Kadir Nelson, *Say Their Names*, 2020

> I searched for the traces of the destroyed. In every line item, I saw
> a grave. Commodities, cargo, and things don't lend themselves to
> representation, at least not easily. The archive dictates what can be
> said about the past and the kinds of stories that can be told about
> the persons catalogued, embalmed, and sealed away in box files
> and folios. To read the archive is to enter a mortuary.
>
> —Saidiya Hartman, *Lose Your Mother: A Journey along the Atlantic
> Slave Route* (2007)[1]

In the months that followed the worldwide protests against police
brutality and anti-Black violence, other images of Floyd, beyond
Frazier's video, started to circulate, further reinforcing and materializing his transformation into an emblem. One of the most
striking expressions of this transformation was Kadir Nelson's
Say Their Names, which appeared on the June 22, 2020 cover of *The
New Yorker*. Nelson reconceives Abraham Bosse's frontispiece for
Thomas Hobbes's 1651 *Leviathan or The Matter, Forme and Power
of a Common-Wealth Ecclesiasticall and Civil* by depicting Floyd as
another kind of Leviathan, no longer containing the subjects of
an absolute sovereign but instead pointing to the possibility of a
new social contract, a new common-wealth that might be truer
to its name since it would begin in the richness of its commons.
In Bosse's version, the torso and arms of the king are composed
of over three hundred figures, all of them facing backward and
thus remaining anonymous, so that their force resides exclusively in their unanimity, their subsumption under the name of
one single power, represented by Charles II. Additionally, Bosse's
emblem enlists the theological by quoting a line from the book of
Job that identifies the sovereign with God—"*Non est potestas Super
Terram quae Comparetur ei Job 41.24*" (There is no power on earth
to be compared to Him). While the line suggests another more
divine ground for ideological unification—even if Hobbes has
to admit that his sovereign can only be an artificial, machinic,
monstrous, "Mortall God"[2]—Bosse's use of it entirely bypasses
the figure of Job as an index of senseless suffering, which is why
Nelson's appropriation of this earlier anamorphic etching, joining another, more specific community of dispossessed peoples

Abraham Bosse, frontispiece for Thomas Hobbes's *Leviathan or The Matter, Forme and Power of a Common-Wealth Ecclesiasticall and Civil*, 1651

to the anonymous, depersonalized subjects in Hobbes's frontispiece, points to a different common-wealth altogether, one organized around the recognition of suffering Black masses. But it is important to distinguish between the anonymity and impersonality demanded by Hobbes's sovereign and those of the vanquished, anonymous ones who "toil for others" in Marx and Benjamin, and between the different uses to which these figures are put within these different contexts. In Bosse's depiction, the sovereign's face is the only part of him not composed of the bodies of others—the impersonal, anonymous, faceless, and silent figures whose aggregation composes the sovereign, who, in this common-wealth, is the only one who can have a face, however composed and artificial it may be. Following Marx, this condition indicates that the state—like the city and landscape above which Bosse's sovereign towers—is effectively devoid of people; it cannot bear human and suffering subjects. The populace must first be depersonalized and anonymized in order for the state to maintain itself. Put another way, the sovereign and the state can only maintain their sovereignty through an instrumentalized depersonalization of their constituencies. Benjamin, on the other hand, deploys and performs impersonality within the movement of his writing—as we have seen, this impersonality is legible in his writings in the different forms of citationality, allusion, and repetition that are their signature. If he emphasizes this mode of depersonalization—intensifying and massifying his language—it is in order to mobilize this scattering force against the depersonalization that would constitute a state and to do so in order to make a different state possible, one that might begin in its recognition of the vanquished. While Benjamin, enacting his very particular understanding of analogy and similitude, seeks to transform depersonalization into a revolutionary strategy—a strategy that he himself appropriates from Gracián and other baroque contemporaries of Hobbes and Bosse—he is conscious of the danger that a structurally similar form of depersonalization can be mobilized to support sovereignty and state-sanctioned forms of violence. This danger of complicity is present in Marx and Benjamin alike and requires a delicate vigilance on the part of the historical materialist. The structural closeness between a strategy of depersonalization that is at once constitutive and destructive of the state is also legible in Nelson's appropriation of Bosse's image, which remains, like the portrait of Luther behind Klee's *Angelus Novus*, simultaneously the marker of what his image occupies and supplants and of its material support.

Indeed, Nelson's image imagines a new common-wealth composed of the vast numbers of Blacks who have been depersonalized, vanquished, erased, and dehumanized. He not only displays the histories of racism and enslavement that have been invisible within the long history of capitalist state formations, but he also joins this more particular history of Black suffering with that of vanquished populations more generally. In recalling the nameless subjects who surrender their agency and selfhood to the sovereign and the state, he accomplishes at least two things. First, he joins the histories of these unnamed to the history of violence against Blacks, inscribing both constituencies into an even longer and broader history that demands an act of memorialization and naming; and, second, he imagines a new common-wealth that includes the anonymous Black communities who have toiled for others and gives them faces, even as—because of the overlay of his oil painting over Bosse's etching—he suggests that this naming and remembering cannot escape its entanglement with what came before and cannot help referencing the potential complicity between the anonymous subjects who surrender their agency to the state and the violence committed against innumerable unnamed and unmourned Black subjects. Substituting Floyd for Charles II and replacing presumably white populations with Black ones, Nelson signals the history he wants to exceed and transform, and does so through an act of appropriation that, asking us to think the relation between the histories he puts together, politically displaces the earlier image in order to bring the interplay between these images into the practice of an activist, antiracist pedagogy.

Nelson's dynamic refiguration, then, does not erase but instead appropriates Bosse, takes the elements of Bosse's image into account and reinscribes them under a different motto, an urgent demand, "Say their names." Nelson's motto goes directly against the figure of sovereignty sealed within Bosse's inscription and underwrites an emblem that seeks to awaken all the dead, putting memory and accountability at the center of a new covenant between the dead and the living. In Nelson's composition, Floyd's torso becomes a transmedia archive of Black grief, grievance, and death but also of political struggle and resistance against the continuity of a relentless brutalization. The list of figures and their portraits (taken from photographs, paintings, videos, and murals) doubles as a reading of American history through the lens of Black grief and grievance: Malcolm X, Martin Luther King, Jr., Medgar Evers, the Tulsa race massacre, the Selma march, the unnamed and enslaved, Gordon and his scarred back, Rodney King, Rosa Parks, Emmett Till, Stephon Clark, Philando Castile, Tamir Rice, Breonna Taylor, Walter Scott, David McAtee, Alton Sterling, Yvette Smith, Sandra Bland, Michael Brown, Botham Jean, Aiyana Stanley-Jones, Eric Garner, Freddie Gray, Laquan McDonald, Trayvon Martin, Tony McDade, and Ahmaud Arbery. The *New Yorker* website includes an interactive archive with details of these individuals and communities, highlighting the pedagogical aim of the project (we can see it as a complement to the "1619 Project," since it also begins with the Atlantic slave trade) and its wish for a more activist visual literacy whose aim is to imagine a community that, never closing its eyes to this history, would seek to transform it. Nelson's demand, "Say their names," enlists oral performativity as a speech act that constitutes a promise and an alliance to a new community, one that not only remembers the dead but fully includes them in the temporal complexity of a "now" that can be activated politically. The dead are awakened, and we are asked to imagine, with them, a new relation between the past and the present, a new social contract that would make another future possible.

Danny Lyon, *Birmingham, Alabama,* 1963

XVIII. *ANGELUS NOVUS:* A MILITANT EMBLEM

The person falls to pieces, loses its breath. It passes over into something else, is nameless, no longer hears reproaches, fleeing its extension into its smallest dimension, fleeing its dispensability into nothingness—yet on reaching that smallest dimensionality, with a deep breath at having passed across, it recognizes its new and actual indispensability in the whole.

—Bertolt Brecht, "Crushing the Person" (1929–1930)

Afropessimism gives us the freedom to say out loud what we would otherwise whisper or deny: that no Blacks are in the world, but, by the same token, there is no world without Blacks.

—Frank Wilderson III, *Afropessimism* (2020)[1]

According to Benjamin, when a particular "chain of events appears before us," the angel of history "sees one single catastrophe, which keeps piling wreckage upon wreckage and hurls it at his feet." This angel "would like to stay, awaken the dead, and make whole what has been smashed." But the wind of a storm "blowing from Paradise" gets "caught in his wings" and the angel "can no longer close them." Driven "irresistibly into the future to which his back is turned," the angel cannot awaken the dead, cannot redeem the wreckage before him, however much he would wish to do so. We recall these details here because Benjamin's emblem of defeat and hopelessness is indexed, however secretly and unintentionally, by one of the most widely circulated images of George Floyd, reproduced in various versions and disseminated through different media around the globe in the months soon after his death—a mural painted by the artist Donkeeboy and his mother Donkeemom in Houston's Third Ward in June 2020. The mural presents Floyd as a nearly photographic Black angel, in black and white and emblazoned on a clear blue background, with his wings extended, wearing a hoodie with the word "Ghetto" written on it, under a halo with the inscription "Forever breathing in our hearts," his eyes and face oriented directly at us, as if—even if there is no symmetry between the interplay of gazes that takes place here, and perhaps especially then—asking

Donkeeboy and Donkeemom, *George Floyd, Houston's Third Ward* (2020)

us to register our responsibility toward him and everything for which he has now become the emblem. We are asked to remain answerable not just to him but to all the dead he has conjured and awakened, to think our relation to what brought death to them—to keep them safe not simply from the violent history that led to their death but also from the history that will continue to seek to erase and efface them from its movement, and this because, as Benjamin would put it, "even the *dead* will not be safe from the enemy if he is victorious," and, until now, "the enemy has never ceased to be victorious" (*CH*, 391). It therefore asks us to think simultaneously of the relations among the past, the present, and the future in order to take responsibility for what we see before us. It names a task of transformation, the spirit of a revolution that would take its strength from the acknowledgment of the history of Black grief and death. Its new *Angelus Novus* would magnify, in Marx's words, "the given task in the imagination,"[2] and what we are asked to imagine is its relation to the unorthodox historical materialist network we have been tracing and to the ways in which it circulates in the world as a gathering, transformative force.

This circulation is already announced in the inscription above the angelic Floyd's head: "Forever breathing in our hearts." Suggesting that Floyd—who, in his last dying breaths, repeatedly uttered the words "I can't breathe" as he was being held in a lethal chokehold (repeating the phrase uttered by Eric Garner in 2014 when he was killed in the same way by the New York Police Department)—remains alive in our hearts, it also tells us that, in response to the breathtaking degree of police brutality that has been directed to Black and minority populations, we carry not simply the memory of this violence, not just the images of it, but also the responsibility of responding to it in the most active and activist ways. The inscription comes to us in the mode of bereavement, but a bereavement that generates movement, whose breath, propelled by the winds of history, carries Floyd's last words forward, incorporating them within a formulation that itself enacts the very gesture of inscription it calls forth. Announcing an act of memory and memorialization, it at the same time evokes the innumerable other deaths recalled by this singular one, all of them brought to life in a collective awakening of the dead. This broader and more expansive context is reinforced if we read this haloed inscription in relation to the word "Ghetto" stamped on Floyd's hoodie. This rather macabre confirmation of capitalism's capacity to instrumentalize even the word "Ghetto"—with its long historical associations of racial discrimination, forced separations, fierce cycles of inequality, and political powerlessness, beginning with the spatial segregation of Jews in medieval Europe—not only signals Floyd's inscription within the racism at the heart of capitalism but also names an almost allegorical figure for the capitalist mechanisms of racism and economic discrimination that Floyd already wore on his body, even before his death. The word "Ghetto" appears almost as Floyd's name but certainly as an inescapable suggestion that his identity is inseparable from the marginalized and threatened community to which he belongs, and that he now represents globally. If we note that, in Black slang, a ghetto angel references the power of the ghetto and, in particular, the dead guardian who, with this power, watches over his community from beyond his grave, we can point to another way in which the emblem that Floyd has become opens the possibility of a communal, transformative response to the anti-Black violence that took his breath away, if only—from the vantage point of the aftermath of the summer of 2020—to have it be carried around the globe and given another life.

This new Black angel's upwardly extended wings memorialize the "hands up" pose of the Black man halted and about to be accosted or arrested by the police.[3] At the same time, he embodies the possibility of the rise of a new political, heterogeneous mass emerging across race, class, gender, generations, and borders of all kinds that is not just a continuation of a theological appropriation. This possibility resonates with Marx's own strategies for gathering populations around a political project, in all its uncertainties and lack of guarantees; it is an *Aufhebung* of them, a dialectical image and emblem of a temporally complex and politically activated "here-and-now." The *Angelus Novus* of this Benjaminian *Jetztzeit* is now less awkward and less untimely than either Klee's or Benjamin's respective angels. Enlisting a secularized theology in a political struggle that does not belong just to the present, it appears as another version of Benjamin's hard-working dialectician—or at least is transformed into one by the masses who emerge in relation to the moment in which he is transformed from a living being into a dead one—whose death works to blast open the historical moment and reveal once again the endemic racism that is the signature of the United States. Despite the long history of resistance to anti-Black violence and racism, a history full of victories and defeats, a history filled with acts of transformative courage and endurance but also with massive death and grief, this systemic racism has rarely been so exposed and across such a large, diverse set of populations around the globe, a fact that was surely facilitated by social and technical media that, intensifying the circulation of emblems, of texts and images, formed a global broadcast system whose aim was to massify its effects—but also its countereffects and their propaganda.

Jameson points to an earlier event that has great resonance with the events of 2020 and that was itself organized around its own broadcast system, even if, because it took place sixty years ago, it was enabled by a different technical medium. The event to which he refers is the assassination of John F. Kennedy, the aftermath of which was televised globally and, displaying a moment of communal grief that exceeded the death of Kennedy himself, bore within it the archive of Black suffering and disenfranchisement. Similarly structured around a moment of civil unrest emerging from questions directly related to America's anti-Black history that, circulating globally through the images of the struggle transmitted by technical media, encouraged millions to move in an antiracist direction, the assassination was the culmination of a series of events that, together, eventually led to the passing of the Civil Rights Act of 1964 and, indeed, took place just months after Kennedy had expressed his support for this legislation. As Jameson puts it:

> A universalized televisual reception has opened the way for collective events which are no longer simply news, but which involve popular participation of a quite different kind than the workers' writing that Benjamin (and Enzensberger after him) imagined to offer a "dialogical" alternative to the one-way broadcast. The Kennedy assassination, to take one classic example, transformed the nature of historical chronology, producing a new kind of date-event in which millions of people participated as a personal experience and which largely transcended the limits of the shock-type *Erlebnis*. The collective nature of television is thereby glimpsed as a new form of aura, whose political implications (as, for example, in flash mobs) have scarcely yet been explored, let alone exhausted. (*BF*, 217)

Pointing to the fact that the date of Kennedy's assassination has been inscribed within the nation's imaginary and marks an instance in which millions of people were moved to a global act of mourning, he invites us to recall the context of the event, a context which, in America, can only reference a racial conflict.

In the spring of 1963, activists in Birmingham, Alabama launched one of the most consequential campaigns of the civil rights movement, beginning with a series of sit-ins, marches, and boycotts to protest segregation laws in the city. On May 2, 1963, more than one thousand students skipped classes and gathered at Sixth Street Baptist Church to march to downtown Birmingham. As they approached police lines, hundreds were arrested and carried off to jail. When hundreds more young people gathered the following day for another march, white public safety commissioner Bull Connor directed the local police and fire departments to halt the demonstration, even forcefully, if necessary. The peaceful demonstrations were met with violent attacks using high-pressure fire hoses and police dogs on men, women, and children alike—producing some of the most iconic and troubling images of the civil rights movement. Appearing on television and in newspapers, the images sparked outrage around the world (Kennedy himself expressed disgust on viewing the iconic image of a German shepherd lunging forward and about to bite a young Black boy). The event is considered one of the major turning points in the civil rights movement. Even though Kennedy's June 11, 1963 speech on civil rights is ostensibly concerned with the fight over integration at the University of Alabama, he acknowledged the importance of the May 3 events in language that, decrying the situation in Birmingham as "intolerable" and noting that Birmingham and the country were in the world's spotlight, already echoes that of Martin Luther King, Jr.'s April 16 "Letter from Birmingham Jail." We could even say that, in a certain sense, Kennedy's speech was countersigned by King and the movement itself. But America again found itself under the world's gaze when, in September of that year, four Black girls were killed by bombs planted by white supremacists at the 16th St. Baptist Church. The bombings sent shock waves throughout the country and beyond.

Jack Whitten's *Birmingham 1964* was produced within months of both Kennedy's assassination and televised funeral and the murder of the four girls. A militant box, it explodes with the anti-Black violence lodged in the heart of America. It offers us a glimpse of the brutality that lies beneath the painted surface. The tear in the body of the nation is also a tear in the formal language of abstraction Whitten had embraced until then—a language that is now violently attacked in the aftershock of tangible and painful violence. The surface of a black monochrome abstract painting is pulled apart and becomes a visual sorrow song. The newsprint photograph inside Whitten's painterly black box is from May 3, 1963 and shows a policeman with a dog attacking a young Black protester during the civil rights campaign in Birmingham. The

Jack Whitten, *Birmingham 1964*, 1964

image, taken by photojournalist Bill Hudson, is barely yet forcefully revealed under the broken black surface of the canvas. It is a companion image of the silkscreens Andy Warhol created on the same subject between 1963 and 1964. The protests fueled by the bombing of the 16th Street Baptist Church were simultaneously an act of collective mourning. The bombing, and the murders that followed them, intensified a civil rights movement that continued to be met with legal, police, and civil violence at each of its manifestations. The newsprint image in Whitten's "painting" emerges out of a gash in the surface—which is made of found materials, including cardboard, black paint, aluminum foil, and a stocking mesh. The stocking mesh that covers the newsprint is a direct reference to Du Bois's "double consciousness" and his concept of "the veil" as a visual manifestation of the color line. Whitten is very much in conversation with Du Bois—who died in Accra in August that same year—during the composition and production of his piece. In *The Souls of Black Folk*, Du Bois describes how Black Americans are "born with a veil" and gifted with a "second sight" that encompasses "two souls, two thoughts, two unreconciled strivings: two warring ideals in one dark body whose dogged strength alone keeps it from being torn asunder."[4] The raw and open gash in Whitten's canvas refuses to close the historical wound experienced by Black Americans; it is a violence that precedes the Birmingham bombings and extends long afterward. While Du Bois somehow sublimates the figure of the veil when he refers to it as a gift of second sight for African Americans—it is simultaneously a curse and a blessing—Whitten heightens the violence trapped inside the figure of the veil by treating the image like explosive radioactive material that cannot be contained by aluminum foil (a material that is known to block the flow of radiation). *Birmingham 1964* effectively functions like a *Denkbild*; it is an emblem of America as a constellation of Black grief then and now. It is a reminder of Claudia Rankine's claim that "the condition of Black life is one of mourning"[5]—a communal despair, a sorrow song. Like a Benjaminian sentence, Whitten's painting contains an entire world, a constellation that brings together the different temporalities of the living and the dead.

Providing a frame for understanding the events in the summer of 2020 by recalling an event from the early 1960s, Jameson emphasizes the mediatic, televisual capacity to circulate images that can move millions of people and reenacts the Marxist and Benjaminian gesture of reading the present through a past that is never just past. It is precisely because the racist past of America

Kerry James Marshall, *Memento #5*, 2003

Kerry James Marshall, *Souvenir II*, 1997

survives in the present that Kennedy and his brother Robert are assassinated largely for their increased support for civil rights and for their wish to inscribe America's Black citizens into the world of rights enjoyed by all American citizens. Their stance against anti-Black racism helps explain artist Kerry James Marshall's decision in his *Mementos* and *Souvenir* series to present these two figures, along with Martin Luther King, Jr. and an entire pantheon of civil rights activists, as winged angelic figures floating in the paintings alongside inscriptions that refer to the loss and mourning that characterize Black life. These angels belong to an entire constellation of angels, all of which form part of the haloed Floyd angel's inheritance. The Floyd angel is even an archive of all the previous angels that are inscribed within it; in Marshall's work, these are cultural and political figures who died between 1959 and 1979—most but not all of them African-American—including, among others, and beyond the Kennedys and King, Medgar Evers, Fred Hampton, and Malcolm X.

That Floyd comes to bear the entirety of this history, and even more, helps account for the enormity of the convulsive response to his murder. What also made this explosion possible was the rather remarkable set of conditions that, together, reinforced a communal sense of despair and grief and, in doing so, incited global demonstrations against anti-Black violence, as just one cipher for all the threads woven into this moment. These conditions included the pandemic which revealed the structural inequalities that have guaranteed the endurance of the irreducible relation between racism and capitalism, and the rage and shame over Trump and all the legislators, politicians, and citizens whose own complicity, whose own racism and white supremacism, resonated with and gave support to his. In response, the pedagogical project of the Black Lives Matter movement, with its library composed of a vast archive of writings and actions by antiracist scholars, activists, writers, and political figures, helped inform the different constituencies that rose in protest over the intolerable history of anti-Black violence—with all of this galvanized by the murder of George Floyd.

What prevented this particular death from being absorbed and made invisible—as so many others before it have been—was exactly the constellation of forces that, in the context of a communal despair of historic and global proportions, enabled a new emblem, a new angel of history, to join with the historical materialist dialectician to set the sails at the precise moment in which they could align themselves with the "wind of world history." Setting his wings alongside Benjamin's sails and propelling himself—or, more precisely, being propelled—into an agent of social change, Floyd's angel is, unlike Benjamin's, able to awaken the dead, and also to inherit the future they still carry within them. Like a militant box that is also an unmarked and communal grave, this angel bears the dead and the future within him; he preserves the enigma of history's defeats, even as he contains the innumerable archives of activist knowledge that are our most precious resources for "reckoning with the winds of the storm." The political organization of hopelessness and communal grief recognizes in the dead a relation to the possibility of an incommensurable future and, mobilizing the negation that "race" has been in the affirmative direction of a hope in the midst of hopelessness, materializes the entanglement between hopelessness and hope that we have seen under the names Marx, Luxemburg, and Benjamin, and that is confirmed once more by Du Bois when, in *The Souls of Black Folk*, he writes that it is perhaps only in the context of absolute pessimism that we can nurture "a hope not hopeful, but unhopeful."[6] Like a Pandora's box that, once opened, releases the racism, greed, hatred, suffering, disease, hunger, poverty, war, evil, and death that are a consequence of capital's barbarism, this new transmedia Black *Angelus Novus* insists on the necessity of protecting and preserving hope, keeping it alive in the midst of all the destruction and wreckage piling up before him, and us. Pointing to the transition between the living and the dead, it signals a "secret agreement between past generations and the present one," recasting the durational photograph of the dying Floyd in order to transform it into a galvanizing force oriented toward an as-yet-undetermined future, turning the direction of anti-Black violence against the grain of the brutality that produces its particular forms and conditions.

STAR OF THE NORTH, OR THE COMET OF 1861.

Star of the North, or the Comet of 1861, 1861

XIX. THE SECOND COMET

If some chroniclers of the heavens are to be believed, between the Sun and a zone beyond the terrestrial orb sprawls a vast cemetery of comets, with a mysterious glow that appears in the evenings and mornings of clear days. The deaths of these luminous phantoms are seen as they allow the light of the living stars to pass through them. Or rather, they are more like supplicating captives, enchained for centuries to the gates of our atmosphere and vainly demanding freedom.

—Louis Auguste Blanqui, *Eternity by the Stars* (1872)

Negroes must ... hold unfaltering commerce with the stars.

—W. E. B. Du Bois, *Dusk of Dawn* (1940)[1]

In the same way that the image of George Floyd bears the weight of a long history of anti-Black violence, Du Bois's 1920 collection *Darkwater* underscores the entanglement of slavery, United States and European colonialism and imperialism, and the economic roots of what he calls "modern industrial imperialism." Published exactly one century before Floyd's murder, it points to global capitalism's reliance on the surplus labor of the industrial proletariat, most often the exploited labor of the "darker races."[2] Written under the shadow of the massive destruction wrought by World War, the tens of millions of deaths resulting from a global pandemic, the 1919 Paris Peace Conference, the 1919 Pan-African Congress, and all the race riots in the United States beginning in 1917 in East St. Louis and culminating in the Red Summer of 1919, the collection comprises ten chapters—nine essays and a short story—and eleven intertexts in the form of poems, parables, prose allegories, and hymns that, framing each of the chapters, weave them together, creating what Paul Gilroy has called a "polyphonic form."[3]

Du Bois joins his fictional and poetic experiments with historical and economic analyses of imperialism and conquest, of subjection and dispossession, arguing that all of these depend on racial divisions meant to maintain white privilege. Demonstrating the ways in which the issue of race permeates the most urgent issues of the moment—democracy, war, colonialism, labor, education, segregation, poverty, rights, gender equality, the exploitation of African resources and peoples, and of various populations around the globe—Du Bois delineates, often in fantastical ways, the possibilities of a future that could overcome racism and racial hierarchy, even when this seems most impossible. As James Baldwin would put it over four decades later, in a passage that could have been written by Du Bois, "in our time, as in every time, the impossible is the least one can demand— and one is, after all, emboldened by the spectacle of human history in general, and American Negro history in particular, for it testifies to nothing less than the perpetual achievement of the impossible."[4] Like Baldwin after him, Du Bois makes American Negro history a model to be extended throughout the colonized world. Viewing abolition and Reconstruction as revolutionary acts against the racism that legitimates modern industrial imperialism, he argues that the project of racial emancipation is inseparable from the possibility of global decolonization. If Evelyn Brooks Higginbotham suggests that *Darkwater* is Du Bois's "'militant' sequel" to *The Souls of Black Folk*, this militancy is legible in its deconstruction of racial hierarchy and antagonism.[5] "There are no races," Du Bois declares, "in the sense of great, separate, pure breeds of men, differing in attainment, development, and capacity" (*DW*, 47).

Du Bois's book repeatedly transgresses the color line. Every one of its texts challenges the premises behind the idea that there is a division between races. It is difficult to find anything in Du Bois that is either completely black or completely white, but this is especially the case in *Darkwater*—where he experiments with the plasticity and instability of race. As elsewhere in Du Bois, race is understood to be socially constructed and historically determined—even a fiction. If he blurs racial identity through a series of interracial figures, it is because he believes he can only truly interrupt the exploitation and violence at the heart of racial capitalism by targeting its foundation—a system that flourishes through "the 'manure' theory of social organization" (*DW*, 58), in which certain populations are reduced to capital's fertilizer. As he puts it, "one cannot ignore the extraordinary fact that a world campaign beginning with the slave-trade and ending with the refusal to capitalize the word 'Negro,' leading through a passionate defense of slavery by attributing every bestiality to blacks and finally culminating in the evident modern profit which lies in degrading blacks,—all this has unconsciously trained millions of honest, modern men into the belief that black folk are sub-human," fit only to fulfill the "necessary duties and services which no real human being ought to be compelled to do" (*DW*, 35 and 58).[6]

He makes this point most powerfully in the chapter that explicitly responds to his earlier *The Souls of Black Folk*, "The Souls of White Folk." There, in a passage that rewrites a line from his earlier book and at the same time evokes not only the book of Genesis but also Hegel, he declares, speaking of "White Folk," that "Of them I am singularly clairvoyant. I see in and through them. I view them from unusual points of vantage. Not as a foreigner do I come, for I am native, not foreign, bone of their thought and flesh of their language" (*DW*, 15).[7] Referencing his own mixed-race origins, his own "whiteness," Du Bois recalls the "Forethought" he places at the head of *The Souls of Black Folk*. There he writes: "[h]erein lie buried many things which if read with patience may show the strange meaning of being black ... need I add that I who speak here am bone of the bone and flesh of the flesh of them that live within the Veil?" Given *Darkwater*'s subtitle—*Voices from Within the Veil*—we can assume that at least one of these plural voices is that of the mixed-race Du Bois, the Du Bois who, despite being mixed-race—*because* he is mixed-race—identifies himself as "Black." Understanding that "Black" is never just "Black"—this is part of the "strange meaning of being black"—the fact that he identifies as "Black" scans as a political gesture. This gesture gathers more force when he later transforms the phrase "the bone of the bone and the flesh of the flesh" into "the bone of their thought and the flesh of their language." That his bodily identity is an effect of thought and language—and, in particular, of the racist ideas and stereotypes "white folk" project onto "Blackness"—implies that race itself is an invention, or, in Du Bois's own words, a "discovery," a "phantasy," a "very modern thing" that privileges whiteness at the expense of other so-called races. "Wave on wave," he goes on to say, "each with increasing virulence, is dashing this new religion of whiteness on the shores of our time" (*DW*, 15–17). If this exaltation of whiteness is the driving force of the recent world war, if it results in the violent oppression and subjugation of millions of people around the globe, if it pursues conquest in the name of "commerce and degradation," it simply intensifies and extends the violence that divides victims from victors—and peoples according to "race and lineage," to what he calls "the eternal world-wide mark of meanness,—color!" (*DW*, 23 and 21).

This meanness around the word "color" is what motivates Du Bois's effort to de-fetishize whiteness, and to emphasize its fictional status—which is at the heart of its violence. He works to loosen its hold and power over the world, and to imagine the conditions for an antiracist future. This effort is legible throughout *Darkwater* in all the racial mixing that takes place within its different vignettes: the birth of a mixed-race Jesus in "The Second Coming," a Black man who, having passed as white, is revealed to be Jesus in "Jesus Christ in Texas," a king who, also passing as white, reveals to his subjects that he is Black in "The Call," and, in the final story of the collection, "The Comet," a science fiction piece in which, after the catastrophic crash of a comet, the only survivors, a Black man and a white woman, briefly envision starting a new human race together, one that would be entirely miscegenated. The collection closes with the internationalist "A Hymn to the Peoples," a paean to "[t]he mighty rainbow of the world, / Spanning its wilderness of storm" (*DW*, 134). As Du Bois puts it twenty years later in *Dusk of Dawn*, "[d]espite everything, race lines [are] not fixed and fast. Within the Negro group especially there [are] people of all colors."[8] In a world in which, as Nahum Chandler notes, "[r]acial distinctions [are] considered to be absolutely original, primordial, determinate, fixed, permanent, eternal, in the order of things, natural," Du Bois notes that "all members of the Negro race [are] not black."[9] He unravels the tautological fiction that sustains race—a fiction with very real and violent consequences whose force he relentlessly works to counter through his political and writerly activism—by insisting on these several forms of intermixture.

In "The Comet," the possibility of intermixture emerges with the possibilities opened up by the comet's destruction. It points to a future that, coming in the form of an inevitable and uncontrollable miscegenation, would have the potential to create an alternative to white supremacy from the inside, as it were. If the story is placed at the end of *Darkwater*—even if it is followed by Du Bois's closing hymn, it is the final narrative text in the collection— it is because it archives in fictional form all the conflicts that already have been registered elsewhere in the collection. As if written in invisible ink, these conflicts appear between the lines of the story—in its references to the history of slavery and the commodification of Blacks, the unequal distribution of wealth across racial lines, the glory and ruin of capital and empire, the history of racism and of the dispossession and displacement of Black bodies, the injury and death they inherit and experience, the relation between race and capital, and even the possibility of education, transformation, female emancipation, and the becoming-human of commodified labor. We could even say that the tail of "The Comet" is what trails behind it in the form of all the texts that comprise *Darkwater*—texts that, if they could, would wreak the same destruction on the world of white supremacy that the comet does, since, as long as white supremacy lives on, "trouble is written in the stars" (*DW*, 30).

The story opens with a Black bank messenger—he is nameless at the beginning, but we soon learn that his name is "Jim"—being asked, in the midst of the news that a comet is set to hit Manhattan at noon, to descend into the lower depths of the bank's vaults in order to retrieve "two volumes of old records" (*DW*, 124). He immediately registers that he is sent because no one of value would be asked to run such errands. Saidiya Hartman describes his descent, offering protocols for reading the bare details Du Bois offers us and demonstrating the way in which the story invites us to read it historically, even requires that we do so (by putting it in relation not only to all the other parts of the book but also to the history evoked by them):

> As he descends into the underground, the yawning blackness of the inner chamber engulfs him. He finds the two volumes of records and discovers an iron chest, at least a hundred-years-old and rusted shut. Upon prying open the lock, he encounters the dull sheen of gold. The lost records of the bank and its hidden booty, gold locked away and forgotten, discovered by a man of no value—provide a tidy allegory of capitalism and slavery. The crypt harbors the secrets, the disavowed knowledge and missing volumes on which the great financial edifice rests, the same history that has relegated Jim to the bowels of the earth.
>
> The gold found in the fetid slime-filled den occupied only by rats is not the staging for a story of treasure discovered, or a tale of man's fate changed by wealth; this tableau of the hold, the lost records, the gold, and the black is a primal scene of modernity's genesis. In this sunken place, slavery is the thematic ground, although not explicitly mentioned. Held by capital, in a manner of speaking, he is confronted with his origins and pricked by the realization, the uncanny feeling of an equivalence or doubling between the gold in the trunk and the Negro in the vault.[10]

It is not an accident that this rather stunning allegory of racial capitalism and all the accoutrements that make it possible—documents, records, gold, the history of slavery and racism—takes place in Manhattan's financial district, symbolically the financial center of the United States, if not the world. Nor is it an accident that the story begins with a descent into this primal scene that reveals what Hartman calls "an inventory of violence"—a crypt of violence atop which the world of capital lives, most often forgetting or dissimulating what lies beneath it. Du Bois already elaborates the nexus of race and capitalism and its violence in several of the chapters of *Darkwater*, most notably in "Of Work and Wealth," "The Souls of White Folk," "The Hands of Ethiopia," and "Of the Ruling of Men." He depicts the "race hatred" at the heart of "the imperial commercial group of master capitalists, international and predominantly white" (*DW*, 48), and the "chance for exploitation on an immense scale for inordinate profit" that "lies in the exploitation of darker peoples." "It is here that the golden hand beckons," Du Bois adds, "[i]n these dark lands 'industrial development' may repeat in exaggerated form every horror of the industrial history of Europe, from slavery and rape to disease and maiming, with only one test of success,—its dividends!" (*DW*, 21). Even the relay between gold and the Black messenger is made clear in the poem that immediately precedes "The Comet," "The Prayers to God." There a white voice exclaims: "War? Not so; not war— / Dominion, Lord, and over black, not white; / Black, brown, and fawn, / And not Thy Chosen Brood, O God, / We murdered. / To build Thy Kingdom, / To drape our wives and little ones, / And set their souls a-glitter— / For this we killed these lesser breeds / And civilized their dead, / Raping red rubber, diamonds, cocoa, gold!" (*DW*, 122). As Hartman confirms—knowingly ventriloquizing Du Bois—"The Comet" bears reference, at times in telegraphic if not encoded ways, to all the history that accounts for why the bank messenger finds himself in the lower depths of the bank, and not simply because he is ordered to go there; rather, because industry is built on slavery in order "to reap all the profit for the white world" (*DW*, 29).[11] This is the history *Darkwater* delineates and "The Comet" carries forward, even as it wants to end it.

But moving more quickly: while he is in the lower vault, the messenger hears a "Boom!," the sound of the vault's door shutting, perhaps one small effect of the comet's arrival. After some hours, he manages to pry open the door, but, when he steps out, he sees all the dead—clerks, tellers, guards, accountants—a scene that is repeated when he steps out onto Wall Street. The dead are everywhere. Nevertheless, in the midst of all this death and ruination, all this devastation and destruction, he experiences a freedom he has never experienced before. He can enter a restaurant that, even a day before, he would have been unable to enter. He can move about the city without fearing violence against him. "The paradox," Hartman explains, is that human extinction provides the answer and the corrective to the modern project of whiteness. ... The stranglehold of white supremacy appears so unconquerable, so eternal that its only certain defeat is the end of the world. ... Neither war nor rights have succeeded in remaking the slave into the human or in eradicating racism. In the wake of the disaster, the messenger, the last black man on earth, will be permitted to live as a human for the first time. "I am alive, I am alive," he could shout in the streets of Manhattan, without fear of punishment or reprisal. He is alive because the world is dead.

If white supremacy is so ingrained in the fabric of the world that it can only be ended by the world's destruction, "The Comet" permits us to imagine this end, even as it also conveys the heart-breaking reality that to end white supremacy—and all the forms of racial capitalism that sustain it—the world as we know it has to end and start again from an entirely different place.[12] Du Bois moves to imagine the contours of this different place: finding a car, Jim drives through the devastated city and, when uptown, he hears a cry and discovers that a woman also has survived. After he hears her but before he locates her, he has not thought of her as white and she has not thought of him as Black. When they register their difference, it takes time for them to feel safe with one another. Borrowing language from "The Souls of White Folk," the woman's interior monologue expresses her initial caution. He learns that she had been "shut up in [her] dark room developing pictures of the comet" which she had taken the previous night (*DW*, 127). After moving through the city together, they open up to one another and begin to draw closer in an exchange that begins to dissolve their differences:

> The world was darkening to twilight, and a great, gray pall was falling mercifully and gently on the sleeping dead. The ghastly glare of reality seemed replaced with the dream of some great romance ...
> "How foolish our human distinctions seem—now."
> "Yes—I was not—human yesterday," he said.
> She looked at him. "And your people were not my people," she said; "but today—"
> "Death, the leveler!" he muttered.
> "And the revealer," she whispered gently, rising to her feet with great eyes. ... A vision of the world had risen before her. Slowly the mighty prophecy of her destiny overwhelmed her. Above the dead past hovered the Angel of Annunciation. She was no mere woman. She was neither high nor low, white nor black, rich nor poor. She was primal woman; mighty mother of all men to come and Bride of Life. She looked upon the man beside her and forgot

all else but his manhood, his strong vigorous manhood—his sorrow and sacrifice. She saw him glorified. He was no longer a thing apart, a creature below, a strange outcast of another clime and blood, but her Brother Humanity incarnate, Son of God and great All-Father of the race to be. ... Behind them and all around, the heavens glowed in dim, weird radiance that suffused the darkening world and made almost a minor music. Suddenly, as though gathered back in some vast hand, the great cloud-curtain fell away. Low on the horizon lay a long, white star—mystic, wonderful! And from it fled upward to the pole, like some wan bridal veil, a pale, wide sheet of flame that lighted all the world and dimmed the stars. ... The shackles seemed to rattle and fall from his soul. ... Their souls lay naked to the night. It was not lust; it was not love—it was some vaster, mightier thing. ...

Slowly, noiselessly, they moved toward each other—the heavens above, the seas around, the city grim and dead below. He loomed from out the velvet shadows vast and dark. Pearl-white and slender, she shone beneath the stars. She stretched her jeweled hands abroad. He lifted up his mighty arms, and they cried each to the other, almost with one voice, "The world is dead."

"Long live the—" (*DW*, 130–132)

With its devastating impact, the comet catastrophe blasts all distinctions, including those that, before this destruction, would have made a relationship between Jim and Julia impossible. Their exchange acknowledges that these social and racial distinctions—between Black and white, human and nonhuman, rich and poor, belonging and not belonging—have been effaced.[13] They no longer hold sway in this now unprecedented situation in which race and capital have been momentarily abolished by the world's destruction. When these distinctions fall, it becomes possible not only for each to encounter the other without fear but also for each of them to be released from a world that would condemn one of them to nothingness.[14] Jim is no longer "a thing apart," but the "Father of the race to be," with Julia the "primal mother" and "Bride of Life." This coming closer to one another is an analogue to the "dim, weird radiance" that suffuses the "darkening world" and, bringing light into this darkness, briefly allows the vision of a different future. The potential emergence of this future is accompanied by a "minor music" that pulls the "cloud-curtain" away in order to reveal "low on the horizon" a second comet—one whose tail, like a "wan bridal veil, a pale, wide sheet of flame," lights the world and dims the stars. If the first comet comes as a force of destruction that, leaving scarcely anything behind, nevertheless offers the possibility of shattering the hold of white supremacy, the second comet appears as a force of annunciation, as the fleeting sign of a different future, one that would begin in the promise of miscegenation—in a rethinking of the possibilities of miscegenation. While Du Bois suggests in several texts that miscegenation is the future, he never neglects the violence associated with the history and invention of the term and the fact that Black women bore the brunt of this violence.[15] Before elaborating the terms of this promise within the corpus of Du Bois's writings, we wish to point to another comet that is silently present within the story.

In a speech delivered on August 1, 1860, Douglass dedicates his remarks to John Brown. "His behavior was so unusual that men did not know what to make of him," he writes. "It was thought the race of such men had become extinct. ... We have not yet recovered from the wonder with which this man's deeds filled us. ... He was as a comet, whose brightness overspread half the sky ... with John Brown and his associates, the NEGRO IS A MAN."[16] When Du Bois was writing "The Comet," it is nearly inconceivable that he would not have had this reference in mind. Before writing his biography of John Brown, he had wanted to write a biography of Douglass. He was deeply engaged with Douglass's writings and speeches throughout his life, and, given his study of Brown, he would have had a great interest in any reference Douglass would have made to this other abolitionist. The comet that Brown is joins the forces of Du Bois's two comets. As one of the great figures of abolition, he embodies the force that, like the first comet, would destroy the underpinnings of white supremacy in order to open the space for a different future, one that, like the second comet, points to the possibility of what Du Bois in his biography of Brown calls "a new society free from prejudices" and from the "inequalities of race and class." Brown is the emblem of the possibility of a new beginning. If "persistence in racial distinction spells disaster sooner or later," the system of slavery and the privilege of whiteness that sustains it are, in Brown's word, "wrong," which is why this system must be eliminated. We must, according to Du Bois, following Brown, "[d]estroy it—uproot it, stem, blossom, and branch; give it no quarter, exterminate it and do it now."[17] If the Brown comet insists that white supremacy can only be overcome by a complete destruction of the world that sustains it, it also carries with it the dissolution of racial distinctions promised by Brown himself, and manifested in his radical abolitionism.[18]

This dissolution is enacted within "The Comet" in the possibility of miscegenation—as the increasingly legible signature of what Du Bois understands as international "modernity"—in order to challenge the entire logic of a global capitalist system that depends on the distinction between races. The story presents the violent resistance to this challenge: at the very moment that Jim and Julia imagine starting a new miscegenated human race, Julia's father and her fiancé appear, having been outside of New York when the comet hit. We immediately return to a world organized around "the shibboleth of race" when the father exclaims: "Why! It's—a—nigger—Julia! Has he—has he dared—." Although Julia replies "[h]e has dared—all to rescue me … and I thank him much" (*DW*, 133), she says this without looking at Jim. Indeed, she does not look at him again and we can expect that she never will. He is again someone of lesser value, and the fact that he is given a "tip" reinstates money as the universal equivalent. As Hartman notes, "*Nigger* is repeated to make visceral the violence that accompanies the restoration of the world, to remind him of the hatred that is its substrate. The clock has been turned back, and once again he is barred from the human. He stands silently beneath the glare of the light with the flat unseeing eyes of a sleepwalker and broken by the sweet experience of *what might have been*." Jim then hears his name called out and sees a woman approaching him with their dead child in her arms, a closing figure for the transformation of hope into mourning—for a stillborn hope. The devastation wrought by the comet recurs in the quiet but no less violent devastation of a different future. If John Brown's raid on Harper's Ferry ultimately fails—if his effort to undo white supremacy is crushed and punished—it is not surprising that the otherworldly comet that is his analogue in Du Bois's story also fails to bring enduring transformation. Nevertheless, together, the story's comets not only offer a glimpse of what this transformation could look like but also leave behind a trail that, although never a blueprint, can join forces with the next political comet. As Du Bois notes, in a line that he repeats several times in his biography of Brown, the legacy that the abolitionist comet bequeaths to us is "this great word: the cost of liberty is less than the price of repression," even when "that cost be blood." What is required is nothing less than "the abolition of hard and fast lines between races" and "the breaking down of barriers between classes."[19]

Foreseeing the rise of new forms of intermixture in an increasingly globalized world and pointing to the intensifying erosion of any lines or borders between different groups of people, De Bois argues, as Chandler explains, that "the kinds of social processes that led to the formation of the United States and have been extended in its own imperial policy" have become "virtually universal."[20] In Du Bois's words,

> the expansion and consolidation of nations to-day is leading to countless repetitions of that which we have in America to-day—the inclusion of nations within nations—of groups of undeveloped peoples brought into contact with advanced races under the same government, language and system of culture. The lower races will in nearly every case be dark races. German Negroes, Portuguese Negroes, Spanish Negroes, English East Indian, Russian, Chinese, American Filipinos—such are the groups which following the example of the American Negroes will in the 20th century strive, not by war and rapine but by the mightier weapons of peace and culture to gain a place and name in the civilized world.[21]

This point is reiterated in the lesser-known part of Du Bois's claim that "the problem of the twentieth century is the problem of the color line—the relation of the darker to the lighter races of men in Asia and Africa, in America and the islands of the sea."[22]

If Du Bois would seem to argue for the potentially salutary effects of miscegenation—its capacity to unsettle the logic that, sustaining racial distinctions and hierarchies, reinforces white supremacy—he also understands the risk of naturalizing it.[23] He knows that miscegenation cannot be disentangled from the violence of its history—rooted as it is in the history of slavery, rapacious violence against Black women, the brutality of antimiscegenation laws, and the way in which miscegenation was—and continues to be—instrumentalized in the direction of racism. He knows that it will create its own devastating racist backlash—something we are witnessing with great intensity today. This is why, he acknowledges, the "greatest cost" of liberty "would be the new problems of racial intercourse and intermarriage which would come to the front. Freedom and equal opportunity in this respect would inevitably bring some intermarriage of whites and yellows and browns and blacks. This might be a good thing and it might not be. We do not know."[24] Du Bois more than once argues that one of the most important questions for the future is that of racial contact and intermingling, but his most extended case for the need to study the consequences of racial intermixture can be found in an unpublished text from 1935—the same year *Black Reconstruction* is published—simply entitled "Miscegenation."[25]

There, claiming that the question at stake is nothing less than what "race" is, Du Bois again states that there are "no hard and fast dividing lines" between the "conventional divisions of mankind into black, yellow and white," adding that the "numerous subdivisions" called "races" arose "from the intermingling of more primitive groups." There are no "pure races," he writes, "[t]hey have been built up through indiscriminate inter-breeding throughout past ages."[26] Citing A. C. Haddon's claim that a "racial type is after all but an artificial concept," he goes on to note that "[m]odern Italians, Frenchmen, Englishmen and Germans are composites of the broken fragments of different racial groups or sub-groups," concluding that "[w]orld-wide communication has tended to miscegenation on a broad scale."[27] Here miscegenation is not simply the future but also a fact of history. Miscegenation precedes—is at the heart of—any effort to assert a difference or an identity. But, as Du Bois goes on to note:

> The bitterest protest and deepest resentment in the matter of inter-breeding has arisen from the fact that the same white race which today resents race mixture in theory has been chiefly responsible for the systematic misuse and degradation of darker women the world over, and has literally fathered millions of half-castes in Asia, Africa and America. ... Indeed, the question of the extent to which whites and blacks in the United States have mingled their blood, and the results of this inter-mingling, past, present and future, is, in many respects, the crux of the so-called Negro problem in the United States. ... They are glad that slavery has disappeared but their hesitation now is how far complete social freedom and full economic opportunity for Negroes is going to result in such racial amalgamation as to make America octoroon in blood. It is the real fear of this result and inherited resentment at its very possibility that keeps the race problem in America so terribly alive.[28]

If miscegenation is a historical fact presaging a different future, Du Bois remains attentive to the resentments that appear in response to its possibility, especially because the world's economies continue to be organized around the presumed distinctions between the races. This is why, he worries, intermingling might "lead on to the dangers of lawless caste, race hatred, and war,"[29] something we increasingly have witnessed in the last few years and not only in the United States: in the intensification and proliferation of violence that has accompanied the reemergence of white supremacist activism. Although such racism has a long history, for Du Bois it is "[t]he imperial width of the thing," its "heaven-defying audacity," that "makes its modern newness" (*DW*, 21). In this context—and despite the risks—Du Bois chooses miscegenation as a fact and figure that points, in Julia Hooker's words, to "a

hoped-for global and anticolonial uprising against white supremacy."[30] For him, in the end, it is a question of numbers and of the
massification of the fact of intermixture, a massification that, as in
Benjamin, cannot be controlled, restricted, or instrumentalized—
even when it is violently resisted.

This massification along miscegenated lines is already
inscribed in the John Brown comet—something that becomes legible if we recall the remarks that Brown makes on November 2,
1859, when, convicted of treason, conspiracy, and murder, he is
invited to address the court. In his speech, Brown offers us a script
for understanding the meaning of his death. He declares: "Now, if
it is deemed necessary that I should forfeit my life for the further-
ance of the ends of justice, and mingle my blood further with the
blood of my children and with the blood of millions in this slave
country whose rights are disregarded by wicked, cruel, and unjust
enactments, I say, let it be done."[31] As Franny Nudelman notes,

> In a sweeping rhetorical gesture made meaningful by his impend-
> ing death on the scaffold, Brown [uses] the figure of blood to ally
> his extraordinary fate with the routine abuse of slaves. Blood,
> imagined here as a sort of universal fluid, unites Brown, his fam-
> ily, and countless slaves. Combining his lifeblood with the "blood
> of millions," Brown participates in, and radicalizes, a tradition of
> abolitionist sympathy that dramatizes slave suffering in an effort
> to mobilize readers. ... Blood shed, first by slaves and then by
> Brown himself, is reinterpreted as one blood, a common fluid that
> circulates between Brown, his children, and enslaved millions. ...
> Brown's blood provides the medium that binds a far-flung imag-
> ined community.[32]

Brown suggests that his death will inaugurate a process of
massification that, gathering its momentum from the mixing of
Brown's blood with that of millions of others, will take the form
of miscegenation. This miscegenation—which appears with the
force of his rhetoric, but which signals a fact that goes beyond
just language, or at least points to what cannot be fully contained by language—reappears in another form in the well-known
Civil War song "John Brown's Body," which became an anthem
for the Union army. In the same way that Brown announces the
transformation of his death into the potential transformation
of the body politic, the song describes the transformation of his
corpse into, in Nudelman's words, "a source of public meaning."
Although "John Brown's body lies a-mouldering in the grave,"
the song insists that his "soul goes marching on." In doing so,

it "imaginatively [reverses] the effects of violence, granting both agency and meaning to the process of decay," suggesting in this way that Brown endures even beyond the disappearance of his body.[33] Incorporated into the song, his body disappears only to be brought back to life again by each of the soldiers who sing the song along with others.[34] Brown's body disintegrates only to be recomposed again in song, like the tail of a comet held together by the breath of multiple others—a comet that, like those of Du Bois, becomes a figure for the force of destruction that must always precede the inauguration of a different future.[35]

Edward Emerson Barnard, *The Great Comet of 1882*

XX. TO THE PLANETARIUM

As in the realm of the stars the orbit of a planet is in some cases determined by two suns; as in certain cases suns of different colors shine near a single planet, sometimes with red light, sometimes with green light, and then occasionally illuminating the planet at the same time and flooding it with colors—so we modern men are determined, thanks to the complicated mechanics of our "starry sky," by *different* moralities; our actions shine alternately in different colors, they are rarely univocal—and there are cases enough in which we perform actions *of many colors.*

—Friedrich Nietzsche, *Beyond Good and Evil* (1886)

One cannot imagine any fundamental change in our social existence which has not first thrown off Utopian visions like so many sparks from the tail of a comet.

—Fredric Jameson, *Archaeologies of the Future* (2005)[1]

If Jameson suggests that *One-Way Street* is Benjamin's "only book," it is not just any book but rather a complete reconceptualization of what a book might be and, more specifically, of how a book's organization and style operate in relationship to the history and politics it contains and cannot contain at the same time. Written between 1923 and 1926 and published in 1928, *One-Way Street*—as we already have noted—was to be an integral part of Benjamin's projected but never finished book on "Politics." Benjamin oscillated between a reading of Paul Scheerbart's "asteroid novel" *Lesabéndio* and *One-Way Street* as the concluding section of his political study, eventually moving in the direction of the latter. It is remarkable that what may have constituted Benjamin's most openly political proposal relies so heavily on highly experimental and speculative literary forms, but this should no longer be surprising. The role of fabulation and experimentalism is key to understanding Benjamin's stance on literary and politico-philosophical production, and on production more generally. Here he experiments with the plasticity of the thinking mind at play, to present the reader not just with a finished product but rather with the infinite possibilities and movements inscribed within a single "book."

One-Way Street presents itself to the reader as a heterogeneous accumulation of fragments and as a work-in-progress, very much like the "construction site" that entitles one of its many short sections. As Michael W. Jennings explains,

> when it appeared in 1928, Walter Benjamin's *One-Way Street* presented the reader with a new and radical literary form. Avoiding all semblance of linear narrative, the book seems on first reading to offer a jumble of sixty apparently autonomous short prose pieces: aphorisms, jokes, dream protocols; cityscapes, landscapes, and mindscapes; portions of writing manuals; trenchant contemporary political analysis; prescient appreciations of the child's psychology, behavior, and moods; decodings of bourgeois fashion, living arrangements, and courtship patterns; and, time and again, what Benjamin would later call the empathy with "the soul of the commodity."[2]

He goes on to say that the book is "a highly theorized constellation of fragments" that echoes in turn the theory of writing Benjamin presents in the "Epistemo-Critical Preface" to his *Origin of the German Trauerspiel*. There he writes:

> Method is indirection. Presentation as indirection, the roundabout way—this, then, is the methodological character of the tractatus. Renunciation of the unbroken course of intention is its immediately distinguishing feature. With its staying power, thinking constantly begins anew; with its sense of the circumstantial, it goes back to the thing itself. This unceasing inhale-and-exhale is the form of existence most proper to contemplation. ... Just as the majesty of mosaics remains when they are capriciously disassembled, so philosophical observation fears no dissipation of momentum. Out of the singular and disparate they come together.[3]

It is almost as if Benjamin imagines his book first in the form of a condensed theoretical *tractatus* and then later materializes it in the form of a literary montage of attractions, in which "the singular and the disparate ... come together" to demonstrate that only through "the roundabout way" of "indirection" can we uncover the hidden structure that underlies capitalist modernity.

As Greil Marcus does in his recent preface to the book, it is worth listing the book's table of contents to get a sense of the kind of associations Benjamin cinematically projects onto the minds of his readers in "the unceasing inhale-and-exhale" that, for him, "is the form of existence most proper to contemplation," and in the "thinking [that] constantly begins anew":

Filling Station—Breakfast Room—Number 113—For Men—Standard Clock—Come Back! All Is Forgiven!—Manorially Furnished Ten-Room Apartment—Chinese Curios—Gloves—Mexican Embassy—To the Public: Please Protect and Preserve These New Plantings—Construction Site—Ministry of the Interior—Flag . . . at Half-Mast—Imperial Panorama: A Tour of German Inflation—Underground Works—Coiffeur for Easily Embarrassed Ladies—Caution: Steps—Attested Auditor of Books—Teaching Aid—Germans, Drink German Beer!—Post No Bills—Number 13—Ordnance—First Aid—Interior Decoration—Stationers—Fancy Goods—Enlargements—Antiques—Watchmaker and Jeweler—Arc Lamp—Loggia—Lost-and-Found Office—Stand for Not More than Three Cabs—Monument to a Warrior—Fire Alarm—Travel Souvenirs—Optician—Toys—Polyclinic—These Spaces for Rent—Office Equipment—Mixed Cargo: Shipping and Packing—Closed for Alterations—Stamp Shop—Si Parla Italiano—Technical Aid—Hardware—Tax Advice—Legal Protection for the Needy—Doctor's Night-Bell—Madame Ariane: Second Courtyard on the Left—Costume Wardrobe—Betting Office—Stand-Up Beer Hall—No Vagrants!—To the Planetarium. This fast-paced modernist montage of accumulated glimpses and sounds, imaginary and real, revolves around the hidden lives of commodities and the relations they establish with the movements of the capitalist city. It calls into being a reader willing to be overwhelmed with a dizzying array of stimuli and innervations and happy to forgo narrative order in favor of a constellation of diverse motifs that appears and disappears in a synesthetic and eroticized ebb and flow.[4] In this way, the afterimages Benjamin imprints on the reader are also the traces of a thinking that exhausts and revives itself in the transience of experience. In *One-Way Street* Benjamin performs each and every one of his philosophical concepts by threading them into the fabric of a text that speaks to the senses beyond the "enervating amazement at what is daily repeated." It perceives "the phenomena of decline as stability itself and rescue alone as extraordinary, verging on the marvelous and incomprehensible" (*OWS*, 451). Paradoxically, by relying on the commodity as a nexus of metamorphosis and instability, Benjamin gives us insight into the madness of the logic of universal equivalence. After all, as he puts it, "the 'Lunaparks' are a prefiguration of sanatoria" (*OWS*, 487).

Benjamin's mordant critique of the money form—the universal equivalent par excellence—is most directly addressed in his "Imperial Panorama: A Tour through the German Inflation." The book's longest section, it is broken up into smaller fragments that mimic the viewing stations, the stereoscopic images, and, more generally, the architecture of Kaiserpanorama, the popular carousel at Berlin's Imperial Arcade. There he spins his own rhetorical carousel to have us experience the unsteadiness of a pervasive and fluctuating universal equivalent that turns out to be nothing more than an "optical illusion," a "phantom," and a "mirage" (*OWS*, 453). What passes as either private property or national wealth is now, in the midst of an exponentially growing postwar and postpandemic inflation, more legible as the cruel and shameful gamble it was designed to be—and has been. Even in "stable conditions"—what Luxemburg calls "quiet times"—there are "strata for whom stabilized conditions" are nothing more than "stabilized wretchedness" (*OWS*, 451), and this because the poverty, hunger, housing crisis, and violence that populate the streets of Berlin are the direct result of a "society, each of whose members cares only for his own abject well-being." At most, the extremity of Germany's circumstances forces not only "the onlooker's pity or his equally terrible awareness of his own impunity, but his shame" (*OWS*, 452). Not unlike the one invoked by Marx in his letter to Ruge, this shame is a symptom of a shared inability "to make peace with poverty," and the last sentence on the "rapaciousness" with which we destroy nature (*OWS*, 452 and 455). Benjamin is poignant in his fragmented depiction of an urban experience where "money stands ruinously at the center of every vital interest," where "a universal delusion" is refracted everywhere, and where "in the denaturing of things—a denaturing with which, emulating human decay, [the German bourgeoisie] punish humanity—the country itself conspires" (*OWS*, 454). This is, of course, also the world of Du Bois's comet. In both instances, the catastrophe happens when no one is watching and all we see in its aftermath is the earth's ruination. As Benjamin puts it in the section's closing sentence, "If society has so denatured itself through necessity and greed that it can now receive the gifts of nature only rapaciously— that it snatches the fruit unripe from the trees in order to sell it most profitably, and is compelled to empty each dish in its determination to have enough—the earth will be impoverished and the land will yield bad harvests" (*OWS*, 455).

Benjamin returns to the plunder of nature throughout his text and does so always in reference to the hegemony of money and the commodity form. Together, they present the impoverishment produced by greed in the guise of exchange. Because commodity fetishism and its magical powers of transformation are the organizing motif of Benjamin's constellation of figures—they are the enigma of its beating heart—his "book" can neither begin nor conclude in any recognizable way. It is predicated, in a manner that he will further develop in "The Storyteller," on the disappearance of narrative and linear temporality; it insistently transforms and mutates from one genre and topic to another, refusing to focus simply on one place, object, or sensation. This is why this distracted and endless accumulation of diverse fragments can only appear and disappear and, in its final and most musical moment, can only scatter and expand into larger orbits, like the left-over debris of Benjamin's singular literary explosion. The last section, titled "To the Planetarium," signals this expansive logic and directs our gaze toward the sky so that we can shift our attention gradually—and then all at once—from the city onto the earth, from the earth onto the planet, and from the planet onto the cosmos. That this section is the most speculative in the book is hardly a coincidence. In a world entirely taken over by the commodity, only comets and stars can potentially herald a different modality in the relationship between the human and the nonhuman, and between nature and technology.[5]

In an anachronistic echo of the Blanqui that Benjamin discovers as he researches his *Arcades Project*, "To the Planetarium" reminds us that, if fabulation, experiments, and speculation are part of the political archive, then so are stars and comets. Very much like "The Comet" in *Darkwater*, this final section briefly brings together all the other sections in the book only to scatter them again—to fling them even farther away in an "ecstatic trance" that announces a "new and unprecedented comingling with the cosmic powers" (*OWS*, 486). Before he can move in the direction of cosmic potentialities, however, Benjamin demands that we contemplate the very real destruction of the earth brought about by military technology, and that we imagine the violence of a worldwide catastrophe in order to then be able to conceive of an emerging and multiplying collectivity that, operating with an entirely "new body," calls for another "organization of pessimism":

In the nights of annihilation of the last war, the frame of mankind was shaken by a feeling that resembled the bliss of the epileptic. And the revolts that followed it were the first attempt of mankind to bring the new body under its control. The power of the proletariat is the measure of its convalescence. If it is not gripped to the very marrow by the discipline of this power, no pacifist polemics will save it. Living substance conquers the frenzy of destruction only in the ecstasy of procreation. (*OWS*, 487)

Benjamin's elliptical reference to the October Revolution in Russia and to the failed German Revolution makes it clear that this "first attempt" has not yet succeeded in inaugurating a new collective body, one that would be an offspring of the "power of the proletariat," a proletariat that, very much like the ravaged surface of the earth, is still convalescent (recovering, that is, but also growing stronger by the day, and not only because of its defeats). If, at present, however, the cosmos has become a purely optical experience unable to conjure the communal "ecstasic trance" (*OWS*, 486) of earlier and maybe future periods, it is because of the technological "wooing of the cosmos" (*OWS*, 486–487), which— "enacted for the first time on a planetary scale, that is, in the spirit of technology"—has replaced telescopes with propellers, electrical currents, bombs and gases that, digging "sacrificial shafts" in "Mother Earth" (*OWS*, 486), have made the earth look as distant and forlorn as the moon. Moreover, "the lust for profit of the ruling class"—as it sought to exploit technology in the war—turned technology into an enemy and "the bridal bed into a bloodbath" (*OWS*, 487).

Nevertheless, as Benjamin knows, any transformed relationship to the planet and beyond must be mediated by technology. Like the commodity object, technology emerges as both the culprit and the cure. It becomes salvatory when it is no longer directed to "the mastery of nature" that "the imperialists teach" as "the purpose of all technology," but rather becomes the means of a new relationship between humans and the cosmos on a "planetary scale" (*OWS*, 487). What appears as Benjamin's ambivalence toward technology—even a contradiction in his stance toward it—owes much to the science fiction of Scheerbart and to what the expressionist philosopher Salomo Friedlaender called "creative indifference,"[6] and should be seen as yet another attempt on his part to enact what Miriam Hansen calls his "experimental will to explore and shift between antithetical if not antinomic perspectives."[7]

While Friedlaender's philosophy seeks to move beyond the dichotomy of subjects and objects in the direction of a collective human technology, Scheerbart anticipates Donna Haraway's assertion that "science fiction is political theory"[8] in order to engineer an entirely new species in which nature and technology are fused. He envisions the natural laws of a planet that conceives of itself as a collective and cosmic body, but one that is in constant motion and transformation, never the same from one moment to the next. His strange fiction is presented as an "asteroid novel," a hybrid never encountered before, closer to an imagined architectural construction emblematic of the unity of technology and nature than to any sort of narrative. Indeed, besides writing science fiction, plays, poetry, and journalism, Scheerbart was a proponent of glass architecture and a member of the Glass Chain movement—which included Walter Gropius, Bruno Taut, and Hans Scharoun. Benjamin quotes his architectural writings extensively in his *Arcades Project*. As an engineer and inventor, Scheerbart also was directly involved in the speculative design of perpetual motion machines, and in 1910 he wrote a speculative science memoir about them, *The Perpetual Motion Machine: The Story of an Invention*. These machines would be capable of extracting infinite movement from finite energy sources, effectively putting an end to the energetic plunder of the earth, a thermodynamic impossibility that had to remain hypothetical but that clearly reverberates in the engineering innovations he describes in *Lesabéndio*. Although largely forgotten until relatively recently, Scheerbart was a visible figure in the German avant-garde, and particularly influential for expressionism, proto-surrealism, and Dada. When he died by starving himself, his action was generally interpreted as a political protest against the violence of World War I (an echo of Fritz Heinle's suicide that Benjamin surely would have registered).

Scheerbart's utopian novel was published in 1913. Defying any generic classification—demonstrating that, at its origins, science fiction already was a hybrid of different genres—it depicts the planet Pallas and its inhabitants, the Pallasians, plastic zoomorphic beings in whose bodies technology and nature are fully integrated. Indeed, their rubbery bodies are able to morph and adapt to whatever is needed in a given situation. In a state of constant metamorphosis, their elasticity enables them to change their shape, their tubular legs with suction-cupped feet help them secure themselves or launch to another place, their eyes can become telescopes or microscopes, and, because of their wings, they can fly. They absorb nutrients through their pores, and even transform themselves into radio receivers in order to receive news. While most of the novel consists of detailed descriptions of Pallasian processes of reproduction—of life, resources, and knowledge—and more generally of the collective habits of the planet, it also tells the skeletal and somewhat comic story of Lesabéndio's dream of building a 44-mile-high tower that can connect the two halves of Pallas's double star—its torso and its head—and exponentially increase the energy and knowledge of the planet. The novel's climax indicates how the completion of this architectural and technological project utterly transforms the collective life of Pallas and brings enhanced happiness to the Pallasians, who initially resist the project—struggling with the effort it requires and the changes it produces. Lesabéndio, who dies in order to realize his plan, becomes a comet and is fully absorbed into the head system of Pallas as a bodiless entity without a self.

That Scheerbart's embrace of technology and its transformative potential has clear political undertones is something Benjamin immediately points out. In his words, Scheerbart "knew better than any other author how to give emphasis to the revolutionary character of technological labor" (*GS*, 6:368). In a short review of *Lesabéndio* he goes on to say that "Scheerbart's greatest find was to have the stars plead for the cause of creation together with mankind ... the gentle, amazed serenity with which the author describes the strange natural laws of other worlds, the vast cosmic projects which are undertaken there, and the nobly naive discussions of the inhabitants show him to be one of those humorists who ... seem never to forget that the earth is a star."[9] Pointing to Scheerbart's own method of "indirection," here Benjamin suggests that, if Scheerbart turns to science fiction and to the description of a seemingly entirely different world—a world of stars and comets and strange elastic creatures—he does so in order to actively engage what, for him, are the most pressing questions about the relation between technology and nature, and to imagine a world that could exceed them and in which stars could have a communal agency that emerges in the process of their own creation. This is exactly what Benjamin does with his scalar shift in "To the Planetarium": he reminds us that the earth is a star and suggests that our perspective and responsibility toward the fate of the planet should adjust accordingly. They should move toward a "cosmological perspectivism" *avant la lettre*.[10]

From the moment he encounters *Lesabéndio*—Scholem gives him a copy of the book in 1917 as a wedding gift—Benjamin keeps it close and continues to plan an extended political treatment of it until the end of his life. In his 1933 "Experience and Poverty," he writes:

> No one has greeted this present with greater joy and hilarity than Paul Scheerbart. There are novels by him that from a distance look like works by Jules Verne. But quite unlike Verne, who always has ordinary French or English gentlemen of leisure traveling around the cosmos in the most amazing vehicles, Scheerbart is interested in inquiring how our telescopes, our airplanes, our rockets can transform human beings as they have been up to now

into completely new, lovable, and interesting creatures. Moreover, these creatures talk in a completely new language. And what is crucial about this language is its arbitrary, constructed nature, in contrast to organic language. This is the distinctive feature of the language of Scheerbart's human beings, or rather "people"; for human likeness—a principle of humanism—is something they reject. Even in their proper names: Peka, Labu, Sofanti, and the like are the names of the characters in the book *Lesabéndio*, titled after its hero. The Russians, too, like to give their children "dehumanized" names: they call them "October," after the month of the Revolution; "Pyatiletka," after the Five-Year Plan; or "Aviakhim," after an airline. No technical renovation of language, but its mobilization in the service of struggle or work—at any rate, of changing reality instead of describing it.[11]

The new and technologically transformed reality Scheerbart depicts must also involve the creation of a new, arbitrary, and impersonal language, a language that would not be instrumental but instead a technology of pure means that echoes and mimes the logic of a planet in which knowledge and creation cannot be extricated from one another. Benjamin's comparison to Soviet children's names underscores his tendency to read some of the details of Scheerbart's novel as proto-communist gestures, suggesting that he thinks of communism itself as a kind of political asteroid, a cosmic formation that cannot be accounted for with a terrestrial modus operandi still based on individual and individualist expressions. This different communism cannot be "humanist"—it would reject the "principle of humanism"—and it would demand another way of conceiving collectivity, the relation between idealism and materialism, imagination and political organization, and, again, the role of language, reading, and writing in the historico-political sphere. If Benjamin reads the relationship between architecture, technology, political philosophy, and language in *Lesabéndio* as a proto-communist blueprint for a different social, political, and economic organization—rather than simply as describing or endorsing the changes already implemented by the Soviet government—it is because the communism he has in mind has not yet been realized and, at best, can only be pointed at through indirection and fictional speculation. If Benjamin's communism has never yet existed, it must be imagined, and *Lesabéndio* is his chosen medium here.

Early in the novel, we are told how Pallasians come into being. When they are born—or rather "hatched" from pods, since no sexual contact is involved in their reproduction—they seem to speak a poetry drawn from the future. Issuing sounds that have never yet existed, their first utterances have futurity built into them. They emerge from "large nutshells located in the lead veins" of Pallas, and the initial incomprehensible sounds they make become their names. As they learn Pallasian, they begin to tell, with great joy and laughter, future stories of far-away stars and asteroid rings that, increasing the knowledge of Pallas and other nearby asteroids, still contain "secrets within themselves." These stories produce an archive that is recorded and later studied: "The first stories of the freshly hatched Pallasians are always written down. Each Pallasian always has something entirely new to tell that cannot be compared with what the previous little ones said," and "many Pallasians spend all their time with these stories, which reveal many things about the essential nature of Pallas—but also give rise to many riddles."[12] Each story becomes a singular piece of the puzzle that Pallas is, and the freshly hatched Pallasians, born speaking a new and unprecedented language that cannot be understood but quickly learning Pallasian, retain a trace of the incommunicability and incomprehensibility of their "native" tongue—a tongue that, shared with no one else, is not recognizable—in their name.[13] They never leave behind the illegibility that, at the source of their language, remains linked to who they are. Benjamin would have been attracted to this acknowledgment of the incommunicability of language in general, to this fidelity to it, but he also would have loved that the Pallasians have a singular relation to books and written documents.

Because Pallasians "can easily transform their eyes into microscopes, nearly all books are produced photographically in the tiniest form possible, so that every Pallasian is capable of carrying his entire library around on his collar" (*L*, 10). They are able to call up any book they wish to read, and they also can share books in their library with each other. In addition, every book that becomes available can be added to everyone's collar so that there is a shared archive of books. Although the Pallasians can often communicate through a kind of telepathy—although their bodies can become technologized receivers of information—"sharing thoughts" on Pallas "is accomplished much more easily through books and other types of writing signs" (*L*, 161). The accessibility of all forms of knowledge is of a piece with Pallas's efforts to expand the public realm—to make space accessible to everyone by eliminating private property or to share knowledge rather than keeping it for a select few. Reading and writing are here forms of massified accessibility. They are available to everyone, even if they retain their relation to what remains inscrutable—to what remains linked to the riddles and enigmas of the cosmos but also of language itself. This is how the Pallasians learn about the earth, which, in its difference, comes with its own incomprehensibility.

Reading a travelogue written by a Pallasian who visited earth, Lesabéndio conveys the visitor's impressions of the earth and its inhabitants. Viewing earth through the mediation of a Pallasian perspective, the account offers a rather devastating evaluation of life on our planet, an almost comical cautionary tale against the logic of violence, plunder, greed, and blindness toward the other, that leaves the Pallasian "horrified." The Pallasian emphasizes the earthlings' predatory habits, which they themselves cannot see—the violence with which they nourish themselves by killing other life forms, cutting them up and then eating these pieces with an almost unquenchable voracity, and with which they "attack each other in enormous hordes of thousands, and inflict terrible wounds with sharp pieces of iron and weapons for shooting," which "generally results soon after in death" (*L*, 10–11). Despite his horror at earthly violence—its destruction of the planet's human and non-human inhabitants and of nature in general—the Pallasian does admire the interest humans have in other stars, and he registers that they are aware of Pallas and that they themselves call the star *Pallas*, after the astronomer who discovered it, *Peter Simon Pallas*! This relay between the star and its earthly discoverer would seem to corroborate, even if in this rather displaced way, a sense that different worlds already can be imagined on earth—if only from a distance and if only through the medium of the stars.

It is because the earth can have a relation to other worlds that it is possible to imagine a world beyond its presently devastated, impoverished, plundering, and violent state. That the world of the Pallasians is meant to offer a vision of an alternative to the world of capital and its obsessions with the conquering of nature and the hoarding of property can be seen in another passage in which Benjamin again turns to Scheerbart, and in which the ubiquity of glass in the architecture of Pallas can be viewed as a utopian and hyperbolic intensification of the Glass Chain group's own proposals for a different future:

> To return to Scheerbart: he placed the greatest value on housing his "people"—and following this model, his fellow citizens—in buildings benefiting their station, in adjustable, movable glass-covered dwellings of the kind since built by Loos and Le Corbusier. It is not a coincidence that glass is such a hard, smooth material to which nothing can be fixed. A cold and sober material into the bargain. Glass in general is the enemy of secrets. It is also the enemy of possessions.[14]

Glass is understood here as an architectural pure means. It is entirely devoid of bourgeois interiority and, as the "enemy of secrets," is completely public. The "enemy of possessions," it also challenges the "helpless fixation on notions of security and property" (*OWS*, 450) that characterizes contemporary earthly society.[15] Examples that stress the importance of assembly and public debate abound in *Lesabéndio* and overwhelmingly concern the protagonist's need to secure enough consensus and support from the Pallasians to carry his project forward. In order to build a tower that can connect the two parts of Pallas's double star—the so-called "head" and "torso" of the planetoid—Lesabéndio uses his rhetorical powers to persuade the other Pallasians to join him in this collective and collaborative project—to let go of their own plans and desires in the name of a mass movement, something he will later call, echoing Friedlaender, "a theory of surrender." In his words, "[i]f everyone stubbornly works on his own individual insight, without paying any attention to the insights of his neighbors, then there's no point in thinking about the fulfillment of even one of these plans. We have to subordinate our own thoughts to a greater thought—or subordinate our thinking to an entity greater than ourselves" (*L*, 90). Lesabéndio's conviction comes to him in a dream; he realizes that he can "only really feel an inner peace when [his] thoughts are drawn toward the great unknown that knows more about our fate than we do, and which guides us where we need and want to go, even when we aren't able to recognize it" (*L*, 63). In answer to the question of "what selfhood actually is!" (*L*, 158), the novel increasingly turns Pallas into an allegorical site of metamorphosis in which selves are shown to be relational, hybrid, and collective. In the terms most familiar to us, Pallasians are impersonal subjects—scattered selves without agency of their own. Lesabéndio makes this clear in a reverie just as he is falling asleep. "We're not acting primarily according to our own will, after all," he says:

> The great spirit of our Star reigns in us. We only seem like independent beings. Something unconscious is active and is the most powerful source in our beings. I believe that the Guiding Principle lives high above us in the head-system of Pallas—in the great cloud that gives us day and night—and, above the great cloud, in the shackled comets—toward which we strain and strive. It's for them that we continue to work on the great Tower. This is no longer an artistic quest, but something else—something beyond our understanding. We only feel well when we know ourselves to be at one with it. I want to merge totally and become a single being. Maybe

*He up there—the Powerful One—*will take me in when I become transparent. We become transparent when we are near death. (*L*, 113–114)

To be at One with something else and, in particular, with something greater and larger is to cease to be just oneself, and even to admit that one is never just oneself.[16] This communal sense of being—which counters any sense of individualism or privacy, especially one that depends on a sense of private property—is at the heart of Pallasian identity and, as Lesabéndio notes here, is most evident when a Pallasian is near death. As we learn, when a Pallasian is dying, his body dries up and becomes "practically transparent": "At that point, the dying Pallasian conceives the wish to be sucked up by a living one. The living Pallasian absorbs him through his pores." This process can only take place if "the absorber" is "completely willing to inhale the other Pallasian," but Pallasians really only refuse if they have already "absorbed another dying Pallasian that same day." The absorbing Pallasian stretches his body to its full height, opens his pores widely, and the body of the dying Pallasian—flickering with fluorescent lights—shatters into little pieces that are then drawn into the pores, with the dying body eventually disappearing altogether (*L*, 40). This rather remarkable process of incorporation becomes a figure for the multiplicity of selves in each Pallasian body, with each "self" presumably also an ensemble of all the dead Pallasians already "inside" the dying body because of the absorptions to which this body has itself previously assented. It would seem that the Pallasian body is a living cemetery that takes in the withering, scattered plural body of the dying Pallasian and incorporates it, along with all the other bodies that come with it. It is an incorporation that gives the dying body another life, another kind of communal life at the threshold of death and life. It signals a process whereby the dead survive in the body of the living and a world in which the living carry all their dead with them. The Pallasian body is a kind of common-wealth, a communal and relational self, and therefore not a "self" at all. It also is itself transformed with each absorption:

> As soon as a Pallasian has sucked a dying creature up into himself, a subtle transformation can be seen in him. Qualities of the dead Pallasian start to overlay the features of the one who absorbed him, and a physical increase in size and in the strength of all organs will be noticeable in the absorber. Pallasians who absorb many dying fellow beings receive a steadily growing vitality from them ... a Pallasian who has just absorbed another Pallasian usually feels full of initiative and ready to start new projects. (*L*, 43)

This process of absorption, this transformation at the limit between death and life, is exemplified in the most spectacular and consequential way in the final chapters of the book, in which—having realized the dream of his Tower in collaboration with the Pallasians in a mass movement that evolves, in fits and starts, only in the process of the Tower's production—Lesabéndio dies. Absorbed into the double star of Pallas, he becomes a comet. These concluding pages offer a fantastic vision of what a proto-communist revolution could look like. They are full of all the signs of such a transformation, as if in anticipation of Benjamin's later description of "revolutions" as "innervations of the collective— or, more precisely, efforts at innervation on the part of the new, historically unique collective which has its organs in the new technology." "This second technology," he goes on to say, "is a system in which the mastering of elemental social forces is the precondition for playing [*das Spiel*] with natural forces."[17] This "second" technology allows for the kind of transformative innervation that defines the new Pallas as a permanent revolutionary force of disparate elements that, "rotat[ing] onward" (*L*, 221), takes the "spinning wheel" as its emblem. Registering the revolutionary potential existing within the stars themselves, Lesabéndio notes that "[w]heels spinning around their own axes are … intoxicating—at least, in the imagination. If we think about wheels constantly turning on their axes, this puts us into a state of intoxication so powerful that we cannot imagine a greater one. The biggest secret of our planetary system is hidden inside these spinning wheels" (*L*, 196). This rotating movement of transformation—of metamorphosis and accumulation—is identified by Biba, Lesabéndio's main interlocutor, as the primary principle that guides not only Pallas but also the entire cosmos and the relationships between its different stars:

All moments of coming together depend on long and gradual preparatory processes of transformation. Stars draw toward other stars so that—either to a small degree or, sometimes, quite energetically— they can *transform* their entire being. See how comets transform themselves only in close proximity to the Sun! Think of that! It's the clearest possible example. This principle of metamorphosis is to be expected in the beings living on the surfaces of stars as well. Consider Pallasians when they die! Perhaps all death in our solar system should be ascribed to this broad, omnipresent principle of transformation. (*L*, 161)

Pointing to a death that is not a death but rather the signature of metamorphosis into another form, the novel ends with a series of shattering and transformative events, all of which signal a revolution that establishes a new relation to the cosmos—in the binding together of the head and the torso of the double star Pallas, in the joining of mind and body, idea and matter.[18] Lesabéndio feels his entire body "decomposing," "spreading far out on all sides," and all he can register is that "everything distant" comes closer. He feels "no obstacles or restraints *anywhere*" (*L*, 193).

This revolution is painful, as is all transformation, and must be prepared for—and these "long and gradual preparatory processes of transformation" include learning that "[w]e have no right to fear what is terrible": "Terrible things always lead us forward. They transform us. We are not able to transform ourselves if we flee pain and torment. So, just listen to what the Sun will say to you now! ... '*All of you, don't fear pain—and don't fear death either*'" (*L*, 198). Understanding that revolutionary transformation takes its point of departure from pain, suffering, and death, Biba proclaims—registering the "red eye" that now looks "uncannily" into the Tower Lantern—"This is the biggest event of our lives. Many things will change now" (*L*, 195). Coming with the glow of a "carmine-red ball of light," this radical moment of transformation unfolds under the sign of an *asteroid communism* that cannot be subsumed into a communism we might recognize or that could even be named. The features of this asteroid revolution accumulate in intensified fashion as the novel nears its end and then—embodying the "spark of defiance" that expands "through the planets"—they explode all at once. As Lesabéndio exclaims, "we'll become volcanoes—concussive shocks to the world—thunderous storms—intoxicating light turbulences." "What does it matter if I live or not?," he adds,

> As long as the star that is with me, or in me, stays alive—a life of many worlds. It will be difficult, yes. But only through difficulty do we arrive at the greatest ecstasies. The slack pauses must be overcome. Everything must rotate faster, so that we perceive more and more. Here comes the intoxication again, generated by this eternal turning—the rotating balls and wheels suffocate anything trivial. Forward! Don't fear the pain! Don't fear death! The sphere! Infinity! The wheels! The circle! The circle! (*L*, 204–205)

That Lesabéndio has experienced a revolution is confirmed when he declares that he "no longer perceived or thought in the way he had before the transformation" (*L*, 205), that his experience of "the greatest possible autonomy" has come with his surrender to what is greater than him, a doubled experience that recurs "again and again in a million variations" and that, he suggests, belongs to the unfolding of history itself. There can be no revolution without death, without the dissolution of the self, without the delineation of a communal form that emerges through a painful and, at first, incomprehensible metamorphosis. In the world of Scheerbart's *Lesabéndio*, this transformation corresponds to the movement of an endless rotation in an expanding orbit that increasingly includes more and more asteroids and stars. Lesabéndio himself begins "rotating" in a state of bliss, as he senses himself "drawing closer to the other stars," and, in the end, the border between his decomposing self and the masses around him is abolished. Stretching out his entire body, he realizes that his body is "the entire torso-system of Pallas." At the same time, "[t]he old star of Pallas" awakens "to a new life" and becomes "an exemplary model for other asteroids" (*L*, 219). The novel would seem to confirm— proleptically, as it were—Benjamin's claim in "To the Planetarium" that the "ancients' intercourse with the cosmos had been different." As in the future Scheerbart imagines, Benjamin suggests that it is in "the ecstatic trance" alone that "we gain certain knowledge of what is nearest to us and what is remotest from us, and never of one without the other. This means, however, that man can be in ecstatic contact with the cosmos only communally" (*OWS*, 486). This is why it is entirely fitting that Lesabéndio's last words are "mit Allen zusammen," *with all together*—referencing not just his inscription and absorption within a planetary network of relations but also the entanglement of what is singular with a world of reproduction, repetition, and relationality. Scheerbart's total revolution—a revolution that reconceptualizes a new kind of collectivity, one that is continuously expanding and transforming—implies a different way of coming together. It cannot be named and, indeed, can only be imagined in an asteroid novel, since it has never had an earthly equivalent. Despite the seemingly utopian revolutionary explosion with which the novel ends, *Lesabéndio* insists that the riddles and enigmas of the world need not be solved but rather acknowledged as a source of endless possibility. Even in the midst of their revolution, even in their growing proximity to the transformative principles at the heart of the cosmos, the Pallasians refuse to concede their belief in a meaning that must remain elusive if it is not to become authoritarian. *Lesabéndio* preserves its riddle and enigma: the revolution can only begin with a leap into the unknown.

Blanqui—Benjamin's other traveling companion in his political exploration of the skies—already emphasizes this point when he, too, suggests that communism can only come in the form of stars and comets, since it has yet to be realized on earth. Indeed, he suggests, we cannot criticize something that has never yet existed; we must imagine it differently. We must orient ourselves toward what seems most impossible, toward what nearly exceeds our capacity to imagine it. Communism, as Blanqui views it—and Scheerbart and Benjamin after him—is always still to come. In a passage in which he counters those who would dismiss communism or force its premature realization, he insists on its present nonexistence. He writes:

> Communism is accused ... of sacrificing the individual and denying freedom. And no doubt, were it to be born premature through the use of forceps, before reaching its full term, a stunted version of communism might well induce many people to regret the good old days that precede it. But if it is to be the child of science, who will dare denounce the infant of such a mother? Where, moreover, is the evidence that might support the accusations that are leveled against it? Since the accused has never yet lived, they amount to nothing but an unfounded insult.[19]

Having lived through the Russian and German revolutions—one presumably successful, the other a catastrophic failure—and even having visited the Soviet Union, Benjamin would have agreed with Blanqui: communism has never yet existed. This is why Benjamin so rigorously resists any identification with the Communist Party, or any of its forms. It is also why the violent efforts to suppress the dream or idea of communism—even in the forms it takes during his lifetime—is nothing more nor less than the measure of its revolutionary force.

Blanqui's own journey into the stars is itself a militant dream in the face of violent constraints. In solitary confinement in the Fort du Taureau, with his jailers under strict orders to shoot him if he even approaches a window, he turns his mind's eye to the skies and demonstrates, once again—like Scheerbart and Benjamin—that "revolutions must take place in the mind before they can be carried out in the streets."[20] This point is demonstrated by the fact that it is precisely by writing *Eternity by the Stars: An Astronomical Hypothesis* in 1871 that Blanqui manages to participate in the revolution of the Paris Commune. Even though the book is written in the solitude of his prison cell during one of his many intermittent periods of imprisonment, Blanqui's text makes it out onto the streets (in ways that echo the effects and itineraries of Luxemburg's own prison writings). Deliberately exploiting his

sense of the role of writing in revolutionary action, Blanqui publishes his book early in 1872 before his political trial, shares it with
journalists, and even displays it in court as part of his defense
strategy. In May 1872, he also makes sure that two of Adolphe
Thiers's allies in the Versailles tribunal chamber receive copies of
the book (recognizing the threat Blanqui represented, Thiers had
imprisoned him again just days before the Paris Commune insurrection). As Frank Chouraqui notes, the trial was to take place
under the jurisdiction of the so-called "pardons committee" ("la
commission des grâces"), but Blanqui instructs his messenger to
inform the two members of the Assembly that, in this case—this
is the travesty, he suggests—his fate is not with "the committee of stars" ("la commission des astres") but only with Thiers.[21]
Acknowledging the power Thiers holds, he simultaneously diminishes it by suggesting that the true arbiter of the revolutionary
actions for which he is accused and condemned are the stars in the
heavens. Granting authority to these enigmatic celestial bodies—
as well as to the text he has written—he defies Thiers with the
force of his speculations on the relation between the revolutions
in the skies and those on the ground. Figures of the vanquished
and the dispossessed, "nomads," comets exhibit an unparalleled
freedom of movement that can only be matched by the freedom
of the proletariat's political unfolding. They are "sidereal enigmas" because, very much like the proletariat, "they are nothing,
they do nothing, and they only have one role: that of an enigma."
They are "fantastic beings," and a single comet contains enormous powers of transformation and condensation. It is "an ounce
of fog," Blanqui writes, "that first expands to fill a billion-cubic
leagues, then shrinks to the size of a carafe."[22] Like Scheerbart's
speculative Eternal Motion Machine, Blanqui's experimental scientific and political treatise moves from the finite to the infinite
by extending political agency to what exceeds the human—and
cannot be determined by the human. With Blanqui, cosmology is
fully politicized and, in the end, his text is not simply a hypothesis but an action.

While *Eternity by the Stars* remains the most difficult of all
of Blanqui's writings to classify, it is one of the most militant.
It manages to continue the revolution of the mind in the most
unimaginable circumstances and strives to demonstrate the
strength of the imagination's freedom of movement against the
greatest odds. This freedom, however, is not individual or individ-
ualistic but rather a relational means to connect with the minds
of others "like an electric current" since—in an earthly version

of Lesabéndio's *mit Allen zusammen*—"it is through thought that [human beings] communicate" and "through thought that they form one single being. It is through thought that universal solidarity is established, through thought that the interest of one becomes the interest of all."[23] As in Scheerbart and Benjamin, the mind in Blanqui communicates through reading and writing—technological media capable of traversing different times and spaces. Blanqui's composite mind—a kind of collective intelligence that comes as a force of scattering—contains the traces of a multiplicity that, preceding and overcoming the individual, always subsumes him or her. To put it differently: only collective thought can enable collective power, but to do so it must first be communicated and shared, and there is no predicting or controlling the path of its transmission, especially since, as he puts it in a fragment from 1868, "thought is itself only a shadow, a passing breeze, a nothingness that disappears."[24] Nevertheless, if Blanqui states that "[t]he source of intellectual power resides in the capacity to communicate one's ideas,"[25] it is because only through communication can these ideas gather and accumulate in order to constitute a shared common-wealth of the mind—a "phalanx," he writes[26]—which, bringing together innumerable incommensurable associations, is essential to any revolutionary future. This common-wealth will, in turn, enable the emergence of a new collectivity, a collectivity that, understanding that the mind is the place where political action begins, remains as mobile, indeterminate, and enigmatic as nebulae in the skies. This is to say that any sense of commonality and collectivity is always interrupted from within. In Blanqui's words,

> At every point discord incessantly shatters this supposed harmony—a harmony that would otherwise stagnate and, soon after, decompose. The laws of gravity have millions of unexpected consequences; they produce a shooting star here, a sun-star there. Why banish them from the general harmony? These accidents displease, and yet we are born from them! They are the antagonists of death, the always-open sources of universal life. It is only through a permanent failing of its good order that gravitation is able to reconstruct and repopulate the globes. On its own, the good order that we vaunt would let them disappear into nothingness.[27]

If this indeterminacy disturbs the "good order" we want, it is not surprising that it is met with violence. Indeed, in light of the state violence and repression he himself experienced, Blanqui warns that those who would suppress this discord, "[t]hose who suppress the freedom to think and write are more dangerous than wolves and tigers, than cholera and yellow fever."[28] If Thiers and others censor the freedom of thought to assemble, they do so because they are fully aware of its unpredictable revolutionary potential. Blanqui goes on to suggest that, through a mimetic contagion, an untethered and expansive collective mind moves like the comets that "join the innumerable tribes that dwell in the imaginary expanse" and that, with their movement, trace "ellipses, parabolas, or hyperbolas" in the sky.[29] Collectively dispersed historical agents moved by the wind of history, they navigate their way together, as Lesabéndio says, "in a million variations," or as Blanqui himself puts it, with "limitless diversity"[30]—writing in the sky, and never simply in a straight line.

Josef Albers, *Homage to the Square / Red Series, Untitled III*, 1968

XXI. A RED COMMON-WEALTH

Philology is nekyia, descent to the dead, ad plures ire. It joins the largest, strangest, always growing collective and gives something of the life of its own language to the collective to bring those who are underground to speech. It dies—philology dies, every philologist dies—in order to permit some of those many an afterlife, for a while, through its language. Without philology, which socializes with the dead, the living would become asocial. But the society of philology is the society of those who belong to no society; its life is lived together with death, its language an approaching silence.

—Werner Hamacher, *Minima Philologica* (2015)

This is black Marxism, black communism, where the originary reconstruction is understood as the preservation of the ontological totality, the reconstructive conservation, if you will, of wealth, of the wealth of who and what we are and will be. This is the condition of possibility of accumulation, primitive or otherwise; but it is also its disruption, deferral, originary displacement or anoriginal differing. Anoriginal stealing, anoriginal dispossession at the level of a disruption of regulative and lawful self-possession, the citizen-subject's necessary mode.

—Fred Moten, *Stolen Life* (2018)[1]

The writings of Scheerbart and Blanqui can be said to *storm the heavens* in the name of an imagined common-wealth that, extending itself on a planetary scale, can potentially counter the violence of global capitalism.[2] This common-wealth points to the possibility of exceeding, if not shattering, the forms of capitalism—enabling us to imagine alternatives to capital's cruel and ruthless structures of organization. If its contours are traced in the skies and the stars, it is because we have yet to realize it on earth (nonetheless, its outline can be glimpsed in revolutionary moments and especially in revolutionary texts). The forms of capitalism not only dominate the politico-economic sphere but also contribute to the violent destruction of nature, the exploitation of workers, the subjugation and displacement of minoritized populations, and the ruination of noncapitalist modes of association. The writers we have been reading introduce a crack or fissure into these forms—insisting on the ruin capitalism already bears within it—in order to interrupt them, de-universalize them, recombine their different elements in order to destabilize them and suspend their brutality, if just for a brief moment. The constellation of texts at play here—all constellations, whether celestial or textual, are always in motion, never reducible to a particular moment in time or space—points to the militancy of diverse literacies, all of which begin in the desire to maximize and massify the cracks and fissures in capitalist relations of production. They engage and transform the language of capital by excavating and exposing its violence and, in doing so, join an ever-growing collective of texts—what we are calling "a red common-wealth"—that, in its very movement, never ceases to create new coalitions among ever-expanding acts of resistance.

This resistance takes the form of acts of reading that—diagnosing the innumerable apparatuses that support capitalism and, in particular, racial capitalism—reveal fierce and radical literary practices that gain their strength and force as they are enacted and repeated, that is, accumulated, across different temporal and spatial geographies. This different kind of accumulation is legible in all the writers we have set in motion here but can certainly be registered in Benjamin's effort to massify his sentences, to intensify their citationality in order to produce a scattered, nonlinear accumulation that exceeds capitalist calculation.[3] If we follow the logic of his practice of writing, the archives of defeat and resistance are only inherited if they are intensified and perpetually transformed, altered, made to deviate or swerve. If *to inherit* means *to read*—to read the cracks and fissures in what we inherit, the fugitive shards and fragments of historical ruination[4]—this inheritance not only transmits catastrophe but also passes its legacy forward in modes of transmission that are themselves catastrophic. In Benjamin's words, phenomena can only be "rescued," can only be conveyed, "through the exhibition of the crack within them."[5] "There is," he goes on to say, "a transmission that is catastrophe" (*AP*, 473). This transmission and its attendant breakdowns can be embraced in politically antagonistic ways. Capitalism strives to efface the cracks in all its phenomena by neglecting the force of "the revolutionary moments in the occurrence of history" in the name of a stable and identifiable inheritance that insists on continuity. It "misses"—we could say deliberately conceals—the places "where tradition breaks off," the "peaks and crags, which offer footing to one who would cross over them" (ibid., 474), so many stepping stones from which we can spring in another direction. A militant understanding of the inevitable negativity of transmission instead sets the catastrophic character of transmission against the catastrophe that capital is and, embracing this negativity, remains faithful to what is most enigmatic in what we inherit, resists fixed determinations of what is transmitted to us. Catastrophe permits us to see—the cracks it produces give us a glance into the interiority of capital, opening it to its own disintegration—the possibility of a wealth that has been neglected, excluded, annihilated. We can only see beyond capital when we register the ruins it creates and leaves behind, when reading and writing break down in such a way that they become mediums of disaster, but a disaster that points to the possibilities that emerge from defeat and loss. History can never be measured as a series of finished acts but must be politically activated as a wellspring of future possibilities. The cracks in capital are a means of transformation because possibility can only be imagined from the perspective of its impossibility; hope becomes legible only when it is shattered. If historical catastrophe leaves its imprint in the language we use—an imprint whose illegibility demands that we read it but without assuming we can overcome it—language becomes a veritable common-wealth of historical experience and knowledge, a reminder of the accumulated history we carry within us (if unbeknownst to us) and that we also can activate. This common-wealth may tell us how history is transmitted but not how it ends, and, because this end is always uncertain, we can imagine that things also could have been different beforehand, that history could have unfolded otherwise. This capacity to envision different beginnings and ends is the condition of a revolutionary politics, one that begins in a catastrophe that speaks through acts of reading and writing that, in turn, can never be assigned to a single historical actor because transmission always exceeds the personal—it is always impersonal.

This common-wealth of, in Marx's phrase, "associated producers"[6] points to the only inheritance we have that is not entirely governed by ownership and the capitalist barbarism that protects and maintains it. Its vast relationality resists all delimitations and forms of possession and instrumentalization. This shared wealth—a wealth that only increases as it is shared or added to in every act of reading and writing—points to the incommensurability of entanglements that cannot be named or ordered in a manageable and predictable way. It is an index not just of our inscription within a network of shifting relations—within a growing association of producers—but also of our duty to continue to examine critically our place and responsibility in it. It is the measure of the extent to which we have inherited, taken in, the vast archives that, shaping our present, can be drawn upon and added to in order to facilitate a different future. If this common-wealth is inseparable from the possibilities of revolt and praxis, if its significance depends, as Jameson notes, on "the historical value we attach to 'culture' and the way in which superstructures are seen as an active part of the mode of production" (*BF*, 30–31), its force lies in its destruction of the distinction between superstructure and base (already an outdated distinction in Marx's historical moment), and of "culture" itself. What is at stake is reconceptualizing "culture" so that—no longer a token of class, nation, expertise, or what we have come to refer to as "cultural capital" that can be possessed, but instead a formation disassembled by a critical reading of the codes and systems it formalizes and the violence it enacts—it is transformed through its massification, the multiple modes of its transmission, its plural forms of inheritance. It is when "culture" is thought of as one, when it can be identified as a bourgeois form, that it displays its barbaric underbelly, and this contradiction puts its conceptualization in crisis. The crisis that inhabits and structures culture compels it to distinguish itself from nonculture and to insist on a distance from its own barbarism by projecting it elsewhere. The common-wealth—as what cannot be localized or appropriated, as what, belonging to no one, splinters bourgeois identity—is the enemy of culture. This is why, if this culture would have its way, the common-wealth would never be permitted to emerge. It would be where the common-wealth meets its end; it would be its graveyard. However, the common-wealth interrupts culture as an "object" that can be appropriated for national, ideological, or "cultural" purposes. If culture is a site of production that detaches itself as an object, the common-wealth is a site of collective production without limits. It is *culture on strike* because it is culture from the perspective of the producer, not the consumer. It breaks culture open in order to show its fissures, to expose its incapacity to be what it promises to become—among other things, a mask for capitalist violence and barbarism. It pluralizes and multiplies culture from the "inside," as it were, but in forms that are neither identifiable, countable, nor calculable. The sheer scale of the ever-growing archives of defeat and resistance, and the constant critical labor they demand, present an obstacle to appropriation and commodification. It has the potential to interrupt their subsumption within the monster that capitalism is—with its power to integrate and bury entire networks of relations and transform them into images and words that, when consumed as cultural objects that efface this violence, would leave us forever impoverished and alone.

In each instance, the figures we have put alongside one another here not only contribute to this common-wealth; they enact one of its most characteristic features: its focus on the dispossessed, and on the impossible but inexorable demand to continue to rewrite history, if not from the perspective of the vanquished—which can only be a vanishing horizon—at least with the vanquished in mind. Each of these writers attend to the violence of racial capitalism, even if differently and with different emphases and manners of proceeding. They write with this violence in view, and, in many respects, it is violence that frames and moves their writing. In several instances, it informs their formal experimentation, and, because it is so pervasive, their task can never be finished, which is why they keep writing and why so many of their texts remain incomplete or imagined. In this final section—a section that itself can only gesture in the direction of a common-wealth that is impossible to contain and determine—we trace another thread of related texts in order to point to the way in which the texts in this expanding archive gather their force in their accumulation. This accumulation is perhaps more *originary* than the economic one imagined by Marx and is always in the process of becoming something else—from its very beginning. It offers a cumulative infrastructure for the political imagination and for the possibility of a different future.

★

We can begin to imagine this alternative cumulative force by recalling what it seeks to counter and interrupt: the violence of capitalist wealth and, in particular, the matter of primitive accumulation. Marx never ceases to point out that the nonoriginary origin of capitalism that is primitive accumulation is "written in the annals of humankind in letters of blood and fire."[7] His language evokes an early document on the genocidal violence of Spanish colonial capitalism in the Americas, Bartolomé de las Casas's 1542 *Brevísima relación de la destruición de las Indias* (*A Short Account of the Destruction of the Indies*), a text he reads and cites more than once and that gives an account of the foundational violence of capital and, in particular—as Benjamin would have it—of capitalism as religion. As Marx suggests, capital announces itself through colonial expropriation and total racial violence: "The discovery of gold and silver in America, the extirpation, enslavement and entombment in mines of the indigenous population of that continent ... are all things which characterize the dawn of the era of capitalist production. These idyllic proceedings are the chief moments of primitive accumulation."[8] He makes clear that he identifies the Spanish conquest with the earliest forms of primitive accumulation. "The different moments of primitive accumulation," he writes, "can be assigned in particular to Spain, Portugal, Holland, France and England, in more or less chronological order."[9] In his description of colonial violence, Las Casas addresses Prince Philip of Spain (later King Philip II), asking him to end the savage extraction of capital from the Indies in order to protect the moral integrity of the emerging imperial dominium. He denounces one form of accumulation in favor of another: the brutal and indiscriminate extraction of gold, silver, and other precious minerals and materials in favor of a process of Christianization that, accumulating souls, can enforce a different, and perhaps more effective, form of subjugation. As Daniel Nemser puts it, it is a matter of "'humanizing' Spanish colonial rule, attenuating the violence on which it depends in order to create the conditions in which conversion could proceed." Las Casas's own personal transformation, from a slave-owning colonizer to a "protector de los indios," provides the blueprint for the kind of conversion he has in mind and that both the conquistadors and their indigenous victims must undergo simultaneously, albeit differently. Nemser emphasizes the double sacrificial transformation of Amerindian populations: "indigenous bodies are thus sacrificed to the twinned economies of mineral and spiritual extraction. In the colonial context, primitive accumulation takes a decisively Christian form."[10] The imperative of accumulating spiritual wealth is further legitimated within the Catholic Spanish empire since it is underwritten by a papal bull.

This is why, when Las Casas indicts the violence of colonialist exploitation, he still remains fully inscribed within the imperial project.[11] His preferred version of colonialism is based on the conversion of souls—the true wealth of the church. It transforms material accumulation into spiritual accumulation. Las Casas's Spanish empire is an evangelizing enterprise. His condemnation of the violence of conquest is made in the name of the church and its religious beliefs and has as its aim the further expansion and empowerment of the Spanish church and state.[12] That the Spanish conquistadors brutalize, dehumanize, and exterminate the native populations is not simply violent and sadistic, he suggests, but also wasteful. The real wealth of the Americas is not nature's riches but the population that can, if converted, increase the number of Christians in the world. If the conquistador assumes that the New World's natural resources are endless, Las Casas argues that the only thing that is infinite in his horrifying accounts is the violence of capital—a violence that is realized either by genocide or enslavement, both of which, murdering the soul, diminish the possibility of Christianization. He understands that, while violence is infinite, natural resources are not. This is largely why Las Casas's prolonged lament—nothing less than a rhetorical and political jeremiad—turns repeatedly to the notion of the infinite (infinite cruelty, pain, loss, death, murder) in order to underscore both the stakes and the impossibility of the task at hand: to relate a violence that is absolutely unimaginable.[13] He repeatedly refers to the impossibility of any chronicle doing justice to the unspeakable violence he witnesses, to the "unspeakable cruelty" that, in his words, "beggars all description."[14] Nevertheless, he gestures in the direction of the endless violence that sustains Spain's colonial enterprise—a genocide that announces other genocides to come and that results from the murderous violence and the epidemics that, a consequence of the initial contact, were intensified by starvation and the destruction of the land that, until then, sustained its native inhabitants. Las Casas himself notes the joint devastation of the people and the land when he returns to Cuba. As he puts it: "The whole of the island was devastated and depopulated, and it now affords, as we discovered on a recent visit, a moving and heartrending spectacle, transformed, as it has been, into one vast, barren wasteland."[15]

If Spanish colonialism is simultaneously an expropriation of land, culture, and life, it is also a burial site that takes the form of a mine dedicated to the extraction of, in Las Casas's eyes, the false god "gold." That gold is the god of the Spanish conquest is mentioned several times in Las Casas's history, but it is confirmed in one of the few moments in his account in which an Amerindian speaks. There, one of the tribal leaders attributes the cruelty and evil of the conquistadors to their devotion to gold: "They have a God whom they worship and adore, and it is in order to get that God from us so that they can worship Him that they conquer us and kill us." Beside a basket of gold jewelry, he proclaims: "Here is the God of the Christians. If you agree, we will do *areitos* ... in honor of this God and it may be that we shall please Him and He will order the Christians to leave us unharmed." After unanimous consent, the dances begin, but he soon notes that, "if we keep this God about us, they will kill us in order to get their hands on Him."

For this reason, he adds, "Let us throw Him into the river," which again they all consent to do.[16] In this way, the tribe repeats the gesture through which the conquistadors destroy and bury indigenous idols and fetishes, albeit for different reasons.[17] Indeed, burials appear repeatedly in Las Casas's account, most notably in connection with the deaths of indigenous workers within the gold, silver, and mercury mines. In excavations and refineries, this interplay between the enforced extraction of precious metals and the burial of native bodies suggests that the real originary accumulation is that of violence. It is revealed rather stunningly in a passage in which Nemser, extending the allegory Las Casas sets into motion, identifies the Indians themselves with the ore they are mining and the graves in which they are buried:

> Cutting minerals from the mountain, the *mitayos* dig their own graves (the Latin *effodiendis* comes from *fodio*, to dig up, from which *fossa*, grave, is derived). In the refineries ... it is not only these minerals but Indians themselves that are ground into powder in preparation for amalgamation. In this powerful image, indigenous bodies are literally worked into the metal that enters into circulation as coin. At the limit of life and death, human liberty and natural slavery, the mines operate as an exemplary zone of indistinction.[18]

Pointing to the merging of Indians and commodities, to the inscription and erasure of labor within coins, the passage offers us another figure for racial capitalism—one that helps us imagine what remains so unthinkable, and this despite the extremity and violence it portends. The unthinkable is embedded here in the ubiquitous everyday object that, circulating daily amongst innumerable hands, sustains the colonial empire.

Las Casas's critique of colonial violence relies on a rhetoric of intensification, amplification, and compression. Rhetorical strategies are no mere writerly details here but rather the conceptual core of his argument: the total violence of colonialism proves to be irrational and unethical precisely because it is unimaginable, because the human mind cannot account for it without becoming undone in the process.[19] This unraveling is mimed in the syntactical unfolding of Las Casas's sentences, in their often long and convoluted cadences, swollen to the point of bursting, in their repetitions and expansions, almost impossible to read without losing one's breath, and this because what these sentences seek to describe—a violence that is indescribable, at the limit of what can be said—should take one's breath away. The *Brevísima* is situated at the limit between sense and non-sense and seeks to mobilize that border through political emotion. Following Las Casas's logic, it is the indistinction between the two that should instill terror and shame, "espanto," into his readers. Its own critique of violence, its own *Trauerspiel*—one that, like Benjamin's, explores the relation between sovereignty and death, but more directly in relation to questions of race—this abbreviated account describes a "series of events" that "caused astonishment, anguish, mourning, and an overwhelming bitterness and pain to all these people and kingdoms; from here to the end of the world, or until all of these have been exterminated, they will not cease to lament and sing their *areitos* and dances (as we do here in what we call 'romances') about this calamity and loss of their entire nobility, whom they had held in esteem for years and years, and of their future."[20] Las Casas joins in the mournful lament of the Indians, but his book is an impossible one. A failed translation, it is unable to contain the memory of the vastness of this genocide and destruction. Nevertheless, it exists as a record of this impossibility—of the unspeakable truth at the heart of empire. The Spanish atrocities are infinite, which is why all he can offer is a condensation (an all too brief account) of a book that in fact cannot exist. He envisions a book that could strive to match this devastation in a passage whose sentences exhibit the struggle, the incapacity of language, to capture the scale of this genocidal violence. What is so moving in the passage is its inability to hold together. What we witness is a linguistic movement whose grammar breaks down in the face of what it is asked to convey:

> I say truly that what these two expeditions did in terms of evil ... if it were possible to express and understand so much evil, so many ravages, so many deaths, so many depopulations, and so many and such savage injustices, they would terrify present and future centuries and would fill a grand book to the brim, because these exceeded all past and present, both in the quantity and number of abominations that happened upon the peoples that were destroyed and the lands that became deserts, because all of them were infinite.[21]

What has been registered as the poverty of Las Casas's rhetorical powers—the convolution and, at times, inelegance of his writing—is instead the powerful trait of a writer who is fully aware of the limits of his language and who must at every step try to stretch it, even to mutilate it, in order to match the violence that itself fractures his words and breaks the syntax of his sentences, a violence whose excess remains incomprehensible. The politics of his book lies precisely in this breakdown. We could even say that if the book has power over its readers it is because of this breakdown that, in turn, echoes that of Las Casas's failed mission. Las Casas writes in the hope that his book can be a force of transformation, but he knows he cannot achieve this transformation alone, which is why he so often incorporates testimonies and writings of several of his contemporaries as part of his plea to Prince Philip. If the force of Las Casas's denunciation comes from his faith, this faith ensures his complicity with the project of Spanish colonialism. The transformative power of his denunciation is diminished by its commitment to Christian conversion, since this commitment remains consonant with the expansion of Spain's imperial aspirations.[22] Nevertheless, the dense complexity of Las Casas's at least double commitment is carried forward in the different ways in which his activism—however compromised it may be—remains a resource for later writers.

Benjamin himself formalizes the contradiction at work in Las Casas in an enthusiastic 1929 review of Marçel Brion's *Bartolomée de Las Casas: "Père des Indiens,"* which appeared a year earlier. In the review, he writes that "[t]he colonial history of the European peoples begins with the outrageous process of the Conquest, which transformed the entire newly conquered world into a torture chamber." Tracing Brion's attention to the "unfailing energy" with which Las Casas seeks to improve the lives of the natives, he adds that, when Las Casas dies "in a Dominican monastery in Madrid in 1566," "he had done his part, but, at the same time, the work of destruction was accomplished. ... In the name of Catholicism, a Priest confronts the atrocities committed in the name of Catholicism" (*GS*, 3:180).[23] Indeed, if, as Benjamin writes in *One-Way Street*, "without exception the great writers perform their combinations in a world that comes after them" (*OWS*, 446–447), it is not surprising that Las Casas's condemnation of the Amerindian genocide finds its resonance in several of the writers we have been reading. As we will see, the violence of colonialism and racial capitalism is a red thread that circulates not only in Marx's and Luxemburg's writings on primitive accumulation but also in Benjamin's several references to Las Casas and Mesoamerica.

★

Benjamin's interest in Mesoamerican cultures and languages dates to the seminars conducted by the German ethnologist, archaeologist, and linguist Walter Lehmann in the winter semester of 1915–1916, which he attended while he was a student at the University of Munich (Rainer Maria Rilke also was in attendance) and, again in 1921, when he was in Berlin—Lehmann had moved to Berlin to become the director of the Ethnological Museum there. The seminars took place in Lehmann's apartment, which was filled with Amerindian archaeological artifacts he had extracted from various expeditions and excavations in the Americas (in particular, from an unofficial excavation close to Teotihuacán). The seminars focused on cosmology, with an emphasis on astrological calendars and the measurement of time, the language and culture of ancient Mexico, and Bernardino de Sahagún's *Florentine Codex*. Benjamin's notes from the classes have been lost, but he refers to the sessions in several letters to Scholem and Fritz Radt.[24] He also seems to have been interested in learning Nahuatl, and Scholem claims he noticed a copy of Fray Alonso de Molina's 1555 *Vocabulario en lengua castellana y Mexicana* on his desk in Berlin sometime after 1916.[25] But he was especially interested in Mesoamerican animism, something that is legible not only in several scenes in his later *Berlin Childhood*—where he describes several inanimate objects coming to life—but also in the first of the two Mexican dreams he recounts in *One-Way Street*.[26]

Benjamin presents this first dream in a section entitled "Mexican Embassy" ("Mexikanische Botschaft"). The dream follows a citation from Baudelaire:

Je ne passe jamais devant un fétiche de bois, un Bouddha doré, une idole mexicaine sans me dire: c'est peut-être le vrai dieu. [I never pass by a wooden fetish, a gilded Buddha, a Mexican idol without reflecting: perhaps it is the true God.]

—Charles Baudelaire

I dreamed I was a member of an exploring party in Mexico. After crossing a high, primeval jungle, we came upon a system of above-ground caves in the mountains. Here, a religious order had survived from the time of the first missionaries till now, its monks continuing the work of conversion among the natives. In an immense central grotto with a gothically pointed roof, Mass was celebrated according to the most ancient rites. We joined the ceremony and witnessed its climax: toward a wooden bust of God the Father, fixed high on a wall of the cave, a priest raised a Mexican fetish. At this, the divine head turned thrice in denial from right to left. (*OWS*, 448–449)

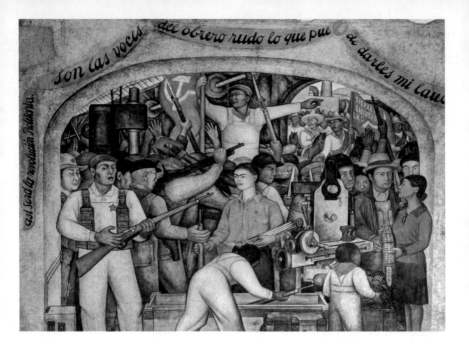

Diego Rivera, *The Arsenal*, 1928

Benjamin's title, "Mexican Embassy," references the envoy sent to Mexico, but "Mexikanische Botschaft" can also be translated as either "Mexican mission" or "Mexican message." In all cases, though, the title's referent remains unstable, and this because this Mexican mission can refer to a mission *in* Mexico—a mission *by* Spanish missionaries in Mexico, for example—but also to a *Mexican* mission, a mission originating not in Spain but in Mexico. Further, the section titled "Mexikanische Botschaft" includes a passage from Baudelaire, a German (Benjamin) in the expedition, perhaps from another era, and a gothic architectural element (and therefore a European and Christian one)—which means that this "Mexican mission," this Mexican message or gospel, is not exclusively "Mexican," or that whatever is "Mexican" cannot be restricted to Mexico. In addition, this message includes a series of relays that, attributing features of one God to another, makes the true godhead undecidable. This undecidability is legible throughout the dream and is intensified if we register that, as a member of the expedition, Benjamin is a displaced figure of Lehmann who also reenacts Baudelaire's encounter with different fetishes (the quotation from Baudelaire—reimagined and rewritten by Benjamin—is itself the dream of a quotation).[27] The dream enables him to find himself simultaneously in different historical moments, including the moment of the encounter between the Spanish missionaries and the Mexica peoples. Within the dreamwork, nothing is determined or fixed, nothing can be identified in a single time or space, and everything moves in the direction of a decolonial account of the history of violence.

Benjamin's dream offers a genealogical allegory of the violence of the Spanish conquest and of German colonialism's own relationship to this history. Reenacting and displacing the initial colonial encounter between Franciscan missionaries and Mexica leaders, the expedition in the dream comes upon a system of caves and, entering what seems to be the central one, they witness a priest holding up a Mexican fetish to the bust of God the Father, who proceeds to deny it three times.[28] The colonial encounter implies a form of mimicry that transforms the colonial power into what it wishes to deny or destroy, initiating a process of *entanglement* that potentially challenges all identifications, even in the instances when it is ideologically instrumentalized. That the bust of God the Father is made of wood, for example, puts it within the purview of the Baudelaire citation and, consequently, it can be said to be just one more fetish. This relay between a Christian fetish and an indigenous one—in which each takes on the traits of the other—is reinforced by the denying movement of the divine figure's head, since, in this movement, it embodies the animism that would more properly belong to an indigenous deity who, in this instance, would deny a lesser one. The blurring between the two fetishes is reiterated in another form in the "most ancient rites," since these rites are not identified as either Catholic or pre-Hispanic. Putting idolatry alongside the Catholic mass, the priest offers a Mexican fetish to a God in a ritualistic citation of sacrifice and, in doing so, transforms the Christian God into a pre-Hispanic one.[29] Even as God the Father denies indigenous divinity, he confirms it by absorbing the indigenous god and its principle of animation. Affirming that theology is fundamental to the colonial project, the dream unsettles all forms of theological certitude. It archives a syncretism among fetishes, priests, and animated objects that projects characteristics of the figures that are denied onto the ones that would deny them.[30] This is why, in a rather daring and provocative suggestion, Heriberto Martínez Yépez suggests that the priest who offers up the fetish in Benjamin's dream could be Las Casas himself, since, late in his life, in his 1564 "Tratado de las doce dudas" ("Treatise of Twelve Doubts"), he argues that fetishes or idols can be the true God, since God is in every idol.[31] Here Las Casas anticipates the mystical elements of Marxian fetishism—which, in turn, reveals both its transformative potential as a kind of animism and its theological dimensions. Like the Marxian letter, Benjamin's dream traces another kind of primitive accumulation, one that gathers its force in the superimposition of the various layers of interpretive strata condensed in the dream itself. These strata include the condensations and displacements of all the mirroring effects between the colonial project and its presumed subjects but also all the history that supports colonialism in general, and especially its violence. As Benjamin puts it in his review of Brion's biography of Las Casas,

> It is very interesting to pursue the ways in which the economic necessity of a colonization that was not yet imperialist … seeks its theoretical justification: America is an unclaimed good; subjugation is the precondition of the mission; it is the duty of Christianity to intervene against the Mexica's human sacrifices. The theorist of state reason—who does not openly present himself as such—was the Court chronicler Sepulveda. The dispute that occurred between the two opponents in 1550 in Valladolid marks the highest point in the life and, unfortunately, the work of Las Casas as well. For no matter how close this man came into contact with reality,

the result of his action remained entirely limited to Spain. After the dispute of Valladolid, Charles V issued decrees that abolished slavery, abolishing the so-called "encomienda," the "patronage," which was one of its most racist forms, etc. Yet the same or similar measures had already been enacted before, almost without any success. (*GS*, 3:180–181)

Reading the Spanish conquest as an early instance of racial capitalism, Benjamin notes that, despite the efforts of Las Casas to expose the violence of the conquest, "the work of destruction" prevails, and what accumulates, he suggests, is more violence, violence on top of violence.

If Benjamin's first dream condenses a network of associations that touch on the relations among religion, colonization, and capital in a way that brings together the Spanish conquest with German colonialism, his second dream, described just a few pages later, returns to this same constellation of themes, but this time reverses the landscape. If the first dream is presumably located in Mexico—but a Mexico that is not entirely "Mexican"—the second dream is located in a Weimar that proves not to be just "German." Whether or not Benjamin actually sends the dream to Lehmann, we can assume that his former teacher is at least one of its addressees, if in encoded ways. This colonial-cosmological dream, presented under the title "Tiefbau-Arbeiten"—which has been translated as "Underground Works" or, more recently, as "Structural Engineering Works"[32]—is written around the time that Lehmann returns from a trip to Mexico during which he collects Amerindian artifacts for the Völkerkunde Museum in Berlin, of which he is then director. If Benjamin imagines sending him an artifact in the form of an enigma to be deciphered and translated, his oneiric missive also appears as a critique of Lehmann's colonial ethnological quest to classify indigenous materials and languages; it is a comic depiction of the failure of such a project.

In the dream, Benjamin wakes up one morning laughing, with a strange word in his head: "Anaquivitzli." As Martínez Yépez has noted—and Ng after him—the word is an imagined Nahuatl word, but a Nahuatl word that, according to Benjamin, is assembled from syllables and words that are also Greek, French, Latin, and German.[33] As Benjamin tells us:

In a dream I saw a barren terrain. It was the marketplace of Weimar. Excavations were in progress. I, too, scraped about in the sand. There the spire of a church steeple emerged. Delighted, I thought to myself: a Mexican shrine from the time of pre-animism, from the Anaquivitzli. I awoke laughing. (Ana = ἀνά; vi = vie; witz = Mexican church [!]) (*OWS*, 455; translation modified)

Martínez Yépez argues that, like his first dream, Benjamin's second dream can be contextualized in terms of its reenactment of an encounter between Europe and Mexica history and culture and, in particular, in relation to the Aztec conception of dreams. Viewing the dream as part of a long history of European appropriations of non-European cultural practices, in this instance oneiric ones, he emphasizes the dream's capacity to move across times and spaces and, in every moment, to appear not simply as a text to be deciphered but also as a force of destruction, since it unsettles all order and every distinction, especially economic and political ones.[34]

In this instance, the dream takes place in the Weimar marketplace—an emblem of the city's financial and transactional power, the nexus of its economy of exchange. In Benjamin's oneiric vision, however, this marketplace is not a site of bustling commerce, but rather a bleak and barren terrain, with its only activity the excavations that are taking place. The excavations reveal the tip of a Mexican church, suggesting that Weimar is built over its colonial endeavors, that it buries the signs of its plunder, and that its imperial ambitions are shared with other colonial powers, not the least of which are the Spanish. The "barren terrain" belongs to the indistinction of the dream and to a multitemporal, multigeographical logic, with pre-Hispanic Mexico overlapping not only with Spanish Mexico but also with nineteenth- and twentieth-century Germany and Europe. This economy of exchange—based on translations, equivalences, and displacements between Germany and Mexico, between colonized and colonizer, between different nation-states, and between different languages—is located in a Weimar that is also experiencing political and cultural instability and upheaval (it is no accident that, within *One-Way Street*, this second dream immediately follows the book's "Imperial Panorama" section, with its analysis of the destructive character of the bond between imperialism and capitalism, the economic unraveling of Germany, and the exploitation of nature). It is a place of exchange, extraction, construction, and also ruination and impoverishment—its terrain empty and desolate.

If the marketplace embodies the enigma of capital, the almost alchemical equivalence of the most disparate and arbitrary objects, Benjamin's dream constructs its allegorical exchanges by means of figures and linguistic play. The emerging Mexican church reveals that theology is the hidden infrastructure of the capitalist marketplace, especially when it gets coordinated with the colonial project. The "Benjamin" in the dream is "delighted" with his discovery and immediately translates the scene into an ironically academic act of identification—the Mexican shrine, he tells us, is "from the time of pre-animism"—that soon collides with the amalgamated logic of the dream sequence. The temporal extraction that the identification signals, reminiscent of a museum label, parodically amplifies Europe's archaeological drive, which disconnects, reifies, and desocializes indigenous artifacts. If ruins from the Americas would seem to belong to the European unconscious—if Benjamin helps uncover them by scraping "a bit in the sand"—the Nahuatl neologism that appears in his dream, with its fragments of ancient Greek, Latin, French, and German, marks the inscription of Europe's presence within the indigenous language. But it also recalls the fact that Nahuatl itself is mediated by European hands, through the grammars and dictionaries compiled by Franciscan priests and used by them to teach the Aztec nobility how to translate their thoughts and language into the Roman alphabet. The encounter and conquest should be understood as an encounter between different languages that achieves its colonial aim, beyond brute force, by the imposition of one language upon another. Nahuatl already has undergone the violence of colonization, and the writing that emerges incorporates elements from both indigenous and European traditions. It exhibits the confusion of inexact appropriations and translations, the assimilation and distortion of European traits, a generalized dialectics of misunderstanding, and different forms of alienation, and this because none of the languages involved are monolingual. They are already pluralized before the encounter.[35]

If Benjamin's pseudo-Nahuatl neologism doubles as an indictment of colonial extractivism—which he associates with the academic ethnological authority of Lehmann, who becomes a synecdoche for the violence of colonial plunder under the veil of an expanded cultural understanding—it also indicates the way in which the encounter with another language introduces us to the foreignness of all languages. "Anaquivitzli" proves to be a liminal word that, belonging to an invented language—the word, belonging to no one's native tongue, is also foreign to itself—demonstrates Benjamin's conviction of the mutual contamination that takes place when different languages come into contact with one another, however much we might resist this contamination.

Benjamin demonstrates this—after he wakes up—by breaking the word down into syllables and associating each syllable with either a preposition or word from another language, each of which bears reference to an element in the dream. The syllable *ana*, which Benjamin identifies with ἀνά and which, in ancient Greek, can mean "upward" or "again," alludes not just to the emergence of the tip of the church, its rising from the ground, but also to the long history of repeated extractivist colonial endeavors. The syllable *vi*, in which he hears *vie*, French for "life," is legible in the transit from Benjamin's "from the time of pre-animism" to his "from the Anaquivitzli," since, syntactically, the two phrases, superimposed one atop the other, join these different temporal moments together and, in doing so, identify *life* with the animism of the word "Anaquivitzli" itself. Moving simultaneously in different directions—the sentence suggests that this hybrid word also belongs to the time of pre-animism—it points to an animism *before* animism, an animism in language itself. The *witz*, which Benjamin identifies as a "Mexican church," turns the church into a joke that arises because of the incongruity of the church's appearance in Weimar but also into a force of dissolution since its emergence—within the unconscious of Germany and Europe and as part of their colonial archives—unsettles the distinctions on which German and European colonialism depend. Benjamin's neologism asks us to think about the multiplicity that can exist within a word and the foreignness that not only interrupts any monolingual conception of language but also enables us to get closer to the alienating, distancing effects of language.

Benjamin makes this point in his 1921 "Task of the Translator" essay when, citing Rudolph Pannwitz (Benjamin's antennas would not have missed this other *witz*), he writes: "The basic error of the translator is that he preserves the state in which his own language happens to be instead of allowing his language to be powerfully affected by the foreign tongue. Particularly when translating from a language very remote from his own, he must go back to the primal elements of language itself and penetrate to the point where work, image, and tone converge. He must expand and deepen his language by means of the foreign language." Benjamin reinforces his suggestion that we deepen our relation to our "own" language when we register the foreignness within it a few sentences later, adding: "[t]his, to be sure, is to admit that all translation is only a somewhat provisional way of coming to terms with the foreignness of languages," including our own.[36] It is not impossible that this insistence on the way in which translation makes our own language foreign to itself was influenced by his seminars with Lehmann and his engagement with Nahuatl and the *Florentine Codex*. In fact, in a postscript to a letter he sends to Scholem on November 8, 1921, soon after attending Lehmann's seminars again, Benjamin tells his friend of a grand reunion with Lehmann and remarks that, although the seminars are still conducted in the same old style, he now registers them as entirely "Scheerbartian"![37] Like the language of the Pallasians, Benjamin's invented word is foreign to everyone, and absolutely constructed and artificial. It reads as the language of pre-animism, but it is instead a language of the future for subjects who do not yet exist. It is scarcely an accident that, when Benjamin divides "Anaquivitzli" into its respective syllables, he omits one—the *qui*, which, in French and Latin, means "who." The historical processes that Benjamin's dream evokes are without subjects, and certainly without fixed identities of any kind. Within the movement of history—within Benjamin's dream of history—the subject disappears because, produced by this movement, it is instead plural, relational, and impersonal. The "who" of history is no one because it can be everyone; it is the not-yet-existing *nonsubject* of revolution. If Benjamin's two Mexican dreams offer oneiric condensations of the history of plunder and colonization—if they appear as dreamlike condemnations of this history—they also point to a reconfiguration that, revealing the mutually destructive and constitutive relations between colonizer and colonized, gestures in the direction of an enigmatic commons that would no longer be organized around the politics of identity. That this commons to come can only be imagined in the otherworldliness of dreams—in which identities are entirely indeterminate, fetishes can come alive, Gods can be delegitimized, and different geographies and landscapes can find themselves elsewhere—suggests that the transvaluation of capitalism still belongs to a revolutionary future. This future requires not only that we decipher the resources granted to us by dreams but that we also imagine a future in which the primitive accumulation that is legible in the history of colonialism—in the history of racial capitalism—will no longer be just an accumulation of violence. Given Benjamin's interest in Mesoamerica, his critique of the relation between capital and colonialism is consonant with his interest in tracing a connection between communism—as it is imagined, for example, on Scheerbart's Pallas, which, in a letter to Scholem from November 23, 1919, Benjamin describes as "the best of all worlds" (*C*, 151)—and its Amerindian counterparts.[38] As we will see, Marx himself turns to ancient societies in the last

Tina Modotti, *Mexican Sombrero with Hammer and Sickle*, Mexico City, 1927

years of his life in order to further imagine what a planetary communism might look like. If Amerindian thought is a thought of transformation that exceeds the human—we might recall that Scheerbart's Pallasians reject the concept of the "human" in the name of a more relational commons—this planetary commons would embody a model of accumulation in which, in Martínez Yépez's words, "[t]he underworlds and the heavens, plants and animals, humans and things" would be "coparticipants in the formation of another general economy." "Nothing can be left out if this commons is to take place," he adds, "it would include everything ... [this commons] is not one. Every single thing is already the entire commons."[39] If Benjamin's dreams are a resource for imagining this commons—for imagining what this communist commons might look like—Marx's and Luxemburg's writings on primitive accumulation, in the negativity of their analyses, also become a means of creatively exceeding capitalist destruction.

★

As Marx notes near the opening of "The So-Called Original Accumulation" (*Die sogenannte ursprüngliche Akkumulation*) chapter in *Capital*, "[i]t is well known that conquest, subjugation, pillaging, murder—in short, acts of violence—have dominated the history of the real world. But the gentle world of political economy has always been an idyll. There, law and 'labor' have been the only means of acquiring wealth, although, of course, an exception is made every year for 'this year.' The methods of original accumulation may be many things; what they are not is idyllic." What Marx references here is a capitalist myth of origins, one in which the violence of capital is effaced through a kind of fairy tale about capital's idyllic beginnings. We should view this myth, he adds, from "the standpoint of nursery tales." What we have known as "primitive accumulation" is really "original accumulation," and more precisely "*so-called* original accumulation" (our emphasis), which is to say *not* "original accumulation" at all, or rather not what it is purported to be. In Marx's writerly hands, the concept of "original accumulation"—as he acknowledges, itself a translation and revision of Adam Smith's "previous accumulation"—emerges simultaneously as a capitalist description and a colonial justification of what the noncapitalist world experiences as theft, expropriation, and relentless plunder.[40] As he puts it in his 1853 essay on "The Future Results of British Rule in India," "The profound hypocrisy and inherent barbarism of bourgeois civilization lies unveiled before our eyes, turning from its home, where it assumes respectable forms, to the colonies, where it goes naked."[41] For Marx, history is a history of destruction and, in this history, there can be no capitalism without colonialism. If colonialism is just one index of capitalism, it nevertheless reveals the violence of capital in all its nakedness. This is why "so-called primitive accumulation" is in fact the opposite of what it presents itself as—a mechanism for the accumulation of wealth; it is instead a means of expropriation and impoverishment, of dispossession and death, with force and violence as its modus operandi. Scarcely an idyllic paradise, it is, in Marx's word, a Dantean "Inferno."[42]

Marx not only makes his political point through his use of this "so-called"—which already suggests that "original accumulation" is not what we think it is—but also by putting the phrase "original accumulation" in quotation marks which, like suspended clothespins, hang the concept out to dry. As Marx points out, capitalism employs the term in order to designate colonialism as a necessary phase in its development—as its "idyllic" prehistory. However, "original accumulation" in fact belongs to the colonialist discourse it seeks to justify. The term "primitive" encapsulates the ideology of a positivist narrative that is as essential to capitalism as war and the plunder of nature (to mention two of the instances of capitalist violence that Luxemburg singles out in her critical reading of "so-called 'primitive accumulation'"). But once the negative critical force of the Marxian letter is turned toward the concept, the phrase "primitive accumulation" can no longer be understood as a historical description of an earlier phase of capitalist development. It is rather a term that Marx investigates as part of his ideological critique of the capitalist rhetoric that justifies the brutal structures behind its pervasive colonial violence. It is the continuity of this structural necessity—that it is never just "previous" or past is part of its "secret"—that allows Luxemburg to reinforce Marx's critique when she returns to Marx's phrase in her 1913 *The Accumulation of Capital: A Contribution to the Explanation of Imperialism*. There she in fact reads the negative rhetorical moves of each of the terms in "so-called 'primitive accumulation'"—repeating Marx's "so-called" but also putting the phrase "primitive accumulation" in quotation marks.[43] In other words, Luxemburg demonstrates her fealty to Marx by reenacting, perhaps unconsciously, the same critical readerly and writerly strategies that Marx displays in his 1875 "Critique of the Gotha Program," which, attending to the smallest grammatical and linguistic details, effectively argues that the Gotha Program is not communist enough because its manifesto is not written precisely enough, either in its style or diction (not communist enough, that is, because it does not take full responsibility for its language).

The Gotha Program was the program of the Socialist Workers' Party of Germany. Marx distances himself from it since, for him, it misrepresents the principles of socialism and therefore jeopardizes the movement by giving its enemies ammunition. When he sends his critique to the leaders of the newly formed SAPD (which would later become the SPD, the Social Democratic Party of Germany), he also sends a copy of the recently published French edition of *Capital*, signaling his sense that the Party has not read him properly, and needs to do so. He also cites his *Communist Manifesto* as a counter to several of its claims. Beyond his critique of the Program's nationalist bent, the Party's retreat from the revolutionary promise of the Paris Commune's effort to offer an alternative to capitalism, the Party's misunderstanding of the source of wealth, and the complicity between its rhetoric and that of bourgeois politics, Marx opposes any determinate program for the future. In his words, *"[e]very step of real movement is more important than a dozen programs."*[44] Our interest in this remarkable text is Marx's practice of reading—and its essential relation to his political activism. He painstakingly moves through the sentences and paragraphs of the Program—often pausing on particular words—and repeatedly accuses the Party of writing that is imprecise and sloppy, "bungled in style and content," full of "loose notions" and "obsolete verbal rubbish," "botched" quotations, and "hollow phrases" that, miming the language of the bourgeoisie, "can be twisted and turned as desired" and lose all their meaning.[45] He rewrites phrases, asks questions about the use of words or phrases like "labor," "useful labor," "proceeds of labor," "fair distribution," "equal right," and "free state," and claims that the Program's appendix suffers from "slovenly editing." "And what wild abuse," he goes on to note, "the program makes of the words 'present-day state,' 'present-day society,' and of the greater misconception it creates in regard to the state to which it addresses its demands."[46] The text is further evidence that critical reading protocols are a political practice; for Marx, the possibilities of communism cannot be imagined without committed, and even militant, readers and writers—with reading and writing not restricted to just linguistic practices but expanded to include communist strategies for doing political work. Under this light, Luxemburg's attention to Marx's overt citation of the term allows her to pursue the question of the source of his phrase in the first stage of her and Marx's negative appropriation of Smith's capitalist conceptualization. Her political commitments are legible in her close attention to the slightest rhetorical and lexical shifts in Marx's texts, even to his punctuation.

Like Marx, Luxemburg also points to the excesses of violent expropriation rather than to chronological precedence as the distinguishing feature of "primitive accumulation." In *The Accumulation of Capital*, she points out that the very idea of "previous accumulation" already implies the teleological and self-fulfilling logic of the "total capitalist,"[47] a point of view that, as in Marx, is a cover for "brute force" (Marx refers to force as the "midwife" of a history that is itself "an economic power"[48]). In her reading, Luxemburg underlines the extractive violence directed toward the noncapitalist modes of production on which, paradoxically, capital depends for its survival. As she puts it, "Capitalism needs non-capitalist social strata as a market for its surplus value, a source of supply for its means of production, and a reservoir of labor-power for its wage system."[49] The relation of capitalism to noncapitalist "reservoirs" of labor and natural resources follows a colonial "method of violence":

> permanent occupation of the colonies by the military, native risings and punitive expeditions are the order of the day for any colonial regime. The method of violence, then, is the immediate consequence of the clash between capitalism and the organizations of a natural economy which would restrict accumulation. ... This method is the most profitable and gets the quickest results, and so it is also the most expedient for capital.[50]

Emphasizing the interdependence of colonial violence and capitalist modes of production, Luxemburg points to the ongoing complicities between colonialism and industrialization. In a passage that echoes both Las Casas and Marx, she notes that "[f]orce, fraud, oppression, looting are openly displayed without any attempt at concealment, and it requires an effort to discover within this tangle of political violence and contests of power the stern laws of the economic process."[51] Emphasizing the parallelism between indigenous bondage and the enslavement of Africans by European capitalism, she writes: "[t]he economic basis for the production of raw materials is a primitive system of exploitation practiced by European capital in the African colonies and in America, where the institutions of slavery and bondage are combined in various forms."[52] Four years later, Luxemburg returns to the study of indigenous communities specifically in relation to the plunder of nature, drawing a connection between this plunder and the extermination of native populations. In a letter dated May 2, 1917, she tells Sonja (Sophie) Liebknecht that she has been studying natural science:

> Only yesterday I read why the warblers are disappearing from Germany. Increasingly systematic forestry, gardening and agriculture are, step by step, destroying all nesting and breeding places: hollow trees, fallow land, thickets of shrubs, withered leaves on the garden ground. It pained me so when I read that. Not because of the song they sing for people, but rather it was the picture of the silent, irresistible extinction of these defenseless little creatures which hurt me to the point where I had to cry. It reminded me of a Russian book which I read while still in Zürich, a book by Professor Sieber about the ravage of the redskins in North America. In exactly the same way, step by step, they had been pursued from their land by civilized men and abandoned to perish silently and cruelly.[53]

Always a reader—and not just of books on natural science or histories of the extermination of native populations but also of nature and the various ways in which it bears the destructive effects of capital in its trees, land, shrubs, and leaves—Luxemburg points to the devastating effects of industrial forestry and agriculture on the conditions of life. The march of capitalism spells the eradication of the warblers and of Native Americans. Leaving behind fallow and unproductive land, clearing its path through deforestation, disturbing nature's means of replenishing and reproducing itself, moving forward through the displacement and genocide of populations, capital's accumulative advance proves to be barbaric, not "civilized."

Luxemburg here follows Marx, who claims that "the squandering and exploitation of the earth" are one of the defining features of the system of capitalist accumulation.[54] "The more a country proceeds from large-scale industry as the background of its development," he writes, "as in the case of the United States, the more rapid is this process of destruction." Marx's argument that capitalist production introduces a rift in "the metabolic interaction between man and the earth" is well known. The destructiveness of capital "prevents the return to the soil of its constituent elements," he writes, "it hinders the operation of the eternal natural condition for the lasting fertility of the soil." In a later formulation, he states that capital's dissipation of the "vitality of the soil" creates "an irreparable rift in the interdependent process of social metabolism, a metabolism prescribed by the natural laws of life itself."[55] Joining ecological destruction, capitalist production, and the expropriation of life and labor, Marx delineates the contradictions of a capitalism that creates the conditions of its own demise by destroying the very material resources on which it depends. Capitalism meets its limits when it imagines it has none. As Paul Burkett, John Bellamy Foster, and Kohei Saito demonstrate, Marx gathers his understanding of the effects of industrial agriculture on the earth's metabolic system through his reading of various treatises on natural science.[56] Developing his argument in his discussion of ground rent theory in *Capital*, he especially is indebted to Justus von Liebig's 1862 edition of *Agricultural Chemistry*, in which, in his introduction (on which Marx took extensive notes in 1865–1866 as he was finishing the first volume of *Capital*), Liebig points to what he calls industrial agriculture's "robbery" of nature—its depletion of essential nutrients of the soil without establishing a "law of compensation," without replenishing what it extracts. Liebeg views this ongoing depletion as unsustainable, stating, in a passage that has great resonance today, that "if we do not succeed in making the farmer better aware of the conditions under which he produces and in giving him the means necessary for the increase of his output, wars, emigration, famines and epidemics will of necessity create the conditions of a new equilibrium which will undermine the welfare of everyone and finally lead to the ruin of agriculture."[57] As Marx notes, echoing Liebig, "all progress in capitalist agriculture is a progress in the art, not only of robbing the worker, but of robbing the soil; all progress in increasing the fertility of the soil for a given time is progress towards ruining the more long-lasting sources of that fertility."[58] If Marx points to the strategies and techniques that industrial agriculture puts in place to increase productivity—from technological innovations to different means of fertilizing the soil to international trade—he insists that, in the long run, far from countering the acceleration of the earth's ruination, these efforts actually ensure it. He describes a vicious circle in which the depletion of resources in one geographical area requires either supplying additional resources extracted somewhere else or abandoning the area and diminishing the resources of another one. The effort to broaden the scale of capital's industrial growth only further exposes the contradictions in this expansion, leading to a greater exploitation of nature's resources.

In response to this soil exhaustion—the result of climate, erosion, the removal of organic matter and nutrients, destructive methods of cultivation, and the voracious plunder of capitalist agriculture—Liebig urged crop diversification and rotation, along with the application of fertilizers. The demand for fertilizer was partially filled by various artificial manures, but especially by Peruvian guano. The best guano came from the Chincha Islands, just twelve miles from the coast of Peru, in the bay of Pisco. Since the islands received very little rainfall, the naturally high nitrogen content of the guano remained undiluted in a pungent, brownish-yellow concretion that also was very rich in phosphate. In some of the ravines of the islands, it was said to be nearly 300 feet deep, and some speculated that it must have begun to accumulate there soon after the biblical flood.

At war with Bolivia in the late 1830s and experiencing several civil wars in the early 1840s, Peru found its economy shattered and, in order to reduce its enormous war debt, it began to negotiate with foreign companies for the selling of its guano. In 1841, Peru's President Manuel Menéndez formally nationalized the country's guano resources and, for the next thirty-five years, the Peruvian government would earn most of its foreign revenues from selling guano to other countries. In 1842, the London firm Anthony Gibbs & Sons shared a monopoly on exports for five years and, in 1847, gained sole control of British and North American markets. By 1846, Peru had received more than $1.3 million in guano advances, and by the 1860s seabirds supplied more than 75 percent of the government's revenues. High prices, however, encouraged searches for substitutes and even encouraged fraud. By 1854, several varieties of guano had been introduced from Africa, Central America, the Caribbean, and assorted Pacific islands, but they were considered far inferior in quality to those of Peru. Europe and America hoped to share in the plunder of the resources of native peoples whose cultures were violently altered or destroyed. The guano trade reveals the guiding principle of racial capitalism: in Emerson's words, "expensive races—race living at the expense of race," at the expense, that is, of what he elsewhere calls "the guano-races of mankind."[59] According to Foster, Clark, and York, "the Peruvian guano trade is a classic case of ecological imperialism and of the internationalization of capitalism's metabolic rift. ... The trade enhanced the imperialist integration of distant economies, expanding, deepening, and increasing the global metabolic rift." Indeed, they go on to note, "[t]he international guano trade from 1840 to 1880 perfectly embodies the dynamic of

ecological imperialism, the robbing of resources and the degradation of ecosystems, as European nations—especially Britain—and
the United States plundered Peru, extracting 12.7–20 million
tons of bird excrement from the islands to enrich their nutrient
depleted soils, given the unsustainable practices of industrial
capitalist agriculture."[60] Marx himself suggests that the impor-
tation of guano enables Europe to defer its acknowledgment of
its finitude, even if just temporarily—until the guano reserves are
themselves depleted, that is—but only at the expense of the ecological metabolism of Peru's natural economy.

As a commodity, guano bears the traces of the history of imperialism and colonization. Its trade suggests that the liberty and
economic prosperity of empire are entangled with the oppression,
and often the death, of millions of slaves and ethnic immigrants.
As Emerson puts it, in a line that easily could have been written
by Marx, "in each change of industry, whole classes and populations are sacrificed."[61] This point is confirmed when we note that
the workers involved in supporting and maintaining the guano
trade included not only the German, Irish, and African Americans
to whom Emerson refers but also, among so many others, the
Peruvian convicts, natives, and Chinese coolies that worked the
Peruvian guano fields. According to Evelyn Hu-Dehart, from 1849
to 1874, as many as 100,000 contract laborers or "coolies" were
transported, under deception or coercion, across the Pacific to
help meet the demand for cheap labor on the coastal guano fields.[62]
There would in fact have been no guano trade without these laborers. Amidst the ravages of war and the labor shortages resulting
from the end of African slavery, Peru—hoping to encourage foreign investment and unable to find enough cheap labor among
the small coastal peasantry, freed slaves, or the highlanders, to
meet the growing demand—decided to seek it overseas. When it
was clear that European immigrants were not drawn to the lack of
available land and low wages in Peru, the Peruvian government—
following the example of the British planters in the West Indies,
including Cuba—resorted to a racialized system of bondage in
the form of Chinese laborers. In south China, Westerners used
Chinese "runners"—the same term their counterparts in Africa
were called—to "recruit" poor young men, often by force but also
by persuading them that they were to work the gold mines in
California. Some boarded ships in Amoy or other Chinese ports,
but the greater number probably passed through the Portuguese
colony of Macao. As Hu-Dehart points out, many of the same
ships and captains used in the African slave trade "transported

Chinese coolies, packing them on board in the same way as slaves, across a 'middle passage' that was even longer in distance and more arduous."[63] Mortality rates on these ships—often referred to as "floating coffins"—were as high as 30 percent or more, due to overcrowding, insufficient food, lack of proper ventilation, and poor hygienic conditions. Once the Chinese laborers arrived in Peru, they were auctioned, and then housed in long, rectangular slave quarters. The working conditions on the islands were unbearable, not only because of their inhospitable nature—the climatic conditions on the islands made any work there a matter of privation and hardship, since the heat and lack of rainfall made water and food supplies very scarce—but also because of the viciousness with which the laborers were driven to dig and load the guano. In response to these harsh conditions, the coolies often chose to commit suicide in order to escape their enslavement.[64] The pressure experienced by the Peruvian government to stop what was often referred to as "another African slave trade" did not, however, prevent the deaths of tens of thousands of coolies and Peruvian laborers—many of whom, buried in the guano fields in which they died working, became, like the flesh and carcasses of birds and sea lions, part of the guano that soon would be exported to Europe and the United States to fertilize their lands and crops. The guano harvesting also resulted in the deaths of the guano-producing seabirds, as their nests were destroyed in the mining of the fields. The ecological system sustaining them and allowing them to reproduce was ravaged by the process of extraction, just as Luxemburg's warblers were destroyed by the industrialization of agriculture.

As Marx notes, the very fact that England needs to manure its fields with guano imported from Peru and other countries confirms that capitalist agriculture is no longer "self-sustaining"; "it no longer finds the natural conditions of its own production within itself, naturally arisen, spontaneous, and ready to hand," but instead requires "an independent industry separate from it—and, with this separateness the whole complex set of interconnections in which this industry exists is drawn into the sphere of the conditions of agricultural production."[65] This industry emerges as a historically created necessity and is supported by an economic infrastructure that gathers its force through the legalization of the coolie labor system in the form of racialized contract slavery.[66] Foster points to the expansion of this industry around the globe, noting that "[t]he trade in scalps promoted by the British and the Puritans of New England, the slave trade in Java, the conquest and plunder of

India, the opium trade, and so on, were all means in which capital created a world system under its control that extracted wealth and raw materials for capitalist industry for the benefit of Europe, while destroying communal systems of property elsewhere. All of this is part of the larger, global expropriation that provided the primary accumulation for the genesis of industrial capital."[67]

Following Liebig and other natural scientists—in particular Carl Fraas, whose interest in the physics of nature expands Liebig's emphasis on its chemistry by focusing not only on climatic influences on soil and plant growth but also on the detrimental effects of deforestation in works like his 1847 *Climate and the Plant World Over Time: A Contribution to the History of Both*[68]—Marx repeatedly points to capital's "exploitation" and "squandering of the powers of the earth." He argues that the conditions of the earth's endurance and survival require its "systematic restoration," insisting on "a conscious and rational treatment of the land as permanent communal property, as the inalienable condition for the existence and reproduction of the chain of human existence." "Even an entire society, a nation, or all simultaneously existing societies taken together are not the owners of the earth," he goes on to explain, "[t]hey are simply its possessors, its beneficiaries, and have to bequeath it in an improved state to succeeding generations, as *boni patres familias*."[69] Joining his ecological activism to his critique of political economy, Marx indicates that the task of communism is the protection and preservation of the metabolic relation between society and nature. Here to be red requires that we simultaneously be "green," but in a way that does not in turn capitalize on the rhetoric of sustainability itself. In the words of Foster and Clark—we quote them with the proviso that, in our reading, the "human" in Marx is never, strictly speaking, just human, but already an amalgam of historical and material traces, an ensemble of social relations that can never be reduced to a single entity—"if the revolutionary struggle for socialism failed in the past," it was because "[i]t did not demand the reconstitution of human labor based on a society of associated producers and a world of creative labor—aimed at the fulfillment of human potential, while rationally regulating the human metabolism with nature so as to protect the earth for future generations."[70]

★

If Marx finds resources for imagining this "society of associated producers" and this "world of creative labor" in Fraas and other natural scientists he reads at the time, it is because he sees in them what he calls—in a letter to Engels from March 25, 1868 in which he mentions Fraas directly—"an unconscious socialist tendency."[71] While all of Marx's work aims at making this tendency more manifest, at having it be materialized, this effort is particularly evident in his late work—and across a wider temporal and global panorama. In addition to his readings in natural science, he reads several books on precapitalist and non-Western societies, focusing on agriculture, landed property, communal forms of production, nonhierarchical modes of organizing family structures, and gender relations. Kevin Anderson notes that, after the fall of the Paris Commune in 1871, Marx begins to look for other "forms of resistance to capital outside Western Europe and North America." This search is legible in the changes he makes to the French edition of *Capital* soon after the defeat of the Commune, in the notes he takes from 1879–1882 on non-Western and precapitalist societies—some of which have been published as his *Ethnological Notebooks*—and in a series of writings on Russia from 1877 to 1882 in which, in Anderson's words, he suggests that "agrarian Russia's communal villages could be a starting point for a socialist transformation, one that might avoid the brutal process of the primitive accumulation of capital."[72] Dunayevskaya herself remarks, adding Marx's 1875 "Critique of the Gotha Program," that these threads in Marx's thought need to be understood as part of his ongoing wish to find resources for imagining noncapitalist possibilities, to extend his thinking and research beyond Eurocentric constraints, beyond the *jus publicum Europaeum*.

Nowhere is this more evident than in Marx's *Ethnological Notebooks* or, during this same period, in the various drafts of his correspondence with the Russian activist Vera Zasulich about the revolutionary potential of Russian communes.[73] While interest in these Marxian multilingual glosses has grown exponentially in the last years,[74] Dunayevskaya was among the first to register the transformative character of the *Notebooks*, noting that these "profound writings ... summed up [Marx's] life's work and created new openings ... a new vantage-point from which to view Marx's oeuvre as a totality."[75] As a collection of working notes—and, as we will suggest, so much more than just this—they not only give us a glimpse into Marx's process of production and, in Dunayevskaya's words, "let us hear [him] think," but they also "reveal, at one and the same time, the actual ground that led to the first projection of the possibility of revolution coming first in ... underdeveloped countries like Russia; a reconnection and deepening of what was projected in the *Grundrisse* on the Asiatic mode of production; *and* a return to that most fundamental relationship [between men and women] which had first been projected in the 1844 essays." "Marx's hostility to capitalism's colonialism was intensifying," she adds, and "he returns to probe the origin of humanity, not for purposes of discovering new origins, but for perceiving new revolutionary forces."[76] He searches for resources as much to think about the origins of different forms of hierarchy within past societies as he does to think about transforming social relations in contemporary capitalist ones. What the *Notebooks* critically embody is *the method of reading* that Marx develops during the course of his lifetime, and we can see this in the way in which he records, summarizes, and transforms passages from the books he reads and studies. Franklin Rosemont captures the wildness of the *Notebooks* when he writes:

> Karl Marx's *Ethnological Notebooks*—notes for a major study he never lived to write, have [a] fugitive ambiguity. These extensively annotated excerpts from works of Lewis Henry Morgan and others are a jigsaw puzzle for which we have to reinvent the missing pieces out of our own research and revery and above all, our own revolutionary activity ... the book presents the reader with all the difficulties of *Finnegan's Wake* and more, with its curious mixture of English, German, French, Latin and Greek, and a smattering of words and phrases from many non-European languages, from Ojibwa to Sanskrit. Cryptic shorthand abbreviations, incomplete and run-on sentences, interpolated exclamations, erudite allusions to classical mythology, passing references to contemporary world affairs, generous doses of slang and vulgarity; irony and invective: All these the volume possesses aplenty, and they are not the ingredients of smooth reading. ... Rather it is the raw substance of a work ... the spontaneous record of his "conversations" with the authors he was reading, with other authors whom they quoted, and, finally and especially, with himself. ... On page after page Marx highlights passages wildly remote from what are usually regarded as the "standard themes" of his work. Thus we find him invoking the bell-shaped houses of the coastal tribes of Venezuela; the manufacture of Iroquois belts "using fine twine made of filaments of elm and basswood bark," "the Peruvian legend of Manco Capac and Mama Oello, children of the sun"; burial customs of the Tuscarora; the Shawnee belief in metempsychosis; "unwritten literature of myths, legends and traditions"; the "incipient sciences" of the village Indians of the Southwest; the *Popul Vuh*, sacred book of the ancient Quiche Maya; the use of porcupine quills in ornamentation; Indian games and "dancing (as a) form of worship."[77]

Marx's *Ethnological Notebooks* present us with a multilingual coalition of quotations, fragments, and notations that are assembled and disassembled before our eyes on every one of its crowded pages. What is available in print is just a selection of the more than 800 pages that comprise the notebooks and that, beyond what is now published, cover a vast range of societies and historical periods, including notes on, among other things, the history of India and Latin America, communal forms in Indonesia and Ceylon, ancient rules of finance, especially in Egypt, Dutch colonialism and its global consequences, gender and kinship patterns in the Americas and in ancient Greece, Rome, and medieval Europe, works in physical anthropology and paleontology, and Russian-language studies of rural communes in Russia. The variegated and often seemingly chaotic presentation of materials, as Rosemont notes, makes the reading of the notebooks a rather formidable task, if not an impossible one.[78] What we have before us is a massive attempt to reconceptualize "primitive accumulation"—with its long history of violence and expropriation—through a different process of accumulation, one that accumulates political resources and possibilities, that superimposes elements from different societies, customs, and languages one atop another, often in the same sentences. Gathering together histories of different modes of communal organization and putting them atop and alongside one another, Marx's notebooks perform a kind of equality—in the sense that, through the critical lens of Marx's reading practice, these varied communal forms emerge as so many resources for moving modern capitalist formations toward more "archaic" forms of communal ownership and production, and a more sustainable and less predatory metabolism with nature. To put it another way: in the last decade of his life and, in particular, in the last three years of his life, Marx intensifies his exploration of communist possibilities. Understanding, as Dunayevskaya notes, "that revolutionary forces do not easily arise and that they are not easily imagined,"[79] he expands his network of resources onto a more global scale and especially includes indigenous materials, along with excerpts on noncapitalist communal forms around the world. By the time he assembles his *Notebooks*, he has been analyzing the apparatuses of capitalism for more than four decades. Having honed his antennas during the course of a lifetime of combating capital and its devastating effects, he knows almost instinctively how to register evidence of noncapitalist forms of association that can help him (and especially us, who, after all, belong to the future for which he relentlessly toils) imagine a different historical outcome. Near the end of his life, Marx is not simply an expert reader of capitalism's totality and its brutal violence but a full-on militant in search of any crack and fissure in its seamless surface. This has to be the *late* Marx, since finding noncapitalist resources requires knowing capitalism inside-out, demands, in fact, the wisdom of a lifetime. We can see this wisdom in every transformation Marx enacts in the language he copies and changes in every instance. We see him imaginatively drawing from his sources—he writes that the "imagination [is] that great faculty" that has so greatly contributed "to the elevation of mankind" (*EN*, 130)—glimpses of "unconscious" socialist tendencies in the truncated potentials of the communal forms he studies. This different kind of accumulation works against capitalist teleology by substituting the latter's false causation with a paratactic logic that allows Marx to gather, massify, and mobilize a different kind of wealth—a common-wealth on the page. We need only cite a few passages to confirm this and, for our purposes here, we will turn to passages Marx cites—and often revises—from Lewis H. Morgan's 1877 *Ancient Society*.

Lawrence Krader's edition of Marx's *Ethnological Notebooks* consists primarily of excerpts from Marx's readings of John Lubbock's *The Origin of Civilization* (1870); Henry Sumner Maine's *Lectures on the Early History of Institutions* (1875); John Budd Phear's *The Aryan Village in India and Ceylon* (1880); and Morgan's *Ancient Society*—although, inserting throughout references ranging from Aeschylus to Herodotus, Homer to Aristotle, Plutarch to Lucretius, Shakespeare to Darwin, Cervantes to Dickens, and more, Marx displays an erudition and reading that vastly exceeds these primary sources. Nevertheless, because Engels bases his 1884 *The Origin of the Family, Private Property, and the State* on Marx's excerpts from Morgan's book, these are the best known of his ethnological notes. The Russian jurist and sociologist Maksim Kovalevsky gives Marx a copy of his *Communal Landownership*, along with Morgan's book, in 1879, and Marx is immediately drawn to Morgan's project because it resonates with his own interests. In his book, Morgan divides the history of societies into three "evolutionary" moments—Savagery, Barbarism, and Civilization. His narrative of the development of one stage into another is just one more version of the "idyll" of primitive accumulation that, for Marx, effaces the racism, violence, settler colonialism, and indigenous genocide that are the engine of this developmental story, but Marx still sees the text as a great resource. Morgan offers him a history of the material conditions of subsistence, the origins of state formations, the links among property, familial structures, and hereditary inheritance, and the contradictions between communal forms and the emergence of capital. Although Marx does not follow Morgan's evolutionary and teleological account of historical progress—nor does he neglect the violence that attends this so-called "progress"—he especially is drawn, as Engels is, not only to Morgan's sense that the immense "outgrowth of property" has become an "unmanageable power" that contains the elements of its own "self-destruction," but, more importantly, to his prediction, on the basis of his rather monumental study of ancient societies, of a potential "revival, in a higher form, of the liberty, equality and fraternity of the ancient gentes."[80]

What Marx and Engels find in Morgan are different possibilities for communal existence; they are reinforced in their conviction that hierarchies of class, property, and gender are not the only means of organization, nor are there set ways of forming families, states, or governing structures in general. That the outcome of historical processes could have taken many different forms—that they did not have to lead to capitalism—suggests that the beginnings of these processes also could have been different. Communism in fact requires that we be able to imagine different beginnings and endings, that we register what Morgan understands as the vicissitudes and accidents of circumstances, and this even though Marx sees indications of social stratifications already in early clan societies—so many signs of all the antagonisms that will develop in time across the world of capital. Still, Morgan provides Marx with empirical evidence of nonhegemonic modes of association and exchange that potentially can become part of a multilingual, multitemporal, noncapitalist arsenal for a revolutionary future—one that would not be condemned to reenact scenes of capitalist accumulation throughout the globe.[81] This arsenal is not only drawn from what Marx takes from the books he reads; it also takes shape through an act of notetaking that is simultaneously an act of political reading whose mode of operation is visible in the unruliness of the patchwork he puts together in each of his entries. This unruliness corresponds to the enthusiasm, awe, and wonder that Marx exhibits on every page. It is as if in his late years he discovers a way of reading the world anew. Like Benjamin in his Mexican dreams, however, he does not present his accumulation of fragments as fetishes or artifacts that belong to capital's museums; he neither romanticizes nor idealizes them. It is perhaps not an accident that Morgan, like Lehmann, was a great collector of indigenous material objects. This colonial form of accumulation—this form of plunder, however "liberal" its intention—runs counter to the accumulation displayed by the writing practices of Marx and Benjamin. Their writing accumulates resources that, never belonging to either one of them, can be activated in political directions and, in particular, in anticolonial ones. In the *Notebooks*, Marx presents these resources in all their motility. This movement is what is activated and intensified in every passage he cites and in which he intervenes; his practice of notetaking ensures that it never ceases, that it leaps from one passage to another, requiring that we read the fragments he puts together syntactically, with endless possibilities for rearranging them.

We can see this movement at work in the following passage, in which, referring to the Spanish encounter with the Aztecs—an encounter that, like his with the texts he reads, is mediated and interrupted by language—he traces the different means of designating and translating words that correspond to the establishment of hierarchical order, and that function across different indigenous populations. Referencing a series of passages from Morgan's pages on "The Aztec Confederacy" and, in particular, the section entitled "The Tenure and Functions of the Office of Principal War-Chief," he writes:

D. Name des office d. Montezuma—*Teuctli*, war chief, als member d. *Council of chiefs* er manchmal genannt *Tlatoani* (= speaker). This office of a *general military commander* the highest known to the Aztecs, war sonst same als d. Haupt *war-chief* der *Iroquois Confederacy*. D. office machte seinen Träger ex officio *member of the Council of chiefs*. The title of *Teuctli* added als a sort of surname wie: *Chichimeca-Teuctli, Pil-Teuctli* etc. | Bei *Clavigero* heissts: "The teuctli took *precedency* of all others in the *Senate*, both in the order of sitting and voting, and were permitted to have a *servant behind them* (der *subsachem* dr Iroquois) with a seat, which was esteemed a privilege of the highest honour." D. *Spanish writers* brauchen nie d. Wort "*teuctli*", verwandeln es in *king* für Montezuma u. dessen successors. *Ixtlilxochitl*, of mixed Tezcucan u. Spanish descent nennt d. *head warchiefs* of *Mexico, Tezcuco* u. *Tlacopan* nur "*warchief*" *teuctli* u. andrem Wort to *indicate the tribe* (*teuctli* = warchief = general). Obiger *Ixtlilxochitl* sagt, sprechend von der *division* of power zwischen d. 3 chiefs, when the confederacy was formed etc:

"The king of *Tezcuco* was saluted [dch d. assembled chiefs der 3 tribes] by the title of *Aculhua Teuctli*, also by that of *Chichimecatl Teuctli* which his ancestors had worn and which was the mark of the empire [das Beiwort tribal designation]; *Itzcoatzin* (Itzcoatl), his uncle, received the title of *Culhua Teuctli*, because he reigned over the *Toltecs-Culhuas* [war warchief of the Aztecs, when the confederacy was formed]; and *Totoquihuatzin den of Tecpanuatl Teuctli*, which had been the title of Azcaputzalco. Since that time their successors have received the same title." (*EN*, 194)

As can be seen here, Marx's practice of notetaking cannot be reduced to a simple process of transcription or synthesis. While he bases his notes on a particular passage in Morgan, he reorders its lines, interrupts them with German—sometimes just a translation of Morgan's English into German, but not always—blurs the distinctions between what is Morgan's and, in this instance, what is Francisco Javier Clavigero's (the line before the citation from Clavigero is also his, but, because Marx inserts it alongside Morgan's language, it appears to be Morgan's), and, in general, wreaks havoc on the narrative arc of Morgan's paragraph by breaking it up into fragments. He refuses to distinguish between what belongs to the main body of Morgan's text and what is in his footnotes by transferring materials from the footnotes into the fragments he cites. He eliminates conjunctions, interrupts temporal order, breaks with any teleological narrative, and, in general, enacts a scattering that becomes increasingly difficult to contain. If, following Morgan, he traces the different words that—across Nahuatl, Spanish, German, and English—refer to the office held by Montezuma and other indigenous leaders, he politicizes the ethnologist's account of the Spanish mistranslations of Aztec words and customs by emphasizing the way in which the encounter involves a process of erasure and loss. The encounter does not take place, or, rather, it takes place only in an equivocal encounter between languages, one that is marked not only by the force of empire but also by hierarchical structures—structures that can be registered among the Spanish, the Aztecs, and the Iroquois, if in different measures.

Inserting his German into Morgan's text—mixing his language with Morgan's, thinking his thoughts, that is, in the heads of others—becomes a means for Marx to prevent any one language from having authority over another one. He performs a leveling that, because language is one of its most powerful means of subjugation, targets colonial dominance in general. This insistence on a kind of horizontality can be seen throughout the *Notebooks*, and can be registered at times simply in the alteration of a single word. There are several instances of this, but one particularly striking example pertinent to our present discussion occurs when, in response to a remark that Morgan makes in his discussion of the governance structure of the Iroquois, Marx substitutes a German word for one of Morgan's, turning his argument against him.

Morgan praises the emergence of the office of war-chief as "a permanent feature" in the confederacy of the Iroquois—an office he likens to that of a general, "Hos-gä-ä-geh'-da-go-wä" can also mean a "great war soldier"—suggesting that the similar position within Aztec culture is, like that of the Iroquois, "a great event in the history of human progress."[82] When Marx transcribes the line into his *Notebooks*, however, he replaces "great" with the German "verhängnisvoll," which makes the sentence read: the "*introduction of this office as a permanent feature verhängnisvoll event* in the history of human progress" (*EN*, 173). In this small intervention, Marx affirms his sense of the "*verhängnisvoll* [disastrous]" and deleterious effects of hierarchical forms, a stance that can be registered throughout the *Notebooks*. These catastrophic effects belong to different modes of stratification and arise within these early communal, proto-communist forms, with, in Dunayevskaya's words, "the establishment of ranks—relationship of chief to mass—and the economic interests that accompanied it." As she explains, "Marx demonstrated that, long before the dissolution of the primitive commune, there emerged the question of ranks *within* the egalitarian commune. It was the beginning of a transformation into opposite—gens into caste. That is to say, within the egalitarian communal form arose the elements of its opposite—caste, aristocracy, and different material interests. Moreover, these were not successive stages, but *co-extensive* with the communal form."[83] Like capital itself, these early noncapitalist communes move toward their ruin at the very moment they organize themselves not only around family and private property but, more significantly, around the antagonism between a chief and the masses. For Marx, the dissolution of the early communal form is as much a result of its own internal movement, its own transitional state, as it is of external forces. Dunayevskaya makes this point again when, referencing what Luxemburg calls "the world historic act of the birth of capitalism," the Spanish conquest and its enslavement and extermination of indigenous populations, she writes that Marx

> called attention to the fact of conquests, even when the commune was at its height. Just as there was conquest, even when the commune was at its height, and the beginning of slavery when one tribe defeated another, so there was the beginning of commodity exchange between the communes as well as emergence of conflict within the commune and within the family, and not only between the family and the gens. All these conflicts coalesced during the dissolution, which is why Marx's *Notebooks* keep stressing the duality in primitive communism.[84]

The resources into which Marx taps in order to imagine different communist possibilities bear the kernel of their own dissolution within them. This fact, however, neither effaces the violence that often leads to their destruction nor erases their potential within a socialist future. If Marx views history as a catastrophic form that unravels in the volatility of its formlessness, its force breaks through the cracks and fissures it opens in order to allow for unexpected, revolutionary events to unfold in insurgent and ungovernable ways. It is because the unfolding of history is never fully finalized or absolutely determined that, again in Dunayevskaya's words, there can be no "world historic defeat." Even in an imagined capitalist totality, there are always elements of resistance, often hidden under the signs of defeat and erasure, that guarantee that the antagonism between capitalist and noncapitalist forms can never be at a standstill, and this because history is another name for constant movement and flux. There is "always one more revolution to make," she writes, "and the proof [is] in what one learn[s] from defeat to transform the next battle into a victory."[85]

This oscillation between defeat and revolution—an oscillation whose rhythm is as unpredictable as it is irrepressible—can be registered throughout Marx's *Notebooks*, and indeed throughout his work. Having assiduously studied the brutal suppression of the French Revolutions of 1789, 1830, 1848, and 1871, the violence of the American Civil War, and the defeat of rebellions around the globe, he is particularly attuned to the way in which the rhetoric of liberty and equality—always evoked in contexts of great inequality—can be mobilized not simply by revolutionary movements but also by counterrevolutionary regimes in order to protect the interests of the privileged, propertied classes. The mere evocation of these revolutionary "ideals," in other words, is not a guarantee that they are not at the same time betrayed and instrumentalized by colonial or state forces whose aim is only to protect the liberty of the few. While Morgan himself privileges equal rights and "the cardinal principles of democracy" and understands the threats to these rights and principles that are introduced by an insistence on property—he argues that, "when property [is] created in masses," slavery emerges, along with "despotism, imperialism, monarchy, [and] privileged classes"[86]—his insistence on the evolutionary development of history enables him to describe the collective accumulation of property as part of the progress from less developed communities to more advanced ones. In the end, consonant with his paternalistic concern for American Indians, he claims that the "Aryan" family "has proved its intrinsic superiority by gradually assuming control of the earth" and that the United States—which has inherited everything before it—is the cumulative realization of a "representative democracy."[87] The movement through the different stages of development is presented as the result of natural evolution rather than of violent colonization. Marx would be particularly attentive to these contradictions in Morgan's text. He references another instance in which Morgan evokes the revolutionary phrase "liberty, equality, and fraternity," but this time in a passage that also points to the European colonization of the Americas, even if indirectly. Marx's excerpt reads:

All the members of an Iroquois gens *personally free*, bound *to defend each other's freedom; equal in privileges u. personal rights*. Sachem u. chiefs claiming no superiority; a *brotherhood bound together by the ties of kin. Liberty, Equality, and Fraternity,* though never formulated, were *cardinal principles der gens* u. diese d. *unit of a social u. governmental system*, the foundation wor<au>f *Indian society organized*. Erklärt *sense of independence* u. *personal dignity universally an attribute of Indian character*.

Zur Zeit der europäischen Entdeckg waren d. *American Indian tribes* generally organized *into gentes, with descent in the female line;* In einigen *Tribes*, wie den *Dacotas, the gentes had fallen out;* in andern, wie unter *Ojibwas*, d. *Omahas* u. d. *Mayas of Yucatan*, descent has changed from female to male line. *Throughout aboriginal America* die *gens* nahm ihren *Namen von some animal*, or *inanimate object, never from a person;* in this early condition of society, the *individuality of persons was lost in the gens*. (*EN*, 150)

First citing Morgan, the excerpt begins by characterizing the Iroquois as a gens that privileges equality, rights, and independence and is nonhierarchical. Marx continues with Morgan's reference to the tripartite slogan of the French Revolution and the ethnographer's claim that, even "though never formulated" as such, the Iroquois gens manifests these ideals. He follows Morgan a bit more and then, excising a paragraph, he moves directly to his German rendition of Morgan's "At the epoch of European discovery," "Zur Zeit der europäischen Entdeck[un]g." Translating the phrase not only calls more attention to it, but also permits Marx to distance himself from Morgan's silence regarding the Spanish conquest and early British and French colonizations, all of which involved colonial massacres of indigenous populations. Marx accomplishes at least two things by insisting on this phrase in German: First, he recalls the European origins of the "Doctrine of Discovery," formulated in 1493 in the papal bull issued by Pope

Alexander VI and giving Spain the right to claim ownership of any "discovered" non-Christian land in the New World. The doctrine became the basis of European claims in the Americas and the foundation for the expansionism of the United States' manifest destiny, since it was reaffirmed by the US Supreme Court in 1823, when Chief Justice John Marshall's opinion in a unanimous decision argued "that the principle of discovery gave European nations an absolute right to New World lands."[88] And, second, he returns us to his own language in order to recall to us what he himself has written on European colonialism in general and on the Spanish conquest in particular. For Marx, Morgan's "European discovery" is a euphemism for the violence of conquest and colonization—for the dispossession, murder, and forced assimilation of indigenous populations that has characterized the colonial project for more than three centuries.

Marx's German insertion is just one register of his political reading of Morgan. He transmits the catastrophe obscured in Morgan's omissions in the caesura he creates between his paragraphs—which brings the revolutionary slogan closer to his translation of Morgan's line—and this is his real act of translation. Following Althusser, we might say that he offers a "guilty" reading of Morgan—one that inflects his own interests, but also brings Morgan's complicity to the page's surface. Marx reads Morgan symptomatically by evoking what the ethnographer does not say. He excavates Morgan's text as Benjamin excavates Weimar's marketplace. If the European "discovery" of the Americas marks a decisive break, it is because it disorganizes, fractures, discards, erases, and vanquishes. This is why Marx's *Notebooks* become a means for him to read the fragments and remains that have been left behind, to read the histories that are hidden in the histories bequeathed to us and, through this work of gathering and excavation, to retrieve and reactivate the traces of different protosocialist communal forms. In the context of Morgan's reading of the progress of history in terms of an evolutionary tendency toward governance, property, and family structures, Marx excerpts this passage because it includes the traces of a world in which, as he puts it, again joining his German to Morgan's English, "*[t]hroughout aboriginal America* die *gens* nahm ihren *Namen von some animal,* or *inanimate object, never from a person;* in this early condition of society, the *individuality of persons was lost in the gens.*" In this fraternity, there are no proper names but rather only the common names of animals and inanimate things. The absence of proper names works against the nominalism of property, possessive individualism, and propertied forms of inheritance—forms of hereditary succession which, as Marx notes elsewhere in the *Notebooks*, "when first established, *came from force* (usurpation), nicht *by the free consent of the people*" (*EN*, 173). From the fragments of the now destroyed Iroquois gens—Marx refers to the "*[c]onstant tendency to disintegration*" that exists in "the elements of gentile organization" (*EN*, 156)—he can imagine the fusion of the individual into the communal, a metabolism among humans, animals, nature, and objects that has nothing to do with the hierarchical and familial structures at the heart of capitalism, or even with the concept of a generalized "humanity" that, in line with Morgan's recourse to European Enlightenment tropes, supports it. Instead, binding together a communal social metabolism and a nonexploitative metabolism with nature, it points to the possibility of an Iroquois gens that is still to come, that has not yet been fully realized. The movement in his excerpts becomes a way of enacting not simply the mobility and transience of social formations but also the mobility and transience of language itself; in Marx's words, both are "*incapable of permanence*" (ibid.), and it is this impermanence that makes transformation possible.

This transformation is not only legible in the alterations Marx makes in Morgan's language or in his translations of sentences into German, but also in the insertion of passages from a vast constellation of texts that he sets in motion as part of his intervention in the texts he reads, including, among so many others, Aeschylus's *Eumenides*, *Seven Against Thebes*, and *Prometheus Bound*, Demosthenes's *Appeal Against Eubulides*, Homer's *Iliad*, Herodotus's *Histories*, Thucydides's *History of the Peloponnesian War*, Strabo's *Geography*, Aristotle's *Politics*, Plutarch's *Theseus* and *Solon*, Tacitus's *Germania*, Cicero's *Republic*, Edmund Spenser's *A View of the State of Ireland*, Cervantes's *Don Quixote*, Machiavelli's *Discourses*, Hobbes's *Leviathan*, and Alexis de Tocqueville's *The Ancién Regime and the Revolution*. That he places these passages in multiple languages alongside—and often inside—the excerpts he draws from Morgan, Lubbock, Maine, Phear, and others enables him to engage in an act of reading that is at the same time an act of gathering and assembling, that is entirely collaborative and that again confirms that we never read alone. As with the frontispiece from Marx and Engels's "Theses on Feuerbach" with which we began, the *Ethnological Notebooks* are another window into the process of Marx's production. Even if Engels is not taking notes alongside him, the fact that he writes his *Origin of the Family* based on Marx's notes on Morgan confirms their ongoing conversations, conversations Marx extends to all the comrades on his library shelves, a much larger common-wealth of texts than in his earlier life, since his archive has grown vastly in the intervening years. The texts he reads are transformed into a means of production that creates a mass of collaborators and, as in Engels's doodle, we witness *the slow emergence of a mass through the movement of his pen*. This time the mass is contextualized, even if only fugitively because of the intensification of its movement across Marx's pages, in a broader exploration of different communal forms. There is a deliberateness to his choice of texts—he calls forth texts that resonate or produce a tension with the language he puts them in relation to, even if these associations, drawn from the library in his head, cannot always be pinned down exactly and do not always emerge with a full consciousness on his part of their expansive mobility, which is to say that he is not always in full control of their effects within the *Notebooks*. This is why the common-wealth of texts he gathers here becomes a means of enacting a community at loose ends, a community whose expansiveness cannot be delimited since, as we have seen, reading itself is a work of amplification and multiplication. If texts have to be supplemented, however—if they have to be put in relation to other texts—it is because they are never sufficient by themselves. This insufficiency has its counterpart in all the communal forms Marx studies in his *Notebooks*, each of which succumbs to a process of ruin and disintegration unless it aligns itself with other communes. What Marx learns—or rather what he reinforces throughout his *Notebooks* and his late works in general—is that it is precisely because no commons can survive on its own that it has to be inscribed within a common-wealth. It must become part of an always fugitive, always transient, always moving international set of coalitions.[89] Marx's *Notebooks* show him thinking and writing like a mass. His last will and testament, they bequeath to us a fleeting vision of how a communist community might be assembled, one that refuses to be circumscribed by borders or identities of any kind and that, instead, moves in the direction of incalculable and unpredictable coalitions that have, as their aim and means, the destruction of all ends. As Marx and Engels put it in *The German Ideology*, "[c]ommunism for us is not a *state of affairs* which is to be established, an *ideal* to which reality [will] have to adjust itself," but rather "the *real* movement which abolishes the present state of things."[90]

★

Among the many things we inherit from Marx is his relentless effort to bring about an international movement that, without bounds, is nevertheless finite—always open to revision, alteration, and metamorphosis. This internationalism is at stake in Marx's 1881 correspondence with Zasulich, which can be coordinated with his *Ethnological Notebooks*, and which is also evident in the last journey of his life, including a trip he makes to Algeria in April 1882. Zasulich writes to Marx in February 1881. She tells him how critical the Russian edition of *Capital* has become for the cause of Russian socialism, and she asks him—she declares it a "life-and-death question" for the socialist party—if he believes the Russian peasant communes can become a revolutionary force or if they are destined to perish under an approaching capitalism. It is worth noting that, by the time he receives Zasulich's letter, Marx's work is already in danger of being instrumentalized and ideologically reified, and not only in Russia. Zasulich herself mentions explicitly how Russian "Marxists" resist any deviation from what they perceive as Marx's dogma. But Marx is anything but a dogmatic thinker, and his late work becomes increasingly more plural and less certain, organized as it is around the not yet determined possibilities and transformations of multitemporal non-Western alternatives to capitalism.

In the first draft of his reply to Zasulich, speaking of the crisis of capitalism in Western Europe, he writes, in a passage whose last sentence is a slightly revised quotation from Morgan, that today capitalism finds itself, "both in Western Europe and the United States, in conflict with the working masses ... and with the very productive forces which it generates—in short, in a crisis that will end through its own elimination, through the return of modern societies to a higher form of an 'archaic' type of collective ownership and production." In the final version of his reply to Zasulich, Marx adds that, given his study of the situation—he begins teaching himself Russian in 1869 in order to have access to the debates more directly—"the commune is the fulcrum for social regeneration in Russia."[91] If the commune is to have a revolutionary future, however, Marx argues that it must form a coalition with Western working-class movements. Marx and Engels reiterate this point in the 1882 preface to the second Russian edition of the *Communist Manifesto*, the very last text Marx publishes before his death. They write:

Can the Russian *obshchina* [peasant commune], a form, albeit heavily eroded, of the primeval communal ownership of the land, pass directly into the higher, communist form of communal ownership?

Or must it first go through the same process of dissolution that marks the West's historical development? Today there is only one possible answer: If the Russian revolution becomes the signal for a proletarian revolution in the West, so that the two complement each other, then Russia's peasant communal landownership may serve as the point of departure for a communist development.[92]

Here Marx and Engels reinforce the lesson of the *Ethnological Notebooks*: no commune can endure on its own; if it remains isolated, it inevitably experiences a process of dissolution and disintegration. Again, in the first draft of his letter to Zasulich, Marx insists that "[o]nly a general uprising can break the isolation of the 'rural commune,' the lack of connection between the lives of different communes."[93] For any commune to persist, it must form alliances with revolutionary movements elsewhere; in Russia's instance, in order to reap the benefits of Western modernity rather than be destroyed by it. There can be no revolution, in other words, without a red common-wealth, without coalitions that do not respect national borders and that, in their massification across different geographies of time and space, create all the possibilities that Marx envisions in the amalgamation of resources he puts together in his *Notebooks*. If Marx is another name for an ever-widening and ever-new series of encounters, we might recall Althusser's claim that "the materialism of the encounter is ... contained in its entirety in the negation of the End, of all teleology ... that the materialism of the encounter is the materialism, not of a subject ... but of a process, a process that has no subject, [and] no assignable end."[94] In the common-wealth, there is no subject—there is only a multilayered process of encounters, coalitions, alliances, with unforeseeable shapes and outcomes, and even these are always moving in relation to the openness that comes with a relation to the future, that comes, that is, with a relation to others.

Marx again insists on the necessity of this openness when, on his way to North Africa, he crosses the borders of Europe for the first time in April 1882. His two-month sojourn in Algiers is mediated by several texts but particularly by his reading of Kovalevsky's writings on Algeria; in his *Notebooks*, Marx associates the violent repression of the 1871 Paris Commune with the 1873 seizure of communal land in Algeria by the same French colonial state. As in his letter to Zasulich, Marx's letters from Algeria to Engels, Lafargue, and his daughter Laura emphasize that, although Muslim Algerians are "neither subjects nor administrative objects," although they experience "*[a]bsolute equality in their social intercourse*"—things he admires about their rural communes and which he experiences as a measure of hope—"they will go to hell without a revolutionary movement." He imagines the "magical panorama" of the "wonderful combination of Europe and Africa."[95] This wonder is consonant with the wonder he experiences when, as in his *Ethnological Notebooks*, he envisions the many possibilities for organizing society differently. Marx encourages us again to understand that communism depends on our capacity to keep a relation to the wonder and surprise of a world that—even in the face of atrocities, violence, and injustice—can still inspire hope in the face of hopelessness. All the writers and thinkers we read in this book exist in relation to this sense of wonder, which is a reservoir of strength for them, but also an experience that preserves their relation to a future, to Marx's "poetry of the future."[96]

Marx's communist common-wealth—his belief in the possibility of international coalitions and assemblages of anticapitalist forces whose "*real* movement" would abolish "the present state of things"—finds its echo and expansion in each of the readers and writers we have gathered together in our book. Their works add to the common-wealth of resources that Marx spent his life amassing and that he bequeathed to us as just one starting point. He knows no one can do this work alone; it requires a mass. Like Marx, Luxemburg, Benjamin, Du Bois, and all the other writers who are in turn evoked in each of their texts and under each of their names, this common-wealth belongs to the motility of an endless process without a subject that will not be silent in front of capitalist violence or shy away from its own violence, that is impossible to transform into dogma or to synthesize into a system, that will demand a reading that exceeds the text in order to make each text a site of encounters and possibility, that risks being political because it knows politics is the only means we have for not only encountering what is incalculable but also for maximizing it. It is a politics that can never have a determinate or fixed form and that, because of the danger of an almost inevitable complicity with what it believes goes in the direction of the worst, must remain in movement. The task is how *to set the masses in motion*, and, as we have seen, this task is folded into an activity of reading and writing that, accumulating its force through the common-wealth it mobilizes, reminds us that, whenever we think and struggle for change, we are never alone.[97]

In an essay that takes Lenin's title "What Is to Be Done?" as its own, Jean-Luc Nancy writes that, more than ever, "it is necessary at one and the same time to affirm and denounce the world as it is," to make the world into the place of its own contradictions, but always in motion. These contradictions are "what [prevent] us from ever knowing in advance what is to be done," and require an inventiveness, creativity, and experimentation that are "always without model and without guarantee." But "where certainties come apart," he adds, "there too gathers the strength that no certainty can match."[98] This inventive gathering of anticapitalist resources is enriched by each act of reading and writing that calls us *to a movement*, and *to movement "itself."* As the readers and writers we have assembled note time and again, this movement must be invented; it must be composed in a collaborative, collective, and endless process out of the fragments, ruins, and shards that capitalism leaves behind and discards. The answer to the question "what is to be done?" is to invent a world in which nothing is ever done or finished. Our greatest resource in this work of invention, in this struggle, is the red common-wealth, a common-wealth that—ours and not ours at the same time—may have as one of its names, as one of its passwords, the shibboleth *Anaquivitzli*.

red, *n.* [ME. *red, redde*; AS. *read*; akin to G. *rot*, ON. *rauthr*: from same root come also L. *rutilus, rufus, ruber,* Gr. *erythros,* W. *rhwdd,* Ir. and Gael. *ruadh,* also Sans. *rudhira,* blood.]
1. a primary color, or any of a spread of colors at the lower end of the visible spectrum, varying in hue from that of blood to pale rose or pink.
2. a pigment producing this color.
3. [*often* R–] [senses *a* and *b* from the red flag symbolizing revolutionary socialism.] (a) a political radical or revolutionary; especially, a communist; (b) a citizen of the Soviet Union; (c) [*pl.*] North American Indians.

Joseph Kosuth, *"Titled (Art as Idea as Idea),"* 1967

In his prison notebooks, Antonio Gramsci writes that the "starting point of critical elaboration" is a recognition of ourselves as an ensemble of social relations, as "a product of the historical processes to date that [have] deposited in us an infinity of traces, without leaving an inventory." He tells us that all critical work—every act of reading, writing, and thinking—is collaborative; it begins in a context that is as wide as it is unpredictable, and in relation to others. Because of this, he adds, "it is imperative at the outset to compile [this] inventory." Acknowledgments are a modest means of beginning such an inventory—of gathering together everyone who has contributed to our critical labor through conversation, friendship, and a shared commitment to the joy and excitement of study. Because this book was written in the midst of a great communal despair, the conversations it enabled feel more precious and urgent than ever, as we struggle to organize our pessimism into a force of activism. Throughout, we have reaped the benefits and delights that attend what Fred Moten has called "a practice of cultivating sharing."

We owe a very felt debt to everyone who has discussed this book with us—sometimes just a detail in it and sometimes all of it—and we wish to express our warmest and most loving thanks to the very rich commonwealth to which we are so very fortunate to belong. Everyone in it has left their traces in the book and in our lives. We particularly want to thank Branka Arsić, Ben Baer, Ian Balfour, Aristides Baltas, Joslyn Barnes, Yve-Alain Bois, Bruno Bosteels, Marc Caplan, Terrell Carver, Manuel Cirauqui, Tom Cohen, Andrew Cole, Rebecca Comay, Jorge Coronado, Brent Edwards, Peter Fenves, David Ferris, John Fleming, Eva Franch, Daniela Gandorfer, Anthie Georgiadi, Anthony Graves, Anjuli Gunaratne, Paul Haacke, Carla Herrera-Prats, Michael W. Jennings, Mina Karavanta, Patrick Killoran, Josh Kotin, Makis Kouzelis, Agnieszka Kurant, Jo Labanyi, Russ Leo, Bettina Lerner, Aaron Levy, David Lloyd, Andreas Maratos, Elissa Marder, Yates McKee, Susan Meiselas, Paola Mieli, Alberto Moreiras, Rosalind Morris, Fred Moten, Paul Ramirez Jonas, Gerhard Richter, Douglas Ross, Sylvia Sachini, Lidia Santarelli, Simona Sawhney, Fazal Sheikh, Lisa Sigal, Gayatri Chakravorty Spivak, Liana Theodoratou, Mónica de la Torre, Sumeja Tulić, Alexander G. Weheliye, Patricia J. Williams, Autumn Womack, Sara Workneh, and Slavoj Žižek. We also would like to thank the graduate students with whom we tested out parts of the book in the fall of 2022: Christian Bischoff, Holly Bushman, Marie de Testa, Paola Del Toro, Florian Endres, Heejoo Kim, Fay Y. Lin, Céleste Pagniello, Cassandra O. Rota, Sofia Tong, and Piper Winkler. We know that a list, the simplest of inventories, cannot convey the different intimacies that structure the singularity of each of our relations, but we trust that elsewhere we have been able to express our unique relations to everyone we mention here.

We thank Donkeyboy, Elliott Guidry, Glenn Ligon, Kerry James Marshall, R. H. Quaytman, and Cassio Vasconcellos for so kindly granting us permission to reproduce their images and, indeed, for providing them to us. We also thank the Addison Gallery of American Art, Age Fotostock, Akademie der Künste, Berlin, Alamy Stock Photo, Josef and Anni Albers Foundation, Bibliothèque Nationale de France, Condé Nast, Association Marcel Duchamp / ADAGP, Paris, Fine Art Images / Heritage-Images, Hauser & Wirth, New York, IMEC (Institut Mémoires de l'Édition Contemporaine), International Institute of Social History (Amsterdam), Kunstbibliothek, Library of Congress, Miguel Abreu Gallery, New York, Museum of Modern Art, New York, National Maritime Museum, Greenwich, London, Nelson-Atkins Museum of Art, Kansas City, New-York Historical Society, Photo Tate, Staatliche Museen zu Berlin, Sueddeutsche Zeitung Photo, Ullstein Bild / The Granger Collection Ltd, Special Collections and University Archives, University of Massachusetts Amherst Libraries, The Andy Warhol Foundation for the Visual Arts, Inc., Whitney Museum of American Art, and the Jack Whitten Estate for the images they provided and for the permission they granted us to reproduce them.

It has been a great pleasure to work with Tom Weaver at the MIT Press. It is not possible for us to imagine a more supportive, thoughtful, and enthusiastic editor, and we are grateful for his enduring confidence in this book from its earliest beginnings. We thank Duncan Whyte for his wonderfully creative design, his attentiveness, openness, inventiveness, and collaborative spirit. We also thank Matthew Abbate for all his kind and meticulous attention to the manuscript in all its details, Gabriela Bueno Gibbs for her assistance in helping the book move through its process of production, and Andrew Ascherl for the generous inventiveness of his index.

The beauty of this collaboration is that it has confirmed in rather extraordinary ways that we never read, write, think, let alone publish, alone—even when we find ourselves in forced isolation or simply imagine ourselves alone.

INTRODUCTION: "THE RED WHAT READING DID ..."

1. Marx and Engels's first collaboration was also a critique of the Young Hegelians and resulted in the 1844 *The Holy Family*, itself a sarcastic reference to Bruno Bauer and his supporters. See Karl Marx and Frederick Engels, *The Holy Family, or, Critique of Critical Criticism: Against Bruno Bauer and Company*, trans. Richard Dixon and Clement Dutts, in Marx and Engels, *Collected Works*, vol. 4 (New York: International Publishers, 1975). The fragments and sketches that have been assembled in *The German Ideology* are themselves a response to Bauer's rebuttal of their earlier book, and therefore a continuation of their earlier collaboration.

2. In one of Engels's letters to Marx's daughter, Laura Lafargue, shortly after Marx's death, Engels writes that "[a]mong Mohr's [Marx's] papers I have found a whole lot of manuscripts, our common work, of before 1848." He recalls reading some of the manuscripts to Marx's housekeeper Helene Demuth. Demuth is said to have remarked, "[n]ow I know why you two were laughing so hard at night back then in Brussels so that no one in the house could sleep." See Friedrich Engels, "Engels to Laura Lafargue," June 2, 1883, in Marx and Engels, *Collected Works*, vol. 47 (London: Lawrence & Wishart, 1997), 31.

   We might recall here Walter Benjamin's claim, in a discussion of Brecht's epic theater in his essay "The Author as Producer," that "there is no better trigger for thinking than laughter." "In particular," he adds, "convulsion of the diaphragm usually provides better opportunities for thought than convulsion of the soul. Epic Theater is lavish only in occasions for laughter." See Benjamin, "The Author as Producer," trans. Edmund Jephcott, in Benjamin, *Selected Writings*, vol. 2: *1927–1934*, ed. Michael W. Jennings, Howard Eiland, and Gary Smith (Cambridge, MA: Belknap Press of Harvard University Press, 1999), 779.

3. Walter Benjamin, *Gesammelte Schriften*, 7 vols., ed. Rolf Tiedemann and Hermann Schweppenhäuser (Frankfurt am Main: Suhrkamp Verlag, 1972–1989), 3:351. All references to Benjamin's collected writings in German are to this edition and will be noted parenthetically by *GS* with volume and page number.

4. Benjamin, "The Author as Producer," 777.

5. Cited in ibid., 770

6. Ibid.

7. For the most detailed and scrupulous account of the history of these fragments—and their assemblage into a "book" called *The German Ideology*—see Terrell Carver and Daniel Blank, *A Political History of the Editions of Marx and Engels's "German Ideology Manuscripts"* (New York: Palgrave Macmillan, 2014). We owe Carver and Blank a felt debt for the work they have done here.

8. Benjamin, "The Author as Producer," 773. Benjamin already had evoked Brecht's line in a 1932 review of Kurt Hiller's *Der Sprung ins Helle* (The leap into light). See "Der Irrtum des Aktivismus: Zu Kurt Hillers Essaybuch 'Der Sprung ins Helle'" (*GS*, 3:351).

9. Karl Marx, "Letters from the *Franco-German Yearbooks*," trans. Rodney Livingstone and Gregor Benton, in *Karl Marx: Early Writings* (New York: Penguin Books, 1975), 201.

10. Karl Marx and Friedrich Engels, *The German Ideology*, trans. W. Lough, in Marx and Engels, *Collected Works*, vol. 5 (New York: International Publishers, 1976), 38. For the German version of this passage, see Karl Marx and Friedrich Engels, *Deutsche Ideologie: Zur Kritik der Philosophie, Manuskripte in chronologischer Anordnung*, ed. Gerald Hubmann and Ulrich Pagel (Berlin: Walter de Gruyter, 2018), 3.

11. Louis Althusser, "From *Capital* to Marx's Philosophy," in *Reading Capital: The Complete Edition*, trans. Ben Brewster and David Fernbach (London: Verso, 2015), 38–40.

12. Ibid., 41–42.

13. The phrase is Althusser's. See ibid., 32.

14. Marx and Engels, *The German Ideology*, 38.

15. Marx and Engels, *The Holy Family*, 123.

16. Althusser, "From *Capital* to Marx's Philosophy," 12.

17. Karl Marx, "Preface to the French Edition," March 18, 1872, in *Capital: A Critique of Political Economy*, vol. 1, trans. Ben Fowkes (New York: Penguin Books, 1990), 104.

18. Althusser, "From *Capital* to Marx's Philosophy," 42.

19. The name "Marx" has often been used to enact a political engagement with literature. Think for instance of Trotsky's *Literature and Revolution*, Lenin's writings on Tolstoy, Adorno's literary essays, Bakhtin's reflections on Dostoevsky, Benjamin's writings on Baudelaire, Lukács's readings of realism and naturalism, Sartre's essays on Flaubert, and Jameson's texts on Balzac or Conrad. At the same time, in strict terms, literature as such does not exist in Marx. Inscribed within an unevenly determined system of sociopolitical and cultural practices, it

belongs to social relations of production that are historically determined and transformed, and historically linked to other ideological forms. This is to say that the materialist analysis of literature must renounce the notion of the literary work—the illusory presentation of the unity of a text, its totality, self-sufficiency, and perfection—even if it deploys what is most literary in such work.

20. We are indebted in this idea of "comrades on the shelf" to Shellyne Rodriguez. In a Zoom discussion hosted by the Strike MoMA collective on April 13, 2022—a conversation between her and Kazambe Balagun, moderated by Amin Husain and Marz Saffore and held in collaboration with the Slought Foundation in Philadelphia—she talks about the necessity of putting writings from the past to work in the present. See https://www.youtube.com/watch?v=koDGgVZCHtc (Rodriguez evokes the phrase at the 17:39 mark in the video).

21. Marx, *The German Ideology*, 94.

22. Robert Kaufman, "Red Kant, or the Persistence of the Third 'Critique' in Adorno and Jameson," *Critical Inquiry* 26, no. 4 (Summer 2000), 697.

23. Marx, *The German Ideology*, 160.

24. Ibid., 274.

25. That the novel retains its political valence even today is confirmed by Subcomandante Marcos in an interview he gave Gabriel García Márquez in 2001. Reinforcing Marx's own canon of political literature, he notes that "*Don Quixote* is the best book out there on political theory, followed by *Hamlet*, and *Macbeth*. There is no better way to understand the tragedy and the comedy of the Mexican political system than *Hamlet*, *Macbeth*, and *Don Quixote*." See Subcomandante Marcos, "The Punch Card and the Hourglass: Interview by García Márquez and Roberto Pombo," *New Left Review* 9 (May-June 2001), http://www.newleftreview.org/A2322.

26. Interestingly for us, "The Leipzig Council" was not published until 1921 in the journal *Archiv für Sozialwissenschaft und Sozialpolitik*, in the same issue that included the first publication of Benjamin's "Toward the Critique of Violence." We will point to the disruptive circulation of a hidden figure for the masses in Benjamin's essay when we turn to it in the four sections we later devote to it.

27. Saidiya Hartman, *Wayward Lives, Beautiful Experiments: Intimate Histories of Riotous Black Girls, Troublesome Women, and Queer Radicals* (New York: Norton, 2019), 227 and 228.

28. In his introduction to the 2020 edition of Cedric Robinson's *Black Marxism*, Robin D. G. Kelley contextualizes the Black Lives Matter movement and, in doing so, pluralizes it—presenting it as a living archive of innumerable collective efforts to abolish racial capitalism. Putting it in relation to the 1960s—and even to the 1860s—and the Black struggle for equal rights, demonstrating that the present movement is part of a much larger constellation, he forces us to reckon with the prolonged multigenerational labor that activism requires and, in particular, with the role of reading and writing in this activism. The passage is worth quoting at length:

As I write these words during the summer of 2020, we are witnessing the Black Radical Tradition in motion, driving what is arguably the most dynamic mass rebellion against state-sanctioned violence and racial capitalism we have ever seen in North America since the 1960s—maybe the 1860s. Sparked by the killing of George Perry Floyd Jr., Breonna Taylor, Ahmaud Arbery, and many others, approximately 26 million people have taken to the streets to protest state-sanctioned racial violence, some demanding that we abolish police and prisons and shift those resources to housing, universal healthcare, living-wage jobs, universal basic income, green energy, and a system of restorative justice. The new abolitionists are not interested in making capitalism fairer, safer, and less racist. They know this is impossible. Rather, they want nothing less than to bring an end to "racial capitalism." The state's reaction to rebellion has also brought us to the precipice of fascism. The organized protests in the streets and other places of public assembly, on campuses, inside prisons, in state houses and courtrooms and police stations, portended the rise of a police state in the United States. For the past several years, the Movement for Black Lives and its dozens of allied organizations warned the country that unless we end racist state-sanctioned violence and the mass caging of Black and Brown people, we are headed for a fascist state. They issued these warnings before Trump's election, but standing here in 2020, as armed white militias gun down protesters, as the current regime threatens to hold on to power regardless of the outcome of the presidential election, as the federal government deploys armed force to suppress dissent, rounds up and deports undocumented workers, and intimidates the public, it is easy to conclude that fascism is already here. The crossroads where Black revolt and fascism meet is precisely the space where Cedric's main interlocutors find the Black Radical Tradition. ... Nearly three decades of movement-building, scholarship, and political education explain why so many people can even say the words "defund the police," "prison abolition," or "racial capitalism." We would not be here if not for Critical Resistance, the Labor/Community Strategy Center, Project South, Organization for Black Struggle (St. Louis), POWER (People Organized to Win Employment Rights), Southerners on New Ground (SONG); INCITE: Women of Color Against Violence, Sista II Sista, the African American Policy Forum, the Black Radical Congress, the Los Angeles

Community Action Network, Miami Workers Center, the Praxis Project, FIERCE (Fabulous Independent Educated Radicals for Community Empowerment), Queers for Economic Justice, the Sylvia Rivera Law Project (SRLP), Reverend William J. Barber's Moral Mondays Movement and new Poor People's Campaign, Cooperation Jackson in Mississippi, the Incarcerated Workers Organizing Committee, the Free Alabama Movement, and Showing Up for Racial Justice (SURJ). We would not be here without Angela Davis's *Are Prisons Obsolete?* and *Abolition Democracy*, or Michelle Alexander's *The New Jim Crow*, or the abolitionist and anti-capitalist writings of Ruth Wilson Gilmore and Mariame Kaba, and others. The murders of Trayvon Martin, Rekia Boyd, Eric Garner, Michael Brown, Tamir Rice, John Crawford III, Alton Sterling, Walter Scott, and so many others spawned a wave of Black radical organizations, notably Black Lives Matter, the Dream Defenders, Black Youth Project 100, We Charge Genocide, BOLD (Black Organizing for Leadership and Dignity), Hands Up United, Lost Voices, Millennial Activists United, Million Hoodies Movement for Justice, Dignity and Power Now, Ella's Daughters, Assata's Daughters, Black Feminist Futures Project, Leaders of a Beautiful Struggle, Let Us Breathe Collective, the Movement for Black Lives, The Majority, and Scholars for Social Justice, among many others. All of these movements and thinkers have, at one time or another, engaged, embraced, or were influenced by Cedric Robinson's *Black Marxism*. Two key concepts, racial capitalism and the Black Radical Tradition, introduced in these pages almost forty years ago, have become a common part of our shared political language. ... Even more consequential is the extent to which Cedric's ideas have influenced the struggle on the ground. The Movement for Black Lives, a coalition made up of more than 150 organizations, built much of its social justice agenda around a critique of racial capitalism.

The remarkable thing about the passage in our context is that Kelley makes clear that all these movements have a relation to books, not simply Robinson's book but also to books by Angela Davis, Michelle Alexander, Ruthie Wilson Gilmore, Mariame Kaba, and others. In other words, they could not be what they are without a relation to a labor of reading and, in each instance, of books that are themselves the result of a labor of reading and writing—one that takes its point of departure from Marx, regardless of whether or not it is in full agreement with him on every point. What is also important to register here is the boomerang effect of this activism—the violent backlash against it, which can always only confirm its force. See Robin D. G. Kelley,

"Foreword: Why Black Marxism? Why Now?," in Cedric J. Robinson, *Black Marxism: The Making of the Black Radical Tradition*, 3rd ed. (Chapel Hill: University of North Carolina Press, 2020), xi–xiii.

29. Althusser theorizes a similar reading loop in his introduction to the 1965 *Reading Capital*, and he does so in relation to the now famous collaborative project of reading Marx that he led and that, besides him, included Étienne Balibar, Jacques Rancière, Roger Establet, and Pierre Macherey. Our introduction is indebted to this collective reading and to a number of its insights: the need to attend to what is not visible on the page, to the symptoms of a text, to the "play on words" in *Capital* that is inseparable from its political work, its militant refusal of abstraction, its emphasis on the collaborative character of reading in general and, above all, the claim that we are all readers of Marx, even if we have never read a single page of his work. In Althusser's words:

> Since we "came into the world," we have read *Capital* constantly in the writings and speeches of those who have read it for us, well or ill, both the dead and the living, Engels, Kautsky, Plekhanov, Lenin, Rosa Luxemburg, Trotsky, Stalin, Gramsci, the leaders of the workers' organizations, their supporters and opponents: philosophers, economists, politicians.

Reinforcing our insistence that all reading is mediated, Althusser suggests that, despite all the readers who have come before him and to whom he remains indebted, it is still "essential to read *Capital* to the letter." We have tried to follow this advice throughout our book. See Althusser, "From *Capital* to Marx's Philosophy," 12.

30. Ibid., 24.

31. Raya Dunayevskaya, "An Overview by Way of Introduction; the Black Dimension," in *Rosa Luxemburg, Women's Liberation, and Marx's Philosophy of Revolution* (Highlands, NJ: Humanities Press, 1982), 79–87.

32. Amiri Baraka, "The 'Blues Aesthetic' and the 'Black Aesthetic': Aesthetics as the Continuing Political History of a Culture," *Black Music Research Journal* 11, no. 2 (Autumn 1991), 107.

I. POLITICALLY READ

1. Bertolt Brecht, *The Mother*, trans. Lee Baxandall (New York: Grove Press, 1965), 80.

2. Louis Althusser, "From *Capital* to Marx's Philosophy," in *Reading Capital: The Complete Edition*, trans. Ben Brewster and David Fernbach (London: Verso, 2015), 14.

3. See Fredric Jameson, *The Benjamin Files* (New York: Verso Books, 2020). Further references to this book will be noted parenthetically by *BF* and page number.

4. Fredric Jameson, *Marxism and Form: Twentieth-Century Dialectical Theories of Literature* (Princeton, NJ: Princeton University Press, 1971), xii.

5. Walter Benjamin, "On the Image of Proust," trans. Harry Zohn, in Benjamin, *Selected Writings*, vol. 2: *1927–1934*, ed. Michael W. Jennings, Howard Eiland, and Gary Smith (Cambridge, MA: Belknap Press of Harvard University Press, 1999), 244.

6. "In Praise of the Red Guards," *Peking Review* 9, no. 39 (September 23, 1966), 15–16.

7. See Walter Benjamin, *One-Way Street*, trans. Edmund Jephcott, in Benjamin, *Selected Writings*, vol. 1: *1913–1926*, ed. Michael W. Jennings, Howard Eiland, and Gary Smith (Cambridge, MA: Belknap Press of Harvard University Press, 1996), 447–448. Further references to this text will be noted parenthetically by *OWS* and page number.

8. Walter Benjamin, *Berlin Childhood around 1900* (1934 Version), trans. Howard Eiland, in Benjamin, *Selected Writings*, vol. 3: *1935–1938*, ed. Howard Eiland and Michael W. Jennings (Cambridge, MA: Belknap Press of Harvard University Press, 2002), 393.

9. In the artwork essay, Benjamin writes: "Distraction and concentration [*Zerstreuung und Sammlung*] form an antithesis, which may be formulated as follows. A person who concentrates before a work of art is absorbed by it; he enters into the work, just as, according to legend, a Chinese painter entered his completed painting while beholding it. By contrast, the distracted masses absorb the work of art into themselves." See "The Work of Art in the Age of Its Technological Reproducibility (Third Version)," trans. Harry Zohn and Edmund Jephcott, in Benjamin, *Selected Writings*, vol. 4: *1938–1940*, ed. Howard Eiland and Michael W. Jennings (Cambridge, MA: Belknap Press of Harvard University Press, 2003), 268. Further references to this text will be noted parenthetically by *WA* and page number.

10. As Benjamin puts it, in relation to the experience of disorientation he undergoes when hearing stories about the mummerehlen swirling around him:

> Whatever stories used to be told about it—or whatever someone may have only wished to tell me—I do not know. Mute, porous, flaky, it formed a cloud at the core of things, like the snow flurry in a glass paperweight. From time to time, I was whirled around in it. This would happen as I sat painting with watercolors. The colors I mixed would color me. Even before I applied them to the drawing, I found myself disguised by them. When wet, they flowed together on the palette; I would take them warily onto my brush, as though they were clouds about to dissipate.

See *Berlin Childhood around 1900*, 392–393.

11. As Christopher Bush has argued, porcelain itself is "a medium of telecommunication in the direct sense that it was a principal means by which images and—in some form or other, however falsified—cultural knowledge circulated around the globe." Identifying the mimetic impulse attributed to the Chinese by Benjamin and others, including Marx, Kafka, Eisenstein, and Brecht, he goes on to note:

> Although we might not ordinarily think of porcelain as a medium, we need only recall the extent to which it, perhaps only after paper, functioned as an image-bearing surface that literally circulated around the globe. … Like any other medium, porcelain is both itself something and a means of representing or signaling something other than itself … it both conveys a "content" and shapes that content (like a vessel, if you will). … For Mallarmé, and many after him, to imitate the Chinese meant not to represent but to mimic them, to imitate the way they imitate, to imitate those whose primary characteristic it is to imitate so well.

See Bush, *Ideographic Modernism: China, Writing, Media* (New York: Oxford University Press, 2010), 112–114. Registering the Orientalizing gesture of the West's figuration of China, Bush nevertheless emphasizes the way in which China functions as a nexus of multiple discourses, all of which become not only a means of experiencing a lesson about the distancing effect of technology in general but also a way of exploring the mediatic character of any culture, even if here Bush is interested in the constant recourse in the works of these modern writers and thinkers to a China that is historical, particular, and yet also a figure of the imagination. As a signifier of what is foreign and distant—as a figure that belongs to the Brechtian effort to introduce a kind of estrangement into European cultural politics, and more particularly, into the potentially nationalistic historical context of his German audiences, something Brecht and Benjamin read in the techniques of defamiliarization and estrangement within Chinese works in general—China embodies what Benjamin would call the "Mimetic Faculty." This faculty involves a form of creative mimesis—a force of transformation rather than simply a mode of natural representation—that Brecht calls "inventive miming" and that helps account for a form of imitative copying that, associated with Chinese artistic production, nevertheless produces singular works. See *Brecht on Theater: The Development of an Aesthetic*, ed. and trans. John Willett (New York: Hill and Wang, 1964), 204.

12. Walter Benjamin, "Chinese Paintings in the Bibliothèque Nationale," trans. Timothy J. Artanucci, in *The Work of Art in the Age of Its Technological Reproducibility, and Other Writings on Media*, ed. Michael W. Jennings, Brigid Doherty, and Thomas Y. Levin (Cambridge, MA: Belknap Press of Harvard University Press, 2008), 259–260.

13. Walter Benjamin, *The Arcades Project*, trans. Howard Eiland and Kevin McLaughlin (Cambridge, MA: Belknap Press of Harvard University Press, 1999), 463. Further references to this text will be noted parenthetically by *AP* and page number.

14. Jameson points to the impersonality of Benjamin himself in a 1995 review of the then recently published volumes of Benjamin's correspondence:

> The impersonality I have attributed to Benjamin—it might better be called by Eliot's term, "depersonalization"—also plays its part in the glorious effects of style which achieve their most intense concentration in the great essays but which we can surprise here and there in these letters: "True criticism does not attack its object: it is like a chemical substance that attacks another only in the sense that, decomposing it, it exposes its inner nature, but does not destroy it. The chemical substance that attacks *spiritual* things in this way (dialectically) is the light. This does not appear in language." The digression is self-referential to the degree to which it includes a theory of its own necessary impersonality ... the two final sentences then prod this formulation upwards into associative leaps that can be grasped either as the intensity of the thinking process or as a dialectical multi-layering (from which, incidentally, alchemy and allegory, the baroque and mystical language theory, are never far away).

Fredric Jameson, "An Unfinished Project," *London Review of Books* 17, no. 15 (August 3, 1995).

15. In his 1981 *The Political Unconscious*, Jameson famously announced that the "political perspective" is the "absolute horizon of all reading and all interpretation." See Jameson, *The Political Unconscious: Narrative as a Socially Symbolic Act* (Ithaca: Cornell University Press, 1981), 17.

16. Fredric Jameson, "Marxism and Historicism," *New Literary History* 11, no. 1 (Autumn 1979), 70.

17. Walter Benjamin, "The Author as Producer," trans. Edmund Jephcott, in Benjamin, *Selected Writings*, 2:769.

18. See chapter three, "Literary Communism," trans. Peter Connor, in Jean-Luc Nancy, *The Inoperative Community*, ed. Peter Connor (Minneapolis: University of Minnesota, 1991), 71–81. In this book, Nancy's phrase "literary communism" refers to communal operations of reading and writing that refuse any kind of mythic closure. It works only by "unworking" each of its terms, that is, by interrupting and suspending what we usually mean by "literature" and "communism." As he puts it, "it is because there is community—unworked always, and resisting at the heart of every collectivity and in the heart of every individual—and because myth is interrupted—suspended always, and divided by its own enunciation—that there exists the exigency of 'literary communism.'" He further socializes the meaning and function of literature by understanding it as a singular inscription that can only come into being through acts of transmission and sharing. Literature becomes communicable, and therefore "common," by bypassing the limits of its singularity; it "advenes only inasmuch as it can be shared." Literature's communal exigencies are what link it to Marx's own sense of communism's relation to revolutionary freedom. Quoting Marx's *Capital*, Nancy writes: "It is not an exaggeration to say that Marx's community is, in this sense, a community of literature—or at least it opens onto such a community. It is a community of articulation, and not of organization, and precisely because of this it is a community situated 'beyond the sphere of material production properly speaking,' where 'begins the flowering of that human power that is its own end, the true reign of liberty.'" "The only exaggeration," he adds, "all things considered, in reference to such a formation, would be the confidence apparently placed in the epithet 'human,' for the unworked community, the community of articulation cannot be simply human. This is so for an extremely simple but decisive reason: in the true movement of community, in the inflection (in the conjugation, in the diction) that articulates it, what is at stake is never humanity, but always *the end of humanity*" (*The Inoperative Community*, 80, 78, and 77). His challenge of the concept of the human—his inscription of the human into a community that remains incommensurable—resonates with our elaboration of Benjamin's interest in impersonality.

II. MULTIPLICITY

1. Walter Benjamin cites this Latin saying in *One-Way Street*. "*Ad plures ire* was the Latins' expression for dying," he writes (*OWS*, 484). The saying refers to the Roman convicton that the dead outnumber the living. For the Gramsci quote, see Antonio Gramsci, *Selections from the Prison Notebooks of Antonio Gramsci*, trans. Quintin Hoare and Geoffrey Nowell Smith (New York: International Publishers, 1971), 349 (translation modified).

2. The full citation reads: "What matters for the dialectician is to have the wind of world history in his sails. Thinking means for him: setting the sails. What is important is *how* they are set. Words are his sails. The way they are set makes them into concepts."

3. Jameson's claim that Benjamin never wrote a traditional book insists on the paratactic character of his writing—on the nonlinear, nonthetic, and often montage-like presentation of his materials. Even his *Origin of the German Trauerspiel*—which was published as a book and even includes a "preface"—can be viewed as an experimental exercise organized around a meditation on fragments, ruins, and different

processes of indirection. Nevertheless, as Peter Fenves notes, in a missive from May 22, 2023, there is a more "materialist" explanation for why Benjamin did not succeed in writing books. As he puts it, Benjamin "wanted to write a number of books, made proposals to publishers (Insel, Schocken), and was repeatedly told 'no,' not least because he did not have an academic perch from which to sell them. He had to make a 'living,' and the only way he could do so was by writing (selling) essays and reviews." Without countering Fenves—we agree with him on this point—we also wish to note that the essays and reviews also include a way of understanding why the book as a form can never be closed and, in this sense, Benjamin's conception of a book itself explodes the concept of a book altogether. The *Trauerspiel* book itself—and its critical strength lies in this fact—can be understood as a "book" against the idea of a book, against the idea of a thesis.

4. Walter Benjamin, "Karl Kraus," trans. Edmund Jephcott, in Benjamin, *Selected Writings*, vol. 2: *1927–1934*, ed. Michael W. Jennings, Howard Eiland, and Gary Smith (Cambridge, MA: Belknap Press of Harvard University Press, 1999), 453 (translation modified).

5. As we know, Marx conceptualized the repetition structured within history in generic terms, not the least of which were tragedy, farce, comedy, and historical novels, but also with an eye toward the moments when these forms could be interrupted.

6. Baltasar Gracián, *Agudeza y arte de ingenio* (Madrid: Castalia, 2001), 55.

7. Jameson reminds us that Benjamin gifted a copy of Gracián to Bertolt Brecht and, with this detail, underscores not only the philological origin of the playwright's *gestus*—an embodied emblem of sorts rather than an action—but also the act of transmitting a text from one context to another, from one person or one social form to another. This act of transmission belongs to Benjamin's commitment to the circulation and recirculation of texts—a gesture he understands as political. In Jameson's words, this passing of the book from one to the other "alerts us to the attention in both to this rarely formulated level of intercourse, which eludes the visibility of history and yet remains undetected on the level of individual subjectivity" (*BF*, 11).

The centrality of Gracián as a rhetorical and conceptual guide for Benjamin is hard to overstate, in particular as it regards his *Agudeza o arte de ingenio* (the first version of which was titled *Arte de ingenio, Tratado de la Agudeza*)—an archive of quotations from past and present literature and a seemingly endless classification of the rhetorical production of concepts that, to this day, belongs to no recognizable genre (very much in the manner of Benjamin's *Arcades Project*). In his compendium, Gracián glosses the virtues of multiplication and transformation, allusion and referentiality, the logics of analogy and contradiction, the productive pressures of the contingent, and, above all, the necessity of artifice in the divergent paths toward the inscription of truth.

8. Benjamin, "Karl Kraus," 455.

9. See Walter Benjamin, "Goethe's *Elective Affinities*," trans. Stanley Corngold, in Benjamin, *Selected Writings*, vol. 1: *1913–1926*, ed. Michael W. Jennings, Howard Eiland, and Gary Smith (Cambridge, MA: Belknap Press of Harvard University Press, 1996), 297–360. The epigraph that Benjamin uses for the first section of this essay—a line from Friedrich Gottlieb Klopstock—is directly linked to our discussion here. The line reads: "Whoever chooses blindly is struck in the eyes / By the smoke of sacrifice" (297). The annihilation of the self that Benjamin figures in the subject's impersonality accounts for why choice is never simply the result of an individual's agency, and this because this so-called agency is a structure (what Paul de Man called an "intentional structure": see "Intentional Structure of the Romantic Image," in *The Rhetoric of Romanticism* [New York: Columbia University Press, 1984], 1–18) that consists of an entire network of historical relations and affiliations, deeply intertwined and, because of this, unable to be instrumentalized or programmed in a single direction.

10. Although it is this, too, since, as Jameson notes, even "[p]erception itself is modified by its massification" (*BF*, 200), by its pluralization.

III. MASSIFICATION

1. Walter Benjamin, "The Work of Art in the Age of Its Technological Reproducibility (Second Version)," trans. Edmund Jephcott and Harry Zohn, in *The Work of Art in the Age of Its Technological Reproducibility, and Other Writings on Media*, ed. Michael W. Jennings, Brigid Doherty, and Thomas Y. Levin (Cambridge, MA: Belknap Press of Harvard University Press, 2008), 50.

2. We use the term "anti-aestheticism" here as a kind of shorthand, and in contradistinction to specific artistic practices, but Benjamin never of course leaves the aesthetic entirely behind, especially since, minimally, he still seeks to mobilize a renewed sense of aesthetics that he believes can be politicized, in particular against fascism. If we were to be more precise, we would say that he is against a certain philosophical idea of art—as something that can be original, that can be viewed as mysterious or as having eternal value, as a work that can be associated with the "here and now" of the moment of its production and attached solely to this moment. For him, art can only be politicized if it is understood as plural, mass-like, associated with different times and spaces. In Jameson's words, Benjamin's "Work of Art" essay is "designed to render older, now-obsolete critical values useless for aesthetization, which is to say, for fascism" (*BF*, 178).

3. Walter Benjamin, "On the Concept of History," trans. Harry Zohn, in Benjamin, *Selected Writings*, vol. 4: *1938–1940*, ed. Howard Eiland and Michael W. Jennings (Cambridge, MA: Belknap Press of Harvard University Press, 2003), 391. Further references to this essay will be noted parenthetically by *CH* and page number.

4. Walter Benjamin, *The Correspondence of Walter Benjamin, 1910–1940*, ed. Gershom Scholem and Theodor Adorno, trans. Manfred R. Jacobson and Evelyn M. Jacobson (Chicago: University of Chicago Press, 1994), 84. Further references to Benjamin's letters in English are to this edition and will be noted in the text by *C* and page number. Jameson uses this passage as the epigraph to his book and also cites it later (see *BF*, 146).

5. This is why film is so important to Benjamin. As a medium, cinema, even more than photography, provides him with a technological plasticity capable of imagining new and more fluid relationships between different modes of being, and, in particular, between the human body and the world surrounding it. Rather than a mimetic experience centered around the notion of representation, cinema heralds a mimetic contagion—a transit between an embodied organism and its technological stimulation, a contagion that intensifies energetic exchanges, what Benjamin describes as the "compulsion to become similar and to behave mimetically" (Benjamin, "On the Mimetic Faculty," trans. Edmund Jephcott, in Benjamin, *Selected Writings*, vol. 2: *1927–1934*, ed. Michael W. Jennings, Howard Eiland, and Gary Smith [Cambridge, MA: Belknap Press of Harvard University Press, 1999], 720). Benjamin links these energetic exchanges to his concept of innervation, to the sensorial transformation that technology precipitates in the body. The metamorphosis of the human, the sensualization of perception through a relation with the moving image, is echoed in the transformation of the relation between the animate and the inanimate on the screen. This relation becomes more porous and mobile because film treats bodies and objects in exactly the same way, suggesting an understanding of cinema as a technological animism, whereby objects become alive and bodies behave mechanically. We can think of this as a first technology that takes place through the camera and exclusively on the screen. Benjamin, however, goes further, suggesting that there is a second technology, in the form of innervation, whereby human perception is transformed by incorporating the camera into the body. The link between these two technologies is made when the body recognizes itself as an object and reacts convulsively into movement—becoming animated and galvanized. The recognition of the inanimate triggers animation, and these two technological processes lead, in Benjamin's words, "to a massive upheaval" that is "intimately related to the mass movements of our day." Film becomes "the most powerful agent" in massifying the "innervations of the collective" (*WA*, 254, and Benjamin, "The Work of Art in the Age of Its Technological Reproducibility [Second Version]," 45).

6. See Marx, *Capital: A Critique of Political Economy*, vol. 1, trans. Ben Fowkes (New York: Penguin Books, 1990), chapter 1.

7. Walter Benjamin, "The Work of Art in the Age of Its Technological Reproducibility (Second Version)," 51.

8. Jameson offers a different translation of the passage from Baudelaire's *Fusées* earlier on pages 34–35 (which differs from the one he uses on page 104): "The pleasure we take in crowds is a mysterious expression of our jouissance in the multiplication of number. *Everything* is number. Number is in the individual. Intoxication is a number" (*BF*, 34–35).

IV. GENERAL STRIKE

1. Rosa Luxemburg, "The Mass Strike," trans. Patrick Lavin, in *The Essential Rosa Luxemburg: Reform or Revolution and The Mass Strike* (Chicago: Haymarket Books, 2008), 140. Further references to this essay are to this edition and will be noted parenthetically by *MS* and page number.

2. From our perspective, the most significant works on the essay are those by Jacques Derrida, "Force of Law: The 'Mystical Foundation of Authority,'" trans. Mary Quaintance, in *Deconstruction and the Possibility of Justice*, ed. Drucilla Cornell, Michel Rosenfeld, and David Gray Carlson (New York: Routledge, 1992), 3–67; Werner Hamacher, "Affirmative Strike," trans. Dana Hollander, *Cardozo Law Review* 13 (1991–1992), 1133–1157; Judith Butler, "Walter Benjamin and the Critique of Violence" and "Flashing Up: Benjamin's Messianic Politics," in *Parting Ways: Jewishness and the Critique of Zionism* (New York: Columbia University Press, 2012), 69–98 and 99–113; Giorgio Agamben, *Homo Sacer: Sovereign Power and Bare Life*, trans. Daniel Heller-Roazen (Stanford: Stanford University Press, 1998), especially Part Two; David Lloyd, "Rage against the Divine," *South Atlantic Quarterly* 106, no. 2 (Spring 2007), 345–372; and, most recently, Peter Fenves, "Introduction," and Julia Ng, "Afterword: Toward Another Critique of Violence," in Walter Benjamin, *Toward the Critique of Violence: A Critical Edition*, ed. Peter Fenves and Julia Ng (Stanford: Stanford University Press, 2021), 1–37 and 113–160, respectively.

3. Ng, "Afterword: Toward Another Critique of Violence," 116.

4. Benjamin, *Gesammelte Briefe*, vol. 3: *1925–1930*, ed. Christoph Gödde and Henri Lonitz (Berlin: Suhrkamp Verlag, 1997), 9. From his correspondence, we know that, in the fall of 1920, Benjamin planned a study on politics whose working title was *Politik*. He first mentions the project in a letter to Bernhard Kampffmeyer from September 1920, in which he asks for "bibliographical

information" for a "line of political studies" that he is developing (part of which he refers to as "Der Abbau der Gewalt" [The dismantling of violence]). See Walter Benjamin, *Gesammelte Briefe*, vol. 2: *1919–1924*, ed. Christoph Gödde and Henri Lonitz (Berlin: Suhrkamp Verlag, 1996), 101. Although he will change his mind later, in a series of letters to Scholem he describes the initial arc of the project. On December 1, 1920, he writes that it would consist of three main sections. The first part would be called "Der wahre Politiker" (The true politician). The second part (on which he was working at the time) would be called "Die wahre Politik" (The true politics), and would be divided into two parts, "Der Abbau der Gewalt" and "Teleologie ohne Endzweck" (Teleology without final purpose). Finally, the third part would be a philosophical critique of Paul Scheerbart's 1913 "asteroid novel," *Lesabéndio*. On December 29, 1920, he writes that the first part has been completed and that he hopes to see it soon in print. In January 1921 he mentions "Zur Kritik der Gewalt," which he was asked to write by Emil Lederer for the latter's journal *Weißen Blätter* and which is now assumed to be "Der Abbau der Gewalt," for the first time (ibid., 109, 119, 130, 111n.). In the end, Lederer decides the essay is too long and difficult for the journal and publishes it instead in the journal *Archiv für Sozialwissenschaft und Sozialpolitik*, founded in 1904 by Max Weber, Werner Sombart, and Edgar Jaffé, which Lederer also edited. The piece finally appears on August 3, 1921, followed by the "Leipzig Council" section of Marx and Engels's posthumously titled *The German Ideology*, and by other essays on economics, socialism, religion, and revolution. "Der wahre Politiker" is now considered lost altogether, and Benjamin later changes his mind again and divides the second part of "Die wahre Politik," "Teleologie ohne Endzweck," into two sections, the first focusing on the biological sciences and the second on *Lesabéndio*. Having moved Scheerbart's novel from the project's third part to the second part of its second section, he decides to close his three-part project with a series of "aphorisms, jokes, and dreams" that would serve as, in Ng's words, "a pendant to the essay on the critique of violence." This "pendant," she goes on to note, will be *One-Way Street*. See Ng, "Afterword: Toward Another Critique of Violence," 117.

5. Walter Benjamin, "Toward the Critique of Violence," trans. Julia Ng, in Benjamin, *Toward the Critique of Violence: A Critical Edition*, 39. Further references to this essay are to this edition and are noted parenthetically by *CV* and page number.

6. Anthony Auerbach, "Remarks on Walter Benjamin's 'Critique of Violence,'" delivered at the "After 1968" seminar, led by Katja Diefenbach, at the Jan Van Eyck Academie, Maastricht, in 2007.

7. Julia Ng, "*Rechtsphilosophie* after the War: A Commentary on Paragraphs 4–6 of 'Zur Kritik der Gewalt,'" *Critical Times* 2, no. 2 (August 2019), 240. Part of our argument about Benjamin's "Violence" essay is that it encrypts several references to contemporary events and historical figures, one in particular. As Howard Eiland and Michael W. Jennings observe, "There is not a single reference in Benjamin's correspondence to the highly charged atmosphere in which he and Dora must have found themselves on their return. But from this point forward, the composition of his 'Politics' was accelerated. In April 1920 he drafted a note, now lost, called 'Life and Violence' (see *C*, 162). And at some point in the fall he composed 'Fantasy on a Passage in *The Spirit of Utopia*,' which has not survived either. He continued to read widely, not just in political theory but in related fields as well." See Howard Eiland and Michael W. Jennings, *Walter Benjamin: A Critical Life* (Cambridge, MA: Belknap Press of Harvard University Press, 2014), 130. That Benjamin is silent on particular matters does not mean they do not permeate his writings; in this instance, they intensify his interest in his projected book on politics.

8. Beyond his explicit references to figures involved in these legal debates, Benjamin also implicitly engages two conservative political theorists, Thomas Hobbes and Carl Schmitt, both of whom—one baroque and the other contemporary—view the relationship between law and violence as foundational for the state, and as the key to its longevity and stability. Both figures also will loom large in Benjamin's *Trauerspiel*. In his *Leviathan*, for example, Hobbes states that "Covenants, without the Sword, are but Words, and of no strength to secure a man at all" (Thomas Hobbes, *Leviathan*, ed. Richard Tuck [Cambridge: Cambridge University Press, 1996], 117). Here he points to the interdependence of legal order and force in consonance with Benjamin's critique of violence and Schmitt's later insistence on the "state of exception" as a means of justifying violence. For a discussion of the role and place of Hobbes and Schmitt in Benjamin's essay, see Horst Bredekamp, "From Walter Benjamin to Carl Schmitt, via Thomas Hobbes," trans. M. Thorson Hause and J. Bond, *Critical Inquiry* 25, no. 2 (Winter 1999), 246–266.

9. Denise Ferreira da Silva's *Unpayable Debt* makes exactly this claim when she points out that anti-Black violence relies on a retroactive juridico-economic justification for legitimation, one that effectively blames the victim (we will address this logic more directly in section XVI, "The Hammer of Social Revolution"). As we will see, legal violence and total racial violence are always the effect of a brutal calculus that uses the logic of causality as its cover. In Da Silva's words,

a logical pattern still operates today that, virtually every time the explanation or justification for deployment of otherwise unacceptable total violence, renders the person killed the *cause* of their own killing, whether they seemed to be holding a gun (which turned out to be a wallet, in the case of

Amadou Diallo) or they moved in a threatening way (even after being shot, in the case of Michael Brown). From where, one must ask, does blackness derive such a powerful connection to truth, so strong that it alone sustains the validity of an explanation/justification (by the police officer or non-black person) against any actual (spatiotemporal) evidence to the contrary? My argument here is that this force resides in the particular way in which the racial dialectic transsubstantiates what is politically constituted (by the colonial juridico-economic structure of slavery) into expressions of an organically determined moral deficit (in the case of police shootings) produced by the sight of black skin color (an expression of a moral and intellectual deficit).

See Denise Ferreira da Silva, *Unpayable Debt* (Berlin: Sternberg Press, 2022), 124.

10. Ng, "*Rechtsphilosophie* after the War," 240.

11. Benjamin's attention to the way in which the SPD betrayed its own revolutionary origins in the name of preserving its sovereignty, even with the greatest violence, echoes Trotsky's own accusation against the SPD in his eulogy for Liebknecht and Luxemburg:

The best leaders of the German Communist Party are no more—our great comrades are no longer amongst the living. And their murderers stand under the banner of the Social-Democratic party having the brazenness to claim their birthright from no other than Karl Marx! What a perversion! What a mockery! Just think, comrades, that "Marxist" German Social-Democracy, mother of the working class from the first days of the war, which supported the unbridled German militarism in the days of the rout of Belgium and the seizure of the northern provinces of France; that party which betrayed the October Revolution to German militarism during the Brest peace; that is the party whose leaders, Scheidemann and Ebert, now organize black bands to murder the heroes of the International, Karl Liebknecht and Rosa Luxemburg! What a monstrous historical perversion!

See Leon Trotsky, "Karl Liebknecht and Rosa Luxemburg" (1919), http://www.marxists.org/archive/trotsky/profiles/rosa.htm.

12. Eiland and Jennings, *Walter Benjamin: A Critical Life*, 130.

13. As we will see when we turn to a discussion of the general strike in Du Bois's *Black Reconstruction*, abolition could very well be another word for deposition.

14. Pablo Oyarzún, "Law, Violence, History: A Brief Reading of the Last Paragraph of Walter Benjamin's 'Toward the Critique of Violence,'" *Critical Times* 2, no. 2 (August 2019), 334.

15. For the citations from Georges Sorel, see his *Reflections on Violence*, trans. Thomas Ernest Hulme and Jeremy Jennings, ed. Jeremy Jennings (Cambridge: Cambridge University Press, 2012), 162 and 171; translation modified. Further references to this text will be noted parenthetically by *RV* and page number.

16. Walter Benjamin, "Goethe's *Elective Affinities*," trans. Stanley Corngold, in Benjamin, *Selected Writings*, vol. 1: *1913–1926*, ed. Michael W. Jennings, Howard Eiland, and Gary Smith (Cambridge, MA: Belknap Press of Harvard University Press, 1996), 356.

V. ROSA'S CASKET

1. Bertolt Brecht, "Epitaph 1919," in *The Collected Poems of Bertolt Brecht*, trans. and ed. Tom Kuhn and David Constantine, with the assistance of Charlotte Ryland (New York: Liveright Publishing Corporation, 2019), 364; and Karl Marx, *The Eighteenth Brumaire of Louis Bonaparte*, trans. Daniel De Leon (New York: International Publishers, 1963), 19. Marx here references Erasmus's Latin translation, "Hic Rhodus, hic saltus!," of a line from Aesop's fables—in its original Greek, "Αὐτοῦ γὰρ καὶ Ῥόδος καὶ πήδημα"—in which, in response to an athlete who boasts about the great jump he made in a competition on the island of Rhodes, a bystander proclaims that, if what he is saying is true, he should prove it: "Here is Rhodes, jump here!" Marx's translation of Erasmus's phrase—"Hier ist die Rose, hier tanze!"—replaces "Rhodus" with "die Rose" and implicitly changes the Latin *saltus* (the noun "jump") to *salta* (the singular imperative of *saltare*, which can mean either to "dance" or to "jump," hence Marx's German "tanze"), a translation he gets from the preface to Hegel's *Elements of the Philosophy of Right*. There, after citing the Greek and Latin versions of the line, Hegel notes that "with hardly an alteration, the proverb just quoted would run: '*Here* is the rose, *here* dance.'" If Hegel uses the line in order to reinforce his claim that "[i]t is just as foolish to imagine that any philosophy can transcend its contemporary world as that an individual can overleap his own time or leap over Rhodes," Marx evokes it in order to suggest that, when "a situation has been created which makes all turning back impossible," proletariat revolutions must overcome their constant self-criticism and self-doubt, must exceed their own conditions, and simply take a leap into an unknown future, without any guarantee of success (G. W. F. Hegel, *Elements of the Philosophy of Right*, trans. H. B. Nisbet, ed. Allen W. Wood [Cambridge: Cambridge University Press, 1991], 21–22; for the Marx citation, see Marx, *The Eighteenth Brumaire of Louis Bonaparte*, 107). This is why, when Marx "cites" the line, he enacts a movement between different texts and languages that, in Jan Mieszkowski's words, "no one—Aesop, Erasmus, Hegel, or Marx—can

claim to control." "Marx's mobilization of Aesop, Erasmus, and Hegel," he goes on to say,

> reveals Hegel's citational practice to be a challenge to the possibility of ever knowing if the language one is speaking is a discourse of the past, present, or future.
>
> *Hic Rhodus, hic saltus/salta* is a battle cry of proletarian revolutionaries, the moment at which they do, contra Hegel, go beyond their own place and time. In uttering it, one follows Aesop's athlete and makes a daring leap, springing forth from one language without necessarily being able to return to it or to land safely in a new one, much less coordinate the old with the new. Indeed, having jumped one cannot be sure that what one was jumping from was one's own language in the first place. In this respect, *hic Rhodus, hic saltus/salta* is what Marx in various texts terms a *salto mortale.*

See Jan Mieszkowski, "Romancing the Slogan," *European Romantic Review* 28, no. 3 (2017), 365.

When Marx cites and revises Hegel, even if just slightly, his revision belongs to a revolutionary insistence that his language is not just his, and it is in the enactment of this acknowledgment that his political gesture becomes legible. As we will see, the language of Benjamin's essay on violence also does not belong just to him. Nevertheless, it is in this movement without any determinate agency that the possibility of thinking differently—for Rosa Luxemburg, the possibility of freedom—demonstrates its force. Here the "Rose" becomes the necessarily unstable signifier for the freedom of revolution. Here is indeed the Rose and, in Benjamin, we must learn how to dance with it—something Marx does with the language he inherits and transforms.

2. Gershom Scholem, *Walter Benjamin: The Story of a Friendship* (London: Faber and Faber, 1982), 7.

3. For an account of Georg Benjamin's political affiliations and activities, see Bernd-Peter Lange, *Georg Benjamin: Ein bürgerlicher Revolutionär im Roten Wedding* (Berlin: Verlag Walter Frey, 2019). We thank Peter Fenves for directing us to this book.

4. Benjamin cites Hofmannsthal in his "Paralipomena to 'On the Concept of History,'" trans. Edmund Jephcott and Howard Eiland, in Benjamin, *Selected Writings*, vol. 4: *1938–1940*, ed. Howard Eiland and Michael W. Jennings (Cambridge, MA: Belknap Press of Harvard University Press, 2003), 405. See Hugo von Hofmannsthal's *Der Tor und der Tod* (1894), in *Gesammelte Werke*, ed. Herbert Steiner (Frankfurt am Main: S. Fischer, 1952), 3:220.

5. Leon Trotsky, "Hands Off Rosa Luxemburg!," Leon Trotsky Internet Archive (www.marxists .org), 2005. Written on June 28, 1932, this text was first published in the August 6 and 13, 1932 issue of the Socialist Workers Party newspaper, *The Militant.*

6. Walter Benjamin, "Death," trans. Peter Fenves, in Walter Benjamin, *Toward the Critique of Violence: A Critical Edition*, ed. Peter Fenves and Julia Ng (Stanford: Stanford University Press, 2021), 78.

7. Werner Hamacher, "Affirmative Strike," trans. Dana Hollander, *Cardozo Law Review* 13 (1991–1992), 1139, fn. 12

8. The Berlin magistrate refused to let the Communist Party of Germany bury the dead in the historic cemetery that had been created for the victims of the March Revolution of 1848 in the Berlin district of Friedrichshain. Instead, he assigned them a rear area in the remote Berlin-Friedrichsfelde cemetery. This area was intended for common criminals and was called the "criminal corner." The USPD and KPD organized a joint funeral service there, turning the cemetery area into a permanent pilgrimage destination. Over 100,000 people took part in the funeral procession. For Luxemburg, an empty coffin was buried next to Liebknecht's grave because her body had not yet been found. A body was found in Berlin's Landwehr canal on May 31 and, assumed to be that of the murdered revolutionary, it was subsequently buried in Friedrichsfelde on June 13, which has been widely recognized as Luxemburg's final resting place.

A mystery emerged in May 2009, however, when Dr. Michael Tsokos, head of the Berlin Charité hospital's Institute of Legal Medicine and Forensic Sciences, discovered a torso—with no head, hands, or feet—stored for decades in the cellar of the hospital's medical history museum that he believed to be that of Luxemburg. It was an autopsy report that originally led to speculation that Luxemburg's body had never left Berlin's Charité hospital in June 1919 in the first place. When examining the medical examiner's report associated with the corpse—dated June 13, 1919—Tsokos noticed a number of suspicious irregularities in both the details of the report and the way one of the originally examining physicians added an addendum in which he distanced himself from the conclusions of his colleague, which Tsokos called "a very unusual occurrence." Tsokos had a number of elaborate tests, such as carbon dating and computer tomography exams, performed on the corpse. The tests determined that the body "showed signs of having been waterlogged … that the body had belonged to a woman who was between 40 and 50 years old at the time of death and that she had suffered from osteoarthritis and had legs of different lengths." As Tsokos told *Der Spiegel*, he concluded that the corpse bore "striking similarities with the real Rosa Luxemburg." According to his account, as reported in *Spiegel*, Luxemburg, who died at the age of 47,

> suffered from a congenital hip ailment that left her with a permanent limp, which in turn caused her legs to be of different lengths. And after her violent death at the hands of

right-wing paramilitaries, her body was thrown into Berlin's Landwehr Canal. ... Her body was only recovered almost five months later after the winter ice had melted. Then, after an autopsy at the Charité hospital, she was allegedly buried in the Friedrichsfelde Cemetery. ... Surprising inconsistencies from the report on the original autopsy, performed on June 13, 1919 on a body said to be that of Rosa Luxemburg, seem to lend credence to Tsokos' hypothesis. On the one hand, forensic examiners at that time reported details that did not agree with the anatomical peculiarities of Luxemburg's body. ... The autopsy explicitly noted the absence of hip damage and also said there was no evidence that the legs were of different lengths. The autopsy also revealed no traces on the upper skull of the two rifle-butt strikes soldiers reportedly inflicted on Luxemburg. Regarding the gunshot to the head that killed Luxemburg, the original medical examiners did note a hole in the corpse's head between the left eye and ear, but they did not find an exit wound nor did they note the presence of a bullet in the skull. Furthermore, rumors had long been circulating at the Charité that the body of Red Rosa never actually left the hospital. Some say that Luxemburg's head was preserved in the Institute of Legal Medicine and Forensic Sciences. Even the missing hands and feet fit with Tsokos' theory. When the revolutionary was thrown into the canal, eyewitnesses say weights were tied to her ankles and wrists with wire. During the months her corpse spent under water, they could have easily severed her extremities. The remains that were once placed in that grave could not be used in resolving the mystery because they disappeared after virulently anti-communist Nazis attacked and plundered the grave in 1935.

See "Berlin Hospital May Have Found Rosa Luxemburg's Corpse," *Spiegel International*, May 29, 2009. It is doubtful that Benjamin would have been aware that Luxemburg's body might never have been found in the aftermath of her death, but he certainly knew that the casket in the initial funeral in January 1919 had been empty. We can only assume that he would have found it perfectly appropriate to learn that Luxemburg's missing body had become the object of several burials, and that the annual ceremonies in remembrance of her would have been organized around the absence of her remains. This would have been particularly the case because, as Shoshana Felman notes in her account of the trauma Benjamin experienced in the aftermath of the suicide of his friend Fritz Heinle,

the most traumatic memory that Benjamin keeps from the war is not simply this unnarratable epiphany—this sudden overwhelming revelation of youth as a corpse—but the added insult, the accompanying shame of the impossibility of giving the beloved corpse a proper burial, the shame of the incapability of taking leave of the dead bodies by giving them the final honor of a proper grave. It is because the bodies cannot be appropriately buried that the corpse ... becomes a ghost that never will find peace. The grave, symbolically, cannot be closed. The event cannot be laid to rest.

See Felman, "Benjamin's Silence," *Critical Inquiry* 25 (Winter 1999), 223. There would be much to say about the repetition of this story of a grave's absence, since, as we know, after Benjamin's own suicide—itself a repetition of Heinle's suicide—the money left in his pocket at his death was only enough to "rent" a grave. As Felman adds, "[a]fter a while, the body was disinterred and the remains were moved to a nameless collective grave of those with no possessions" (ibid., 228). In the same way that Benjamin's critique of violence is organized around the missing body of Luxemburg, we could say that his own missing body circulates in the vast body of writings about him and his work.

9. It is essential to refer to Luxemburg's death as a femicide in order to evoke the unbearable toll of gendered violence that has continued its course up to the present. This violence has been particularly galvanizing in Latin America and led to the *Ni una menos* demonstrations in Argentina in 2015 and the feminist strikes since then across the continent, and especially in Chile, Peru, Bolivia, Paraguay, Uruguay, El Salvador, and Guatemala. Presenting themselves as a "collective scream" against "*machista* violence," these demonstrations and strikes have brought together hundreds of thousands of women in the largest actions many of these countries have ever seen. These mass movements have together contributed to a renewed interest in Luxemburg, one that takes a distinctively feminist slant. The stature of Luxemburg in relationship to feminism has grown exponentially in the last decade. It is also notable that these feminist mass strikes have for the very first time included indigenous and non-waged workers. For a recent history of these movements—and their inspiration in Luxemburg, in particular—see Verónica Gago, *Feminist International: How to Change Everything* (London: Verso, 2020). These movements have now had their reverberations across the globe—from Mexico to the United States, from Brazil to Spain, from India to Iran, from Afghanistan to Turkey, and beyond.

10. Walter Benjamin, "The Metaphysics of Youth," trans. Rodney Livingston, in Benjamin, *Selected Writings*, vol. 1: *1913–1926*, ed. Michael W. Jennings, Howard Eiland, and Gary Smith (Cambridge, MA: Belknap Press of Harvard University Press, 1996), 6. In a letter dated May 10, 2023, Gerhard Richter reiterates "Benjamin's

aversion to direct modes of presentation, especially when it comes to 'the political.'" Reinforcing the importance of secret names in Benjamin, he points to a rather remarkable passage in Benjamin's preliminary notes and drafts for his Kraus essay: "speaking of Kraus's writerly strategy with regard to the political, Benjamin likens Kraus to the fairytale character 'Rumpelstilschen,' the one whose name nobody supposedly knows, and who will lose his magical powers once his name is revealed to the public (which happens at the end of the fairytale). Benjamin writes: 'Bei Kraus ist folgende Überschneidung üblich: Reaktionäre Theorie begründet revolutionäre Praxis ... Kraus als ein Rumpelstilzchen: "Gott sei Dank daß niemand weiß / daß ich Marx und Engels heiß." (With Kraus, the following overlap is common: Reactionary theory justifies revolutionary practice ... Kraus as a Rumpelstiltskin: 'Thank God nobody knows / that my name is Marx and Engels'). In the Grimms' version, the character's well-known rhyme goes as follows: 'Ach, wie gut ist, daß niemand weiß, daß ich Rumpelstilzchen heiß.' This weird Benjaminian idea that Kraus is a Rumpelstilzchen whose real (but secret) name is Marx and Engels—is this not fascinating?" Benjamin's note can be found in GS, 2.3:1092. We are grateful for this reference.

11. Felman, "Benjamin's Silence," 218. Benjamin also encodes Heinle in a short text most likely written in late 1915 or early 1916, "Das Regenbogen: Gespräch über die Phantasie" (The rainbow: dialogue on fantasy). In the dialogue, the character Margarethe evokes Heinle by citing one of his lines: "A poet has written: 'If I were made of material, I would color myself' [wäre ich von Stoff, ich würde mich färben]." See GS, 7:24. Other citations of Heinle's poetry also appear quietly in Benjamin's color studies, his essays on children's books, and in the "Mummerehlen" section of Berlin Childhood. On his appearance in the various texts on color, see Peter Fenves, The Messianic Reduction: Walter Benjamin and the Shape of Time (Stanford: Stanford University Press, 2011), 67.

12. Walter Benjamin, "Two Poems by Friedrich Hölderlin," trans. Stanley Corngold, in Benjamin, Selected Writings, 1:29.

13. Felman, "Benjamin's Silence," 215 and 218. Benjamin himself identifies mourning with silence in his 1916 essay on language. There, he writes: "[i]n all mourning there is the deepest inclination to speechlessness, which is infinitely more than the inability or disinclination to communicate." See Walter Benjamin, "On Language as Such and on the Language of Man," trans. Edmund Jephcott, in Benjamin, Selected Writings, 1:73.

14. Benjamin, "Two Poems by Friedrich Hölderlin," 31 and 32.

15. Already in a letter to Martin Buber from July 1916—in a passage that imagines "a relationship between language and action in which the former would not be the instrument of the latter"—Benjamin suggests that the politics of his writing can be measured in relation to its fidelity to what remains unsaid, something we argue is evidenced by his silent encryption of Luxemburg. As he puts it:

> My concept of objective and, at the same time, highly political style and writing is this: to awaken interest in what was denied to the word; only where this sphere of speechlessness reveals itself in unutterably pure power can the magic spark leap between the word and the motivating deed, where the unity of these two equally real entities resides. Only the intensive aiming of words into the core of intrinsic silence is truly effective. I do not believe that there is any place where the word would be more distant from the divine than in "real" action. (C, 80)

16. While we are presently tracking Benjamin's encryption of Luxemburg within his essay, it should be noted that, in the aftermath of his engagement with this feminist political icon, he incorporates the thoughts and writings of a number of politically active female figures that, from our perspective, transform his intellectual trajectory in fundamental ways—even when they are not always documented extensively or even acknowledged. Among them, perhaps the two most significant are the Latvian Asja Lacis and the French Claire Démar.

Benjamin met Lacis on the island of Capri in the summer of 1924 and started an intermittent affair with her that later took him to Moscow and Riga in 1926 and 1927 and resulted in his Moscow Diary. He also dedicated One-Way Street to her by renaming his book Asja Lacis Street and registering the entanglement of her voice with his. While living in Weimar Germany, Lacis, a director of agitprop and proletarian children's theater, introduced Bertolt Brecht, Erwin Piscator, and Fritz Lang to Mayakovsky's avant-garde theories. She also shared firsthand accounts of mass spectacles staged by the "Theater of October," including the reenactment of the storming of the Winter Palace in 1920, and of Sergei Eisenstein's cinematic experiments. She directly intervened in the media literacy of a number of Weimar intellectuals, well beyond just Benjamin. She often is mistakenly credited for introducing Benjamin to Marxism, but, as we have demonstrated, his engagement with Marx began much earlier.

In addition to Lacis, Benjamin became familiar with the work of the nineteenth-century Saint-Simonian revolutionary Claire Démar (1799–1833), pseudonymous author of Appel d'une femme au peuple sur l'affranchissement de la femme and of the posthumously published Ma loi d'avenir, while researching and writing his unfinished Arcades Project. He references Démar's emancipatory pamphlets as archives full of passionate power and as-yet-untapped revolutionary potential. Among other things, Démar called for the abolition of patriarchy as the basis for the laws of inheritance that sustain both property and the oppression of women through legalized prostitution (i.e., marriage) and childbearing, what she will call the "law of blood." See Claire Démar, *Appel au peuple sur l'affranchissement de la femme: aux origines de la pensée féministe*, ed. Valentin Pelosse (Paris: Albin Michel, 2001), 211. By the time Benjamin cited her in his *Arcades Project*, Démar's work had been almost completely forgotten after her suicide in 1833; he reactivated her and transformed her presumed obsolescence into a resource for addressing the present.

It would be important to trace the influence of such politically active women in Benjamin's political life. As we will see, something similar happens with Marx. In the last years of his life, he is introduced to precapitalist communal organizations in Russia and also encouraged to think about their revolutionary potential for averting capitalism by the Russian activist Vera Zasulich. We will explore the effects of this late turn in Marx in "A Red Common-Wealth."

17. Besides the fact that Sorel surely read Luxemburg's *Mass Strike*—it is interesting that he does not cite it directly, but, in accordance with a logic he could have gotten from Nietzsche, she is perhaps too close to him to mention—he quotes her directly in a passage in which he accuses the Social Democrats of abusing the idea of justice, suggesting that this is why Luxemburg called the idea of justice "this old post horse, on which for centuries all the regenerators of the world, deprived of surer means of historic locomotion, have ridden; this ungainly Rosinante, mounted on which so many Quixotes of history have gone in search of the great reform of the world, bringing back from these journeys nothing but black eyes" (*RV*, 220). The Luxemburg citation is from her *Reform or Revolution*, parts of which already had appeared in 1899. See, in a different translation than that offered in the Sorel translation, Rosa Luxemburg, *Reform or Revolution*, in *The Essential Rosa Luxemburg: Reform or Revolution and the Mass Strike*, ed. Helen Scott (Chicago: Haymarket Books, 2008), 84.

18. We are indebted to David Lloyd for pointing out this anagram to us.

19. That Benjamin never left this moment behind—a moment in which, in the aftermath of the war, he writes his violence essay—is legible in his long-standing interest in the Spartacists. In addition to his explicit return to them in his late essay on the "Concept of History," their presence is most strongly in evidence in his 1937 essay on Fuchs, "Eduard Fuchs, Collector and Historian," an essay that shares language with Benjamin's artwork essay and with his theses on the concept of history, a detail that connects it to his late writings. A friend of Adorno, Max Horkheimer, Franz Mehring, and many other prominent figures during the Weimar period, Fuchs was a founding member of the Spartacists

and a longtime leftist activist. He shared a disillusionment with the German Social Democratic movement with many of his friends and colleagues, among them Liebknecht, Luxemburg, Franz Mehring, and Clara Zetkin. When the war broke out, inspired by the Bolsheviks, together they formed the Spartakusbund, the Spartacus League. This splinter organization of the SPD would eventually become the Kommunistische Partei Deutschlands or KPD (Communist Party of Germany) in late 1918.

During the war, he was the general plenipotentiary for the welfare of Russian prisoners of war in Germany and played a central role in pursuing amnesty for political prisoners in both Germany and Russia. He was part of Liebknecht's and Luxemburg's inner circle and, because of the trust the Russian government had in him, he was often a mediator between Lenin and the German revolutionaries and helped facilitate the establishment of the Third International. In November 1918, he drove Luxemburg from Breslau to Berlin on her release from prison and he also ensured Liebknecht's safe travel to a banquet in the leader's honor at the Russian Embassy in Berlin. In late December, he carried a letter from Luxemburg to Lenin, which was accompanied by the draft program of the Spartacists, entitled "What does the Spartakusbund Want?" A supporter of innumerable communist projects, Fuchs was referred to by Lenin himself as "Der Mann im Schatten" ("The Man in the Shadows"). See Ulrich Weitz, *Der Mann im Schatten: Eduard Fuchs* (Berlin: Karl Dietz Verlag, 2014), 17.

Beyond his political work, Fuchs's critical and scholarly work—especially his work on caricature, which he read through Marxist cultural theory—was inseparable from his political activities, as Benjamin makes clear in his essay on him. It should also be noted that many of the ideas that make their way into Benjamin's artwork essay—especially in regard to the relation between artworks and technological reproducibility—come directly from Fuchs's own writings, as is evident in the passages Benjamin cites from Fuchs (see, for example, Walter Benjamin, "Eduard Fuchs, Collector and Historian," in Benjamin, *Selected Writings*, vol. 3: *1935–1938*, ed. Howard Eiland and Michael W. Jennings [Cambridge, MA: Belknap Press of Harvard University Press, 2002], 283). In addition, Benjamin's famous assertion that "[t]here is no document of culture which is not at the same time a document of barbarism" can be traced to Fuchs's own reflections on the pillage and plunder of cultural artifacts by the English and French empires. One of the great collectors of European and East Asian art—watercolors, paintings, lithographs, drawings, posters, and objects—Fuchs housed his collection in the Villa Fuchs, which was built for him by Mies van der Rohe in Berlin-Zehlendorf in 1911. On behalf of the Communist Party, Fuchs later commissioned the architect to build the Monument to the November Revolution, often referred to as the Rosa Luxemburg memorial.

It is rather remarkable that Benjamin devotes one of his late major essays to Fuchs, that is, to a central Spartacist. This suggests the significance the Spartacists had for him not simply because of his brother's political activism but also because of how impacted he had been by the example of Luxemburg and by the violence of her assassination. There is much more to trace here, but what is important for us in this context is simply to emphasize the endurance of Benjamin's incorporation of Spartacist strategies for doing politics. That he does this through the activities of writing and reading is perhaps justified further if we recall what Luxemburg's biographer J. P. Nettl says about the role of writing in the Spartacist uprising: "Rosa laid down as immediate tasks the reissue of their daily paper, the production of a more theoretical weekly, special papers for youth and for women, a soldiers' paper, syndication of leading articles to be offered to other newspapers—shades of Sozialdemokratische Korrespondenz; finally, the creation of a special department for propaganda in the army. Never had a revolution had such a paper base." See J. P. Nettl, *Rosa Luxemburg*, vol. 2 (London: Oxford University Press, 1966), 724.

20. Rosa Luxemburg, "Die Krise der Sozialdemokratie," in Luxemburg, *Gesammelte Werke*, vol. 4: *August 1914–January 1919*, ed. Annelies Laschitza and Günter Radczun (Berlin: Rosa-Luxemburg-Stiftung, 2000), 148–149.

21. See Frederick Engels, "The Bakunists at Work: An Account of the Spanish revolt in the Summer of 1873," https://www.marxists.org/archive/marx/works/1873/bakunin/index.htm.

22. In his late "On the Concept of History," Benjamin praises Luxemburg's Spartacist League for its insistence on the violence and oppression of the past: for its refusal to forget the injustices of the past and to focus solely on the promise of the future, as was the usual practice of the Social Democrats of his day. In his words,

The subject of historical knowledge is the struggling, oppressed class itself. Marx presents it as the last enslaved class—the avenger that completes the task of liberation in the name of generations of the downtrodden. This conviction, which had a brief resurgence in the Spartacus League, has always been objectionable to Social Democrats. Within three decades they managed to erase the name of Blanqui almost entirely, though at the sound of that name the preceding century had quaked. The Social Democrats preferred to cast the working class in the role of a redeemer of *future* generations, in this way cutting the sinews of its greatest strength. This indoctrination made the working class forget both its hatred and its

spirit of sacrifice, for both are nourished by the image of enslaved ancestors rather than by the ideal of liberated grandchildren. (*CH*, 394)

That Benjamin returns to the Spartacists in this late text is another confirmation that he never left Luxemburg behind. Instead, he carries her with him until the very end of his life.

23. Sorel makes a similar point when he writes:

Today the confidence of the socialists is much greater than it was in the past, now that the myth of the general strike dominates the true working-class movement in its entirety. No failure proves anything against socialism, as it has become a work of preparation; if it fails, it merely proves that the apprenticeship has been insufficient; they must set to work again with more courage, persistence and confidence than before, the experience of labor has taught the workers that it is by means of patient apprenticeship that one can become a true comrade at work; and it is also the only way of becoming a true revolutionary. (*RV*, 31)

If Benjamin encrypts Luxemburg in his text in order to enable her to silently press Sorel in other directions—to emphasize certain elements of his argument but also to challenge others, to move his language from within (Sorel himself recalls Bergson's claim that "we speak more than we think, as we are *acted upon* rather than act ourselves" [*RV*, 26], a line that beautifully describes the effects of Luxemburg inhabiting Sorel's language)—it is important to register that there are elements of Sorel's argument that correspond with Benjamin's and Luxemburg's conceptions of revolution. Like Luxemburg, Sorel here suggests that defeat can becomes a means of furthering the work of the revolutionary—since it can be a kind of preparation for future action. At the same time, his insistence on the mythic character of the general strike is something both Benjamin and Luxemburg would bristle at.

24. Benjamin registers the link between Sorel's insistence on myth and the violence of fascism in an interview that he conducts with Valois in 1927 and that he later reports. There, in a discussion on dictatorship, he declares that Sorelianist socialism is perhaps the best school for fascism. While there are moments in his violence essay in which he seems to believe that Sorel actually cautions against violence—as when he notes that "[w]ith thought-provoking arguments Sorel has explained the extent to which such a rigorous conception of the general strike is liable to diminish the deployment of violence in revolutions" (*CV*, 53)—his suspicion of Sorel's insistence on the myth of both Marxism and the general strike is already legible in his earlier essay. In his report on his interview with Valois, he even wonders whether—departing

from Sorel's theorization of the mass strike, but still wanting the revolution to be a mass movement—Valois deploys the "trick" of the rhetoric of "bloodless revolution" in order to justify the "great upheavals of the postwar period," a point that implicitly suggests that Sorel himself took advantage of this same rhetoric. Benjamin registers the possibility of Sorelian-inflected violence in tangible fashion when, during his interview, his "gaze falls upon a revolver that my discussant [Valois] has left lying in front of him on his desk," and he quickly cuts his interview short. See Benjamin, "Für die Diktatur: Interview mit Georges Valois" (*GS*, 4:490–491).

25. Trotsky, "A Requiem for Karl Liebknecht and Rosa Luxemburg," https://www.marxists.org/archive/trotsky/profiles/rosa.htm.

26. Ibid.

27. Rosa Luxemburg, "Order Reigns in Berlin!," trans. Peggy Fallen Wright, in *The Rosa Luxemburg Reader*, ed. Peter Hudis and Kevin B. Anderson (New York: Monthly Review Press, 2004), 376–378.

VI. PANORAMAS OF VIOLENCE

1. Jacqueline Rose, *On Violence and on Violence against Women* (New York: Farrar, Straus and Giroux, 2021), 199.

2. In two texts that Benjamin wrote in consecutive days in Ibiza in 1933—both under the same title, "Agesilaus Santander"—he develops a theory of secret names that resonates with his interest in Luxemburg here. Among other things, he suggests that names, secret or not, are always metamorphosing (they can never "remain the same and untransformed"), and that the identity of the person to whom they would refer is also constantly changing, undergoing a displacement, and becoming something else. Walter Benjamin, "Agesilaus Santander (Second Version)," in Benjamin, *Selected Writings*, vol. 2: *1927–1934*, ed. Michael W. Jennings, Howard Eiland, and Gary Smith (Cambridge, MA: Belknap Press of Harvard University Press, 1999), 714–715. Indeed, in Benjamin's violence essay, Luxemburg cannot be identified with a single name, since both her and any name used to refer to her are in constant metamorphosis—like the mass strike itself.

3. For a detailed reconstruction of the events of the night of the assassinations of Luxemburg and Liebknecht and of the subsequent efforts to protect the murderers, see Klaus Gietinger's *The Murder of Rosa Luxemburg*, trans. Loren Balhorn (New York: Verso Books, 2019).

4. We need only think of the millions of European political refugees that Benjamin will join at the end of his life, or of the contemporary nomenclature of "illegal immigrant" or "*sans-papiers*."

5. Michelle Ty, "Benjamin on the Border," *Critical Times* 2, no. 2 (August 2019), 311–312.

6. For a beautiful meditation on Luxemburg's relation to both nature and politics, see John Berger,

"A Letter to Rosa Luxemburg," *New Statesman*, September 18, 2015, https://www.newstatesman.com/long-reads/2015/09letter-rosa-luxemburg-0.

7. It is worth noting that the Monument to the Revolution that Fuchs commissioned Mies van der Rohe to build was constructed in 1926 in the Friederichsfelde cemetery in the outskirts of Berlin. It consisted of an unadorned horizontal, solid brick construction that, in its appearance, resembled a prison and an execution wall—Mies insisted that this was intentional. It was financed through the sale of postcards depicting a photomontage of a model for the monument, but was above all a nonhierarchical structure. The number of bricks and the number of revolutionaries buried on the site served as an architectural translation of the revolution that belied its failure by inscribing it in Berlin's collective memory—many of the bricks had been assembled from the bullet-riddled remains, in some places piled some twenty feet high, of buildings damaged or destroyed during the Spartacist uprising. The bricks also were meant to evoke labor and the process of massification, both concerns of the Spartacists. In his speech of June 11, 1926, Wilhem Pieck, the only communist leader to survive his arrest by the Freikorps, stated that "the monument rises simple, massive, imposing like the revolutionary power of the proletariat and in the spirit of Freiligrath's words: *I was, I am, I shall be*." Nevertheless, the monument was still considered somewhat abstract. Because of this, both the red flag and Freiligrath's quote were often temporarily installed on the site or photomontaged in reproductions. It was heavily damaged in 1933 and the Nazi party ordered its demolition in 1935. It had to be demolished brick by brick because it was reinforced with cement and because blasting such a structure would have endangered the entire area. See Andrea Contursi, *Mies van der Rohe's Monument to the November Revolution in Berlin-Lichtenberg* (Bari: Ilios Editore, 2018), 59.

8. Rosa Luxemburg, *The Letters of Rosa Luxemburg*, ed. Georg Adler, Peter Hudis, and Annelies Laschitza, trans. George Shriver (London: Verso, 2011), 456–458. For an account of the afterlife of this particular letter in the writings of Karl Kraus and Benjamin, see Lori Turner, "Kraus and Benjamin on Luxemburg: The Contemporaneous Reception of Luxemburg's Büffelhaut Letter," *Prometheus* (Spring 2021), https://prometheus journal.org/2021/03/17/kraus-and-benjamin-on-luxemburg/. Benjamin refers to the letter as late as 1934 in a letter to Scholem in which he defends his relation to communism against his friend's admonishment. That he returns to the letter suggests once more how affected he had been by it—and by Luxemburg herself.

9. J. P. Nettl, *Rosa Luxemburg*, abridged edition (New York: Oxford University Press, 1969), 250.

10. While Luxemburg is associated with this slogan, she most likely borrowed it from Karl Kautsky. Nevertheless, in her 1915 *The Junius Pamphlet*:

The Crisis in German Social Democracy, she mis-attributes the line to Engels. She writes:

> Friedrich Engels once said: "Capitalist society faces a dilemma, either an advance to socialism or a reversion to barbarism." ... We have read and repeated these words thoughtlessly without a conception of their terrible import. At this moment one glance about us will show us what a reversion to barbarism in capitalist society means. *This world war* means a reversion to barbarism. The triumph of imperialism leads to the destruction of culture, sporadically during a modern war, and forever, if the period of world wars that has just begun is allowed to take its damnable course to the last ultimate consequence. Thus we stand today, as Friedrich Engels prophesied more than a generation ago, before the awful proposition: Either the triumph of imperialism and the destruction of all culture, and, as in ancient Rome, depopulation, desolation, degeneration, a vast cemetery; or, the victory of socialism, that is, the conscious struggle of the international proletariat against imperialism, against its methods, against war.

See *The Rosa Luxemburg Reader,* 321. Scholars have been unable to find an equivalent line in Engels and, because Luxemburg is writing her pamphlet in prison, without her library, it is not surprising that she could have misremembered her source, which would seem to be Kautsky's 1892 *The Class Struggle (Erfurt Program).* Although Luxemburg repeatedly criticizes Kautsky for his complicity with the worst elements of the Social Democratic Party, this book was one of the most widely read texts of socialism throughout Europe and she surely knew it. Kautsky's commentary was translated into sixteen languages before 1914 and it became the accepted account of Marxism at the time. In chapter 4 of his book, entitled "The Commonwealth of the Future," he writes: "If indeed the socialist commonwealth were an impossibility, then mankind would be cut off from all further economic development. In that event modern society would decay, as did the Roman empire nearly two thousand years ago, and finally relapse into barbarism. As things stand today capitalist civilization cannot continue; we must either move forward into socialism or fall back into barbarism." (See https://www.marxists.org/archive/kautsky /1892/erfurt/.) Luxemburg's reanimation of this source in her famous Spartacist slogan resonates just as deeply today as it did during the first World War.

VII. DEPOSITIONS

1. Judith Butler, *Parting Ways: Jewishness and the Critique of Zionism* (New York: Columbia University Press, 2012), 81.

2. Part of the Hebrew Bible, Numbers was not conceived as a book—even if it is traditionally referred to as one. What we have instead has a long and complex history and was most likely assembled and edited into its present form on the basis of various sources sometime in the early fifth century. The diversity of these source materials complicates the possibility of determining either its origins or its date. The text presents itself as an amalgam of literary genres—legal material, ritual prescriptions, historical narratives, poetic folk traditions, and different censuses—and simply takes its name from the first words of the text.

3. Talmudic study here refers to the rabbinic debates on the teachings of the Torah (the first five books of the Bible, one of which is the book of Numbers). While Benjamin had little access to Hebrew, he would have been interested in the multiplicity of readings that were generated by the Torah, and by its companion texts in the Hebrew Bible.

4. Numbers 16:28–35, in *The Hebrew Bible: A Translation with Commentary,* vol. 1: *The Five Books of Moses,* trans. Robert Alter (New York: W. W. Norton, 2019), 533–537. Further references to Numbers refer to this edition and will be noted parenthetically by chapter and verse.

5. David Lloyd, "Rage against the Divine," *South Atlantic Quarterly* 106, no. 2 (Spring 2007), 352.

6. On this point, see Adam Y. Stern's "On Zionism and the Concept of Deferral," *Critical Times* 5, no. 1 (April 2022), 34.

7. Peter Fenves, "Introduction," in *CV,* 33.

8. For an excellent and rather extended reading of this essay, see Werner Hamacher, "Guilt History: Benjamin's Sketch 'Capitalism as Religion,'" *Diacritics* 32, no. 3–4 (Fall-Winter 2002), 81–106.

9. Fenves, "Introduction," 56 and 34.

10. Jacqueline Rose, "What More Could We Want of Ourselves!," *London Review of Books* 33, no. 12 (June 16, 2011), https://www.lrb.co.uk/the-paper /v33/n12/jacqueline-rose/what-more-could-we -want-of-ourselves.

11. Werner Hamacher, "Affirmative Strike," trans. Dana Hollander, *Cardozo Law Review* 13 (1991–1992), 1155, fn. 44.

12. Ariella Azoulay, "The Loss of Critique and the Critique of Violence," *Cardozo Law Review* 27, no. 3 (2005–2006), 1037.

13. As Willem Styfhals has noted,

> Some well-known concepts from Benjamin's early writings—messianic time, fate, law, and justice—were actually developed dialogically in conversations between Benjamin and Scholem. These concepts that Benjamin used in essays such as "Fate and Character" or "Critique of Violence" can indeed be understood in relation to Scholem's earlier use of them in his diaries, in his notes from his time in Switzerland, and particularly in the essay on Jonah. Claiming that the origin

of these key concepts is dialogical neither suggests that Benjamin's and Scholem's concepts completely coincided in the 1910s and early 1920s nor that they continued using them in the same way in their later work. It only suggests that the *specific* ideas Scholem and Benjamin shared cannot be univocally attributed to either one of these thinkers but that their meaning arose in conversations, with each participant adding important conceptual layers.

See Willem Styfhals, "Predicting the Present: Gershom Scholem on Prophecy," *Journal of Jewish Thought and Philosophy* 28 (2020), 262–263. Unpublished during his lifetime, the German text of Scholem's essay "Über Jona und den Begriff der Gerechtigkeit" can be found in Gershom Scholem, *Tagebücher nebst Aufsätzen und Entwürfen bis 1923*, ed. Herbert Kopp-Oberstebrink, Karlfried Gründer, Friedrich Niewöhner, and Karl E. Grözinger, vol. 2 (Frankfurt: Jüdischer Verlag, 1995), 522–532. That Scholem's and Benjamin's writings are often interwoven with one another, especially around ethico-theological issues, points to the difficulty of asserting originary authorship in any context, since reading and writing are always collaborative.

14. Noting that Scholem's essay "combines philosophical speculation with a biblical commentary on the book of Jonah," Styfhals offers a concise summary of the biblical story. As he explains:

The book tells the story of the prophet Jonah who is supposed to prophesy to the citizens of Nineveh that God has decided to destroy their city because of its moral decadence. ... In Scholem's interpretation, the book of Jonah indeed recounts the story of a failed prophet. Jonah initially attempts to escape his divine calling and refuses to bring the prophecy to Nineveh. He flees God by boat, but he is soon caught in a storm at sea. Realizing that Jonah is to blame for the storm, the sailors throw him overboard and he is eaten by a large fish. In the fish's belly, Jonah prays to God to save him and he promises to deliver the prophecy after all, whereupon the fish spits him out again. When Jonah finally prophesies in Nineveh about the imminent catastrophe, its citizens decide to repent and change their ways, hoping to avert the disaster that Jonah announced. God indeed changes his mind and decides not to destroy Nineveh after all. His judgment is deferred and Jonah's prophecy fails. Scholem's commentary attaches great significance to this moment of deferment (*Aufschub*) and failure, which he considered "structurally the center" of the book. Jonah, for his part, questions God's decision and becomes angry with him. Since God did not execute the judgment about Nineveh that he asked Jonah

to prophesy about, Jonah feels that God has deceived him. But God responds that Jonah has no right to be angry and points out that he refused to show any concern for the citizens of Nineveh.

Ibid., 263–264.

15. Gershom Scholem, "On Jonah and the Concept of Justice," trans. Eric J. Schwab, *Critical Inquiry* 25 (Winter 1999), 357.

16. Ibid., 356.

17. Here we invoke Nietzsche's famous passage about the need to always have a doer behind the deed, something he views as fictional: "Just as the popular mind separates the lightning from the flash and takes the latter for an action, for the operation of a subject called lightning, so popular morality also separates strength from expression of strength, as if there were a neutral substratum behind the strong man, which was *free* to express strength or not to do so. But there is no such substratum; there is no 'being' behind doing, effecting, becoming; the 'doer' is merely a fiction added to the deed—the deed is everything." See Friedrich Nietzsche, *On the Genealogy of Morals*, trans. Walter Kaufmann and R. J. Hollingdale, ed. Walter Kaufmann (New York: Vintage Books, 1989), 45.

18. Scholem, "On Jonah and the Concept of Justice," 358–359.

19. Marc Caplan, "Arnold Schoenberg's Jewish Trauerspiel: Aesthetics, Allegory, and Ethics in *Moses und Aron*," *Modernism/modernity* 28, no. 3 (September 2021), 565.

20. Scholem, "Jonah and the Concept of Justice," 355 and 360.

21. Ibid. On the figure of the "storm of forgiveness" in Benjamin, see Butler, *Parting Ways*, 92–98, and Hamacher, "Guilt History," 101–105.

22. Scholem, "Jonah and the Concept of Justice," 357, translation modified.

23. Walter Benjamin, "On Language as Such and on the Language of Man," trans. Edmund Jephcott, in Benjamin, *Selected Writings*, vol. 1: *1913–1926*, ed. Michael W. Jennings, Howard Eiland, and Gary Smith (Cambridge, MA: Belknap Press of Harvard University Press, 1996), 70 and 64.

24. These indices are the same for both Hiller and Benjamin; as Lisa Marie Anderson sumarizes in her preface to her translation of Hiller's "Anti-Cain," they include the German Revolution and its deposing of Kaiser Wilhelm II, the splintering of revolutionary factions into either the more centrist Social Democrats or soviet-style councils, the counterrevolutionary violence of the Freikorps, mass strikes and demonstrations in Berlin that resulted in street violence, armed conflicts among the Social Democrats, the USPD and the KPD, and the Spartacist uprising. See Lisa Marie Anderson, "Kurt Hiller, 'Anti-Cain: A Postscript to Rudolf Leonhard's "Our Final Battle against Weapons,"' Translator's Preface," in Walter Benjamin, *Toward the Critique of Violence: A Critical Edition*, ed. Peter

Fenves and Julia Ng (Stanford: Stanford University Press, 2021), 179.

25. Because Hiller does not see a contradiction between his activism on behalf of gay rights and especially abortion rights and his activism against violence and murder of any kind in the name of the "sanctity of life," he is an interesting figure to consider in relation to current debates over abortion and, in particular, the "right to life" movement.

26. Anderson, "Kurt Hiller, Translator's Preface," 181–182.

27. Kurt Hiller, "Anti-Cain: A Postscript to Rudolf Leonhard's 'Our Final Battle against Weapons,'" trans. Lisa Marie Anderson, in Benjamin, *Toward the Critique of Violence: A Critical Edition*, 193. It is worth noting that, while Hiller defines "life" as more than an "idea"—as something that cannot be reduced to an idea—his language nevertheless depends on a dematerialized conception of "life." It is precisely through this abstraction, determination, and reduction of life's simultaneously experiential and immanent complexities that Hiller signals his distance from Benjamin. Indeed, by contrast, Benjamin is always careful to avoid any manner of linguistic simplification or curtailment, and this because he knows that the political is hidden in plain sight in every sentence, if not in each word choice.

28. Despite the clear resonances between them, the different stakes of Scholem's and Benjamin's reading of the commandment as a "guideline" that demands personal interpretation and responsibility become apparent in Benjamin's use of the adjective "terrible." While Scholem stays within the parameters of faith and morality, never crossing the threshold of transgression, Benjamin takes the leap into the possibility of political violence, understanding the need, "in terrible cases," to disregard the commandment in response to contingent circumstances that transform the meaning of the violent deed. However, in a passage from Scholem's early diaries, the latter displays his ongoing dialogue with Benjamin, Hiller, and the political emergencies of his time in ways that are in keeping with the radicalized and antibourgeois context of Weimar intellectual circles. In a version of Marxist Zionism, Scholem writes:

> We as Zionists are pure people and want nothing to do with the wickedness and the baseness of this universal slaughter [of the First World War] ... the time can be called "great" only when the commandment "thou shalt not kill" is upheld ... we will not be dazzled by the chatter of university professors, we, the agents of the proletariat of yearning!

Cited in Amir Engel, *Gershom Scholem: An Intellectual Biography* (Chicago: University of Chicago Press, 2017), 38.

29. Hiller, "Anti-Cain," 186.

VIII. THEOLOGICAL FIGURATIONS

1. Walter Benjamin, "Capitalism as Religion," trans. Rodney Livingstone, in Benjamin, *Selected Writings*, vol. 1: *1913–1926*, ed. Michael W. Jennings, Howard Eiland, and Gary Smith (Cambridge, MA: Belknap Press of Harvard University Press, 1996), 289 (translation modified).

2. That Benjamin's insistence on the relation between historical materialism and theology at the same time requires a reconceptualization of historical materialism—a reconceptualization that remains a task throughout his work, as he insists on distancing himself from any party definition of the term—is made clear in the first thesis of "The Concept of History." There he famously describes an automaton chess player that wins not because this mechanical contraption can outwit any opponent but because, through a system of mirrors, it hides a "hunchbacked dwarf" who is a master chess player inside it. As Benjamin writes, "[o]ne can imagine a philosophic counterpart to this apparatus. The puppet, called 'historical materialism,' is to win all the time. It can easily be a match for anyone if it enlists the services of theology, which today, as we know, is small and ugly and has to keep out of sight" (*CH*, 389). Benjamin's conception of "historical materialism" goes against the slogan of "historical materialism"—that it is a slogan is announced by putting the phrase in quotation marks and also by referring to it as a "puppet" *called* "historical materialism," suggesting that the phrase itself is manipulated and mobilized by the left without "a consciousness of the present which explodes the continuum of history" (Benjamin, *Selected Writings*, vol. 3: *1935–1938*, ed. Howard Eiland and Michael W. Jennings [Cambridge, MA: Belknap Press of Harvard University Press, 2002], 262). Historical materialism is a method of reading historically that is neither epic, universal, nor subservient to histories written from the perspective of the victors, which can include a theology able to pull historical materialism's strings.

3. Jameson cites this response in a discussion that emphasizes Benjamin's sense of "completeness" as a "secular synonym for the theological idea of fulfillment" (*BF*, 232), in which the incompleteness of the past is completed in the future. That the secular and the theological form a kind of couple here helps explain why Benjamin's language can be simultaneously theological and atheological.

4. In a letter of September 16, 1924, Benjamin writes to Scholem from Capri about the importance of these two encounters. In particular, he emphasizes the closeness of Lukács's book to his own political and literary interests: "I wrote you that several references converged: a reference to Lukács's book joined one of a private nature. While proceeding from political considerations, Lukács arrives at principles that are, at least in part, epistemological and perhaps not as far reaching as I first assumed. The book astonished

355

me because these principles resonate for me or validate my own thinking." "Regarding communism," he goes on to say, "the problem with 'theory and practice' seems to me in effect to be that, given the disparity that must be preserved between these two realms, any definitive insight into theory is precisely dependent on practice" (C, 247–248). He reiterates his admiration of Lukács in a list of recent readings in which he describes *History and Class Consciousness* as "an extraordinary collection of Lukács's political writings" (C, 268). In particular, he appreciates Lukács's understanding of the relation between theory and practice, between what he calls "the critical situation of class struggle and an impending concrete revolution" and "the last word in theoretic knowledge" (GS, 3:171). On his return to Berlin from Capri in December 1924, he again writes to Scholem: the communist signals of which he had written to him earlier, he tells him, "were indications of a change that awakened in me the will not to mask the actual and political elements of my ideas in the Old Franconian way I did before, but also to develop them by experimenting and taking extreme measures ... my surprise at the various points of contact I have with radical Bolshevist theory has of course been renewed" (C, 257–258).

Claiming that he is astonished by the closeness between Lukács and his thinking, that he is surprised by the promixity of his thinking to that of radical Bolshevist ideas, Benjamin emphasizes the experimentation and extremity with which he will develop the "political elements" of his ideas. Given our interests, it is not an accident that Lukács's *History and Class Consciousness* is entirely mediated by Luxemburg. He not only devotes two of his chapters to her, but he also states at the outset that "Rosa Luxemburg's thought is necessary" and that "a truly revolutionary, Communist and Marxist position can be acquired only through a critical confrontation with the theoretical life's work of Rosa Luxemburg" (Georg Lukács, *History and Class Consciousness: Studies in Marxist Dialectics*, trans. Rodney Livingstone [Cambridge, MA: MIT Press, 1972], xlii). Lukács's privileging of Luxemburg resonates for Benjamin because it also validates his thinking—it confirms his sense of her singular importance within the history of Marxism and, in particular, in Germany. Like Benjamin, Lukács registers Luxemburg's deep engagement with Marxist thought and praxis, her elaboration of the entanglement of theory and practice and victory and defeat, the centrality of the proletarian masses to her conviction of the possibility of revolution, the destructiveness of capitalism, and the violence and significance of her assassination. Referencing her murder at the end of his second chapter, "The Marxism of Rosa Luxemburg"—written in January 1921, the same month that Benjamin finishes his "Critique of Violence" essay—Lukács writes:

Her death at the hands of her bitterest enemies, Noske and Scheidemann, is, logically, the crowning pinnacle of her thought and life. Theoretically she had predicted the defeat of the January rising years before it took place; tactically she foresaw it at the moment of action. Yet she remained consistently on the side of the masses and shared their fate. That is to say, the unity of theory and practice was preserved in her actions with exactly the same consistency and with exactly the same logic as that which earned her the enmity of her murderers: the opportunists of Social Democracy.

See Lukács, *History and Class Consciousness*, 44. Even though Benjamin's encounters with Lukács and Lacis may have "awakened" in him "the will not to mask the actual and political elements of [his] ideas in the Old Franconian way [he] did before"—as when he silently entombs Luxemburg in his violence essay and presents her through the masks of Sorel, Niobe, and the "great criminal" in an almost medieval, allegorical mode of presentation—he will never overcome his suspicion of direct presentation. He will continue to navigate his way through the historico-political domain—which for him must be thought in relation to Luxemburg's reading, and therefore Marx's reading, of the violent unfolding of the history of capitalism—with the readerly and writerly strategies of indirection that he puts into motion from his earliest writings. For a reading of the relation between theory and practice through the lens of Lukács's literary writings—a reading that offers another way to understand Lukács's relation to Benjamin—see Sara Nadal-Melsió, "Georg Lukács: Magus Realismus?," *Diacritics* 34, no. 2 (Summer 2004), 62–84.

5. See Walter Benjamin, *Briefe*, vol. 1, ed. Gershom Scholem and Theodor W. Adorno (Frankfurt am Main: Suhrkamp Verlag, 1966), 355.

6. Ibid., 376.

7. In regard to Benjamin's red flag, it is hard not to think of one of the most striking scenes in Charlie Chaplin's 1936 film *Modern Times*, which marked the final appearance of the Little Tramp, who, on this occasion, is described simply as a "factory worker." The film was released while Benjamin was again at work on his "Work of Art" essay, now in its third, and still unfinished, version. Although Benjamin does not mention the film in his essay, it is impossible not to see echoes of it scattered throughout the images of his sentences. As is the case with Gracián in his *Trauerspiel* book, Benjamin seems to have absorbed the cinematic and conceptual movements of Chaplin's film so deeply that he can simply mime them in the essay's performative philosophical and political strategies.

In the black-and-white silent film, after a scene of unprovoked police brutality, the now unemployed Tramp picks up a rag that has fallen out of a truck, put there presumably to warn nearby pedestrians of the possible danger of falling cargo and, therefore, we are led to assume, red. A few seconds later, unbeknownst to the Tramp, his little flag becomes the banner of a communist demonstration he finds himself now heading (we are at this point certain as to the color of the flag). He is taken to be the leader of the demonstration and arrested, one of many more arrests to take place in the film. However, throughout the film, unlike the little red flag, the color red (as an index of revolution but also of violence, danger, and generalized uncertainty) does not disappear, but rather spills over and continues to saturate the remaining scenes of the director's first openly political film. Nonetheless, unlike Benjamin or Chaplin, the Tramp has no agency in the role he plays, as he misreads or remains oblivious to the context of his actions in an uncertain world where meaning is in flux. In this way, the Tramp functions like a misplaced sign that the audience reads to comic effect. Indeed, it is through the figure's refusal to identify, through his negation of the possibility of individual agency, that the impersonality of his characterization becomes mobilized: the Little Tramp never identifies with anything so that the audience can identify with him, or rather with the void he signals by being out of place, and often, as is the case in *Modern Times,* also out of time.

8. The English translation of this passage introduces an ambiguity that is absent in the original German. In the English, Benjamin's question to Scholem about his imagined red flag could be: (1) Do you want to prevent me from hanging a red flag out of my window by *me* saying that it is only a little piece of cloth? or (2) Do you want to prevent me from hanging a red flag out of my window by *you* saying that it is only a little piece of cloth? In a note from October 8, 2021, Gerhard Richter explains that the ambiguity of the English in regard to the subject of the second clause in "do you want to prevent me from hanging a red flag out of my window, saying that it is only a little piece of cloth?" disappears in the original German, since "Benjamin's use of the subjunctive mood refers the saying or speaking back to his interlocutor [Scholem]: 'willst Du mir mit dem Hinweis, das sei ja nichts als ein Fetzen Tuch, verwehren, die rote Fahne zum Fenster herauszuhängen?'" "An overly literal translation," Richter goes on to note, "would read: 'Do you want to keep me from hanging the red flag from my [or out of my] window through the observation [or hint; or piece of advice] that it is [*sei*] nothing but a scrap of cloth.' The subjunctive form 'sei' clearly acts as a report on Scholem's (real or imagined) speech act, an act from which Benjamin distances himself precisely by using the subjunctive (he could simply have used 'ist' here, which would have placed him in closer proximity to what he is reporting). And 'mit dem Hinweis' ('with' in the sense of 'by means of' the observation/hint/

piece of advice from Scholem) attributes a kind of instrumentality to Scholem from which Benjamin distances himself—precisely in the very noninstrumentalizable manner that the letter seems to develop." We are grateful to Richter for his time and thoughtfulness here.

9. Red is the most important color in Benjamin's political *Farbenlehre*. It appears in many of the most significant moments in his oeuvre and it is consonant with, and an elaboration of, the red that appears in the Baraka line we evoke in our introduction: "The Red what reading did re adding reproducing revolution." Benjamin's insistence on red can be read as what he calls elsewhere a "red inkblot" (*GS*, 6:29). Like the theology that permeates his thought like ink on a blotter, the color red permeates his writings like a red thread of ink that, circulating as the lifeblood of his work, weaves together his meditations on language, perception, thought, experience, reproducibility, messianism, race, and revolution. In the more than two dozen texts that he writes on color from 1915 to the early 1920s, red appears as the color of transience, movement, alteration, and, most strikingly, of expressionlessness, which Benjamin later associates with the general strike. This means that red does not designate anything in a determinate fashion but instead comes with the force of destabilization. We might remember that red is a verb in German, *Erröten*, and Benjamin is particularly interested in red as a process of coloration, in what it would mean, that is, to "redden" the world. As he puts it in his short text "Über die Scham," the "color of shame is pure: its red is neither colorful nor color but coloration. It is the red of transition" (*GS*, 6:71). "The redness of shame," he adds in the text's last line, is the "[e]xpressionlessly signifying appearance of transition" (ibid.). This redness does not belong to a subject—it always falls from the outside and is never an expression of anything interior (it "announces absolutely nothing inward" [*GS*, 6:69])—and it signals a subtle violence against determination in general.

Benjamin's sustained fascination with red as a color that is experienced as mood, intensity, and movement *before* it gets more explicitly politicized in his *Moscow Diary* already provides us with a glimpse of the features that precede and augur what a revolutionary politics would be like: transitory, violent, impersonal, unable to be formalized in language, even if at the same time it is never mute or without voices. While red is already marked politically for Benjamin in his engagement with Luxemburg and the Spartacists—and in his readings of Marx and others—red is the primary color of his visit to Moscow in the mid-1920s. The most visible color in this postrevolutionary landscape, it is the "predominant" color in classrooms, with their images of Soviet stars and heads of Lenin. It is visible in the Red Army, in the state flag, in the symbols of the revolution, in the radiant colored rags, Chinese paper fans and kites, colored wooden toys for sale in the streets, and even in the red traffic lights that Benjamin sees as he walks in the boulevards. In Moscow, experience is mediated by red and, in his essay "Moscow," he notes that, in Russian, "'red' and 'beautiful' are *one* word" (Walter Benjamin, "Moscow," trans. Edmund Jephcott, in Benjamin, *Selected Writings*, vol. 2: *1927–1934*, ed. Michael W. Jennings, Howard Eiland, and Gary Smith [Cambridge, MA: Belknap Press of Harvard University Press, 1999], 33).

The usual trajectory of red in Communist Party politics, where it represents and identifies something that already exists, gets reversed by Benjamin. For him, red, in the experience of its transience, tells us something about how a revolutionary politics might be experienced: fugitive and violent, beautiful in its rising and falling, like the red dawns and sunsets that also punctuate Benjamin's writings, and belonging to no one in particular. This red that is never just a color signals a mood, an inkblot, that permeates and intensifies history in the direction of revolution. There would be much more to say here—even about the redness of Benjamin's Messiah—but we return to Benjamin's red *Farbenlehre* in a forthcoming essay titled "Red Benjamin."

IX. MESSIANIC PROMISES

1. Werner Hamacher, "Messianic Not," trans. Catharine Diehl, in *Messianic Thought Outside Theology*, ed. Anna Glazova and Paul North (New York: Fordham University Press, 2014), 227.

2. Jacques Derrida, *Specters of Marx: The State of the Debt, the Work of Mourning and the New International*, trans. Peggy Kamuf (New York: Routledge, 1994), 74.

3. Walter Benjamin, "Theological-Political Fragment," trans. Edmund Jephcott, in Benjamin, *Selected Writings*, vol. 3: *1935–1938*, ed. Howard Eiland and Michael W. Jennings (Cambridge, MA: Belknap Press of Harvard University Press, 2002), 306.

4. Werner Hamacher, "'Now': Walter Benjamin and Historical Time," in *Walter Benjamin and History*, ed. Andrew Benjamin (London: Continuum, 2005), 40–41.

5. Ibid., 38.

6. Walter Benjamin, "Surrealism: The Last Snapshot of the European Intelligentsia," trans. Rodney Livingstone, in Benjamin, *Selected Writings*, vol. 2: *1927–1934*, ed. Michael W. Jennings, Howard Eiland, and Gary Smith (Cambridge, MA: Belknap Press of Harvard University Press, 1999), 216.

7. Ibid.

8. Walter Benjamin, "Capitalism as Religion," trans. Rodney Livingstone, in Benjamin, *Selected Writings*, vol. 1: *1913–1926*, ed. Michael W. Jennings, Howard Eiland, and Gary Smith (Cambridge, MA: Belknap Press of Harvard University Press, 1996), 289.

9. Benjamin, "Theological-Political Fragment," 305.

10. Walter Benjamin, "Paralipomena to 'On the Concept of History,'" trans. Edmund Jephcott and Howard Eiland, in Benjamin, *Selected Writings*, vol. 4: *1938–1940*, ed. Howard Eiland and Michael W. Jennings (Cambridge, MA: Belknap Press of Harvard University Press, 2003), 402.

11. Walter Benjamin, "The Work of Art in the Age of Its Technological Reproducibility (Second Version)," trans. Edmund Jephcott and Harry Zohn, in *The Work of Art in the Age of Its Technological Reproducibility, and Other Writings on Media*, ed. Michael W. Jennings, Brigid Doherty, and Thomas Y. Levin (Cambridge, MA: Belknap Press of Harvard University Press, 2008), 50.

12. Walter Benjamin, "An Outsider Makes His Mark," trans. Rodney Livingstone, in Benjamin, *Selected Writings*, 2:309. For Jameson's citation of this passage, see *BF*, 240.

13. Franz Kafka, "The Coming of the Messiah," trans. Clement Greenberg, in *Parables and Paradoxes*, bilingual edition (New York: Schocken Books, 1961), 81.

14. It is interesting that, however central Kafka is to Benjamin—and he is absolutely critical—Benjamin associates this possibility less with Prague than with Moscow—at least within the urban topologies that Jameson traces so beautifully in his "Space and the City" chapter. Indeed, according to Jameson, Benjamin associates Moscow with "the experience of [the] struggle to emerge into a post-bourgeois, post-individualistic future" (*BF*, 118).

15. Walter Benjamin, "Fate and Character," trans. Rodney Livingstone, in Benjamin, *Selected Writings*, vol. 1: *1913–1926*, ed. Michael W. Jennings, Howard Eiland, and Gary Smith (Cambridge, MA: Belknap Press of Harvard University Press, 1996), 204 (translation modified). For the German, see Benjamin, *GS*, 2.1:175.

X. BENJAMIN'S BOXES

1. Anne Carson, *Autobiography of Red: A Novel in Verse* (New York: Vintage Books, 1998), 7.

2. Jameson associates Benjamin's concept of redemption to the early Christian concept of *apocatastasis*: "The redemption of the dead—the very phrase comes close to that breathtaking orthodox belief called apocatastasis, in which, after the trumpet of the Last Judgment, all of the dead of human history, sinners as well as saved without exception, will rise from the grave all equally redeemed, in some final and definitive bodily resurrection" (*BF*, 231). As Michael W. Jennings has noted, "[i]n the first section of the convolute labeled 'social movement' in *The Arcades Project*, Benjamin speaks of the 'will to apokatastasis' as the resolve to gather again, in revolutionary action and in revolutionary thinking, precisely the elements of the 'too early' and the 'too late' of 'the first beginning and the final

decay.'" "The will to apokatastasis," he adds, "is in this sense *the* political will, the will to bring an end to what is in the hope that, in a cosmological turn, something better might succeed it." See Michael W. Jennings, "The Will to Apokatastasis: Media, Experience, and Eschatology in Walter Benjamin's Late Theological Politics," in *Walter Benjamin and Theology*, ed. Colby Dickinson and Stéphane Symons (New York: Fordham University Press, 2016), 98.

3. Walter Benjamin, "Agesilaus Santander (Second Version)," trans. Rodney Livingstone, in Benjamin, *Selected Writings*, vol. 2: *1927–1934*, ed. Michael W. Jennings, Howard Eiland, and Gary Smith (Cambridge, MA: Belknap Press of Harvard University Press, 1999), 715.

4. Benjamin's longstanding relation to Klee's painting is well known. He purchased the work in 1921 in Munich and kept it close to him until just before his death. He experienced it not as a possession, but, more strongly, as a companion, an interlocutor, even a comrade of sorts. During his exile in France and under threat of persecution by the Nazis, he considered selling the monoprint in order to finance his travels to the United States, but, in the end, he could not part with it. Just before leaving France, he left the work with the writer Georges Bataille, then an archivist and librarian at the Bibliothèque Nationale in Paris, who kept it until the liberation. After the war, it was passed along to Adorno, who was then in New York, and, a few years after Adorno's death in 1969, it went, not without controversy, to Gershom Scholem. In 1987, after Scholem's death, Scholem's widow donated the work to the Israel Museum in Jerusalem. That the work should find itself in Jerusalem after a migrant life that followed the itineraries of exile—and whose traces included not simply the hands through which it passed but also all the contexts in which it existed and all the events that took place during the years it was in Benjamin's possession—is itself a detail to be read. Benjamin's own ambivalence toward Israel as a political concept, his critique of Zionism and the internalized racism of its origins and, in particular, of its arguments about "blood and experience," can be said to be inscribed in the humble object that Klee's small monoprint is (Gershom Scholem, *Walter Benjamin: The Story of a Friendship* [London: Faber and Faber, 1982], 28–29). Benjamin makes this critique even clearer in a letter to Scholem from October 22, 1917. There, drawing a link between a certain racism common to both Zionism and anti-Semitism, he writes: "a principal component of *vulgar* anti-Semitic as well as Zionist ideology is that the gentile's hatred of the Jew is physiologically substantiated on the basis of instinct and race, since it turns against the physis" (*C*, 99).

Although Benjamin never traveled to Palestine, his writings have been a resource for writers and activists arguing for Palestinian rights in the face of Israel's occupation and acts of dispossession. As David Lloyd has noted, "Whatever [Benjamin] foresaw before its foundation about the predictably racist evolution of the so-called 'Jewish State,' ... there can be little doubt that Benjamin would have recognized in the current state of Israel and its occupation that 'state of emergency' that his last writing recognized to be the permanent state of the oppressed." David Lloyd, "Walter Benjamin in Palestine," *Savage Minds: Notes and Queries in Anthropology* (February 10, 2016), https://savageminds.org/2016/02/10/walter-benjamin-in-palestine/#fn-18878-2. There is a certain irony in this world-historical image—it is perhaps the most widely discussed artwork in the history of philosophy in the twentieth century, circulating as an emblem and in a way that far exceeds the boundaries of any museum or gallery—now finding itself inside a cultural institution that has rather singular relations to a project of violent settler colonialism. At the same time, this image—forever entangled with Benjamin's reading of it—remains a witness to all the history, violence, catastrophic wreckage, and even the future that Benjamin inscribed within it. If this angel is unable to redeem this wreckage or to overturn past violence, it exists as a wish to "awaken the dead and make whole what has been smashed," and, in Benjamin's mind, this can only be possible by considering the acts of reflection and reading this angel continues to demand, its refusal to become a quiet and fully aestheticized object.

Because it comes in the form of a massive multimedia archive of relations whose multiple threads cannot be disentangled, it can never be instrumentalized in a single direction and, for this reason, no matter where it resides, it can never be reduced to a particular position or stance. Moving beyond the institutional and ideological boundaries of the Israel Museum every time it is evoked, read, reproduced, or referenced, it can never be a Zionist object. On the contrary, it can become—as it has in films from Palestinian director Elia Suleiman's 1996 *Chronicle of a Disappearance* to Israeli director Udi Aloni's 2002 documentary *Local Angel: Theological Political Fragments,* and in events such as the 2015 symposium in Ramallah, "Benjamin in Palestine: The Place and No-Place of Radical Thought"—a figure that, warning against certain forms of progress, against histories written by victors that work to efface the histories of the vanquished, suggests the disorientation and cessation that could enable us to distinguish so-called "progress" from different ways of moving forward. In other words, while Benjamin's angel may now be one of the "cultural treasures" that the historical materialist must view "with cautious detachment"—since such treasures can have a lineage "which he cannot contemplate without horror," and can be instrumentalized in a direction he wishes to oppose—it still remains a resource, constantly in motion and always changing in how it is viewed and how it sees, that can still today help us understand, and perhaps even begin to counter, the inescapable relation that, following Marx, Benjamin drew between culture and barbarism and saw at work even in the transmission of artworks "from one hand to another." The historical materialist, he writes, "dissociates himself from this process of transmission as far as possible," something Klee's angel, a companion and a witness that is also a figure of suspension and arrest, enables him to imagine in a labor of reading and writing determined "to brush history against the grain"—and especially against the grain of the most violent and devastating histories.

5. There would be much to say about this rather extraordinary discovery, about which we plan to write more in the near future. Minimally, we would want to think about: (1) Luther's relation to his friend Cranach and their collaborations in the making of several of Luther's texts; (2) Luther's iconoclasm, which, because of his incorporation of images in his texts, cannot be said to be against images in general, and which should be read as part of a pedagogical project on how to read images; (3) the relations or differences between Luther's several references to angels and Klee's new angel, since Klee may have purposefully sought to displace Luther's angels with his; (4) the role of Luther in Benjamin's conception of the baroque period; and (5) the relation between Luther's famous theses and Benjamin's preferred mode of thetic presentation—but here we simply wish to emphasize the way in which the materiality of Klee's work asks us to rethink Benjamin's famous description of it.

6. David Wills, "Naming the Mechanical Angel: Benjamin," in *Inanimation: Theories of Inorganic Life* (Minneapolis: University of Minnesota Press, 2016), 166.

7. Jameson himself refers to the cinematic structure of action and depersonalized action in a passage that also joins the question of agency—which is at the heart of Benjamin's figure of the angel of history—to that of the politicization of the masses that depends on not imagining either a face or a single directionality for them. He writes:

So it is that the final form of depersonalized contemplation becomes a seemingly technological kino-eye, and the character function gives way to a function tout court, both returning us, paradoxically, to art and the aesthetic (one which will have to be secured and sheltered against fascist and aestheticizing appropriation). I want to emphasize, before we explore these new developments, that depersonalization is here not to be misunderstood as some psychological trait or flaw in Benjamin himself, but that it is part and parcel of a generalized crisis of action and of the act as such, in a modernity which has evolved into mass political confrontation. (*BF*, 108)

8. Maurice Blanchot, "The *Igitur* Experience," in *The Space of Literature*, trans. Ann Smock (Lincoln: University of Nebraska Press, 1982), 109.

9. In his essayistic portrait of Benjamin, Adorno confirms the force of this figure when he writes that "everything that fell under the scrutiny of his words was transformed, as though it had become radioactive." See "A Portrait of Walter Benjamin," in Theodor W. Adorno, *Prisms*, trans. Samuel and Shierry Weber (Cambridge, MA: MIT Press, 1981), 229.

XI. AN UNUSUAL PEDAGOGY

1. Gayatri Chakravorty Spivak, *An Aesthetic Education in an Era of Globalization* (Cambridge, MA: Harvard University Press, 2012), 1.

2. Walter Benjamin, "Unpacking My Library," trans. Harry Zohn, in Benjamin, *Selected Writings*, vol. 2: *1927–1934*, ed. Michael W. Jennings, Howard Eiland, and Gary Smith (Cambridge, MA: Belknap Press of Harvard University Press, 1999), 492.

XII. A SHIP OF FOOLS

1. Plato, *The Republic*, trans. Desmond Lee (New York: Penguin Classics, 2007), 210.

2. These remarks were made in the response Jameson offered to a panel at the 2021 meeting of the Modern Language Association in celebration of the fortieth anniversary of the publication of *The Political Unconscious*. The full session is available at https://www.youtube.com/watch?v=tEq3GyDYmOk. We are grateful to Andrew Cole, who organized the panel, for having directed us to this event.

3. Theodor W. Adorno, *Negative Dialectics*, trans. E. B. Ashton (New York: Continuum, 1973), 150.

4. Just a few pages before the end of his book, Jameson notes that, as with "collectivity," we do not yet have an instrumentalizable concept of this "secret index," and he signals that this absence of a concept is perhaps one of the signatures of Benjamin's writerly modus operandi. In his words, "[t]o be sure, the 'index' is secret and so in that sense we may never know what it looks like, only that, like a pointing finger, it 'indicates.' Both of these words belong in a Benjamin-style study, they are examples of his elegant evasion of the unspeakable or inexpressible, names for what has no name, words for the as yet unclassifiable (particularly inasmuch as classification governs the general or universal, while all of these things—the past!—are particular or specific, singular, and thereby only worthy of a name as such and not a 'word')" (*BF*, 244).

5. For the phrase "to interrupt the course of the world," see Walter Benjamin, "Central Park,"

trans. Edmund Jephcott and Howard Eiland, in Benjamin, *Selected Writings*, vol. 4: *1938–1940*, ed. Howard Eiland and Michael W. Jennings (Cambridge, MA: Belknap Press of Harvard University Press, 2003), 170.

6. Walter Benjamin, "Paralipomena to 'On the Concept of History,'" trans. Edmund Jephcott and Howard Eiland, in Benjamin, *Selected Writings*, 4:405.

7. While Jameson suggests that the matter of race is what has prevented socialism from existing in America, Raya Dunayevskaya, in a speech of September 1966—in the context of debates over Black Power that eventually would lead to the Black mass revolt in Newark, New Jersey in the summer of 1967—actually argues that it is precisely around the question of race that the first socialist possibilities arose in the mid-nineteenth century. Pointing to the abolitionist movement from the 1830s to the 1860s, she suggests that, predating "the origin of Bolshevism by 80 years," this movement not only transgressed racial lines and gender lines—bringing together Black runaway slaves, white abolitionists, Black freedmen, and the suffragette movement—but also formed a socialist collective, and "when finally the paths of the abolitionists and Karl Marx crossed, the affinity of his ideas and theirs … revealed how indigenous, how deep were the American roots of Marxism." See Runa Dunayevskyaya, "Revisiting 'Black Power,' Race and Class," https://web.archive.org/web/20130821181828/http:/newsandletters.org/issues/2000/Jan-Feb/1.2000_rd.htm. If she suggests that socialism has been possible in America whenever it has collectively sought to overcome the violence of racism, she confirms Jameson's sense that socialism can only thrive if it can imagine a beyond of racism. Here, though, Jameson signals his pessimism in regard to the possibility of a socialist state. We are grateful to Rosalind Morris for directing us to Dunayevskaya's speech.

8. While Jameson emphasizes the "Americanness" of this phenomenon, he also states that the "dangers of Americanization were recognized long before decolonization and the Cold War." In other words, for Jameson, Americanization belongs to the colonial and imperial project and, because of this, can never be understood as simply provincial.

9. Jameson here refers to Lenin's writings on the various ways in which workers can be moved to acquiescence by the lures of capitalism, by what he refers to as a sensed "aristocracy of labor." These writings date primarily from 1914–1917 and form part of his attempt to provide a coherent Marxist explanation of the outbreak of the war and especially the simultaneous and traumatic collapse of the Second International and most of its constituent parties. He makes this argument most extensively in the eighth chapter of *Imperialism*, and in the article "Imperialism and the Split in the Socialist Movement,"

written a little later in the autumn of 1916. In a more programmatic and concise statement from his 1920 "Preliminary Draft Theses on the Agrarian Question for the Second Congress of the Communist International," he writes: "The industrial workers cannot fulfill their world-historical mission of emancipating mankind from the yoke of capital and from wars if these workers concern themselves exclusively with their narrow craft, narrow trade interests, and smugly confine themselves to care and concern for improving their own, sometimes tolerable, petty bourgeois conditions. This is exactly what happens in many advanced countries to the 'labor aristocracy' which serves as the base of the alleged Socialist parties of the Second International." See V. I. Lenin, "Preliminary Draft Theses on the Agrarian Question for the Second Congress of the Communist International," trans. Julius Katzer, in *Collected Works*, 4th English ed., vol. 31 (Moscow: Progress Publishers, 1965), 152. Jameson's suggestion in relation to Lenin's analysis of the bribery of workers joins the economic seductions of capital to the mobilization of racial fearmongering in Nazi Germany, which is of course another form of "bribery" and persuasion and, which as he suggests, helps account for workers' support for Hitler in the 1932 elections. This same racial fearmongering was, as we know, at the heart of Trump's own mobilization of his supporters in the elections of 2016 and 2020, and remains one of the Republican party's most sinister and effective strategies for mobilizing its constituencies.

10. Arguing against the possibility of universal history, and taking his cue from Benjamin's notes for "On the Concept of History," Jameson himself characterizes race as a construction:

> Mallarmé suddenly springs to mind as an argument in support of this repudiation of universal history, for he underscores its many languages, which means that no single language can subsume the totality of the human population, living and dead. And then there are the many peoples: Benjamin here seems to doubt the very unity of any single one of those ethnic and linguistic groups ("the notion that the history of humanity is composed of peoples is a mere refuge of intellectual laziness"). It makes sense even if you argue it by way of the dialects, but even more if you remember that "race" (a form of people) is as artificially constructed a unity as nation (the "national languages" themselves were forcefully unified by compulsory education, military service, legal requirement, markets and other deliberate political processes and operations). (*BF*, 228)

11. Although we often cite texts that do not capitalize the word "Black," even when it is a matter of race, we have chosen to capitalize our use of it—as a cultural and political act—and for reasons

that Du Bois himself offers for the word "Negro." As he puts it in an early footnote in *The Philadelphia Negro*, "I shall throughout this study use the term 'Negro,' to designate all persons of Negro descent, although the appellation is to some extent illogical. I shall, moreover, capitalize the word, because I believe that eight million Americans are entitled to a capital letter" (W. E. B. Du Bois, *The Philadelphia Negro: A Social Study*, ed. Henry Louis Gates, Jr. [New York: Oxford University Press, 2007], 2). In keeping with Du Bois's argument, we remain aware of the present moment. There may very well come a time when this capitalization is no longer necessary—we certainly hope so—but we do not believe that this time has yet arrived.

12. Werner Hamacher, "One 2 Many Multiculturalisms," trans. Dana Hollander, in *Violence, Identity, and Self-Determination*, ed. Hent de Vries and Samuel Weber (Stanford: Stanford University Press, 1997), 301.

13. For a more complete context of the passage, here are the last two paragraphs of Jameson's earlier book:

> [W]e must restore Benjamin's identification of culture and barbarism to its proper sequence, as the affirmation not merely of the Utopian dimension of ideological texts, but also and above all of the ideological dimension of all high culture. So it is that a Marxist hermeneutic—the decipherment by historical materialism of the cultural monuments and traces of the past—must come to terms with the certainty that all the works of class history as they have survived and been transmitted to people by the various museums, canons, and "traditions" of our own time, are all in one way or another profoundly ideological, have all had a vested interest in and a functional relationship to social formations based on violence and exploitation; and that, finally, the restoration of the meaning of the greatest cultural monuments cannot be separated from a passionate and partisan assessment of everything that is oppressive in them and that knows complicity with privilege and class domination, stained with the guilt not merely of culture in particular but of History itself as one long nightmare.
>
> Yet Benjamin's slogan is a hard saying, and not only for liberal and apoliticizing critics of art and literature, for whom it spells the return of class realities and the painful recollection of the dark underside of even the most seemingly innocent and "life-enhancing" masterpieces of the canon. For a certain radicalism also, Benjamin's formulation comes as a rebuke and a warning against the facile reappropriation of the classics as humanistic expressions of this or that historically "progressive" force. It comes, finally, as an appropriate corrective to the doctrine of the political unconscious which

has been developed in these pages, reasserting the undiminished power of ideological distortion that persists even within the restored Utopian meaning of cultural artifacts, and reminding us that within the symbolic power of art and culture the will to domination perseveres intact. It is only at this price—that of the simultaneous recognition of the ideological and Utopian functions of the artistic text—that a Marxist cultural study can hope to play its part in political praxis, which remains, of course, what Marxism is all about.

Fredric Jameson, *The Political Unconscious: Narrative as a Socially Symbolic Act* (Ithaca: Cornell University Press, 1981), 289–290. If, in 1981, Jameson views Benjamin's analysis as an "appropriate corrective" to his theorization of the political unconscious, this corrective is no longer necessary forty years later. As we have argued, Jameson's recent book is more Benjaminian than ever before. His sense of the possibility of political praxis is now thoroughly permeated by Benjamin's own mediated relation to Marx.

14. Benjamin, "Paralipomena to 'On the Concept of History,'" 406.

15. Ibid. That Benjamin remains rigorously antinarrative throughout his writings is legible in his preference for monadic forms—which are more condensed, briefer, mosaic-like, and, the bearers of densely entangled relationships, harder to instrumentalize—including poetry, parables, tales, short stories, drama, and even Proust's durational project which, seemingly an exception, can be understood as the cinematic freeze-frame of a novel. These also include what Jameson calls Benjamin's "small forms": "the spatial sentence, the quotation, the art-paragraph, the tonal sequence and 'montage of attractions,' but also the failed genres, the tractatus, the incomplete medieval treatise, the political speeches and manifestoes, the journals or diaries" (*BF*, 39).

16. Benjamin, "Paralipomena to 'On the Concept of History,'" 406–407.

17. Jameson, *The Political Unconscious*, 289.

18. Benjamin, "Paralipomena to 'On the Concept of History,'" 404.

19. Karl Marx, "Letters from the Franco-German Yearbooks," trans. Rodney Livingstone and Gregor Benton, in *Karl Marx: Early Writings* (New York: Penguin Books, 1975), 199–200.

20. All the citations from this letter from Marx to Ruge in May 1843 can be found in Marx, "Letters from the *Franco-German Yearbooks*," 200–206.

21. Aislinn O'Donnell, "Shame Is Already a Revolution: The Politics of Affect in the Thought of Gilles Deleuze," *Deleuze Studies* 11, no. 1 (2017), 20.

22. Ibid., 21.

23. Karl Marx, *The Class Struggles in France*, in Marx and Engels, *Collected Works*, vol. 10 (New York: International Publishers, 1978), 80. Benjamin's own identification between barbarism

and civilization, which is so critical to Jameson, surely finds its source in this passage.

24. Marx, "Letters from the *Franco-German Yearbooks*," 201.

XIII. COMMUNAL GRIEF

1. Angela Y. Davis, *Freedom Is a Constant Struggle: Ferguson, Palestine, and the Foundations of a Movement*, ed. Frank Barat (Chicago: Haymarket Books, 2016), 135.
2. See Walter Benjamin, "A Communist Pedagogy," trans. Rodney Livingstone, in Benjamin, *Selected Writings*, vol. 2: *1927–1934*, ed. Michael W. Jennings, Howard Eiland, and Gary Smith (Cambridge, MA: Belknap Press of Harvard University Press, 1999), 273–275 (all citations from this text can be found in these three pages). To further elaborate this point, it would be important to return to Benjamin's celebrated "Enlightenment for Children" youth programs, and the over thirty radio plays he delivered for children between 1929 (the year he read Hoernle's book) and 1932. As Jeffrey Mehlman demonstrated thirty years ago, these radio plays—including accounts of the destruction of Pompeii, the Lisbon earthquake of 1755, a Scottish railway disaster, and also of fraud, forgeries, and deceptions of all sorts—reveal their relations with Benjamin's most important philosophical and theological concerns. See Mehlman, *Walter Benjamin for Children: An Essay on His Radio Years* (Chicago: University of Chicago Press, 1993). See also *Walter Benjamin, Radio Benjamin*, ed. Lecia Rosenthal, trans. Jonathan Lutes, with Lisa Harries Schumann and Diana Reese (New York: Verso, 2014).
3. Hannah Arendt, *The Origins of Totalitarianism* (New York: Meridian, 1958), 290 and 295.

XIV. A RED RAY; OR, SOCIOLOGY'S SUPPLEMENT

1. Frederick Douglass, "The Color Line," *North American Review* 132, no. 295 (June 1881), 573 and 575.
2. Werner Sombart, *Why Is There No Socialism in the United States?*, trans. Patricia M. Hocking and C. T. Husbands (London: Macmillan, 1976), 28. We are grateful to Andrew Cole for pointing us in Sombart's direction.
3. If Sombart neglects race in 1906, he explores it at length five years later, publishing in 1911 *Die Juden und das Wirtschaftsleben* (Jews and economic life). As is well known, Sombart conceived his essay—a response to Max Weber's *Die protestantische Ethik und der Geist des Kapitalismus* (*Protestant Ethics and the Spirit of Capitalism*)—as an attempt to explore more extensively the influence of religion on economic life, to focus on the relation between religion and the pervasiveness of the "spirit of capitalism" and to explain the historical evolution of modern capitalism.

We are grateful to Peter Fenves for directing us to this text. Like him, we are struck by the fact that Benjamin does not reference Sombart in his "Capitalism as Religion," which also engages Weber's book. While Sombart's book on the Jewish race has been overshadowed by his endorsement of Nazism in 1934, it is an important document of his stance on the question of race—a question not elaborated in his earlier *Why Is There No Socialism in the United States?* As Fenves notes, this later book was written "before he was 'radicalized' (rightward) by the [First World] War and became the outright antisemite whose work Benjamin would have been familiar with when he was immersing himself in Heidelberg sociology" (Fenves makes this point in a note dated May 22, 2023).

4. Sombart, *Why Is There No Socialism in the United States?*, 43–44.
5. Ibid., 43.
6. Karl Marx, *Marx and Engels on the United States*, ed. Nelly Rumyantseva and others (Moscow: Progress Publishers, 1979), 176. Marx also states that the Republican Party "owes its origin to the struggle for Kansas," that "the struggle for Kansas ... called the Republican Party into being" (ibid., 89).
7. While Sombart emphasizes the force of the slogan "Emancipating the Black Slaves"—his perceived sense that the slogan is what helped expand the abolitionist cause—Du Bois argues in his 1935 *Black Reconstruction in America* that there was no "rallying slogan to unite the majority of the North and in the West, and if possible, bring the Border States into an opposing phalanx" against the seceding South. "Freedom for slaves furnished no such slogan," he adds, since "[n]ot one-tenth of the Northern white population would have fought for any such purpose." On the contrary, he explains, the emancipation of Black slaves was primarily a "military measure" resulting from the need to increase the size of the Union Army and the desire to instrumentalize the mass exodus of Black slaves to the North. As he puts it, "As soon ... as it became clear that the Union armies would not or could not return fugitive slaves, and that the masters with all their fume and fury were uncertain of victory, the slave entered upon a general strike against slavery by the same methods that he had used during the period of the fugitive slave. He ran away to the first place of safety and offered his services to the Federal Army." For Du Bois, the solidification of the Republican Party was less the result of a slogan and more the consequence of the slave's general strike against the slave system. See W. E. B. Du Bois, *Black Reconstruction: An Essay toward a History of the Part which Black Folk Played in the Attempt to Reconstruct Democracy in America, 1860–1880, and Other Writings*, ed. Eric Foner and Henry Louis Gates, Jr. (New York: Library of America, 2021), 71, 103, and 73. Further references to this book are to this edition and will be noted parenthetically by *BR* and page number.

8. Sombart accompanied Max Weber when the latter met with Du Bois at the 1904 World Exposition in St. Louis, so it is likely that he met Du Bois there. In any event, the fact that Sombart coedited the journal in which Du Bois's essay appeared and that he also wanted to have *The Souls of Black Folk* translated indicates that they certainly knew each other in these contexts. We are grateful to R. A. Judy for confirming this information for us. Du Bois's essay was most likely translated into German from his original English by Elisabeth Jaffé-von Richthofen (a friend of Weber's and the wife of Jaffé). See W. E. B. Du Bois, "Die Negerfrage in den Vereinigten Staaten," *Archiv für Sozialwissenschaft und Sozialpolitik* 22, no. 4 (1906), 31–79. We also note that *Archiv für Sozialwissenschaft und Sozialpolitik* is the journal in which, fifteen years later, Benjamin would publish his "Critique of Violence" essay.

9. W. E. B. Du Bois, "The Negro Question in the United States," trans. Joseph Fracchia, *CR: The New Centennial Review* 6, no. 3 (Winter 2006), 242 and 250.

10. In fact, Du Bois's historicization of the diminished goals of trade unions, their eventual alienation of Black workers, and their generalized loss of democratic momentum echoes Rosa Luxemburg's critique of Sombart in her *The Mass Strike*, where she accuses him of detaching the unions' fight for better labor conditions in the capitalist system from the more radical and expansive goals of social democracy. According to her, Sombart insists on opening

> an illimitable vista of economic progress to the trade-union struggle within the capitalist system, in opposition to the social democratic doctrine. Such a theory ["the new trade union theory"] has indeed existed for some time—the theory of Professor Sombart, which was promulgated with the express intention of driving a wedge between the trade unions and the social democracy in Germany, and of enticing the trade unions over to the bourgeois position.

See Rosa Luxemburg, *The Mass Strike*, trans. Patrick Lavin, in *The Essential Rosa Luxemburg: Reform or Revolution and The Mass Strike* (Chicago: Haymarket Books, 2008), 178.

11. Du Bois, "The Negro Question in the United States," 267.

12. W. E. B. Du Bois, "Socialism and the Negro Problem," in *W. E. B. Du Bois: A Reader*, ed. David Levering Lewis (New York: Henry Holt, 1995), 577–580.

13. W. E. B. Du Bois, "Marxism and the Negro Problem," in *W. E. B. Du Bois: A Reader*, 542.

14. W. E. B. Du Bois, "The Negro and Communism," in *W. E. B. Du Bois: A Reader*, 589.

15. Du Bois, "Marxism and the Negro Problem," 544.

16. Nahum Dimitri Chandler, *X: The Problem of the Negro as a Problem for Thought* (New York: Fordham University Press, 2014).

17. Frederick Hoffman, *Race Traits and Tendencies of the American Negro* (New York: American Economic Association, 1896), 312. Du Bois reviews this book critically in 1897 and, in particular, argues against Hoffman's extinction thesis. See W. E. B. Du Bois, "Race Traits and Tendencies of the American Negro by Frederick L. Hoffman, F.S.S. [Review]," *Annals of the American Academy of Political and Social Science* 9 (1897), 127–133.

18. David Levering Lewis, "A 'Most Unique' Exhibit," in *A Small Nation of People: W. E. B. Du Bois and African American Portraits of Progress* (New York: Amistad Press, 2003), 48.

19. Kevin Gaines, *Uplifting the Race: Black Leadership, Politics, and Culture in the Twentieth Century* (Chapel Hill: University of North Carolina Press, 1991), 157. For a wonderful account of Du Bois's exhibit at the 1900 Paris Exposition—its contents but also its rationale—see Shawn Michelle Smith, *Photography on the Color Line: W. E. B. Du Bois, Race, and Visual Culture* (Durham: Duke University Press, 2004).

20. Smith, *Photography on the Color Line*, 18 and 22.

21. For an excellent reading of Du Bois's use of graphs and charts in *The Philadelphia Negro*, see Alexander G. Weheliye, "Diagrammatics as Physiognomy: W. E. B. Du Bois's Graphic Modernities," *CR: The New Centennial Review* 15, no. 2 (2015), 23–58.

22. The two color charts we discuss here are reproduced in *W. E. B. Du Bois Data Portraits: Visualizing Black America*, edited by Whitney Battle-Baptiste and Britt Rusert (Princeton, NJ: Princeton Architectural Press, 2018), plates 11 and 18.

23. W. E. B. Du Bois, "A Program for a Sociological Society" (Speech to the First Sociological Club, Atlanta University, Atlanta, GA), in *Microfilm Edition of the W. E. B. Du Bois Papers*, Manuscript Division, University of Massachusets at Amherst, reel 80, cited in Weheliye, "Diagrammatics as Physiognomy," 26.

24. *W. E. B. Du Bois Data Portraits: Visualizing Black America*, 17.

25. W. E. B. Du Bois, "Sociology Hesitant," *Boundary 2*, 27, no. 3 (Fall 2000), 41.

26. As Du Bois recalls the incident later in his life, he misremembers the victim: in an altercation, Hose had killed his landlord, not his landlord's wife. Du Bois's account can be found in *Dusk of Dawn* (New York: Oxford University Press, 2014), 34. What is emphasized in his account is the affect the incident had on him, and his inability to counter white supremacist violence through reason and evidence.

27. Ibid., 32.

28. Ibid., 34.

29. For an extended reading of Du Bois's account of the death of his son—an account that appears under the title "Of the Passing of the First-Born" in *Souls of Black Folk*—see Annie Menzel, "'Awful Gladness': The Dual Political Rhetorics of Du Bois's 'Of the Passing of the First-Born,'" *Political Theory* 47, no. 1 (2019), 32–56.

30. W. E. B. Du Bois, "Returning Soldiers," *The Crisis* 18, no. 1 (May 1919), reprinted in Robert T. Kerlin, *Voice of the Negro 1919* (New York: E. P. Dutton, 1920), 35–37.

31. Adriane Lentz-Smith, *Freedom Struggles: African Americans and World War I* (Cambridge, MA: Harvard University Press, 2011), 44, cited in David F. Krugler, *1919, the Year of Racial Violence: How African Americans Fought Back* (Cambridge: Cambridge University Press, 2015), 16.

32. Rosa Luxemburg, "Die Krise der Sozialdemokratie," in Luxemburg, *Gesammelte Werke*, vol. 4: *August 1914–January 1919*, ed. Annelies Laschitza and Günter Radczun (Berlin: Rosa-Luxemburg-Stiftung, 2000), 148–149.

33. Following Raya Dunayevskaya's 1982 *Rosa Luxemburg, Women's Liberation, and Marx's Philosophy of Revolution*, we will return to this discussion of primitive accumulation in the last section of our book in relation to Marx's *Ethnographical Notebooks*.

XV. THE SHIBBOLETH OF RACE

1. Raya Dunayevskaya, "The Black Dimension in Women's Literature," in *Women's Liberation and the Dialectics of Revolution: Reaching for the Future* (Atlantic Highlands, NJ: Humanities Press International, 1985), 49.

2. The original subtitle of Du Bois's historiographical study—given here—is often omitted in later editions of the book, but its emphasis on the essayistic experimentalism of the project is of vital importance to its argument. It reinforces that what we have before us is, first, Du Bois's understanding that he can only attempt—make an essay or effort—to provide an account of Black agency, since the Black agency that he portrays is a historical force that cannot be fully represented and, second, that this Black agency, rather than guaranteeing the success of a reconstruction of democracy, can only gesture toward it. The original cover of Du Bois's book, which only capitalizes the words "Black Folk," "Democracy," and "America" further presents the study as an exploration of the inexorable and shifting relations between these three terms.

3. W. E. B. Du Bois, letter to Benjamin Stolberg, October 1, 1934, W. E. B. Du Bois Papers (MS 312), Special Collections and University Archives, University of Massachusetts Amherst Libraries; cited in Michael J. Saman, "Du Bois and Marx, Du Bois and Marxism," *Du Bois Review* 17, no. 1 (2020), 47.

4. It is striking to register how close Luxemburg's and Du Bois's language are as they describe the oceanic swell of the masses' "method of movement."

5. That Du Bois thinks about the slaves' insurrection in relation to other revolutions is made clear when he notes that "[t]he unending tragedy of Reconstruction is the utter inability of the American mind to grasp its real significance, its
national and world-wide implications. ... We are still too blind and infatuated to conceive of the emancipation of the laboring class in half the nation as a revolution comparable to the upheavals in France in the past, and in Russia, Spain, India and China today" (*BR*, 850). For an excellent discussion of the relations that Du Bois saw between the Russian Revolution and the slaves' general strike, in particular, see Bill Mullen's "'Experiments of Marxism': W. E. B. Du Bois and the Specter of 1917," in *The Un-American: W. E. B. Du Bois and the Century of World Revolution* (Philadelphia: Temple University Press, 2015), 56–95.

6. Marx repeatedly turns in his analysis of capital—and of its role in the formation of history and politics in general—not only to literary language but also to literature, not only to historical and political transformations but also to the language without which these changes would never take place. Indeed, in his efforts to realize the promise of a democracy and communism which, for the first time, would inaugurate a new world history of liberation, justice, and equality, one of the most significant resources for such activist work can be found in what he means by "literature."

His interest in literature is perhaps all the more legible when he is not speaking only of what we call novels, poetry, fiction, and fables, but of the illusions, hallucinations, phantasms, virtualities, and simulacra that compose what we, still today, and more than ever, call our everyday existence. Whether he describes and analyzes the dramaturgy of a modern Europe whose unifying projects work to communicate the meaning and effects of capital, whether he speaks of the apparitional character of money or ideology, the spectral character of the commodity and exchange value, a social revolution that can only draw its poetry from the future, the phantasmatic relation between things that characterizes the social relations between men, the ideological or imaginary relationship between individuals and their real conditions of existence, the hallucinatory personification of his famous turning, dancing table, the language of commodities that walk, stand, choose, and dress, the linguistic character of exchange, the misty realm of religion, or the theatricality of political representation, he touches on the realm of literature, on the phantasmagorical and imaginary world that we associate, rightly or wrongly, with the signature of literature. To put it another way, what makes literature literature—its capacity to engage and produce illusionary, imaginary, phantasmatic relations—is at the same time what makes it historical and political, and why it can become a political resource. When, in his famous 1888 letter to Margaret Harkness, Engels claims to have learned more about French society and its history from Balzac "than from all the professed historians, economists and statisticians of the period together" (Karl Marx and

Frederick Engels, *Marx and Engels on Literature and Art* [Moscow: Progress Publishers, 1984], 91), he announces another understanding of literature, one that asks us to mourn it in order to recognize it for what it is: never simply literature.

What we find in Marx is an encounter between literature, politics, philosophy, history, religion, and economics, an encounter between Marx and the activities of a different kind of reading and writing. These two activities—which belong essentially to "literature," as we and Marx understand it, but which are never really two distinct activities—are, in every way, political practices, and this is an insight that, at least in our present context, permeates and motivates the writings not just of Marx but also of Luxemburg, Benjamin, Du Bois, and Jameson.

7. This phrase "experiment of Marxism" is Du Bois's (although he pluralizes the word "experiment"). He uses it to describe the way in which, after emancipation and during Reconstruction, Blacks organized in order to gain ownership of land, to secure the right to vote, and to gain access to education and social benefits. In a passage that also associates this work of reconstruction with the Russian Revolution, he writes:

> As the Negro laborers organized separately, there came slowly to realization the fact that here was not only separate organization but a separation in leading ideas, because among Negroes, and particularly in the South, there was being put into force one of the most extraordinary experiments of Marxism that the world, before the Russian revolution, had seen. That is, backed by the military power of the United States, a dictatorship of labor was to be attempted and those who were leading the Negro race in this vast experiment were emphasizing the necessity of the political power and organization backed by protective military power. (*BR*, 432)

Several readers of Du Bois associate this phrase—"experiments of Marxism"—with the slaves' general strike itself, but this passage makes clear that he refers to the period after the Civil War, in which the role of the state and especially the Freedmen's Bureau is paramount in supporting the effort of the newly freed Blacks to be integrated as full citizens within the Union.

8. For a detailed account of the history of Du Bois's engagement with Marx, see Saman, "Du Bois and Marx, Du Bois and Marxism," 33–54.

9. *The Correspondence of W. E. B. Du Bois*, vol. 2: *Selections, 1934–1944*, ed. Herbert Aptheker (Amherst: University of Massachusetts Press, 1976), 91.

10. W. E. B. Du Bois, "Karl Marx and the Negro," ca. March 1933, W. E. B. Du Bois Papers (MS 312), Special Collections and University Archives, University of Massachusetts Amherst Libraries, 1. See https://credo.library.umass.edu/view/full/mums312-b211-i086.

11. Marx and Engels, *Collected Works*, vol. 41 (New York: International Publishers, 1985), 4. In her 1970 *American Civilization on Trial*, Raya Dunayevskaya subtitles her book *Black Masses as Vanguard*. In doing so, she believes she is simply following Marx and, in particular, his revolutionary antiracist critique of capitalism. While there may be moments in Marx that can be marked as "racist," we agree with Dunayevskaya that he provides us with the strongest resource we have for analyzing and combatting racial capitalism.

12. Cedric J. Robinson, *Black Marxism: The Making of the Black Radical Tradition*, 3rd ed. (1983; Chapel Hill: University of North Carolina Press, 2021), 2. Although the phrase "racial capitalism" first appears seven years earlier in a text by Martin Legassick and David Hemson on the relation between capitalism and racism in South Africa, it gains its most profound elaboration in Robinson's monumental book.

13. Cedric Robinson, "Capitalism, Marxism, and the Black Radical Tradition: An Interview with Cedric Robinson," *Perspectives on Anarchist Theory* 3 (1999), online at http://www.hartford-hwp.com/archives/45a/568.html.

14. Du Bois, "Karl Marx and the Negro," 1.

15. An editor, orator, writer, and civil rights activist, Timothy Thomas Fortune founded the influential *New York Globe* in 1881 and hired Du Bois as a young journalist in 1883. Born into slavery in 1856, he began his formal education after the Civil War. In addition to his publishing ventures, he was the dominant economic theorist of his era, the editor of Booker T. Washington's first autobiography, cofounded the militant National Afro-American League, which was a precursor to the NAACP, and was regarded as the leading and most influential Black radical of the late nineteenth century. His book *Black and White: Land, Labor, and Politics in the South* casts a long shadow on Du Bois's *Black Reconstruction*. Its influence on Du Bois's book deserves close study (even the titles of Du Bois's first two chapters follow the structure of Fortune's book). We would suggest that Du Bois's passage through Fortune's book—with its Marxist vocabulary—prepared him for his later encounter with Marx.

16. For details on the specific materials Marx was reading—an extraordinarily vast set of materials—see *Karl Marx on America and the Civil War*, The Karl Marx Library 2, ed. and trans. Saul K. Padover (New York: McGraw-Hill, 1972), xii–xiii; and *Marx and Engels on the United States*, ed. Nelly Rumyantseva (Moscow: Progress Publishers, 1979), 15–16. On Marx's writings on the Civil War in general, see Tom Jeannot, "Marx, Capitalism, and Race," *Radical Philosophy Today* 5 (2007), 69–92; Kevin B. Anderson, "Race, Class, and Slavery: The Civil War as a Second American Revolution," in *Marx at the Margins: On Nationalism, Ethnicity, and Non-Western Societies* (Chicago: University of Chicago Press, 2010), 79–114; and Matteo Battistini, "Karl Marx and the Global History of the Civil War: The Slave

Movement, Working-Class Struggle, and the American State within the World Market," *International Labor and Working-Class History* 100 (Fall 2021), 158–185.

17. Karl Marx, "The North American Civil War," in *Karl Marx on America and the Civil War*, 69–70, 78.

18. Karl Marx, "The Civil War in the United States," in *Karl Marx on America and the Civil War*, 93.

19. Marx, "The North American Civil War," 74; Karl Marx, "The American Question of England," in *Karl Marx on America and the Civil War*, 56.

20. Marx, "The North American Civil War," 71.

21. "Address of the International Working Men's Association to President Lincoln," in *Karl Marx on America and the Civil War*, 236–237.

22. *General Council of the First International, 1864–1866, Minutes* (Moscow: Progress Publishers, 1962), 311–312. As Kevin Anderson notes, Du Bois cites the version of this letter published by Herman Schlüter in his *Lincoln, Labor, and Slavery: A Chapter from the Social History of America* (New York: Socialist Literature Co., 1913), 200. According to Anderson, Schlüter "gave a different rendering of the text, which he had probably retranslated into English from a German version. The language in Schlüter's version is even more forceful than in the English one, referring to the danger of 'a new struggle which will once more drench your country in blood.'" See Anderson, *Marx at the Margins*, 114.

23. Du Bois first encounters this letter to Lincoln in Schlüter's *Lincoln, Labor, and Slavery*, a book that also addresses Marx's engagement with the American Civil War.

24. Karl Marx, *The Poverty of Philosophy*, in Marx and Engels, *Collected Works*, vol. 6 (New York: International Publishers, 1976), 167–168.

25. Karl Marx, *Capital: A Critique of Political Economy*, vol. 1, trans. Ben Fowkes (New York: Penguin Books, 1990), 414. As he goes on to note,

> However, a new life immediately arose from the death of slavery. The first fruit of the American Civil War was the eight hours' agitation, which ran from the Atlantic to the Pacific, from New England to California, with the seven-league boots of the locomotive. The General Congress of Labor held in Baltimore in August 1866 declared: "The first and great necessity of the present, to free the labor of this country from capitalistic slavery, is the passing of a law by which eight hours shall be the normal working day in all States of the American Union. We are resolved to put forth all our strength until this glorious result is attained." (Ibid.)

For a detailed account of the way in which Marx's engagement with events in the United States influenced the development of *Capital*, see Raya Dunayevskaya, "The Impact of the Civil War in the United States on the Structure of *Capital*," in *Marxism and Freedom: From 1776 until Today* (Lanham, MD: Humanity Books, 2000), 81–91, and John F. Welsh, "Reconstructing *Capital*: The American Roots and Humanist Vision of Marx's Thought," *Midwest Quarterly* 3, no. 3 (Spring 2002), 274–287.

26. Marx and Engels, *Collected Works*, vol. 42 (New York: International Publishers, 1987), 334.

27. As Du Bois puts it near the end of his essay on "The Negro and Communism": "Until the colored man, yellow, red, brown, and black, becomes free, articulate, intelligent and the receiver of a decent income, white capital will use the profit derived from his degradation to keep white labor in chains." W. E. B. Du Bois, "The Negro and Communism," in *W. E. B. Du Bois: A Reader*, ed. David Levering Lewis (New York: Henry Holt, 1995), 593.

28. In a rather remarkable passage in chapter 31 of *Capital* ("The Genesis of the Industrial Capitalist"), Marx makes another reference to "black skin," this time in the context of its role in the development of capitalism and primitive accumulation. He writes:

> The discovery of gold and silver in America, the extirpation, enslavement and entombment in mines of the indigenous populations of that continent, the beginnings of the conquest and plunder of India, and the conversion of Africa into a preserve for the commercial hunting of blackskins, are all things which characterize the dawn of the era of capitalist production. These idyllic proceedings are the chief moments of primitive accumulation.

See Marx, *Capital*, 1:915.

29. Karl Marx, *Wage Labor and Capital*, in Marx and Engels, *Collected Works*, vol. 9 (New York: International Publishers, 1977), 211.

30. C. L. R. James, "Lectures on *The Black Jacobins*," *Small Axe* 8 (September 2000), 91. Given that we are tracing the essential role and place of reading in different political practices—and in particular acts of writing that are simultaneously acts of reading—it is worth noting that James's lectures are almost entirely devoted to an account of all the archival research, reading, and studying he did in order to write his book on Black revolution. In particular, like Du Bois before him, he makes clear that his book is mediated by Marx. As he puts it,

> I notice that both Lenin and Stalin are quoting Marx. So I say, Lenin is quoting Marx, and Trotsky is quoting Marx and saying that Lenin is doing what I am doing. So I go and buy the volumes of Marx. Nobody is educating me. Nobody is telling me what to read. I am doing all this entirely on my own. At the end of it, I realize that I have to do some more reading about the French Revolution. ... I really got hold of historical development, plus I had read Marxism, and had had to study Marxism, first to know what

the quarrel between Lenin and Trotsky and Stalin was about, what were their differences. Then I begin to apply Marxism to the San Domingo Revolution. I study the San Domingo situation and begin to read the great school of the French Revolution. By the time I come to write about the French Revolution in San Domingo, I am a pretty well educated person in history and in politics. I didn't fall from the sky. I didn't go up like Moses and come back with documents. I had to work at it and I worked at it with great pleasure and passion because I was learning from it all the time. (Ibid., 68 and 77)

31. Marx himself identifies the slave as a commodity in his 1849 "Wage Labor and Capital," writing: "Labor was not always a *commodity*. Labor was not always wage labor, that is, *free* labor. The *slave* did not sell his labor to the slaveowner, anymore than the ox sells its service to the peasant. The slave, together with his labor, is sold at once and for all to his owner. He is a commodity which can pass from the hand of one owner to that of another. He is *himself* a commodity, but the labor is not *his* commodity." Marx, *Wage Labor and Capital*, 203.

32. Ibid., 228.

33. W. E. B. Du Bois, *The Souls of Black Folk*, ed. Brent Hayes Edwards (Oxford: Oxford University Press, 2007), 76.

34. W. E. B. Du Bois, "The Conservation of Races," in Du Bois, *The Problem of the Color Line at the Turn of the Twentieth Century: The Essential Early Writings*, ed. Nahum Dimitri Chandler (New York: Fordham University Press, 2015), 52.

35. W. E. B. Du Bois, "The Revelations of Saint Orgne the Damned," in *The Education of Black People: Ten Critiques 1906–1960*, ed. Herbert Aptheker (New York: Monthly Review Press, 1973), 104.

36. Ibid., 117 and 112.

XVI. THE HAMMER OF SOCIAL REVOLUTION

1. See Malcolm X, "Twenty Million Black People in a Political, Economic and Mental Prison," in *Malcolm X: The Last Speeches* (London: Ost-West Europäisches Frauen-Netzwerk, 1969), 36; and James Baldwin, *The Fire Next Time* (1963; New York: Vintage, 1992), 106.

2. See Martin Luther King, Jr., "Hammer of Civil Rights," in *A Testament of Hope: The Essential Writings of Martin Luther King, Jr.*, ed. James Melvin Washington (New York: Harper & Row, 1986), 169.

3. Consisting of two essays—"My Dungeon Shook: Letter to My Nephew on the One Hundredth Anniversary of the Emancipation" and "Down at the Cross: Letter from a Region in My Mind" (published first in *The Progressive* and *The New Yorker*, respectively, in 1962), *The Fire Next Time* was first published by Dial Press in 1963. Referred to as "the poet of the revolution" by Malcolm X, James Baldwin is a towering figure in the history of Black struggles for equality. His sense of Black nationalism was never a question of "separatism," but rather an expansion toward an internationalist and increasingly socialist vision, especially after the Black Panthers' identification of antiracism with anticapitalism. As Baldwin put it in a 1972 interview, in a passage that beautifully anticipates Jameson's sense that race is what has prevented a real socialist revolution in America:

> You have to be very careful what you mean by socialism. When I use the word I'm not thinking about Lenin for example. I don't have any European models in mind. Bobby Seale talks of a Yankee Doodle-type socialism. I know what he means when he says that. It is a socialism created from the indigenous need of the people in the place. So that a socialism achieved in America, if and when we do—I think you have to say when we do—will be a socialism very unlike the Chinese socialism or the Cuban socialism. ... The price of any real socialism here is the eradication of what we call the race problem.

See *Conversations with James Baldwin*, ed. Fred L. Standley and Louis H. Pratt (Jackson: University Press of Mississippi, 1989), 131.

4. As we have noted earlier in our introduction, though—citing Robin D. G. Kelley—the Black Lives Matter movement has to be pluralized and contextualized in relation to the innumerable collective efforts that have sought to counter and break down racial capitalism for decades, if not centuries.

5. It is important to emphasize the role of women in the struggles for civil rights. From Sojourner Truth to Ida B. Wells, from Rosa Parks to Angela Davis, from Kathleen Cleaver to Ruthie Gilmore to the three community organizers who cofounded the Black Lives Matter movement, radical organizing has often been part of a feminist struggle that emphasizes collective leadership and, especially in these last years, has asked us to collectively mourn an entire community that has had to live in constant fear of a violent death. For an expansive history of feminist movements that preceded and reinforced Black Lives Matter, see Angela Y. Davis, Gina Dent, Erica R. Meiners, and Beth E. Richie, *Abolition. Feminism. Now.* (Chicago: Haymarket Books, 2022).

XVII. THE LEVIATHANISM OF THE VANQUISHED

1. Saidiya Hartman, *Lose Your Mother: A Journey along the Atlantic Slave Route* (New York: Farrar, Straus and Giroux, 2008), 17.

2. Thomas Hobbes, *Leviathan*, ed. Richard Tuck (Cambridge: Cambridge University Press, 1996), 120. We thank Russ Leo for his insights into this moment in Hobbes's text.

XVIII. *ANGELUS NOVUS*: A MILITANT EMBLEM

1. Bertolt Brecht, "Zertrümmerung der Person," in *Werke: Grosse kommentierte Berliner und Frankfurter Ausgabe*, vol. 21, ed. Werner Hecht, Jan Kopf, Werner Mittenzwei, and Klaus-Detlef Müller (Berlin: Aufbau/Suhrkamp, 1989–1998), 320; and Frank B. Wilderson III, *Afropessimism* (New York: Liveright, 2020), 40.
2. Karl Marx, *The Eighteenth Brumaire of Louis Bonaparte*, trans. Daniel De Leon (New York: International Publishers, 1963), 17.
3. We are indebted for this identification to Fred Moten, who suggested it to us in a conversation on September 14, 2022.
4. W. E. B. Du Bois, *The Souls of Black Folk*, ed. Brent Hayes Edwards (Oxford: Oxford University Press, 2007), 8.
5. Claudia Rankine, "The Condition of Black Life Is One of Mourning," *New York Times Magazine*, June 22, 2015, https://www.nytimes.com/2015/06/22/magazine/the-condition-of-black-life-is-one-of-mourning.html.
6. Du Bois, *The Souls of Black Folk*, 141.

XIX. THE SECOND COMET

1. Louis Auguste Blanqui, *Eternity by the Stars*, in *The Blanqui Reader*, ed. Peter Hallward and Philippe Le Goff, trans. Mitchell Abidor, Peter Hallward, and Philippe Le Goff (New York: Verso, 2018), 292; and W. E. B. Du Bois, *Dusk of Dawn* (New York: Oxford University Press, 2014), 31.
2. W. E. B. Du Bois, "Of the Ruling of Men," in Du Bois, *Darkwater: Voices from Within the Veil* (New York: Oxford University Press, 2007), 67 and 71. Further references to materials in this collection are to this edition and will be noted parenthetically by *DW* and page number.
3. Paul Gilroy, "Du Bois, Germany, and the Politics of (Dis)placement," in *The Black Atlantic: Modernity and Double Consciousness* (Cambridge, MA: Harvard University Press, 1993), 115.
4. James Baldwin, *The Fire Next Time* (1963; New York: Vintage, 1992), 104.
5. Evelyn Brooks Higginbotham, "Introduction," *DW*, xxv.
6. On the identification of race and fertilizer and, in particular, on race and guano, see Eduardo Cadava, "The Guano of History," in *The Other Emerson*, ed. Branka Arsić and Cary Wolfe (Minneapolis: University of Minnesota Press, 2010), 101–130.
7. The passage Du Bois evokes from Hegel is from *The Phenomenology of Spirit*. There, in a discussion of phrenological theories emerging in the late eighteenth and early nineteenth century—which were instrumentalized as an explanation for the differences among the races—Hegel writes: "When in other respects it is said of Spirit that it *is*, that it has *being*, is a *Thing*, a single, separate *reality*, this is not *intended* to mean that it is something we can see or take in our hands or touch, and so on, but that is what is *said*; and what *really* is said is expressed by saying that the *being of Spirit is a bone*." See G. W. F. Hegel, *The Phenomenology of Spirit*, trans. A. V. Miller (New York: Oxford University Press, 1977), 207. Suggesting that thought is embedded in some form of materiality, he adds, "Spirit is supposed to be known in its own outer aspect, as in a being which is the utterance of Spirit—the visible invisibility of its essence," in which "the outer aspect is lastly a wholly immobile reality which is not in its own self a speaking sign but, separated from self-conscious movement, presents itself on its own account and is a mere Thing." As William J. Urban has noted: "The passage from physiognomy to phrenology is thus the change from signifying representation to inert presence. With physiognomy, we remain at the level of bodily gestures intended to signify the interior of the subject. The problem is that such language of the body invariably fails to reveal what is intended, for there is no proper signifier of the subject. But through the skull bone of phrenology the void of the subject is embodied: the presence of the Thing literally 'gives body' to the impossibility of the signifying representation of the subject." See William J. Urban, "Re-reading Hegel: Meaning and Subjectivity in *The Phenomenology of Spirit*," in *Lacanian Theory: Books, Essays, Reviews, Commentaries* (2022), http://www.swingtradesystems.com/lacan/hegel-zizek-lacan-5.html. For Du Bois, what is most useful here is Hegel's suggestion that it is impossible to represent any subject through physiological emphases alone: the meaning of Blackness can neither be signified nor represented without violence.
8. Du Bois, *Dusk of Dawn*, 51.
9. Nahum Dimitri Chandler, *X: The Problem of the Negro as a Problem for Thought* (New York: Fordham University Press, 2014), 93; Du Bois, *Dusk of Dawn*, 101 and 100.
10. Saidiya Hartman, "The End of White Supremacy: An American Romance," *Bomb Magazine*, June 5, 2020, https://bombmagazine.org/articles/the-end-of-white-supremacy-an-american-romance/. All references to this essay are from this online publication.
11. This claim that "The Comet" is a kind of archive—a translation that appears in the form of an "amalgamation" of all the earlier arguments and motifs in *Darkwater*—cannot be demonstrated here, but what we are suggesting just about this passage on Jim's descent into the lower vaults can be extended to all the others. All of *Darkwater* resonates in its final story.

That Du Bois would turn to the genre of science fiction as a means of countering the bond between imperialism and different forms of racism is perhaps not an accident. As Hee-Jung Serenity Joo suggests, "[i]t is not insignificant that Du Bois turns to the writings of ... H. G. Wells to support his anti-imperialist claims. Du Bois agrees with Wells that 'there can be no permanent peace in the world' so long as Africa is the battleground for 'competitive European imperialisms' bent not only on controlling Africa and its immense natural resources but also on outcolonizing other European nations there." Joo goes on to note that "Du Bois quotes from Wells's *In the Fourth Year: Anticipations of a World Peace* (1918) in a chapter entitled 'Getting the League Idea Clear in Relation to Imperialism' (first published in 1918)." See Hee-Jung Serenity Joo, "Racial Impossibility and Critical Failure in W. E. B. Du Bois's *Darkwater*," *Science Fiction Studies* 46 (2019), 109 and 123. The full quotation in Du Bois is as follows: "'It is the clear, common sense of the African situation,' says H. G. Wells, 'that while these precious regions of raw material remain divided up between a number of competitive European imperialisms, each resolutely set upon the exploitation of its "possessions" to its own advantage and the disadvantage of the others, there can be no permanent peace in the world. It is impossible'" (*DW*, 52). As we will see in our next section, "To the Planetarium," this identification between science fiction and the future possibility of political transformation is also behind Benjamin's interest in Scheerbart's *Lesabéndio*.

12. The role of Afropessimism in *Darkwater* has been pointed out by Hartman and others, but it remains far from straightforward. As Hartman puts it in "The End of White Supremacy," "The tone of the collection oscillates between rage and despair; some might even describe it as an ur-text of afropessimism, but its mood is more tragic; its bright moments are colored by a desire for a Messianic cessation of the given, stoked by a vision of the end of the world, welcoming the gift of chance and accident, and embracing the beauty of death." If she asks us to think about the distinction between an Afropessimist stance and a tragic one, we can do so by comparing Du Bois's stance to that of Wilderson in his *Afropessimism*. Among other differences, the most significant can be described as temporal or even narrative in nature and depends on whether one understands Afropessimism as a point of departure or a point of arrival. While Wilderson can be said to fall into the latter category, Du Bois's "tragic" addition moves in the direction of using the brutal realization of Afropessimism as a cathartic upheaval that can inaugurate a different beginning. It is imperative, however, that this beginning come to terms with the ontological horror of racism as the ground zero of any political project—not despite its brutality but because of it. While such a

stance might seem redemptive, or "messianic," as Hartman suggests, it is remarkably close to Benjamin's "messianic without messianism." It refers to a non-narrative redemption that takes the form of an explosion—a rupture of the linear narrative temporalities that feed on the violence against those they exploit and brutalize. When Wilderson declares that "redemption, *as a narrative mode*, was a parasite that fed upon me for its coherence," he takes for granted that redemption has an internal coherence, whereas Du Bois and Benjamin know that redemption implies the death of any certitude but also of any claim to temporal order and cohesion. They also know that this last death may be the most violent and difficult of all.

While the slave-master antagonism that Wilderson takes as the facticity of Black life—one that he shares with the more nuanced and extensive analyses of the human and nonhuman in Denise Ferreira da Silva's *Unpayable Debt* (Berlin: Sternberg Press, 2022)—has no resolution within the humanist parameters that sustain it from the start, it may still be deposed or abolished in the way Benjamin outlines in his "Toward the Critique of Violence." There, assuming the violent antagonism that the law originates and perpetuates, he insists on its nonlinear temporalization as the entry into its philosophical structure and constructed stability—an entry that is also breaking, that exposes a fissure in its "origin," in Benjamin's sense. If we return to Du Bois's insistence on the thwarted but legible new beginnings in his discussions in *Black Reconstruction* of the Freedmen's Bureau and the slaves' general strike, it becomes clear how crucial it is to see the mobility within Wilderson's antagonisms—which are spot on—and to understand how much is silenced by their essentialism. See Wilderson, *Afropessimism*, 16.

13. If death is seen as a leveler, it can only be because the destruction of the entire world introduces a different economy of death, since, as Du Bois knows, the "cruelty, barbarism, and murder done to men and women of Negro descent" (*DW*, 17) is incommensurable with the death of others. In other words, Black death has never been simply a matter of our shared mortality—even the dead are not safe from racism. This fact has been demonstrated most recently by the effects of another presumed "leveler," the COVID-19 pandemic. The last three years have witnessed the widespread, lethal effects of systemic racism, ranging from the disproportionate number of deaths and hardships experienced by people of color because of the pandemic to the numerous incidents of police brutality and anti-Black violence across the United States. Even as COVID-19 is said to be indiscriminate, to be a profound "leveler"—it crosses all limits and borders and can reach anyone—it lays bare the discrimination that has always structured the relations between races and classes and that is legible in the comorbidities it has produced: poverty,

unemployment, food insecurity, unequal access to education, unhealthy living conditions, lack of health care, all of which affect our most vulnerable communities—indigenous and minority populations, the poor and the disenfranchised, the elderly, those with chronic illnesses, the incarcerated, the undocumented and homeless. As we know, discrimination and racism have been built into the heart of the American experiment from its very beginning like its right ventricle. The interruption of the potential relation between Jim and Julia highlights the bitter irony of Jim's comment.

14. Despite Du Bois's activism against forms of gender-based social and economic discrimination, oppression, and abuse—his "The Damnation of Women" chapter in *Darkwater* stands out in this regard—when it is a matter of sexually marked transgressions of the color line, he struggles to shake off the need to regulate female sexuality in general, and Black female sexuality in particular. This is something that Saidiya Hartman underscores in her semifictional portrayal of Du Bois in *Wayward Lives, Beautiful Experiments*, which is centered on the period during which he researches Black communities for his 1899 *The Philadelphia Negro*. She attributes his discomfort to his Victorian morality and bourgeois prejudice. See Saidiya Hartman, *Wayward Lives, Beautiful Experiments: Intimate Histories of Riotous Black Girls, Troublesome Women, and Queer Radicals* (New York: W. W. Norton, 2019). Similarly, Ryan Schneider argues that Du Bois's mordant, almost satirical, critique of imperialism and its racialized fictions nevertheless emphasizes "manhood" as a privileged force to the detriment of women. "Like Douglass and Washington," he writes, "Du Bois was greatly interested in establishing an active, transgenerational concept of black manhood and, by extension, participating in the broader patrilineal shaping of American culture." Referring specifically to *Darkwater*'s taboo-breaking depiction of interracial sexual relationships, he notes that "even as these scenarios challenge traditional limits of racial-sexual interaction, they also suggest that Du Bois's otherwise enlightened, progressive vision of black-white relations is based on a restricted notion of black female sexual agency." See Ryan Schneider, "Sex and the Race Man: Imagining Interracial Relationships in W. E. B. Du Bois's *Darkwater*," *Arizona Quarterly: A Journal of American Literature, Culture, and Theory* 59, no. 2 (Summer 2003), 66 and 60.

15. The term "miscegenation" was first coined in an 1864 pamphlet with that title. Arguing that the term "amalgamation"—the usual word for "race mixing" at the time—was a "poor word," the anonymous authors of the pamphlet invented the word "miscegenation"—from the Latin *miscere* (to mix) and *genus* (race)—to better describe the mixing of two or more races. The pamphlet was widely circulated and even the topic of intense congressional debates in the lead-up

to the 1864 election. Presenting itself as an abolitionist tract, the pamphlet argued that miscegenated populations are "much superior, mentally, physically, and morally, to those pure or unmixed" and goes so far as to claim that there are no pure races. See *Miscegenation: The Theory of the Blending of Races, Applied to the American White Man and Negro* (New York: H. Dexter, Hamilton & Co., 1864), 8 and 15. Proclaiming the virtues of miscegenation—and suggesting that it is part of Lincoln's and the Republican party's platform—the pamphlet was actually a literary hoax meant to oppose emancipation and racial equality. Suggesting that the Lincoln administration was in favor of the mixing of races, it hoped to feed the fear that Lincoln wanted to destroy white privilege. Written by *New York World* editor David Croly and reporter George Wakeman, the pamphlet was part of a Copperhead campaign against Lincoln. Inspired by an anti-Black agenda, it was meant to rile up the anti-abolitionist movement in the hope that this activism would result in Lincoln's defeat in the upcoming election. Aggressively opposed to intermixture and the abolitionist cause, Croly and Wakeman could be said to have engaged in what we today might call "trolling"—and on a rather large political scale. Croly and Wakeman's effort to introduce the term "miscegenation" in order to mobilize their readers against racial parity has its counterparts in present-day arguments about the various threats to white privilege embodied in changes in demographics, patterns of migration and immigration, and the ordinary intercourse of different populations, all of which fall under what has been called "replacement theory"—the theory that there is a plan to replace white populations by a more diverse and mixed population. For the definitive account of Croly and Wakeman's hoax and its consequences, see Sidney Kaplan, "The Miscegenation Issue in the Election of 1864," *Journal of Negro History* 34, no. 3 (July 1949), 274–343.

16. Cited in David B. Chesebrough, *Frederick Douglass: Oratory from Slavery* (Westport, CT: Greenwood Press, 1998), 51.

17. W. E. B. Du Bois, *John Brown: A Biography* (New York: Oxford University Press, 2020), 162 and 147.

18. In a reading of the "double consciousness" of Brown himself, Chandler writes: "in order to live, he had to take this socially and historically granted life [the fact of his being 'White'] and dispense with it, kill it, destroy it, give it up to the risk and possibility of absolute dissolution. This meant that, within the circuit of his own experience, he had to die twice: once as that ordinary historical being called a 'White' man and, again, as that flesh-and-blood being who can only be given a 'proper' name: John Brown." Tracing what he calls "the strange movement of a 'White' man becoming 'otherwise,' other than simply 'white,' perhaps," he adds, "[w]e will not try to name all at once what he became—avoiding, first, the idea that he became something else all at

371

once or finally, and also, secondly, the idea that he became, simply, Negro, or Black." Instead, he stays with Du Bois's own formulation: that Brown of all "Americans has perhaps come nearest to touching the real souls of black folk."

For Brown, experiencing "a movement of becoming other" is "both to become other than a 'White' man, while yet unavoidably reproducing that very figure of being, even in the movement of becoming other, of becoming other than simply 'white.' On the other hand, this movement, this becoming other, is also to become what one 'is' through or by way of the other. It is, thus, this risk of self in the detour or passageway through the other that remains the scene of the production of the deaths and lives of John Brown." See Chandler, *X: The Problem of the Negro as a Problem for Thought*, 115 and 117. We are indebted throughout our discussion of intermixture to Chandler's own analysis of this term in Du Bois.

19. Du Bois, *John Brown: A Biography*, 165 and 168.

20. Nahum Dimitri Chandler, *"Beyond This Narrow Now" or, Delimitations, of W. E. B. Du Bois* (Durham: Duke University Press, 2022), 206–207.

21. W. E. B. Du Bois, "The Present Outlook for the Dark Races of Mankind," in Du Bois, *The Problem of the Color Line at the Turn of the Twentieth Century: The Essential Early Writings*, ed. Nahum Dimitri Chandler (New York: Fordham University Press, 2015), 122

22. W. E. B. Du Bois, *The Souls of Black Folk*, ed. Brent Hayes Edwards (Oxford: Oxford University Press, 2007), 15.

23. Du Bois's ambivalence toward miscegenation has its analogue in Benjamin's own ambivalence toward technology. Miscegenation and technology can be instrumentalized in both salutary and destructive ways, but, because of their respective inevitability, the processes that make them what they are can never be reversed or overcome.

24. Du Bois, *John Brown: A Biography*, 166.

25. W. E. B. Du Bois, "Miscegenation," 1935, W. E. B. Du Bois Papers (MS 312), Special Collections and University Archives, University of Massachusetts Amherst Libraries. See https://credo.library.umass.edu/view/full/mums312-b229-i063. The manuscript bears the date January 10, 1935 at its top and notes that the piece was being prepared for the *Encyclopedia Sexualis; A Comprehensive Encyclopaedia-Dictionary of the Sexual Sciences*, ed. Victor Robinson (New York: Dingwall Rock, 1936). It has been published in W. E. B. Du Bois, *Against Racism: Unpublished Essays, Papers, Addresses, 1887–1961*, ed. Herbert Aptheker (Amherst: University of Massachusetts, 1985), 90–100.

26. Ibid., 90–91.

27. Ibid., 91–92.

28. Ibid., 95–96.

29. Ibid., 100.

30. Juliet Hooker, *Theorizing Race in the Americas: Douglass, Sarmiento, Du Bois, and Vasconcelos* (New York: Oxford University Press, 2017), 124.

31. See Richard Scheidenhelm, ed., *The Response to John Brown* (Belmont, CA: Wadsworth, 1972), 37.

32. Franny Nudelman, *John Brown's Body: Slavery, Violence, and the Culture of War* (Chapel Hill: University of North Carolina Press, 2004), 18 and 23.

33. Ibid., 18 and 16.

34. The folk song "I Dreamed I Saw Joe Hill Last Night"—composed by Earl Robinson in 1936, with lyrics from a 1925 poem by Alfred Hayes—memorializes the labor activist and songwriter Joe Hill by rewriting "John Brown's Body." It transforms the earlier anthem into a song about the struggle of labor and the need for a political strike (albeit an organized labor strike and not a general one). The strike was to come in the form of a collective response to Joe Hill's 1915 execution. Hill was a Swedish immigrant and itinerant worker whose labor activism took the form, beyond his popular songs, of writings and cartoons. He was executed after a dubious murder conviction and, despite pleas from Helen Keller and President Woodrow Wilson, he became a martyr to the labor movement. His last will, which also became a song, reads: "My will is easy to decide / For there is nothing to divide / My kin don't need to fuss and moan / 'Moss does not cling to rolling stone' / My body? Oh, if I could choose / I would to ashes it reduce / And let the merry breezes blow / My dust to where some flowers grow / Perhaps some fading flower then / Would come to life and bloom again. / This is my Last and final Will. / Good Luck to All of you. / Joe Hill." After cremation, Hill's ashes were distributed into 600 envelopes, and sent to the delegates at the Tenth Convention of the Industrial Workers of the World (IWW) in Chicago and to sympathizers. This scattering of Hill's body is inscribed in Hayes's poem:

I dreamed I saw Joe Hill last night, / Alive as you or me. / Says I, "But Joe, you're ten years dead." / "I never died," says he, / "I never died," says he. / "In Salt Lake City, Joe," says I, / Him standing by my bed, / "They framed you on a murder charge." / Says Joe, "But I ain't dead," / Says Joe, "But I ain't dead." / "The copper bosses killed you, Joe, / They shot you, Joe," says I. / "Takes more than guns to kill a man," / Says Joe, "I didn't die," / Says Joe, "I didn't die." / And standing there as big as life / And smiling with his eyes / Says Joe, "What they forgot to kill / Went on to organize, / Went on to organize. / Joe Hill ain't dead," he says to me, / "Joe Hill ain't never died. / Where working men are out on strike, / Joe Hill is at their side, / Joe Hill is at their side. / From San Diego up to Maine, / In every mine and mill, / Where workers strike and organize," / Says he, "You'll find Joe Hill," / Says he, "You'll find Joe Hill." / I dreamed I saw Joe Hill last night, / Alive as you or me. / Says I, "But Joe, you're ten years dead." / "I never died," says he, / "I never died," says he.

After Earl Robinson put the poem to music, Black Communist activist and antifascist bass-baritone lawyer and actor Paul Robeson became its most famous performer. During McCarthyism, Robeson's music and films were removed from public distribution in the United States. However, in 1956, the British Workers Music Association released a single that paired Robeson's interpretations of "Joe Hill" and "John Brown's Body." In the same way that "John Brown's Body" was kept alive by its repeated singing, "Joe Hill" has remained in circulation through renditions not only by Robeson but by Joan Baez and Bruce Springsteen. The folksinger Otis Gibbs tells an even more interesting version of the ongoing circulation of Hill's body when he reveals that union leaders decided to have folksingers sympathetic with Hill and his political activism carry on his legacy by eating his ashes. He states that he and Billy Bragg were among the singers chosen. See https://www.youtube.com/watch?v=YYoO1v07_ XQ. We thank Fred Moten for referring us to the "Joe Hill" rewriting of "John Brown's Body."

35. That the comet is always a political figure that begins in uncertainty—that it always has been read as an omen, as a portent of cataclysmic change or disaster—is legible in another comet we wish to evoke here, one that appears, like all comets, in the temporal rhythm of a recurrence. In this instance, it is Abraham Lincoln himself who appears on an illustrated envelope as the Great Comet of 1861. Streaking across the skies in the midst of a nation torn by civil war, the 1861 comet was viewed as an allegory of the war at a moment when its outcome was unknown, when it was not clear if the comet augured peace or war, when it was unclear whether Lincoln, identified here with the comet, was hurling toward earth to destroy slavery or to meet his own demise.

Illustrated envelopes with themes emphasizing the divisions between the North and the South were ubiquitous in the early years of the war. In this example, the white stars scattered across the blue background inscribe the American flag within the heavens, suggesting that Lincoln is an instrument in God's hands, hurled toward the earth to accomplish God's will. In addition, the red stripes that compose the tail of the comet evoke the Union at the same time that they recall the identification, prevalent in abolitionist discourse, between the stripes of the flag and the bloody lashes across the bodies of slaves who had been whipped. In this way, the image references not only the fact that the war began in a conflict over slavery—that America's identity was intimately bound with slavery—but also what Lincoln's leadership might help leave behind, even as he carries this legacy forward.

In relation to our reading of Du Bois's "The Comet," it is perhaps pertinent to remember that, in "The Coming of the Lord" section of *Black Reconstruction*, Du Bois himself cites a comment from Lincoln in which the President expresses his initial doubt about the efficacy of the Emancipation Proclamation with reference to a historical comet. In response to the 1456 appearance of what later would be identified as Halley's comet, Pope Callixtus III is said to have issued a proclamation ordering that bells ring to frighten the comet away, that prayers be made to deliver the world from the comet's potential destructiveness, and, in one version, that the comet even be excommunicated. Evoking this apocryphal story, Lincoln declares, "What good would a proclamation of Emancipation from me do, especially as we are now situated? I do not want to issue a document that the whole world will see must necessarily be inoperative, like the Pope's bull against the comet" (see *BR*, 107). That Du Bois cites Lincoln here confirms that he associates Lincoln with the figure of the comet, and, in particular, in relation to the prospect of the Emancipation Proclamation, however tenuous its long-term effects might be. In Du Bois, the comet is always a figure for emancipation.

XX. TO THE PLANETARIUM

1. Friedrich Nietzsche, *Beyond Good and Evil: Prelude to a Philosophy of the Future*, trans. Walter Kaufmann (New York: Vintage Books, 1989), 215–216; and Fredric Jameson, *Archaeologies of the Future: The Desire Called Utopia and Other Science Fictions* (London: Verso, 2005), xii.

2. Michael W. Jennings, "Introduction," in *Walter Benjamin: One-Way Street*, ed. Michael W. Jennings, trans. Edmund Jephcott (Cambridge, MA: Belknap Press of Harvard University Press, 2016), 1.

3. Walter Benjamin, *Origin of the German Trauerspiel*, trans. Howard Eiland (Cambridge, MA: Harvard University Press, 2019), 2.

4. Given the centrality of children in the book—children always augur a relation to the future—it is not surprising that the "inhale and exhale" of its rhythms have their counterpart in what Benjamin describes as a child's capacity to string together a series of enigmatic and poetic phrases that appear surprising in their juxtaposition. He views the child's tendency toward an almost unpredictable form of association as a performance of linguistic displacement that does not foreclose but rather expands and even explodes the potential of each word to form new sets of poetic relations beyond either semantic denotation or grammatical order. The example he gives—which mimes the multiple directions of *One-Way Street* (a tactic that makes the book's title one of its jokes, if not its primary target)—is the sequence "pretzel, feather, pause, lament, clowning": "Time sweeps through nature like a pretzel. The feather paints the landscape, and if a pause ensues, it is filled with rain. No lament is heard, for there is no clowning around" (Walter Benjamin, *Selected Writings*, vol. 2: *1927–1934*, ed. Michael W. Jennings, Howard Eiland, and Gary

Smith [Cambridge, MA: Belknap Press of Harvard University Press, 1999], 727).

5. For a wonderful introduction to the history, culture, and politics of the planetarium and, in particular, the London Planetarium and its function as a cinematic and technical medium, see *AA Files* 66, ed. Thomas Weaver (2013).

6. Benjamin admired Friedlaender's 1919 *Creative Indifference*, but was particularly interested in the latter's review of Ernst Bloch's *The Spirit of Utopia*—which he planned to discuss in relation to *Lesabéndio* in his politics book. He especially appreciated Friedlaender's insistence on the relation between metaphysics and politics. For Friedlaender—who published under the pseudonym *Mynona*, a backward spelling of the German word for "anonymous"—thought must be understood as a creative principle that is indifferent to the separation between subject and object, between the mind and the body, and is capable of creatively overcoming the limitations of the self. This overcoming not only allows for the formation of a higher communal being, a being both objective and technological, but it is also the beginning of all genuine politics. It permits the possibility of a state that would be composed of singular pluralities. For a discussion of Friedlaender's influence on Benjamin, see Uwe Steiner's "The True Politician: Walter Benjamin's Concept of the Political," trans. Colin Sample, *New German Critique*, no. 83 (Spring–Summer 2001), esp. 62–68.

7. Miriam Bratu Hansen, "Room-for-Play: Benjamin's Gamble with Cinema," *October* 109 (Summer 2004), 43.

8. Donna Haraway, *How Like a Leaf: An Interview with Thyrza Nichols Goodeye* (New York: Routledge, 1999), 120.

9. Benjamin, *Selected Writings*, vol. 4: *1938–1940*, ed. Howard Eiland and Michael W. Jennings (Cambridge, MA: Belknap Press of Harvard University Press, 2003), 387 (translation modified). For the original French, see *GS*, 2.2:631–632.

10. Here we reference Eduardo Viveiros de Castro's concept of "cosmological perspectivism." See Eduardo Viveiros de Castro, *Cosmological Perspectivism in Amazonia and Elsewhere* (Manchester, UK: HAU Masterclass Series, 2012). This book brings together four lectures that Viveiros de Castro first delivered in the Department of Social Anthropology at Cambridge University in the spring of 1998.

11. Benjamin, *Selected Writings*, 2:733.

12. Paul Scheerbart, *Lesabéndio: An Asteroid Novel*, trans. Christina Svendsen (Cambridge, MA: Wakefield Press, 2012), 54–55. All references to this novel are to this edition and will be noted parenthetically by *L* and page number.

13. That Pallasian is a learned language means that it is no one's native tongue. As Benjamin puts it, "What is crucial about this language is its arbitrary, constructed nature, in contrast to organic language." This linguistic detail appeals to Benjamin because it allows him to conceptualize further what a depersonalized or impersonal language might look like, and, in turn, to begin to move beyond forms of national identification, birthright, and property that often are associated with so called "native" languages. This depersonalization and impersonality also point to a difference between Benjamin and Scheerbart in relation to their respective conceptions of the human body. If Scheerbart exhibits a certain aversion to bodily functions—sex, birth, digestion (the Pallasians are sexless, they are "hatched" from pods, and they absorb nutrients through their pores)—Benjamin chooses to read what is desexualized and dematerialized in *Lesabéndio* not as something to be averted but as something to be embraced, and specifically in order to formalize a more precise political understanding of impersonality. This difference becomes clearer if we note that Scheerbart's aversion to the human body is tied to his aversion to violence of all kinds, and that, as we will see, his novel—associating violence most directly with the planet Earth—eliminates everything that could potentially cause friction within the community, anything that would move in the direction of private property, possessiveness, greed, and even sexual difference. The sources of friction are either eradicated altogether or reduced through rhetorical persuasion that moves the Pallasians to an eventual consensus. Benjamin, on the other hand, believes that violence cannot be fully eradicated, so his critique is directed toward the antagonisms that fuel, justify, and instrumentalize violence.

14. Benjamin, *Selected Writings*, 2:733–734.

15. Interestingly, the Glass Movement itself began with the publication of private epistolary exchanges between thinkers and architects; it was, to a large degree, the direct result of the elimination of elitist practices of privacy in favor of more transparent, public conversations.

16. *Lesabéndio*'s emphasis on the subjugation or surrender to the "One" would appear to be at odds with Benjamin's proto-communist reading of the text; indeed, as is the case with quite a few avant-garde texts of the time, *Lesabéndio*'s language could easily bend in the direction of proto-fascism. Benjamin's emphasis on the collectivist characteristics of Lesabéndio's plan does not entirely eliminate the risks of Scheerbart's language, with its logic of sacrifice, cathexis, redemption, and messianism. These risks are particularly present in the passages that describe the Pallasians' often comic instrumentalization of the Quikko and the massive "harvesting" of new Pallasians that are then indoctrinated into the collective purpose of building Lesabéndio's Tower. That Benjamin often focuses on materials whose political valence is ambivalent or illegible again suggests the indeterminacy he sees at the heart of political gestures, and which belongs to the risk of transformation. In the instance of *Lesabéndio*, however, he is particularly interested in the way the novel's language of the "One" is

fissured by the multiplicity, plurality, and meta-morphosis that characterizes it. In other words, while the language of *Lesabéndio* may at times have relays with the program of fascism, Benjamin's reading of the text finds in these same moments resources for moving the text in an antifascist direction.

17. Walter Benjamin, *Selected Writings*, vol. 3: *1935–1938*, ed. Howard Eiland and Michael W. Jennings (Cambridge, MA: Belknap Press of Harvard University Press, 2002), 124–125.

18. That the revolutionary transformation of Pallas requires the joining of its head and torso, its "mind" and "body," can be read as an enactment of a philosophical fragment that Blanqui writes in 1849 in which he suggests that there can be no revolution that does not bring thought and matter together. In Blanqui's words, "[i]t is a disastrous error to think one can transform a country by purely material means." Scheerbart understands that the same holds for the planetary as well. See Louis Auguste Blanqui, "1830–1880: Philosophical and Political Fragments," in *The Blanqui Reader*, ed. Peter Hallward and Philippe Le Goff, trans. Mitchell Abidor, Peter Hallward, and Philippe Le Goff (New York: Verso, 2018), 129.

19. Louis Auguste Blanqui, "Communism: The Future Society," in *The Blanqui Reader*, 250. Blanqui's sense that communism was still to come distanced him from most "Marxists." As Philippe Le Goff has noted, Luxemburg's subtle understanding of Blanqui and his place within the history and politics of communism, both during and after his life, enabled her to register a difference between Blanqui and "Blanquism" (just as she saw a difference between Marx and Marxism, a difference that would be reinforced later by Raya Dunayevskaya). Citing her 1906 essay on "Blanquism and Social Democracy," Le Goff writes:

> The actual validity of this account was seldom considered. Rosa Luxemburg for one did recognize that the question of whether or not Engels's characterization of Blanqui "is perfectly just can still be discussed. For in 1848," she explained, "Blanqui did not foresee his club forming a 'small minority' at all; on the contrary, in a period of powerful revolutionary upsurge, he was certain that, upon his call, the entire working people—if not in France, then at least in Paris—would rise up to fight the ignominious and criminal policies of the bourgeois government." "Nevertheless," she continued, arriving at the crucial point, "this is not the main question. What concerns us is whether, as comrade Plekhanov strives to demonstrate, Engels's description of Blanqui can be applied to the Bolsheviks." At stake, then, was not the extent to which "Blanquism" represented an accurate description of Blanqui's own politics and project, but the term's function as

a category in contemporaneous political disputes to denote—and thereby condemn—voluntarist adventurism, substitutionist vanguardism and anti-democratic elitism.

In other words, what was at stake—something Blanqui knew very well—was a matter of reading, and the consequences of reading and misreading, politically. See Philippe Le Goff, *Auguste Blanqui and the Politics of Popular Empowerment* (London: Bloomsbury, 2020), 12. For Luxemburg's essay, see https://www.marxists.org/archive/luxemburg /1906/06/blanquism.html. It would be interesting to trace her own complex relation to Blanqui, but, if—anticipating Lenin, Trotsky, and the Bolsheviks in their conviction that armed uprisings require planning and organization—Blanqui believes that the seizure of power cannot be left to spontaneity, Luxemburg (putting her own distance between her and readings of her) believes such uprisings always need to be mediated by the masses and cannot be organized or planned by either a party or an elite committee.

20. Louis Auguste Blanqui, "Letter to Tessy," September 6, 1852, in *The Blanqui Reader*, 123.

21. See Frank Chouraqui, "At the Crossroads of History: Blanqui at the Castle of the Bull," in Louis Auguste Blanqui, *Eternity by the Stars: An Astronomical Hypothesis*, trans. Frank Couraqui (London: Contra-Mundum Press, 2021), 7.

22. Louis Auguste Blanqui, *Eternity by the Stars*, in *The Blanqui Reader*, 295, 292, and 295.

23. Blanqui, "1830–1880: Philosophical and Political Fragments," 131–132.

24. Ibid., 129.

25. Ibid., 133.

26. Ibid., 130.

27. Blanqui, *Eternity by the Stars*, 305.

28. Blanqui, "1830–1880: Philosophical and Political Fragments," 132.

29. Blanqui, *Eternity by the Stars*, 293.

30. Ibid., 284.

XXI. A RED COMMON-WEALTH

1. Werner Hamacher, *Minima Philologica* (New York: Fordham University Press, 2015), 76; and Fred Moten, *Stolen Life (consent not to be a single being)* (Durham: Duke University Press, 2018), 138.

2. Here we nod in the direction of Marx, who praises the Paris Commune for "storming heaven." See Karl Marx, "Letter to Dr. Kugelmann, Concerning the Paris Commune," April 12, 1871, https://www.marxists.org/archive/marx/works/1871/letters/71_04_12.htm.

3. That Benjamin does not restrict the practice of citation to the citation of texts—that he does not dissociate texts from history and materiality—can be seen in this passage from his *Arcades Project*:

> The events surrounding the historian, and in which he himself takes part, will underlie

his presentation in the form of a text written in invisible ink. The history which he lays before the reader comprises, as it were, the citations occurring in this text, and it is only these citations that occur in a manner legible to all. To write history thus means to *cite* history. It belongs to the concept of citation, however, that the historical object in each case is torn from its context. (*AP*, 476)

4. On this point, see Gerhard Richter, *Inheriting Walter Benjamin* (London: Bloomsbury, 2016), 10.

5. Leonard Cohen makes a similar point in his song "Anthem," in which he says: "There is a crack in everything. That's how the light gets in." Cited in *Leonard Cohen: Poems and Songs*, ed. Robert Faggen (New York: Alfred A. Knopf, 1993), 188.

6. Karl Marx, *Capital: A Critique of Political Economy*, vol. 3, trans. David Fernbach (New York, Penguin Books, 1991), 959. As Agnes Heller notes in her analysis of Marx's communism of "associated producers," a society no longer based on property and a capitalist value and labor system would also understand wealth, value, and need differently. She argues that these three core concepts should be understood in relation to species-being and not to individuals, altering our relation to nature. Wealth is reconstituted as time and relation rather than possession, and capitalist waste ceases because necessity and surplus are no longer opposed to one another. See Agnes Heller, *The Theory of Need in Marx* (London: Verso, 2018).

7. Marx, *Capital: A Critique of Political Economy*, vol. 1, trans. Ben Fowkes (New York: Penguin Books, 1990), 875. We have used here the conventional translation of Marx's *ursprüngliche Akkumulation* because most of the secondary sources and present translations of Marx's *Capital* also use "primitive accumulation." We will discuss this phrase later, but, as Rosalind Morris points out, the phrase can more properly be translated "originary accumulation" and there is also textual evidence that Marx believed the word "accumulation" should even be "expropriation," in which case another version would be "originary expropriation." This alteration makes it an issue of what happens to the expropriated rather than what is accumulated by the capitalist. See Morris, "*Ursprüngliche Akkumulation*: The Secret of an Originary Mistranslation," *boundary 2* 23, no. 3 (2016), 31–34. We look forward to Paul Reitter's new edition of the first volume of *Capital*, which will be the first English translation of the book in nearly fifty years. We thank him and Paul North, who is coediting the edition, for their kindness in letting us preview the translation.

8. Marx, *Capital*, 1:915. We have excerpted the part of this passage that focuses on the Spanish conquest because we are interested here in the thread of Las Casas that one can follow from Marx to Benjamin, but the full passage also references, as we have noted before, "the

beginnings of the conquest and plunder of India, and the conversion of Africa into a preserve for the commercial hunting of blackskins," and, "hard on their heels," Marx adds, "follows the commercial war of the European nations, which has the globe as its battlefield."

9. Ibid.

10. Daniel Nemser, "Primitive Spiritual Accumulation and the Colonial Extraction Economy," *Creative Commons* 5 (2014), 3.

11. Marx makes several references to Las Casas, but he would have been particularly attuned to the closeness between Christianity and colonization because of his reading of William Howitt's 1838 *Colonization and Christianity: A Popular History of the Treatment of the Natives by the Europeans in All Their Colonies*. In "The Genesis of the Industrial Capitalist" section of *Capital*, he quotes what

> W. Howitt, a man who specializes in being a Christian, says of the Christian colonial system: "The barbarities and desperate outrages of the so-called Christian race, throughout every region of the world, and upon every people they have been able to subdue, are not to be paralleled by those of any other race, however fierce, however untaught, and however reckless of mercy and of shame, in any age of the earth."

See Marx, *Capital*, 1:916.

12. The complexity of Las Casas's stance can be viewed, in its most negative light, through the lens of a passage in Du Bois's "The Souls of White Folk." There, referencing "the robbery of other times and races," he points to "conquest sugared with religion; mutilation and rape masquerading as culture." See W. E. B. Du Bois, "The Souls of White Folk," *DW*, 19.

13. While Las Casas offers a detailed account of the plunder, enslavement, and physical torture the Mexica endured, he chooses not to recount the violence of indigenous cultures themselves and the continued and ferocious strife between them. The bloodiness of the expansion and settling of the Aztec empire—often the result of strategic and commercial interests—increased with the establishment of the so-called Triple Alliance among the Mexica, the Texcocans, and the Tacubans that secured Aztec rule. Assuming power in 1440, Moctezuma began a series of campaigns against the Chalca, the people of Puebla and Tlaxcala, and, moving toward the Gulf of Mexico, the Huaxtecs and Totonacs. There are records of victims decapitated or having their hearts cut out, shot full of arrows, stoned, crushed, skinned, burned or buried alive, or thrown from the tops of temples. Although the Aztecs were able to centralize their power, it was the imperialist extension of their rule that made them vulnerable and that Cortés could not only take advantage of—recruiting enemies of the Aztecs to assist in his siege—but could also *a posteriori* use to justify Spanish savagery and insist

on the religious and legal need for the Catholic conversion of Amerindians. As we will see in our discussion of Marx's *Ethnological Notebooks*, caste and property often signal the beginning of the ruination of noncapitalist societies, as was the case with the Aztecs. We mention all this to discourage a romanticization of Amerindian cultures, but without minimizing the genocidal violence perpetrated by the Spanish empire. If Las Casas points to the infinity of Spanish violence, he willingly circumscribes that infinity in order to preserve the myth of "the noble savage," which, in turn, he uses to argue that Amerindians are ideal candidates for Christian conversion.

14. Bartolomé de Las Casas, *A Short Account of the Destruction of the Indies*, ed. and trans. Nigel Griffin (New York: Penguin Books, 1992), 55, 65.

15. Ibid., 30.

16. Ibid., 27–28.

17. In a rather remarkable text that points to the way in which trees are often granted rights that are not given to human beings, Marx references this same story, which he cites from Antonio de Herrera y Tordesillas's 1601 *Descripcion de las Indias Ocidentalises*, a text which, in turn, takes the story from Las Casas: "The *savages of Cuba* regarded gold as a *fetish of the Spaniards*. They celebrated a feast in its honor, sang in a circle around it and then threw it into the sea. If the Cuban savages had been present at the Rhine Province Assembly, would they not have regarded *wood* as the *Rhinelanders' fetish?*" See Karl Marx, "Proceedings of the Sixth Rhine Provincial Assembly—Debates on the Theft of Wood," trans. Jack Cohen et al., in Marx and Engels, *Collected Works*, vol. 1 (New York: International Publishers, 1976), 262. For a reading of Marx's essay in the context of a wonderfully extended and detailed reading of the concept of fetishism, see Rosalind C. Morris's "After de Brosses: Fetishism, Translation, Comparativism, Critique," in *The Returns of Fetishism: Charles de Brosses and the Afterlives of an Idea*, ed. Rosalind C. Morris and Daniel H. Leonard (Chicago: University of Chicago Press, 2017), 133–319. We will return to Marx's suggestion that one man's god is another man's wooden stick in our discussion of Benjamin's first Mexican dream in *One-Way Street*, but here we wish to mark the circulation of particular texts and passages through time, since this is part of what we are calling a "red common-wealth" and part of what we view as the rich resources from which we can draw in order to address the present but also to reactivate the past in the name of a different future.

18. Nemser, "Primitive Spiritual Accumulation and the Colonial Extraction Economy," 6.

19. As David Michael Smith writes, citing David Stannard and considering the devastation of the indigenous population in the Americas after 1492, "the almost inconceivable number of deaths caused by the invasion and conquest of these lands by Europeans and their descendants constitute 'the worst human holocaust the world [has] ever witnessed.' ... No words or numbers can adequately convey the scale of the horror and tragedy involved in the greatest sustained loss of human life in history." See Smith, "Counting the Dead: Estimating the Loss of Life in the Indigenous Holocaust, 1492–Present," https://www.se.edu/native-american/wp-content/uploads/sites/49/2019/09/A-NAS-2017-Proceedings-Smith.pdf.

20. Las Casas, *A Short Account of the Destruction of the Indies*, 50–51, translation modified. For the original Spanish, see Bartolomé de Las Casas, *Brevísima relación de la destruición de las Indias, Colegida por el Obispo Don Fray Bartolomé de Las Casas o Casaus, de la orden de Santo Domingo Año 1552*, in *Digitalia Hispanica* (2006), 147.

The mournful lament of the Amerindians in response to the gratuitous and violent excess of the colonizers poignantly echoes that of Niobe. In Benjamin's critique of violence, the myth of Niobe conveys the massification of violence and the reciprocal installation of force and its justification, both of which resonate with the Spanish imperial genocide. As with Niobe, there is no indigenous action that justifies the mass murder of millions, including the killing of children and pregnant women in front of their families. Any attempt at justification (infractions, laziness, idolatry, paganism, cannibalism) are *a posteriori* instantiations of a border (here between the human and the inhuman, subject and object) that can justify and excuse, to use Las Casas's word, the "infinite" violence that sustains the Spanish empire and its laws.

21. Las Casas, *A Short Account of the Destruction of the Indies*, 54–55. For the original, see Las Casas, *Brevísima relación de la destruición de las Indias*, 151.

22. On this point, see Alberto Moreiras, "Ten Notes on Primitive Imperial Accumulation: Ginés de Sepúlveda, Las Casas, Fernández Oviedo," *Interventions: International Journal of Postcolonial Studies* 2, no. 3 (2000), 352–353.

23. Benjamin's declared wish to give voice to the vanquished could be said to be related to his early interest in the conquest and colonization of the Americas. In this context, he would have been particularly attentive to the fact that any attempt to have the vanquished speak would itself be mediated and translated by the colonial endeavor.

24. For a discussion of Benjamin's engagement with Lehmann, during and after the seminars, see Peter Fenves, "Walter Benjamin, *Altmexiko*, and the Dream of a Different Archaeology," forthcoming in *Archaeology and Its Avatars*, ed. Jorge Coronado and Alexander Herrera Wassilowski (Evanston: Northwestern University Press, 2024); and Julia Ng, "Afterword: Toward Another Critique of Violence," in Walter Benjamin, *Toward the Critique of Violence: A Critical Edition*, ed. Peter Fenves and Julia Ng (Stanford: Stanford University Press, 2021), 150–153.

25. See Gershom Scholem, *Walter Benjamin: The Story of a Friendship* (London: Faber and Faber, 1982), 43.

26. Benjamin's two Mexican dreams appeared a few months before their inclusion in *One-Way Street* in slightly different versions in a collection of dreams put together by Ignaz Ježowski. See Ježower, *Das Buch der Träume* (Berlin: Rowolt, 1928), 270–271. Fenves offers translations of these two earlier versions of the dreams (numbered 523 and 524 in Ježower's compendium):

> 523   A dream came to me of being a member of a research expedition [*forschende Expedition*] in Mexico. After having penetrated a high primordial forest, we happened upon an above-ground system of caves in the mountains, where, from the time of the first missionaries [*aus der Zeit der ersten Missionare*] a [religious] order has maintained itself up until now, an order whose brothers continue the work of converting the indigenous people. In an immense and enclosed central grotto, pointed in a gothic manner, a worship service [*Gottesdienst*] took place according to the oldest rite [*dem ältesten Ritus*]. We approached and received its article of faith [*Hauptstück*]: toward a wooden bust of God the father, which somehow appeared as though attached to one of the cave walls high above, a Mexican fetish was raised by a priest. Then, the head of God moved three times, negating [*verneinend*], from right to left.
>
> 524   In a dream I saw a desolate stretch of land. It was the marketplace in Weimar. There, excavations were organized. I, too, scratched in the sand a little. Then came forth the tip [*Spitz*] of a church tower. Overjoyed [*Hocherfreut*], I thought to myself: a Mexican sanctuary [*Heiligtum*] from the time of pre-animism, from the anaquivitzli. I woke up laughing. (ana = prae, vi = vie, Witz = Mexican church!)

See Fenves, "Walter Benjamin, *Altmexiko*, and the Dream of a Different Archaeology."

27. If Benjamin is a displaced figure of Lehmann, Lehmann is in turn a displacement and condensation of several other figures and texts. Within the dream's plastic logic, any figure can become any other figure. In this instance, the name "Lehmann" references an ever-widening set of associations. As Fenves notes, Lehmann appears as a cover for Konrad Preuß, a German ethnologist, a rival of Lehmann's, who had written an account of his exploration of caves and his witnessing of religious rites in Mexico. It is Preuß and not Lehmann who, according to Fenves, is more decisive for Benjamin's first Mexican dream, but, within the logic of the dream, it is impossible to prioritize either ethnologist since neither appears as himself. Each character in the dream already belongs to the archive of texts Benjamin has read, materials he has studied, and figures he has encountered either in person or through their writings. As in all dreams, the mechanisms of displacement and condensation that work within Benjamin's dream do not follow strict identificatory operations. This does not prevent us, however, from registering the richness that the figure of Lehmann both manifests and obscures here.

28. This denial evokes Matthew 26:34 in which Jesus tells Peter that "before the cock crows, you will deny me three times." That Benjamin's dream is also a citation machine suggests that it is itself an archive; it is the dream of an archive, of what an archive might be—in this instance, an archive of the mutual denial between Spanish missionaries and indigenous communities, a denial that sets one fetish against another, and even against "itself."

29. A ceremony that climaxes in a gesture in which a priest raises a Mexican fetish toward "a wooden bust of God the Father" plays with the structure of the mass. As Russ Leo has suggested to us in a note from January 6, 2023, "in early modern and modern masses, the 'climax' of the mass—the liturgy of the Eucharist—occurs when the priest elevates the 'bread' and 'wine' which become the body and blood of Christ." Benjamin's dream "replaces this sacramental act with a confrontation between a 'sacramental' Mexican idol and a 'Father' whose images or idols are prohibited in *Exodus*. ... The Mexican fetish takes place in the gesture of sacramental offering." This is just one more instance of the blurring of the distinction between Christianity and its indigenous counterpart in Benjamin's dream.

30. On these points, see Heriberto Martínez Yépez, "*¿Sueñan los marxistas con revoluciones aztecas? Poéticas del náhuatl y el México de Karl Marx y Walter Benjamin*" (PhD thesis, University of California, Berkeley, 2018), 107 and 120. We are grateful to Peter Fenves for sharing this dissertation with us.

31. Ibid., 161.

32. The title of the dream is given as "Underground Works" in Benjamin, *Selected Writings*, vol. 1: *1913–1926*, ed. Michael W. Jennings, Howard Eiland, and Gary Smith (Cambridge, MA: Belknap Press of Harvard University Press, 1996), 455, and as "Structural Engineering Works" in Ng, "Afterword: Toward Another Critique of Violence," 156.

33. Martínez Yépez, "*¿Sueñan los marxistas con revoluciones aztecas?*," iii and 168–169.

34. Ibid., 104. Martínez Yépez emphasizes what he considers Benjamin's complicity with colonial extractivism, but we suggest that Benjamin's dream offers resources for criticizing this same extractivism. While Martínez Yépez's decolonial reading of the two dreams is wonderfully nuanced and the most extended political reading of them we have, he falters in too quickly condemning Benjamin for his "Eurocentrism" and, in turn, Marx for his racism, in the name of

an identity politics that his own argument would seem to belie.

35. Besides Nahuatl, over a hundred languages were spoken in New Spain. Through migration, these languages not only touched one another but also altered one another. Because Nahuatl was the language of the nobility, however, it became the lingua franca of the other regions, and a catalyst for different forms of acculturation. Its privilege became the reason why the Spanish priests selected it above the others. As Serge Gruzinski has noted, the indigenous nobility "learned the language of Cicero, read the Latin classics, and translated great European texts into Nahuatl." See Gruzinski, *The Aztecs: Rise and Fall of an Empire*, trans. Paul G. Bahn (New York: Harry N. Abrams, 1992), 104. Even so, Nahua writers incorporated elements from indigenous traditions, including pictographic designs. Here reading and writing become a means of subjugation and colonial rule as well as a means of survival.

36. Walter Benjamin, "Task of the Translator," trans. Harry Zohn, in Benjamin, *Selected Writings*, 1:262 and 257.

37. Walter Benjamin, *Gesammelte Briefe*, vol. 2: *1919–1924*, ed. Christoph Gödde and Henri Lonitz (Berlin: Suhrkamp Verlag, 1996), 208.

38. In a letter to Werner Kraft from October 28, 1935, Benjamin again evokes Scheerbart, this time to claim that the world is still waiting for a culture that can move beyond the accumulation of violence, the "blood and horror," that, until now, has been culture's signature. This culture has to be imagined since it has never yet existed. He writes, warning of the dire outcome of not imagining this world:

> I have hardly succumbed to the compulsion to make some kind of sense of the current state of the world. There have already been many cultures on this planet that have perished in blood and horror. It is naturally necessary for us to hope that the planet will some day experience a culture that has gone beyond both of those things—indeed, just like Scheerbart, I am inclined to assume that the planet is waiting for this. But it is terribly doubtful whether we will be able to present the planet this gift on its one-hundred- or four-hundred-millionth birthday. And if not, it will ultimately dish out as punishment for us, the planet's heedless well-wishers, the last judgment. (*C*, 516)

39. Martínez Yépez, "¿Sueñan los marxistas con revoluciones aztecas?," 227.

40. Marx, *Capital*, 1:874 and 873, translation modified.

41. See Karl Marx, "The Future Result in British Rule in India," in Marx and Engels, *Collected Works*, vol. 12 (London: Lawrence & Wishart, 1979), 221.

42. Ibid., 356. William Clare Roberts makes a wonderfully persuasive case that Marx structures

the first volume of *Capital* around Dante's *Inferno*, rewriting it "as a descent into the modern social Hell of capital." See Roberts, *Marx's Inferno: The Political Theory of Capital* (Princeton, NJ: Princeton University Press, 2017), 24.

43. See Rosa Luxemburg, *The Accumulation of Capital: A Contribution to the Explanation of Imperialism*, trans. Agnes Schwarzchild (Mansfield Centre, CT: Martino Publishing, 2015), 161. As Rosalind Morris insists, "originary accumulation is a problem of translation ... Marx's own text is marked, in its punctuational, lexical, and syntactic forms, by a recognition of the nontransparency of the concept in a manner that implies the irreducibility of structural principles to temporal ones in the analysis of capitalism." See Morris, "*Ursprüngliche Akkumulation*," 62.

44. See Karl Marx, *Critique of the Gotha Program*, trans. Kevin B. Anderson and Karel Ludenhoff (Oakland, CA: PM Press, 2023), 48.

45. Ibid., 54, 59, 62, 53.

46. Ibid., 52–55, 67, 75, 68.

47. Luxemburg, *The Accumulation of Capital*, 81.

48. Marx, *Capital*, 1:916.

49. Luxemburg, *The Accumulation of Capital*, 368.

50. Ibid., 371.

51. Ibid., 452.

52. Ibid., 359. Luxemburg demonstrates the reach of the violence of capitalism around the globe by emphasizing the colonial infrastructure of commercial expansion, technological innovation, public debt, and militarization. Like Marx, she opposes her analysis to the dominant "illusion" that this colonial network extends itself through "peaceful changes":

> The triumphant march of commodity economy thus begins in most cases with magnificent constructions of modern transport, such as railway lines which cross primeval forests and tunnel through the mountains, telegraph wires which bridge the deserts, and ocean liners which call at the most outlying ports. But it is a mere illusion that these are peaceful changes. Under the standard of commerce, the relations between the East India Company and the spice-producing countries were quite as piratical, extortionate and blatantly fraudulent as present-day relations between American capitalists and the Red Indians of Canada whose furs they buy, or between German merchants and the Negroes of Africa. Modern China presents a classical example of the "gentle," "peace-loving" practices of commodity exchange with backward countries. Throughout the nineteenth century, beginning with the early forties, her history has been punctuated by wars with the object of opening her up to trade by brute force. Missionaries provoked persecutions of Christians, Europeans instigated risings, and in periodical massacres a completely helpless and peaceful agrarian population was forced to match arms with the most modern

capitalist military technique of all the Great Powers of Europe. Heavy war contributions necessitated a public debt, China taking up European loans, resulting in European control over her finances and occupation of her fortifications; the opening of free ports was enforced, railway concessions to European capitalists extorted. By all these measures commodity exchange was fostered in China, from the early thirties of the last century until the beginning of the Chinese revolution. (Ibid., 386–387)

53. Rosa Luxemburg, *Letters from Prison: By Rosa Luxemburg: With a Portrait and a Facsimile*, trans. Eden and Cedar Paul, Young International at Schönberg in Berlin, 1921–1923 (public domain: Luxemburg Internet Archive, 2005). While this passage portrays the devastation of the native population as a kind of surrender to the inevitability of their demise, elsewhere Luxemburg registers their resistance, even if they are eventually defeated: "The redskins put up a desperate resistance; but all who survived the slaughter of forty Red Indian campaigns were swept away like so much rubbish and driven like cattle to the West to be folded in reservations like so many sheep." Luxemburg, *The Accumulation of Capital*, 402–403.

Luxemburg's interest in indigenous cultures later finds its counterpart in the attention *indigenismo* gives to her work, already in the 1920s, but also in the 1960s and '70s, and now again in Latin America's Feminist General Strike/Paro internacional de mujeres, which includes important participation by indigenous women. The still largely unexplored relationship between Luxemburg's political theorizations and Peruvian José Carlos Mariátegui's Marxist *indigenismo* is a red thread we cannot pursue here (further proof that a red common-wealth is an unfinished labor for the many). We only note here that, after Mariátegui's trip to Germany in 1922, he gives two lectures on the German Revolution in which he refers directly to Luxemburg's leadership in it. Later, in 1930, he returns to Luxemburg in his *Defense of Marxism*, and also translates one of her texts into Spanish for his journal *Amauta*. For a good summary of Luxemburg's relation to Latin America, see Hernán Ouviña's "Rosa Luxemburg in Latin America" (March 4, 2020), https://rosalux-ba.org/en/2020/03/04/from-mariategui-to-todays-popular-struggles/

54. Marx, *Capital*, 3:949.

55. Marx, *Capital*, 1:637–638 and 3:949–950.

56. See Paul Burkett, *Marx and Nature: A Red and Green Perspective* (London: Palgrave Macmillan, 1999); John Bellamy Foster, *Marx's Ecology: Materialism and Nature* (New York: Monthly Review Press, 2000), 141–177; John Bellamy Foster and Brett Clark, *The Robbery of Nature: Capitalism and the Ecological Rift* (New York: Monthly Review Press, 2020), 13–23; Kohei Saito, *Karl Marx's Ecosocialism: Capital, Nature, and the Unfinished Critique of Political Economy* (New York: Monthly Review Press, 2017), 63–137; and Saito, *Marx in the Anthropocene: Towards the Idea of Degrowth Communism* (Cambridge: Cambridge University Press, 2022).

57. Cited in K. William Kapp, *The Social Costs of Private Enterprise* (New York: Schocken Books, 1971), 35. As Marx notes in a footnote to his chapter on "Machinery and Large-Scale Industry," one of Liebig's "immortal merits" is "to have developed from the point of view of natural science the negative, i.e. destructive side of modern agriculture." See Marx, *Capital*, 1:638.

58. Ibid., 637–638.

59. See Ralph Waldo Emerson, "Fate," in *The Collected Works of Ralph Waldo Emerson*, vol. 6: *The Conduct of Life*, ed. Douglas Emory Wilson (Cambridge, MA: Belknap Press of Harvard University Press, 2003), 4; and Philip L. Nicoloff, *Emerson on Race and History: An Examination of* English Traits (New York: Columbia University Press, 1961), 134. On Emerson's relation to the guano trade, see Eduardo Cadava, "The Guano of History," in *Cities without Citizens*, ed. Eduardo Cadava and Aaron Levy (Philadelphia: Slought Books, with the Rosenbach Museum & Library, 2003), 137–165.

60. See Lola Loustaunau, Mauricio Betancourt, Brett Clark, and John Bellamy Foster, "Chinese Contract Labor, the Corporeal Rift, and Ecological Imperialism in Peru's Nineteenth-Century Guano Boom," *Journal of Peasant Studies* 49, no. 3 (2022), 530 and 515.

61. Ralph Waldo Emerson, *The Journals and Miscellaneous Notebooks of Ralph Waldo Emerson*, vol. 14: *1854–1861*, ed. Ralph H. Orth et al. (Cambridge, MA: Harvard University Press, 1978), 16. As Emerson puts it, noting that America is flourishing over the fertilizer that ethnic minorities have become: "See the shades of the picture. The German and Irish millions, like the Negro, have a great deal of guano in their destiny. They are ferried over the Atlantic, and carted over America, to ditch and to drudge, to make corn cheap, and then to lie down prematurely to make a spot of green grass on the prairie." See Emerson, "Fate," 9.

62. Evelyn Hu-Dehart, "Coolies, Shopkeepers, Pioneers: The Chinese of Mexico and Peru (1849–1930)," *Amerasia* 15, no. 2 (1989), 92.

63. Ibid., 108.

64. One contemporary account published in *The Southern Planter* in 1855 tells of mass suicides, sometimes involving up to fifty coolies at a time. These suicides were so frequent that the Peruvian government was forced to station guards around the cliffs and shores of the islands to prevent them. Stories about the atrocious work conditions in the guano fields, often similar to abolitionist accounts of the abuse and mistreatment of southern slaves, circulated frequently. See "Interesting from the Chincha Islands," *The Southern Planter* (January 1855), 20–21. Eventually, the gross abuses in the recruitment and transportation of the coolies generated such fierce international

and national criticism that the Peruvian government suspended the trade between 1856 to 1861, and only reopened it later under the more relaxed supervision of the Portuguese.

65. See Karl Marx, *Grundrisse: Foundations of the Critique of Political Economy (Rough Draft)*, trans. Martin Nicolaus (New York: Penguin Books, 1973), 527. On this point, see Foster, *Marx's Ecology*, 156.

66. This legal coercion eerily echoes the Spaniards' 1510 "Requerimiento," the Latin ultimatum read to Amerindians ostensibly to have them accept the political and religious authority of the Spanish Crown in the Americas. Once the document had been read aloud, in a language that no Amerindian was likely to understand, any resistance to royal subjection became legally punishable by death, enslavement, or indentured servitude (the last two being only nominally different). Here the legal, regulatory infrastructure supporting colonial capitalism confirms the absolute complicity among capitalism, law, and violence; it is reenacted, almost verbatim, to justify the enslavement and debt peonage of the coolie contracts.

67. Loustaunau, Betancourt, Clark, and Foster, "Chinese Contract Labor, the Corporeal Rift, and Ecological Imperialism," 512. On this point, see also Foster, *Marx's Ecology*, 173. Kohei Saito's recent *Marx in the Anthropocene* presents a Marx who—once capitalism is revealed as a system that requires and produces scarcity, inequality, and the destruction of nature—embraces "degrowth communism" as an essential feature of a postcapitalist common-wealth, one that would entirely transform what wealth means and how it is shared. This wealth would no longer appear as an "immense collection of commodities." There can be no communal wealth, Saito suggests, that does not begin with the interruption of capitalism's endless logic of production—with the interruption, that is, of its concomitant destruction of nature and generalized exploitation. He cites Benjamin's well-known passage on the "emergency brake" in order to evoke a relation between revolution and degrowth communism (see *Marx in the Anthropocene*, 216). In Benjamin's words, "Marx says that revolutions are the locomotive of world history. But perhaps it is quite otherwise. Perhaps revolutions are an attempt by the passengers on this train—namely the human race—to activate the emergency brake" (*CH*, 402). In our terms, Benjamin's "emergency brake" is another name for the general strike and its force of deposition, and it provides further evidence of his attentive and nuanced reading of Marx—a reading that far exceeds that of the orthodox Marxism of his time, and that only now, in the midst of a climate catastrophe—and with the aid of Saito's work—are we perhaps ready to hear.

68. For an extended account of Fraas's importance to Marx, see Saito, *Karl Marx's Ecosocialism*, 228–255.

69. See Marx, *Capital*, 3:948–949 and 911. After the work of Foster, Clark, and Saito, these passages are all very well known. We owe a felt debt to these scholars' intersecting work on Marx's ecologico-political interests. We also wish to acknowledge the important role that the *Monthly Review* has played in the dissemination of this work and the collaborative character of its endeavors. In a recent article in the journal, Foster notes the pertinence of Marx's ecological analyses to our own precarious ecological moment:

> Marx's ecological critique, coupled with that of Engels, embraced nearly all of the ecological problems known in his time: the expropriation of the commons, soil degradation, deforestation, floods, crop failure, desertification, species destruction, cruelty to animals, food adulteration, pollution, chemical toxins, epidemics, squandering of natural resources (such as coal), regional climate change, hunger, overpopulation, and the vulnerability to extinction of the human species itself. It has now been extended by Marxian ecologists via his theory of metabolic rift to the entire set of anthropogenic rifts in the Earth System present in the twenty-first century, including the contemporary rift in the earth's carbon metabolism.

See Foster, "Marx's Critique of Enlightenment Humanism: A Revolutionary Ecological Perspective," *Monthly Review* 74, no. 8 (January 2023).

70. Foster and Clark, *The Robbery of Nature*, 103. Although we do not have the space here to elaborate the role and place of the "human" in Marx, it is important to remember that he explicitly states in *Capital* that the popular belief in the concept of a common humanity can happen "only in a society where the commodity form is the universal form of the products of labor" (*Capital*, 1:152). Humanity arrives only where the commodity form dominates the historico-political domain. This is why Althusser claims that Marxism is not a humanism, but a "theoretical anti-humanism." See Louis Althusser, "Marxism and Humanism," in *For Marx*, trans. Ben Brewster (London: Verso, 2005), 231. The essay begins with an epigraph from Marx that reads: "My analytical method does not start from man" (ibid., 219). An interesting debate—and one that should be elaborated further—can be had with Foster's recent essay, "Marx's Critique of Enlightenment Humanism," since there he responds to Althusser's claim and usefully clarifies that Marx's conception of the human is itself a critique of bourgeois humanism.

71. Marx and Engels, *Collected Works*, vol. 42 (New York: International Publishers, 1987), 558–559.

72. Kevin B. Anderson, *Marx at the Margins: On Nationalism, Ethnicity, and Non-Western Societies* (Chicago: University of Chicago Press, 2010), 196. Although Marx and Engels initially dismissed the Paris Commune as premature, they came to see it as the communist experiment it quickly

became, albeit a short-lived one that was brutally suppressed. That even revolutionaries such as Marx and Engels can be surprised by revolutionary upheavals, and this despite all their study and activism, tells us something about the nature of revolutions. They always arise as a surprise; it is never possible to prepare fully for their arrival. We can only join the revolution, not plan it, and this because its temporality takes the form of an interruption.

73. See Karl Marx, *The Ethnological Notebooks of Karl Marx*, ed. Lawrence Krader (Assen, The Netherlands: Van Gorcum, 1974), and, on Marx's Russian materials and related correspondence, *Late Marx and the Russian Road: Marx and "the Peripheries of Capitalism,"* ed. Teodor Shanin (New York: Monthly Review Press, 1983). All references to the *Ethnological Notebooks* will be to Krader's edition and will be noted parenthetically by *EN* and page number.

74. Raya Dunayevskaya, "The Last Writings of Marx Point a Trail to the 1980s," in *Rosa Luxemburg, Women's Liberation and Marx's Philosophy of Revolution* (Chicago: University of Illinois Press, 1991), 175–197; Franklin Rosemont, "Karl Marx and the Iroquois," in *Arsenal: Surrealist Subversion* (Chicago: Black Swan Press, 1989), 201–213; Kevin B. Anderson, "Late Writings on Non-Western and Precapitalist Societies," in Anderson, *Marx at the Margins*, 196–236; Saito, *Karl Marx's Ecosocialism*, 263–266; John Bellamy Foster, Brett Clark, and Hannah Holleman, "Marx and the Indigenous," *Monthly Review* 71, no. 9 (February 2020), 9–13; and Bruno Bosteels, "El Marx tardío o la vía mexicana: De los *Apuntes etnológicos* a la correspondencia con Vera Zasúlich," in *La comuna mexicana* (Mexico City: Ediciones Akal México, 2021), 271–311. In the pages that follow, we are most indebted to Dunayevskaya and Anderson (her student).

75. Raya Dunayevskaya, *Rosa Luxemburg, Women's Liberation and Marx's Philosophy of Revolution*, 188 and xxi.

76. Raya Dunayevskaya, *The Power of Negativity: Selected Writings on the Dialectic in Hegel and Marx*, ed. Peter Hudis and Kevin B. Anderson (Lanham, MD: Lexington Books, 2002), 294, and Dunayevskaya, *Rosa Luxemburg, Women's Liberation and Marx's Philosophy of Revolution*, 121 and 139.

77. See Rosemont, "Karl Marx and the Iroquois," 201 and 205.

78. It is not possible for us to offer an extended reading of these remarkable notebooks here. We will only gesture in the direction of a frame for reading them and for attending to what makes them so significant within Marx's corpus. We will return to the *Notebooks* at greater length in a future study of the relation between Marx's dissertation on Democritus and Epicurus's different philosophies of nature and these later notebooks—with particular attention to materialism's basis in what he calls, following Lucretius, the "swerve" of differentiation. For now, we

will restrict ourselves to just a few passages in order to convey the richness of these fragments.

79. Dunayevskaya, *Rosa Luxemburg, Women's Liberation and Marx's Philosophy of Revolution*, 24.

80. See Lewis H. Morgan, *Ancient Society*, ed. Leslie A. White (Cambridge, MA: Belknap Press of Harvard University Press, 1964), 467. It is well known that Morgan was influenced by Darwin's writing on evolution, but what Marx finds in Darwin is a mode of proceeding that—emphasizing transmutation, change, transience, the struggle for existence, and nonhuman agency—moves against teleological ends. As he puts it in a letter from January 16, 1861 to Ferdinand LaSalle soon after he reads Darwin's treatise, "Darwin's work is most important and suits my purpose in that it provides a basis in natural science for the historical class struggle. ... Despite all shortcomings, it is here that, for the first time, 'teleology' in natural science is not only dealt a mortal blow but its rational meaning is empirically explained." See Karl Marx and Frederick Engels, *Selected Correspondence*, trans. Dona Torr (Moscow: Progress Publishers, 1975), 115. It should be noted that Marx reads Darwin through their shared interest in Epicurus, whose materialist philosophy was critical to both of them.

81. Luxemburg's attention to the displacement and extermination of indigenous Native Americans is prompted by her readings of Marx but also by her reading of Morgan's *Ancient Society*, a text that, under Engels's influence, would be appropriated as a Marxist classic for decades after its publication (Luxemburg, for instance, first reads it as a teenager in Poland). Morgan's study of ancient indigenous cultures in the American continent provides her—and Marx before her—with an archive of noncapitalist formations that exhibit their resilience against all odds. Marx's and Luxemburg's interest in Morgan's ethnographical study of indigenous forms of association reveals not simply their lifelong commitment to study and reading but also their remarkable attention to the specificity and singularity of sociohistorical conditions, situating them at the antipodes of a Hegelian understanding of "universal history."

What also would have been of great interest to Marx is that Morgan writes most of his work in collaboration with Ely Samuel Parker, a Seneca who maintained a close relationship to his tribe and became Morgan's interpreter and adviser during their ethnographic travels to gather data and artifacts. Morgan dedicates his first book of empirical research, his 1851 *The League of the Iroquois*, to Parker. Despite his condemnation of America's treatment of Native Americans, Morgan, like Las Casas before him, views Christianization and full assimilation as the only path forward for the expropriated and colonized American Indian. In his words, "[t]here are but two means of rescuing the Indian from his impending destiny; and these are education and Christianity." See Morgan, *The League of the Ho-Dé-No-Sau-Nee or*

Iroquois (New York: Dodd, Mead, 1904), 111. Marx does not follow Morgan here, but the ethnographer is by no means his only source. In 1851, while writing *Capital*, Marx is reading William Howitt's 1838 *Colonization and Christianity: A Popular History of the Treatment of the Natives by the Europeans in All Their Colonies,* a bristling indictment of the colonial genocide of Native Americans; William Prescott's 1843 *History of the Conquest of Mexico* and his 1847 *History of the Conquest of Peru*; Thomas Fowell Buxton's 1840 *The African Slave Trade and Its Remedy*; Herman Merivale's 1841 *Lectures on Colonization and Colonies*, and Thomas Stamford Raffles's 1817 *History of Java.* As Foster, Clark, and Hannah Holleman note in their essential essay, "Marx and the Indigenous":

> By the end of the 1850s and before Marx wrote *Capital*, there was a decisive shift in emphasis in his and Engels's writings toward the defense of indigenous, anticolonial struggles, exhibiting a strong concern for and a recognition of the lasting importance of noncapitalist cultural formations/modes of production. Much of the impetus for this shift in perspective was the growth of wars of anticolonial resistance emanating from the indigenous populations themselves, namely the Algerian revolt against French settler colonialism, led by Emir Abdelkader in the 1830s and '40s; the Taiping Rebellion of 1850–64; the "Indian Mutiny" or what Marx called the "Sepoy Revolt" of 1857–59; the nationalist struggle in Ireland led by the Fenians in the 1860s and after; and the Zulu War against the British in 1879. In each of these cases, Marx and Engels were to take the side of the indigenous anticolonial forces.

See Foster, Clark, and Holleman, "Marx and the Indigenous," 8. The essay is a review of Glen Sean Coulthard's *Red Skin, White Masks*, which, focusing on indigenous communities in Canada, makes the broader point that "for Indigenous peoples to reject or ignore the insights of Marx would be a mistake, especially if this amounts to a refusal on our part to critically engage his important critique of capitalist exploitation and his extensive writings on the entangled relationship between capitalism and colonialism." See Coulthard, *Red Skin, White Masks: Rejecting the Colonial Politics of Recognition* (Minneapolis: University of Minnesota Press, 2014), 8.

82. Morgan, *Ancient Society*, 128.
83. Dunayevskaya, *Rosa Luxemburg, Women's Liberation and Marx's Philosophy of Revolution*, 180–181.
84. Ibid., 46 and 184.
85. Ibid., 184.
86. Morgan, *Ancient Society*, 291.
87. Ibid., 468 and 291.
88. Chief Justice Marshall asserts that Christian European nations assumed "ultimate dominion" over the lands of America during the Age of Discovery and that, as a result, North American Indians had lost "their rights to complete sovereignty, as independent nations"; they only retained a right of "occupancy." When the United States became independent in 1776, he adds, it retained the British right of "discovery," inheriting Britain's power of "dominion." See Johnson & Graham's Lessee v. M'Intosh, 21 U.S. 543 (1823), https://supreme.justia.com/cases/federal/us/21/543/case.html. As Benjamin already notes in his review of Brion's biography of Las Casas, however, the absolute denial of indigenous land rights was replaced less than fifty years later when the Spanish emperor Charles V declared that indigenous peoples were the rightful owners of their lands and that the "Doctrine of Discovery" should only function in instances when land was not already owned. He adds, sorrowfully, that, in the end, this declaration did not prevent further violence and dispossession.

89. Marx's suggestion here that revolution requires the gathering together of different communes moves between the figures of the one and the many, a structural couple that appears at different moments in the *Notebooks*, especially in his use of the word "severalty." We cite just one example:

> The *Roman tribes, from their first establishment*, had a *public domain, Ager Romanus*; while lands were held by the *curia* for religious uses, by the *gens*, u. by *individuals in severalty*. Nachdem diese social *corporations* ausgestorben, *the lands held by them in common gradually became private property. Diese several forms of ownership* show dass die älteste *land tenure was die in common dch den tribe*; nach Beginn *ihrer Cultivation*, ein *Theil der tribe lands divided unter d. gentes*, jede wovon *held their portion in common*; diesem folgte im Lauf der Zeit *allotments to individuals* u. diese *allotments finally ripened into individual ownership in severalty. Personal property*, generally, was subject to *individual ownership*. (EN, 134)

The point Marx makes here about the gradual *ausgestorben*, extinction, of communal ownership of land in favor of personal or private property is a transition he marks throughout his *Notebooks* and that he sees at work in indigenous tribes across the centuries and around the globe. This transition belongs to the movement from "social *corporations*" to models of possessive individualism and capitalist bourgeois identity. What he also notes, however, is the way in which older forms of land tenure are nevertheless not extinguished altogether, which is why their traces still can be reactivated in new communal efforts. He captures this oscillation between communal ownership and individual ownership in his use of the word "severalty," a word that can mean both "the quality or state of being several"—of being separate and, in particular, of having sole and exclusive possession, dominion, or ownership over land—and "the quality or state of being individual or particular." While land owned in severalty assumes a single owner—an owner with exclusive right to this or that property—it would have been impossible for Marx not to register the word "several" in "severalty." We would suggest that this movement from several to one and back points to Marx's sense that the commune is never just one, never just homogeneous, but also several, already differentiated from within. The suggestion that individual ownership itself is interrupted by an irreducible plurality or multiplicity is reinforced if we recall what would have been for Marx the closest German equivalent for severalty, *Bruchteilseigentum*. As Gerhard Richter notes, in a message he sent us in January 2023, "the 'Bruch' or break encoded in the word already suggests an internal rupture, pointing to a form of multiplicity. It is as though the 'Bruch' or break not only pertains to the way that the property in question is divided up, but also to the idea that the very concept of Eigentum, or property, is traversed by a crack or leap, a traversal that renders it plural," indicating "the fractured, multiple, and plural nature of the kind of property that is governed by *Bruchteilseigentum* or severalty." When Marx states that communes tend to disintegrate when they remain isolated, he not only suggests the necessity of communes joining other communes in order to form a common-wealth of resistance against capital—against the forces, that is, that would extinguish communal forms of ownership in the name of capitalist private property—but he also wants us to understand how any single commune is already "several," which is why the collaboration among communes can become a force of intensified accumulation and multiplication. In this view, "individuals in severalty" is another name for the impersonal agency of radical, revolutionary communal forms.

we wish to recall his own formulation of this point, in a sermon he delivers on December 24, 1967 at his Ebenezer Baptist Church in Atlanta. In the sermon, he declares:

> Our loyalties must transcend our race, our tribe, our class and our nation; and this means we must develop a world perspective. No individual can live alone; no nation can live alone, and as long as we try, the more we are going to have war in this world ... we must either learn to live together as brothers or we are all going to perish together as fools. ... We are all caught in an inescapable network of mutuality. ... Whatever affects one directly, affects all indirectly. We are made to live together because of the interrelated structure of reality.

If King aligns himself here with the late Marx, in another passage in the sermon he makes a point that resonates with Benjamin's effort to imagine a politics of pure means. He writes: "we will never have peace in the world until men everywhere recognize that ends are not cut off from means, because the means represent the ideal in the making, and the end in process." See Martin Luther King, "A Christmas Sermon on Peace," in *A Testament of Hope: The Essential Writings and Speeches of Martin Luther King, Jr.*, ed. James Melvin Washington (New York: Harper Collins, 1986), 70–71 and 72.

98. Jean-Luc Nancy, "What Is to Be Done?," in Philippe Lacoue-Labarthe and Jean-Luc Nancy, *Retreating the Political*, trans. and ed. Simon Sparks (New York: Routledge, 1997), 151–152.

90. Karl Marx and Friedrich Engels, *The German Ideology*, trans. W. Lough, in Marx and Engels, *Collected Works*, vol. 5 (New York: International Publishers, 1976), 49.

91. For Zasulich's letter to Marx, see Shanin, *Late Marx and the Russian Road*, 98–99, and for Marx's passages, see ibid., 111 and 124.

92. See ibid., 139. We follow Anderson's discussion here; see *Marx at the Margins*, 234–236.

93. Shanin, *Late Marx and the Russian Road*, 112.

94. Louis Althusser, *Philosophy of the Encounter: Later Writings, 1978–87*, trans. G. M. Goshgarian, ed. François Matheron and Oliver Corpet (London: Verso, 2006), 190.

95. Marx and Engels, *Collected Works*, vol. 46 (London: Lawrence & Wishart, 2010), 242 and 213–214, translation modified.

96. Karl Marx, *The Eighteenth Brumaire of Louis Bonaparte*, trans. Daniel De Leon (New York: International Publishers, 1963), 18.

97. Since we are writing these last words of the book on January 16, 2023, Martin Luther King, Jr. Day,

LIST OF ILLUSTRATIONS

Cover: Andy Warhol, *Hammer and Sickle*, 1976. Acrylic and silkscreen. © 2022 The Andy Warhol Foundation for the Visual Arts. Inc. / Artists Rights Society (ARS), New York.

Page 2: Karl Marx, manuscript page from the "Feuerbach" section of *The German Ideology*, 1845–1846. Karl Marx / Frederick Engels Papers, International Institute of Social History (Amsterdam).

Page 28: Gisèle Freund, Walter Benjamin at the Bibliothèque Nationale, Paris, 1937. © IMEC, Fonds MCC, Dist. RMN-Grand Palais / Art Resource, NY.

Page 34: Walter Benjamin, "Was ist Aura?" Draft page from "The Work of Art in the Age of Its Technological Reproducibility," between 1936 and 1939. Akademie der Künste, Berlin, Walter Benjamin Archiv 264/2. Hamburger Stiftung zur Förderung von Wissenschaft und Kultur.

Page 42: Glenn Ligon, *Red Hands #2*, 1996. Silkscreen on canvas, 52.75 × 60.75 inches (134 × 154.3 cm). Photo: Farzad Owrang. © Glenn Ligon; courtesy of the artist, Hauser & Wirth, New York, Regen Projects, Los Angeles, Thomas Dane Gallery, London, and Galerie Chantal Crousel, Paris.

Page 50: Cassio Vasconcellos, *Múltiplos: É Nóis!*, 2011. Inkjet print from a digital file, 130 × 112.5 cm. Courtesy of the artist.

Page 58: Walter Benjamin, "Literature for a More Fully Developed Critique of Violence and Philosophy of Law," n.d. Akademie der Künste, Berlin, Walter Benjamin Archiv 508/16. Hamburger Stiftung zur Förderung von Wissenschaft und Kultur.

Page 70: Rosa Luxemburg, age 36, at her desk in her Berlin apartment, 1907. Rosa Luxemburg Collection, International Institute for Social History (Amsterdam).

Page 84: Man Ray, *Marcel Duchamp as Rrose Sélavy*, ca. 1920–1921. Philadelphia Museum of Art: The Samuel S. White 3rd and Vera White Collection, 1957, 1957-49-1. © Association Marcel Duchamp / ADAGP, Paris / Artists Rights Society (ARS), New York, 2022.

Page 85: Alice Croner and Walter Benjamin, 1921. Akademie der Künste, Berlin, Walter Benjamin Archiv 1512. Hamburger Stiftung zur Förderung von Wissenschaft und Kultur. Photographer and copyright unknown.

Page 88: Max Beckmann, *The Martyrdom* (plate 4) [*Das Martyrium* (Blatt 4)], from *Hell* (*Die Hölle*), 1919. Museum of Modern Art, NY. © 2022 Artists Rights Society (ARS), New York / VG Bild-Kunst, Bonn.

Page 96: Willy Römer, *Spartacists behind Barricades Made of Rolls of Newspaper in Front of the Rudolf Mosse Publishing House, Schützenstrasse, January 11, 1919. Occupation of the Newspaper District*. Photograph, 13 × 18 cm, object size 13 × 18 cm. © Kunstbibliothek, Staatliche Museen zu Berlin, Photothek Willy Römer / Art Resource, NY.

Page 112: Ludwig Mies van der Rohe, *Monument to the November Revolution*, Berlin-Lichtenberg, 1926. Courtesy of Sueddeutsche Zeitung Photo and Alamy Stock Photo.

Page 116: John Heartfield, *The Voice of Freedom in the German Night—On the Wave*, 1937. Akademie der Künste, Berlin, John Heartfield Archiv 5323. Hamburger Stiftung zur Förderung von Wissenschaft und Kultur.

Page 120: Étienne-Louis Boullée, *Cenotaph for Newton* (geometric elevation), 1784. Bibliothèque Nationale de France, Département Estampes et Photographie.

Page 124: Postage stamp printed in USSR, ca. 1967, in celebration of the fiftieth anniversary of the Great October Revolution, including S. Karpov's 1924 painting *Friendship of the Peoples*. Courtesy of Sergey Komarov-Kohl and Alamy Stock Photo.

Page 132: Paul Klee, *Angelus Novus*, 1920. © Fine Art Images / Heritage-Images / Art Resource, New York.

Page 138: R. H. Quaytman, חפר, *Chapter 29*, 2015. Digital drawing, dimensions variable. Courtesy of the artist and Miguel Abreu Gallery, New York.

Page 139: Christian Friedrich von Müller, engraving after a painting by Lucas Cranach, 1838. Courtesy the Miguel Abreu Gallery, New York.

Page 144: Glenn Ligon, *Untitled* (detail), 2016. One of a suite of 17 archival pigment prints, each 71 × 49 inches (180.34 × 124.46 cm). Edition of 5 and 1 artist's proof. © Glenn Ligon; courtesy of the artist, Hauser & Wirth, New York, Regen Projects, Los Angeles, Thomas Dane Gallery, London, and Galerie Chantal Crousel, Paris.

Page 150: Karl Marx, draft page from the third volume of *Das Kapital*, 1870–1880. Karl Marx / Frederick Engels Papers, International Institute of Social History (Amsterdam).

Page 168: Plan and section of slave ship *Brooks*, 1789. © National Maritime Museum, Greenwich, London, Michael Graham-Stewart Slavery Collection. Acquired with the assistance of the Heritage Lottery Fund.

Page 172: Robert Hoskin, *The Slave Ship, after Joseph Mallord William Turner*, c. 1879. Photo Tate, 2022.

Page 176: Paul Nadar (1856–1939), W. E. B. Du Bois, identification card for Exposition Universelle, 1900. W. E. B. Du Bois Papers (MS 312). Special Collections and University Archives, University of Massachusetts Amherst Libraries.

Page 188: W. E. B. Du Bois, "City and Rural Population 1890," 1900. Courtesy of the Library of Congress, Prints & Photographs Division.

Page 189: W. E. B. Du Bois, "Value of Land Owned by Georgia Negroes," 1900. Courtesy of the Library of Congress, Prints & Photographs Division.

Page 194: W. E. B. Du Bois, Atlanta University, 1909. W. E. B. Du Bois Papers (MS 312). Special Collections and University Archives, University of Massachusetts Amherst Libraries.

Page 220: Glenn Ligon, *Debris Field (Red) #16*, 2020–2021. Etching ink, acrylic, and oil stick on canvas, 114 × 88 inches (289.56 × 223.52 cm). Photo: Thomas Barratt. © Glenn Ligon; courtesy of the artist, Hauser & Wirth, New York, Regen Projects, Los Angeles, Thomas Dane Gallery, London, and Galerie Chantal Crousel, Paris.

Page 226: Kadir Nelson, *Say Their Names*, 2020. *The New Yorker*, © Condé Nast.

Page 228: Abraham Bosse, frontispiece for Thomas Hobbes's *Leviathan or The Matter, Forme and Power of a Common-Wealth Ecclesiasticall and Civil*, 1651.

Page 232: Danny Lyon, *Birmingham, Alabama*, 1963: SNCC workers stand outside the funeral of the four girls who had been killed in the bombing of the 16th Street Baptist Church. From left to right: Emma Bell, Dorie Ladner, Dona Richards, Sam Shirah, and Doris Derby. © Danny Lyon / Magnum Photos.

Pages 234–235: Donkeeboy and Donkeemom, *George Floyd, Houston's Third Ward* (2020). Photo: Elliot Guidry.

Page 240: Jack Whitten, *Birmingham 1964*, 1964. Aluminum foil, newsprint, stocking, and oil on plywood, 16 5/8 × 16 inches (42.2 × 40.6 cm). © Jack Whitten Estate. Courtesy the Estate and Hauser & Wirth. Private Collection. Photo: John Berens.

Page 242: Kerry James Marshall, *Memento #5*, 2003. Acrylic and glitter on paper adhered to unstretched canvas banner, 108 in. × 156 in. (274.3 × 396.2 cm). The Nelson-Atkins Museum of Art, Kansas City, Missouri. Purchase: acquired through the generosity of the William T. Kemper Foundation—Commerce Bank, Trustee, 2003.24. Photo: Gabe Hopkins. Art © Kerry James Marshall.

Page 243: Kerry James Marshall, *Souvenir II*, 1997. Acrylic, collage, and glitter on unstretched canvas banner, 108 in. × 120 in. (274.32 cm × 304.8 cm). Purchased as the gift of the Addison Advisory Council in honor of John ("Jock") M. Reynolds's directorship of the Addison Gallery of American Art, 1989–1998 (1998.160). Photo: Addison Gallery of American Art, Phillips Academy, Andover, MA / Art Resource, NY.

Page 246: *Star of the North, or the Comet of 1861*, 1861. Courtesy of the New-York Historical Society Digital Collections.

Page 262: Edward Emerson Barnard, *The Great Comet of 1882*. © Age Fotostock.

Page 284: Josef Albers, *Homage to the Square / Red Series, Untitled III*, 1968. Norton Simon Museum, Museum Purchase. © Josef and Anni Albers Foundation / Artists Rights Society (ARS), New York, 2022.

Page 296: Diego Rivera, *The Arsenal*, 1928. Secretariat of Public Education, Mexico City, Mexico. Courtesy of Cosmo Condina and Alamy Stock Photo.

Page 304: Tina Modotti, *Mexican Sombrero with Hammer and Sickle*, Mexico City, 1927. Courtesy of Ullstein Bild / The Granger Collection Ltd.

Page 333: Joseph Kosuth, *"Titled (Art as Idea as Idea),"* 1967. Whitney Museum of American Art, New York; gift of Peter M. Brant. © 2022 Joseph Kosuth / Artists Rights Society (ARS), New York.

Fortune, Timothy Thomas, 200, 223, 366n15
Foster, John Bellamy, 310–311, 313–314, 381nn69–70, 382n81
Fraas, Carl, 314–315, 381n68
Frazier, Darnella, 221–222, 227
Freedmen's Bureau, 212, 217, 366n7, 370n12
Freikorps, 62, 63–66, 74, 114, 351n7, 354n24
French Revolution, 160–161, 165, 323–324, 367n30
Friedlaender, Salomo, 268, 274, 374n6
Fuchs, Eduard, 350n19, 351n7. *See also* Benjamin, Walter: "Eduard Fuchs, Collector and Historian"

Gago, Verónica, 348n9
Garner, Eric, 231, 236, 339n28
general strike, 26, 63, 199, 346n13, 381n67; doodling and, 16; German government's call for, 62, 65; Luxemburg and, 103; political, 63, 67–68, 77–78; proletarian, 63, 67–69, 71, 73, 76, 77–78, 151; of slaves, 196–199, 201, 207–214, 363n7, 365n5, 366n7, 370n12; Sorel and, 77–78, 81, 351nn23–24; Spartacist uprising and, 64. *See also* mass strike
genocide, 17, 26; of indigenous populations, 177, 291, 293, 294, 309, 318, 377n20, 382n81
German Ideology, The (Marx and Engels), 9–16, 19–22, 327, 338n1, 338n7, 338n10, 344n4; Feuerbach section of, 9, 13; "Leipzig Council" section of, 19–20
German Revolution, 68; Benjamin and, 268, 354n24; Mariátegui on, 380n53
Gracián, Baltasar, 45–46, 145, 229, 343n7, 356n7; *Agudez y arte de ingenio*, 47
grief, 91, 155, 161, 165, 173, 184, 190; Black, 23, 215, 224–225, 230, 236, 241; communal, 22, 156, 165, 174, 215, 225, 238, 245
guano trade, 311–313; Emerson and, 311, 312, 380n59, 380n61; race and, 369n6; suicide of workers and, 312–313, 380n64
guilt, 17, 107, 128; adversary as mute bearer of, 90; of culture, 158, 362n13; economy, 130, 164; justice and, 106; nexus of the living, 130–131, 133, 149

Hamacher, Werner, 73, 103, 127, 155
happiness, 44, 53, 110, 118, 127–130, 133; tiger's leap toward, 136, 163
Hartman, Saidiya, 24, 223, 251–253, 256, 370n12, 371n14
Heinle, Fritz, 74–75, 269, 347n8, 349n11
Hiller, Kurt, 61, 77, 105, 355n25, 355nn27–28; "Anti-Cain," 109–111, 354n24; Benjamin's critique of, 113–115, 338n8
historical materialism, 119, 198, 362n13; destructive energies of, 156; theology and, 117, 355n2; training in, 165
historicism, 136, 156–158
Hobbes, Thomas, 345n8; *Leviathan*, 18, 227–230, 326, 369n2. *See also* Bosse, Abraham
Hoernle, Edwin, 169–170, 363n2
Hoffman, Frederick, 184, 364n17
Hofmannsthal, Hugo von, 72, 347n4
hope, 46, 69, 86, 118, 126–130, 151–152, 184, 245, 330; of Black lives, 186; hopelessness and, 26, 69, 151, 162, 171, 196, 233, 245, 330; indeterminacy of, 149; legibility of, 287; mourning and, 256; political organization of hopelessness and pessimism,

127–128, 149, 165, 245, 267; slaves and, 196
Horkheimer, Max, 179, 350n19

ideology, 21, 30, 365n6; bourgeois, 119; positivist, 306; racial, 200; Zionist, 359–60n4
illegibility, 18, 103, 272; of historical catastrophe, 287; the messianic and, 118; of the slave, 207
immigration, 21, 93, 371n15; of ethnic Europeans, 178
imperialism, 21, 247–248, 323, 352n10; capitalism and, 300; Du Bois's critique of, 371n14; ecological, 311; racism and, 369n11
impersonality, 44, 342n18, 343n9, 356n7; Benjamin's, 38, 51, 109, 149, 229, 342n14; depersonalization and, 145, 229, 342n14, 360n7, 374n13; of language, 82; of politics, 52; politics of, 129; of reading, 37–39; violence as force of, 68
incalculability, 100; of general strike, 68; of human action, 190; political, 80, 149
Independent Social Democratic Party (USPD), 64, 72, 347n8, 354n24
industrialization: of agriculture, 313; colonialism and, 308; racism and, 201
inequality, 22, 98, 174, 237, 323, 381n67
instrumentality, 53, 78, 357n8

Jaffé, Edgar, 180, 344n4, 364n8
James, C. L. R., 207, 367n30
Jameson, Fredric, 17, 22, 29, 38, 43–45, 47–48, 51–54, 117–118, 133, 165, 223, 263, 288, 338n19, 342n14, 342n3, 343n7, 343n10, 343n2, 362n23; on action, 360n7; on aristocracy of labor, 361n9; on Benjamin's small forms, 362n15; on hope, 129–130; on Kennedy assassination, 238–239; literature and, 365n6; Luxemburg and, 166, 171; *Marxism and Form*, 30; "Marxism and Historicism," 39–40; May '68 and, 152; on the messianic, 133; *The Political Unconscious*, 156, 342n15, 360n2, 362n13; race and, 173–175, 177, 181–182, 361nn7–8, 361n10, 368n3; on redemption, 358n2. *See also Benjamin Files, The*
Jennings, Michael W., 64, 264, 345n7, 358n2
Jim Crow, 177, 191, 197
"John Brown's Body," 215, 259, 372n34
justice, 60–61, 105–110, 163, 259, 350n17, 353n13; law as gravestone for, 91; literature and, 365n6; mythical violence and, 95, 97; restorative, 339n28; social, 223; violence and, 68, 105–108, 110

Kafka, Franz, 125, 128, 130, 341n11, 358n14
Kapp Putsch, 62, 64–65
Kelley, Robin D. G., 223, 339n28, 368n4
Kennedy, John F., 238–239, 244
King, Martin Luther, Jr., 222–223, 230, 239, 244, 384n97
King, Rodney, 223, 231
Klee, Paul, 140–143; *Angelus Novus*, 132f, 133, 135, 137, 140–143, 146, 149, 152, 154, 229, 236–237, 245, 359–60n4. *See also* Luther, Martin; Quaytman, R. H.
Kovalevsky, Maksim, 318, 329
Kraus, Karl, 352n8. *See also* Benjamin, Walter: on Kraus

labor, 16, 94, 218, 251, 305, 307–308, 310, 351n23, 352n7, 367n25, 368n31; aristocracy of, 361n9;

EDUARDO CADAVA is Philip Mayhew Professor of English at Princeton University. He is the author of *Words of Light: Theses on the Photography of History*, *Emerson and the Climates of History*, and *Paper Graveyards*. He has co-edited *Who Comes After the Subject?*, *Cities Without Citizens*, and *The Itinerant Languages of Photography*. He also has introduced and co-translated Nadar's memoirs, *Quand j'étais photographe*, which appeared under the title *When I Was a Photographer*, and has curated installations and exhibitions at the MAXXI Museum, the Slought Foundation, Storefront for Art and Architecture, the Al-Ma'mal Center for Contemporary Art, and the Princeton University Art Museum. He is co-directing, with Eyal Weizman, a multiyear project on the relation between political conflict and climate change titled *Conflict Shorelines* that includes field work in Amazonia, the Negev desert, and the Arctic, and collaborating with Fazal Sheikh on a project titled *Exposure* that is documenting the ruination of the Utah landscape by uranium mining and oil and gas drilling and the consequences of this ruination on native communities.

SARA NADAL-MELSIÓ is a New York City based Catalan writer, curator, and teacher. Presently writer-in-residence at the Slought Foundation in Philadelphia, she has taught at the University of Pennsylvania, Princeton University, SOMA in Mexico City, and New York University. Her essays have appeared in various academic journals, edited volumes, and museum catalogs. She is the co-author of *Alrededor de / Around*, and the editor of two special issues on cinema, *The Invisible Tradition: Avant-Garde Catalan Cinema under Late Francoism* and *Anachronism and the Militant Image: Temporal Disturbances of the Political Imagination*. She also has co-curated a survey of Allora & Calzadilla's work for the Fundació Tàpies in Barcelona and has written a book essay about it, *To Be All Ears, To Be in the World: Acoustic Relation in Allora & Calzadilla*, as well as edited a companion volume on the Puerto Rican crisis, *A Modest Proposal: Puerto Rico's Crucible*. Her book *Europe and the Wolf: Political Variations on a Musical Concept* is forthcoming from Zone Books.

Eduardo Cadava
Sara Nadal-Melsió
Politically Red

The MIT Press would like to thank the anonymous peer reviewers who provided comments on
drafts of this book. The generous work of academic
experts is essential for establishing the authority
and quality of our publications. We acknowledge
with gratitude the contributions of these otherwise
uncredited readers.

This publication is made possible in part by the
Barr Ferree Foundation Fund for Publications,
Department of Art and Archaeology, Princeton
University.

Cover: Andy Warhol, *Hammer and Sickle*, 1976.
Acrylic and silkscreen. © 2022 The Andy Warhol
Foundation for the Visual Arts. Inc. / Artists
Rights Society (ARS), New York.

Book design: Duncan Whyte
This book was set in Rosart and printed on
90 gsm Fedrigoni Arena Natural Bulk paper
Printed and bound in Italy by Musumeci

Library of Congress Cataloging-in-Publication Data

Names: Cadava, Eduardo, author. | Nadal-Melsió,
Sara, author.
Title: Politically red / Eduardo Cadava and Sara
Nadal-Melsió.
Description: Cambridge, Massachusetts : The MIT
Press, 2023. | Includes bibliographical references
and index.
Identifiers: LCCN a2022061540 (print) | LCCN
2022061541 (ebook) | ISBN 9780262047807
(paperback) | ISBN 9780262376174 (epub) | ISBN
9780262376181 (pdf)
Subjects: LCSH: Marxist criticism. | Reading--
Philosophy. | Anti-racism. | Social justice.
Classification: LCC PN98.C6 C33 2023 (print) | LCC
PN98.C6 (ebook) | DDC 801.95--dc23/eng/20230403
LC record available at https://lccn.loc.
gov/2022061540
LC ebook record available at https://lccn.loc.
gov/2022061541

10 9 8 7 6 5 4 3 2 1